INTRODUCTION TO

COMPUTER SYSTEMS

INTRODUCTION TO

COMPUTER SYSTEMS

N. A. B. GRAY

PRENTICE-HALL

The program material contained herein or in any further deletion, addenda, or corrigenda to this manual or associated manuals or software is supplied without representation or guarantee of any kind. These computer programs have been developed for student use in a teaching situation and neither the author nor Prentice-Hall of Australia Pty Ltd assumes any responsibility and shall have no liability, consequential or otherwise, of any kind arising from the use of these programs or part thereof.

Prentice-Hall, Inc., Englewood Cliffs, *New Jersey*
Prentice-Hall of Australia Pty Ltd, *Sydney*
Prentice-Hall Canada, Inc, *Toronto*
Prentice-Hall Hispanoamericana, S.A., *Mexico*
Prentice-Hall of India Private Ltd, *New Delhi*
Prentice-Hall International, Inc., *London*
Prentice-Hall of Japan, Inc., *Tokyo*
Prentice-Hall of Southeast Asia Pte Ltd, *Singapore*
Editora Prentice-Hall do Brasil Ltda, *Rio de Janeiro*

Printed and bound in Australia by
the Australian Print Group, Maryborough, Vic.

Cover design by Kim Webber.

2 3 4 5 91 90 89 88 87

ISBN 0 7248 0655 5

U.S. ISBN 0-13-480386-8

National Library of Australia Cataloguing-in-Publication Data

Gray, N.A.B. (Neil A.B.)
    Introduction to computer systems.

    Includes index,
    ISBN 0 7248 0655 5.

    1. Computer. 2. Assembler language (Computer program language). I. Title.
004.2

Library of Congress Cataloging-in-Publication Data

Gray, N.A.B.
    An introduction to computer systems.

    Includes index.
    1. Computers. I. Title.
QA76.G675 1986 004 86-22625
ISBN 0-13-480386-8

Contents

Section III: Input and output

Section IV: Assembly languages and high-level languages

Section V: Extending the CPU

Preface

This text, and associated software package, is designed for a one-semester course at the level 'CS-3: Introduction to Computer Systems' of the ACM Curriculum-78. The prerequisite for entry to such a course is a one-semester introductory course on computer programming (preferably in Pascal). The CS-3 course introduces assembly-language programming, machine organization, and methods of handling input and output (I/O). The main objective of this course is to prepare students for later studies on operating systems; other topics introduced in this course are developed in subsequent courses on the organization of programming languages and compilers.

The software for this course is a computer simulator (the software is provided as part of an instructor's manual). The simulated computer system represents a single bus computer with CPU, memory, disk (using direct memory access), and a variety of other peripheral devices. Optional displays permit students to view the workings of these component parts during program execution. Most of the exercises using the simulator are designed to illustrate aspects of I/O handling, and the problems of coordinating CPU and peripheral device activity.

There are five sections in the course: (1) basic principles, (2) the simulated machine, (3) methods for handling I/O, (4) assembly-languages and high-level languages, and (5) extensions to the simple CPU architecture of the simulator.

The first section of the course covers the architecture and workings of an accumulator-based machine, bits, unsigned and signed binary numbers, and so forth. The actual machine simulated, its instruction set, and addressing modes are covered in the next few chapters.

After introducing the simulated machine, the course focuses on I/O handling. Wait loops for control of simple keyboard and terminal devices are explored first. Then, more sophisticated devices are considered. Buffering schemes are introduced through examples that illustrate how to overlap disk I/O with computations, and how to accommodate sudden bursts of data traffic. The control of several devices by polling loop methods is explored. Finally, interrupt driven I/O is discussed.

The fourth section starts with an examination of the workings of a simple assembler program. More advanced assemblers, macro-preprocessors, and linking-loaders are then described. The review of high-level languages, FORTRAN and languages in the Algol family, is in terms of the computational models that they presume. The computational models for the Algol languages are shown to require significant extensions to the CPU architecture of the simulated machine.

The fifth section examines some of these architectural extensions. More sophisticated instruction repertoires and more elaborate data types are considered. A range of addressing modes is presented – these various addressing modes are justified in terms of the type of high-level programming construct for which they are particularly relevant. Possible enhancements to the I/O handling capabilities of a machine are noted. The Motorola 68000 CPU is used as an illustration of the practical implementation of some of these extensions and enhancements. Finally, the course covers those further extensions to the CPU architecture needed to permit an effective operating system.

Chapter contents

Section I: Basic principles

Chapter 1:   The main components of a simple computer, its bus, memory, CPU, and peripheral devices and their controllers are introduced. The main internal components of the CPU are noted.

Chapter 2:   The operations of an accumulator-based machine are reviewed briefly. The flow of data between memory and CPU is emphasized, as is the need to manipulate addresses as well as program data.

Chapter 3:   The use of bit patterns as a data type is introduced. It is shown how bit patterns can provide an implementation of Pascal sets and, also, of various forms of packed record structures.

Chapter 4:   Methods of using bit patterns to represent several simple data types are reviewed. The data types include sets, characters, and unsigned and signed binary integers. Octal and hexadecimal notations are introduced as a way of representing bit patterns.

Section II: The simulated machine

Chapter 5:   The instruction set of the simulated machine is considered in overview. The first simple practical programming exercises on the simulator are given.

Chapter 6:   The bit-manipulation and test instructions of the simulated machine are examined.

Chapter 7:   The addressing modes of the machine are described.

Chapter 8:   The subroutine-call instruction is presented as a simple, restricted solution to the general problems of subroutine linkage and parameter passing.

Section III: Input and output

Chapter 9:   Input and output using keyboard and terminal are considered. Wait loops are presented as a simple, if wasteful, method of coordinating CPU and device activity.

Chapter 10:   Other peripheral devices including clocks, analog to digitial converters, disks, and tapes are reviewed. The principles of direct memory access are presented.

The coverage of disks and tapes extends to details of how data files might be organized on these media.

Chapter 11: Buffered I/O and polling loop methods of device control are presented.

Chapter 12: The need for an interrupt driven approach to device handling is developed using examples that represent extensions to earlier polling loop programs. The steps of responding to an interrupt by combined hardware and software, by saving the state of the computation, identifying the device, calling a device handler, and returning from interrupt, are illustrated. Two simple example programs are developed. Finally, timing dependent errors are considered. Examples are given of problems that can arise if, for example, there exist variables common to both interrupt handler and main line code.

Section IV: Assembly languages and high-level languages

Chapter 13: The workings of simple absolute loaders and two-pass assemblers are considered. The hand assembly process is followed and used (1) to introduce the need for a first pass through the code to find labels, and a second pass to generate code, and then (2) to explain the lexical analysis processes needed to recognize the various tokens used in an assembly language program. A simple two-pass assembler is examined; code for this assembler is included in Appendix B.

Chapter 14: Some more advanced features of assemblers and loaders are reviewed. These include macros, relocatable code, and the functions of a linking-loader.

Chapter 15: Attention then turns to how high-level languages utilize a machine. First, FORTRAN is examined briefly. It is shown that a static implementation of FORTRAN requires little more than the capabilities of the simulated machine. The need to support recursion in an Algol-derived language is used to introduce stacks. These are shown to provide a basis for a more general approach to storage allocation and procedure invocation irrespective of whether or not recursion is required. Dynamic storage allocation, Pascal's 'new()' and 'free()', is briefly considered and used to justify a heap.

Section V: Extending the CPU

Chapter 16: This is the first of a number of chapters describing extensions to the CPU. Here, three aspects are considered – more instructions, more registers, and more data types. The advantages of a larger instruction repertoire are obvious; more data manipulation instructions are required, and instructions should allow processing of byte, word, and long-word data instead of the word-only processing of the simulated machine. The Motorola 6809 and 68000 CPUs are used to illustrate different ways of providing more registers. Binary-coded-decimal and floating-point data are reviewed. Examples are provided illustrating the round-off problems associated with short floating-point representations.

Chapter 17: The second chapter on extensions to the CPU covers addressing modes and instruction formats. The various addressing modes common to most current microcomputers are explained largely in terms of the types of high-level programming construct that they might be used to realize.

Chapter 18:   Methods of improving the simple interrupt scheme of the simulated machine are considered. Improvements include vectored interrupts and multiple priority levels for interrupts. Memory-mapped I/O is shown to lead to a somewhat cleaner, more systematic machine architecture. The possibility of delegating responsibility for I/O to an I/O processor is noted.

Chapter 19:   In Chapter 15, the needs of Algol-like languages are shown to require extensions to the simple CPU architecture. This chapter shows how the requirements of high-level languages can be satisfied by current microcomputer architectures; the Motorola 68000 is used as the example. The organization of a typical 'computer training board' is also reviewed briefly, and an example program is used to illustrate simple memory-mapped I/O on a system with a Motorola 68000 and 6850.

Chapter 20:   This chapter justifies the inclusion of further hardware capabilities needed (1) to make a distinction between a user-mode and a supervisor-mode for program execution, and (2) to provide some form of memory management. An operating system is first introduced as a set of device-handler routines that may be called by a user application program. It is shown that a system should use interrupts and data buffering to allow the overlap of computation and peripheral activity. Examples are given illustrating that even with overlapped CPU and devices, many CPU-cycles are likely to be wasted on I/O waits. The possibility of multiple tasks being present to soak up wasted CPU cycles is introduced. The presence of multiple tasks leads to the need for supervisor/user-mode distinction and memory management. A simple base/limit register-pair approach to memory management is illustrated. Supervisor calls are then considered. The concept of a process is introduced. Some consideration is given to how processes might use supervisor calls to communicate with an operating system, and how the system might be able to switch CPU attention among a number of processes.

Chapter 21:   Finally, there is a brief introduction to the CPU extensions that are required for more sophisticated memory management systems such as segmentation and paged segmentation.

Further study

The best follow-on text is that by Wakerly, *Microcomputer Architecture and Programming* (Wiley, New York, 1981), which presents a number of examples of actual microcomputer architectures. The texts of Calingaert, *Operating Systems: A User Perspective* (Prentice-Hall, New Jersey, 1982), and of Peterson and Silberschatz, *Operating Systems Concepts* (Addison-Wesley, Massachusetts, 1983) provide descriptive introductions to operating systems. Comer's text, *Operating System Design: The XINU Approach* (Prentice-Hall, New Jersey, 1984), follows with its guide to the practical construction of a realistic operating system.

N. A. B. Gray
November 1986

Section I

Basic principles

1

The structure of a simple computer

The structure of a simple computer is shown in Figure 1-1. This structure epitomizes everything from small personal computers through to medium-sized machines capable of supporting the work of many simultaneous users (as in time-shared systems), or capable of controlling many instruments (as in laboratory or industrial computer-based systems).

Four different types of component are illustrated. First, there is a *bus*. A bus can be viewed as a communications highway consisting of many signal wires. Some of these signal wires carry control signals, others convey individual bits of data, and still others specify the destination of the data being transferred on the bus. The bus joins together the other components of the computer.

The second component is the *memory*, where both the program code and data are stored. Memory is essentially passive. Data in memory should not change. To be changed, data must be taken from memory and sent, via the bus, to the *central processing unit* (CPU).

The central processing unit contains the circuits that decode and execute the instructions of the program code, and the circuits that perform the desired manipulations of data. Further, the CPU usually contains a limited amount of storage for holding the values of the most frequently referenced data elements.

The fourth type of component is represented by the various *peripheral devices* and their *controllers*. Data can be sent to, or received from, peripheral devices. For each such device there will be a controller, which mediates between the device and the computer's bus. Each controller will have specially designed circuitry to convert data from their external form (e.g. a slow sequence of electrical pulses from something like a keyboard, or a particular transient voltage on an *analog-to-digital* converter) into the conventional signals used within the computer.

Bus

Data transferred inside a computer pass over a data highway known as a bus. Simple computers are constructed around a single bus; more elaborate machines may have various buses to allow different data transfers to proceed concurrently. A bus can be viewed as a set of several dozen, maybe as many as 100, parallel wires, each carrying a voltage signal, and include control and timing lines, address lines, and data lines.

Signals on the *control and timing* lines identify what is happening on the bus. Different patterns of signals on the set of control lines will, for example, differentiate between situations where the CPU is trying to read data from memory, from cases where a controller of a peripheral device is trying to place data into memory.

The *address* lines identify locations relevant to data transfers. The address lines can, for example, indicate the address in memory where the CPU is currently trying to store data, or identify a peripheral device controller with which the CPU is trying to communicate.

Finally, the *data* lines are used to carry the data signal. Obviously, voltages of 0 and 1 can encode the bit pattern representing some data element.

Figure 1-1.   The structure of a simple computer

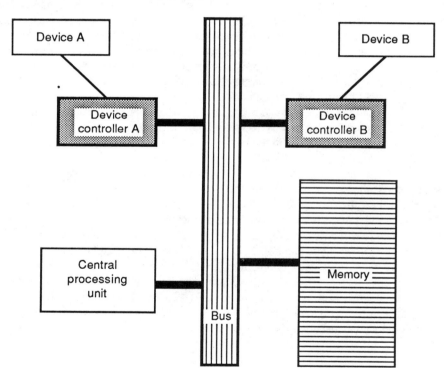

Memory

It is convenient to regard memory as a one-dimensional array of *locations*, or *words*, with each word capable of storing one element of data. A Pascal data structure declaration for memory could be:

```
const    memlimit        = ???;
         bitlimit        = ???;
type     bit             = 0..1;
         word            = array[0..bitlimit] of bit;
var      memory          : array[0..memlimit] of word;
```

The array index number of each word is referred to as its *address*.

Memory sizes vary from a few thousand elements to 16 million or more. Each individual memory element can be viewed as being a set, or an array, of *bits*. If each memory element has n bits then these will be numbered from $0...(n-1)$.

Machines have been constructed with a wide variety of word sizes, that is, values for n. As summarized in Table 1-1, different word sizes are optimal for different applications. Many simple microprocessors are designed to use an 8-bit word; each word in their memory can hold only one character or *byte*. These machines are ideal for tasks that mainly entail the manipulation of characters; for example, intelligent terminals with local editing capabilities will incorporate simple 8-bit machines.

Table 1-1. Typical applications for machines of different word sizes

n	Typical machine application
8	character handling, as in "intelligent terminals", printer controllers etc.
12	simple laboratory instrumentation control
16	laboratory data acquisition, single user workstations, simple time-shared systems
32	general purpose computers for business and scientific applications, large time-shared systems
60	specialized scientific computers

Laboratory computers which acquire and analyze scientific or industrial data are usually 16-bit machines. These machines typically measure voltages (to an accuracy of around one part in 10,000), and accumulate totals and averages for series of measurements. The data being manipulated are usually treated as integers with values in the thousands. Each data element can be represented in a 16-bit word. It is convenient if each data 'fetch' / 'store' operation works with a standard sized data element. An 8-bit machine is less suited to this type of data manipulation because each datum requires more than one byte and hence more than one 'fetch' / 'store' operation. Since a 16-bit word can hold two characters, most machines designed to work with 16-bit data elements have some provision for access to the individual bytes in a word to enable convenient manipulation of character data.

As well as being able to manipulate larger data elements, 16-bit machines have a wider repertoire of instructions and consequently can process data more directly than 8-bit machines. The 16-bit machines have sufficient computing power to serve as individual workstations or even to support multiple users in simple time-shared systems.

The majority of general purpose business computers use a 32-bit word. These machines allow convenient access to the individual bytes within each word and, usually, have some provision for handling data elements that extend over many words (e.g. *floating-point* numbers for scientific calculations that may require two or four words, and strings of characters that may span many words).

In many scientific applications (e.g. in quantum chemistry, weather forecasting, or nuclear physics), one often needs to compute accurately some small difference between large real numbers derived through very extensive calculations. If these computed differences are to be significant then it is essential to use a large number of bits to represent as accurately as possible those real numbers that are being processed. A 32-bit word would not allow sufficiently accurate representation of real numbers (32-bit machines can represent floating-point numbers accurate to only about one part in 10 million); consequently, on a 32-bit machine, such calculations would require multiword data elements. Specialized machines with very long (60-bit) word lengths have been designed to perform these kinds of scientific calculation.

Many other word lengths have been used, and sometimes one can still find a machine with 18-, 20-, 24-, 36-, 40-, or 48-bit words. A few machines are strictly word oriented; each instruction and each data element must occupy exactly one word. Most are more flexible. Machines with short (8-bit, 16-bit) word sizes will have instructions that occupy two or three words of memory. Long word-length machines can pack more than one instruction into a single word.

The size of memory on a computer also reflects its intended application. Memory sizes are usually given in bytes (to allow for direct comparisons of machines which may use quite different word lengths). An intelligent terminal might have only a few thousand bytes. A laboratory computer would typically require tens of thousands of bytes. A small time-shared system will need in excess of quarter of a million while the larger business and scientific computers will have millions of bytes of memory.

On early computers, memories were usually constructed out of magnetic *cores*. Cores were loops of magnetic oxide, threaded through by current carrying wires. Each core loop could be in one of two magnetic states and, consequently, could store one bit of data. Each word of an *n*-bit memory would require *n* cores. The bit values represented by the core loops of a word could be read out (destructively), and the same or new data written back, by sending current through appropriate wires. The time taken to read out the value of a word from memory, and restore it, was the *cycle* time of that memory. A fast core memory had a cycle time of about one millionth of one second or one *microsecond*.

Modern machines use mainly semiconductor memories (though it is sometimes still referred to as *core memory*). These are cheaper to manufacture and are faster, having cycle times of less than half a microsecond (or 500 *nanoseconds*). The only disadvantage of semiconductor memories compared with the older core memory technology is that semiconductor memories are *volatile*, that is, if power to the machine is disconnected then the data stored in memory are lost.

Central processing unit

The most complex component in the computer is its central processing unit (CPU). As illustrated in Figure 1-2, it is useful to distinguish three subsystems within the CPU: the timing and control unit, the arithmetic logic unit, and the high-speed registers.

Figure 1-2. Components of a central processing unit

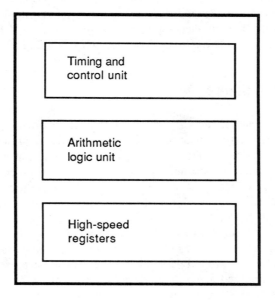

Timing and control unit

The timing and control unit is concerned with the timing of operations, the choice of data manipulation operations, the identification of the data elements that are to be manipulated, the acquisition of those data elements (maybe they have to be obtained from memory), the passing of these data operands to the part of the CPU that will perform the desired operation and, finally, the placing of the result wherever it is supposed to go.

The timing and control unit is best viewed as a sort of *computer within a computer*. Working in a manner analogous to a kind of special purpose computer, these timing and control unit circuits execute wired-in *microprograms* that specify how data can be transferred, instructions recognized, and so forth.

Arithmetic logic unit

It is the arithmetic logic unit (ALU) that actually transforms data, using circuits that perform various arithmetic and logical operations. Possible arithmetic circuits include those for adding two numbers, multiplying two numbers and dividing one number by another. Obviously, such circuits have two inputs and usually one output (an integer division circuit might have two outputs, one output being the quotient and the second for the remainder). The timing and control unit arranges for the data to appear at the right inputs of these circuits, then collects and routes the outputs to their appropriate destinations.

There are also logical circuits for *twiddling* bit patterns including the obvious ones for 'and' and 'or'. In addition, there are usually a number of circuits for shifting the bits in, or rotating the bits around, one word of data.

The more complex computers have more circuits built into their arithmetic logic units. A simple computer might only be able to process integers represented in binary, while a more complex model might also incorporate circuits for manipulating real numbers, or for handling numbers represented in *packed decimal*. Sometimes, these extra circuits are available as add-ons, to be purchased separately if required.

High-speed registers

The final component in the CPU is the high-speed storage. Though some atypical machines can only perform manipulations on data residing in memory (e.g. to add two numbers, both must be brought directly from memory to the two inputs of the adder circuit and their sum sent back and stored in memory), most machines provide a limited amount of high-speed storage for those items of data being processed. Data have to be loaded initially into these high-speed CPU stores, but once there, are available for subsequent manipulation. Calculations can be performed with the intermediate results placed in the high-speed stores. Only the final result needs to be stored back into memory. These high-speed stores are called *registers* (or, sometimes, *accumulators)*.

Some CPUs have only a single register; most machines have 8 or 16. Data in registers can be accessed much faster than data in memory (access times will be in the order of 10 nanoseconds as compared with 500 nanoseconds).

Most machines impose some restrictions on the source and destination of data passing through the circuits in the arithmetic logic unit. Quite commonly, one (or both) input(s) and/or the output from a circuit in the arithmetic logic unit must be data from a register (the second input could be fetched from memory).

Multiregister machines may have additional restrictions on the use of particular registers. A few machines allow the programmer to employ registers in whatever manner is desired (however, there may be conventions regarding usage). On other machines, there may be restrictions wired into the circuitry. For example, one group of registers might be designated as *index* registers to be used only when accessing elements of arrays or other data structures; another register may be reserved as a *stack pointer* for use in all stack-oriented data manipulations and related aspects of program control; only one or two registers, out of a set of four or more, might be usable for holding data and results when performing actual calculations.

The restrictions on data location and register usage must be borne in mind by programmers working at the assembly-language level and by programmers who have to implement code generators for the compilers that will run on a particular machine. Subject to any restrictions on register usage, one attempts to optimize each particular loop construct in a program by reserving CPU data registers for those variables most frequently accessed in that loop.

Apart from the registers used for program data, the CPU contains other high-speed registers. As illustrated in Figure 1-3, there are anonymous registers in the arithmetic logic unit which hold data during manipulation and there are also registers in the timing and control unit.

One of the timing and control unit's registers is the *program counter* (PC). Usually, the program counter contains the address of the next instruction to be executed and, after an instruction is brought from memory, the PC is incremented to the address of the next instruction in sequence. When the program instruction is a 'jump' (corresponding to an explicit 'GOTO' statement in a program, or an implicit 'GOTO' for a 'WHILE' or 'IF...THEN' statement), then the value in the PC is changed and the next instruction is fetched from this new address.

Figure 1-3. Registers in a central processing unit

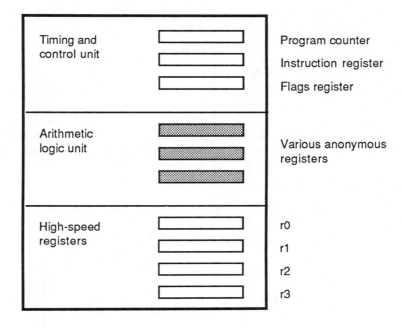

A second register in the timing and control unit is the *instruction register* (IR). Instructions are transferred from memory to the instruction register where they are decoded.

Most CPUs have a *flags* (or *condition codes*) *register* usually comprised of a number of 1-bit flags that encode various status information. Thus, there may be one bit that indicates whether or not the last datum brought from memory, or generated by a data-manipulation operation, was equal to zero. Another 1-bit flag, if set, may indicate that the last arithmetic operation generated a *carry* (just like doing addition when in school, sometimes a carry is generated from one column to the next). Another 1-bit flag may indicate that the CPU is running a program in *user* mode in which there are some restrictions on the range of allowed instructions. These various 1-bit flags are collected together into a flags register. There will be instructions that can test the settings of chosen flags.

Peripheral devices and their controllers

The various peripheral devices and their controllers represent the fourth component of the simple computer. They perform data transfers, and convert data between their external form and a form suitable for computer manipulation. Since they are connected to the main bus, information can pass from a device, through the controller, onto the bus and thence either into data registers in the CPU or, maybe, directly into storage locations in memory.

For each type of device there will be a controller and within the controller there will be a number of registers. A typical controller for a peripheral device contains registers for holding data being transferred to/from the device (*buffer* registers), and for holding 1-bit flags that contain various device *status* information. For example, as illustrated in Figure 1-4, a keyboard controller will have (at least) two registers. There will be an 8-bit data buffer register, which is used to hold a bit pattern that corresponds to the character key pressed on the keyboard. There will also be a 1-bit status register (or *flag* register) that, if set (i.e., is 1), indicates that new data are available. These data can be read when the CPU executes an appropriate instruction. After reading a character, the CPU would clear this *keyboard-ready flag*. When another key is pressed on the keyboard, the

Figure 1-4. Keyboard controller with two registers

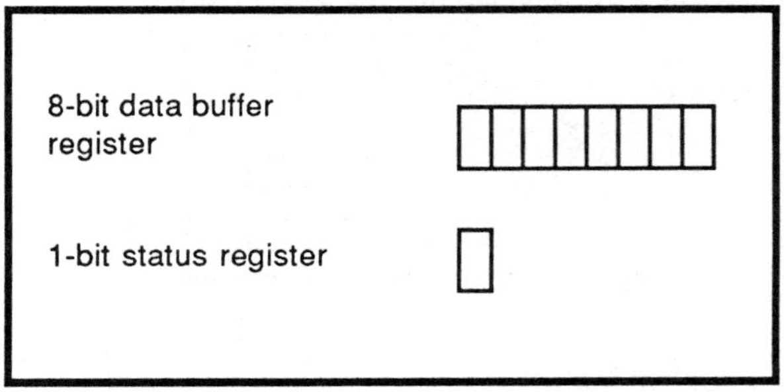

controller would again construct an appropriate bit pattern in its data buffer, and again set its status flag register. A program, running on the CPU, can check whether another character is available by executing an instruction that tests the setting of this keyboard-ready flag.

Controllers for other devices are more complex. For example, a disk controller needs a register to store the number of that block of disk used for the next transfer; another internal flag is needed to indicate whether a 'read' or a 'write' operation is required; and still other registers are needed to record where, in memory, data read from disk are to be placed.

Sometimes, a controller may be shared among a number of similar devices. A computer might for instance have two disk units attached to the same disk controller. The controller would then incorporate a switch that it could use to select which disk unit is to be involved in the next data transfer.

2

An overview of program execution

This chapter provides an overview of the process of program execution as seen at the machine level. Students should already be familiar with the conceptual processes involved in the execution of a program written in a high-level language, such as Pascal. When programming in Pascal, one can focus on the data transformations that the program is to accomplish. But at the machine level, one must also be concerned with the exact way each individual data transformation step will be performed.

Every data transformation step in a program will require (1) determination of where in memory the data elements are located, (2) movement of data from memory into the CPU, (3) performance of the required operation combining the data, and (4) determination of where in memory the result is to be placed, and, then, movement of this result from the CPU back to that memory location. Any machine-level program will involve this kind of detailed description of how data are to be located and manipulated by the CPU.

The coding of the actual data combination step (step 3) is relatively simple. The machine will have circuitry in its arithmetic logic unit for performing the additions, multiplications, or whatever other operations are required. The programmer writing the machine code need only specify the use of the right *instruction*, and hence the appropriate circuit; this part of the programming task is, therefore, similar to coding in a high-level language. But programming at the machine level is more difficult than programming in a high-level language because the programmer must specify the data movements (steps 1, 2, and 4) in full detail.

A simple statement in a high-level language (e.g. 'product:=a[i,j]*b[j,k]') may result in many variables and constants being copied from memory into CPU registers, their combination and, possibly, the storage of temporary results back into memory. The required multiplication operation would be the simplest step in a sequence of a dozen instructions needed to accomplish this data transformation example. For a compiled high-level language, it is the code-generator phase of the compiler that must determine some optimal order for moving data into CPU registers and what results have to be stored temporarily back in memory. A programmer working at the machine level must perform this detailed coding by hand.

In addition to being concerned with the need to move data between memory and the CPU, the machine-code programmer (or a compiler's code generator routines) must also devise appropriate descriptions of memory locations. As well as a repertoire of instructions (that define the arithmetic logic unit circuits to be employed), a machine will have a range of *addressing modes* (each addressing mode being a different way of describing memory locations). Sometimes the address of a data element is known when the program is written; in other cases, it is necessary to calculate, at run time, the address of the datum needed (such is the case when accessing an array element; the address of the datum then depends on the values of array indices). Different addressing modes will distinguish such cases and allow the programmer to specify the location of data.

In this chapter, a prototypical computer model and a fragment of Pascal code are used to illustrate the machine level processes involved in program execution. Instruction repertoires will be reviewed in more detail in Chapters 5, 6, 8 (for the simulated machine), and 16. Addressing modes are considered in Chapters 7 and 17.

A machine to illustrate program execution

Figure 2-1 illustrates the prototypical computer model used for this example. The machine is word oriented; each word in memory will hold one instruction or one data element. The CPU will have a single data register (the *accumulator*), as well as its instruction register, program counter, and flags register. Two-input data manipulation instructions, for example, an addition instruction, will take the current contents of the accumulator as one of their inputs and combine these data with data brought from memory. The result of a data combination operation will be placed in the accumulator.

Figure 2-1.   Architecture of the prototypical computer

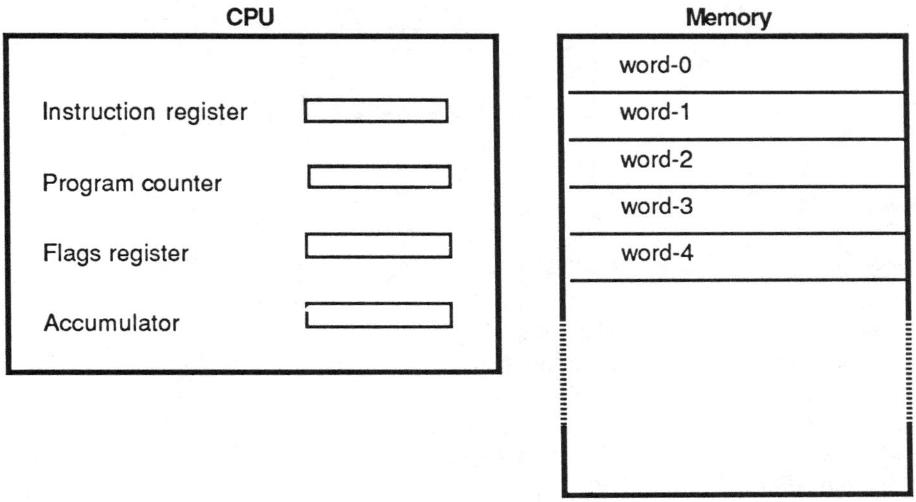

Figure 2-2 illustrates how a program would be arranged in the memory of such a computer. The code would start at a conventional address (here it is presumed to be address 0). Following the code, there would be a few words reserved to hold constants and a larger number of locations reserved for program variables. (A large proportion of memory would, in general, be left unused when a simple program is run by itself on a typical microcomputer.)

The program code will consist of a sequence of instructions. When read and interpreted by the timing and control circuits of the CPU, these instructions will cause the appropriate data transformation circuits to be used to manipulate the program's data.

Figure 2-2. Arrangement of program code and data in memory

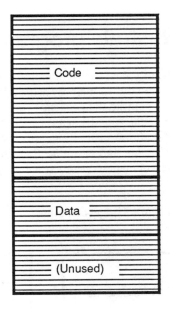

Instructions

The basic types of instruction needed on any *accumulator machine* include:

1. *Data loads and stores.* If data must be manipulated in the CPU, then there must be mechanisms for transferring initial data from memory into the CPU and for copying results back into memory. These instructions will need some description of the address of the memory location that they must reference when loading or storing data.
2. *Data combination.* Addition and logical 'and' are examples of instructions that combine data held in the CPU with data from memory.
3. *Data manipulation.* Data manipulation instructions, such as 'complement' (or logical 'not'), can work solely on data held in the CPU.
4. *Program control.* There must be 'jump' instructions that permit the construction of

loops, 'if...then...else' and 'case' constructs. There must also be 'subroutine call' (procedure call) instructions; both 'jump' and 'subroutine call' instructions require descriptions of particular memory locations. For 'jump' instructions, it is necessary to know where to jump to (i.e. what is the address of the next instruction if it is not in normal sequence); for 'subroutine call' instructions it is necessary to know the address where the subroutine begins.

5. *Testing conditions*. Not all jumps are unconditional, more often it is necessary to express conditional transfers, for example, 'if (num>3) then goto 1234'; a machine's instruction set must include mechanisms for both making tests and using the results of those tests in some conditional jump.

6. *Input and output*. The input data for a program has to be read from some peripheral device, and results sent to some other device; specialized instructions may be necessary for control of devices.

For this example of program execution, the various data transformations, that is, loads, stores, combinations, and so forth, are the most important.

Each of the data transformation instructions in the code of the program will have the structure shown in Figure 2-3. An instruction word is divided into two fields. A fixed number of bits, m, is reserved to specify the data manipulation transformation to be performed. Reserving m bits to define the operation allows for 2^m possible bit patterns and therefore 2^m possible operations. The different bit patterns define the machine operation codes or *op-codes*. On a machine that uses a 4-bit op-code, the code 0000 might represent a command to the CPU to fetch data from memory and place them into the accumulator, that is, a 'load' instruction. Another pattern, for example, 0001, might represent an 'add' instruction, specifying that the data from memory and the data currently in the accumulator be directed to the adder circuit of the arithmetic logic unit.

Figure 2-3. The format of a simple instruction word

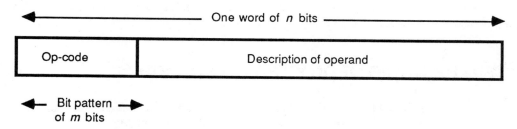

Instruction execution involves three distinct phases: fetch, decode, and execute.

In the *fetch* phase, the timing and control unit of the CPU reads an instruction word from that memory location whose address corresponds to the value held in the program counter. Once brought from memory, this word is placed in the instruction register and then the program counter is updated ready for the next instruction fetch cycle.

The *decoding* phase then commences. The op-code bits are extracted from the instruction register and analyzed. If the op-code corresponds to a data combination instruction, the remaining bits of the word in the instruction register are passed to an address decoder. There, the actual address of the data required is derived.

Finally, in the *execution* phase, the CPU again reads data from memory (at the address determined in the decoding step) and then directs the data into that circuit in the arithmetic logic unit determined in the first part of the instruction decoding step. The execution phase is completed when the results from the arithmetic logic unit are placed into the accumulator.

Defining the operand for an instruction

After the op-code bits have been extracted, the remaining bits of a data transformation instruction hold some description of the operand, that is, the data to be taken from memory and used. Sometimes, these bits of an instruction word may actually represent the data required; more often, these bits can be interpreted to yield the address in memory containing the required data.

It is almost atypical for these operand description bits of an instruction word to define explicitly the address of the location containing the data. Instead, these bits might specify a *relative* address, in effect saying something like *the data are in the fortieth word after the word containing this instruction.* Or the address might be specified relative to the contents of a CPU register, saying something like *the data are in the two-hundredth word after the location identifed in 'base register xx'.* The specification of the address of some data might be quite indirect, for example, the operand description bits might say something equivalent to *the address of the required datum is itself held in the variable which is in a memory location whose address is xxx.*

As well as circuits to decode the op-code part of an instruction word, the timing and control circuits in the CPU include *address decoders*. The address decoder circuits use a few of the bits in the operand description part of an instruction word to recognize the particular addressing mode being used. The remaining bits of the operand description can then be interpreted as representing the data, the explicit address of the data, a relative address for the data, or whatever else might be appropriate.

An example of program execution

The following Pascal program illustrates some simple data manipulations and a *for-loop* construct. (The program does not include any input or output. Machine level I/O is complex, and has therefore been deferred until Chapter 9.)

```
program one;
var   j,sum:integer;
begin
     sum:=0;
     for j:=1 to 10 do
          sum:=sum+j;
end.
```

The first steps in the program involve initialization of the variable 'sum', and initialization of the variables that will be used to control the for-loop. The following pseudo machine code, for the model computer, represents these same initialization steps at the machine level.

```
clear    "sum"
load     "constant 1"
store    "j"
load     "constant 10"
store    "limit"
```

The command words load, clear, and store correspond to the op-code parts of the instructions. The quoted strings, "sum", "constant 10", will be represented in the machine by bit patterns that can be interpreted as specifying the address of a memory location reserved for a variable (either explicitly or implicitly through some relative addressing scheme), or as representing data explicitly. (Details of addressing modes are not important in this example.)

Execution of this group of instructions would accomplish the explicit and implicit initialization steps prior to the for-loop of the Pascal program example. Thus, execution of 'clear "sum"' places the value 0 in that memory location reserved for the variable known as sum. The sequence 'load "constant 1"'; 'store "j"' sets the initial value of the for-loop index. This example machine code refers to a variable, 'limit', that is not defined in the Pascal code. Frequently, a compiler will have to invent and use additional variables to hold such things as the value at which a loop is to terminate. The compiler allocates additional space for such variables and generates code to initialize them. Thus, here the instruction sequence 'load "constant 10"'; 'store "limit"' is used to set "limit" to hold the value that is to be used in the for-loop's termination test. Details of the fetch, decode, and execute steps in instruction execution are illustrated in Figures 2-4 to 2-6.

Code corresponding to the main part of the Pascal for-loop is shown in Figure 2-4. For the purposes of example, some explicit addresses have been assigned to the memory locations containing the various instructions and data elements. The loop is represented by the instructions in memory locations 100-107. Here, the code for the body of the for-loop is followed by a loop termination test. If the termination test is not satisfied, a jump is made back to the top of the loop and the cycle repeated. Note that this way of encoding a for-loop forces the code for the body of the loop to be executed at least once (even in those cases where the termination condition was satisfied prior to first entry).

Figure 2-4 illustrates the state of the computer at the commencement of the fourth cycle through the body of the loop. The program counter (PC) is pointing to the first instruction of the loop, that is, address 100. Execution of the next fetch cycle involves the CPU taking the value 100 from the PC, generating a 'read memory at address 100' request, placing this on the bus and then waiting for the memory to respond. When the memory responds, the data passed back across the bus is directed to the instruction register (IR); the PC is incremented to 101. The resulting machine state would be as shown in Figure 2-5.

Figure 2-4. **Prototypical machine code corresponding to the for-loop of the Pascal example program**

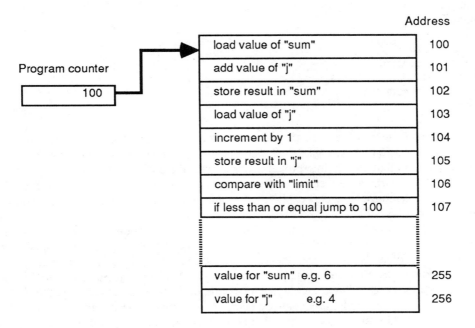

	Address
load value of "sum"	100
add value of "j"	101
store result in "sum"	102
load value of "j"	103
increment by 1	104
store result in "j"	105
compare with "limit"	106
if less than or equal jump to 100	107
value for "sum" e.g. 6	255
value for "j" e.g. 4	256

Program counter: 100

Figure 2-5. **Machine state on completion of an instruction fetch**

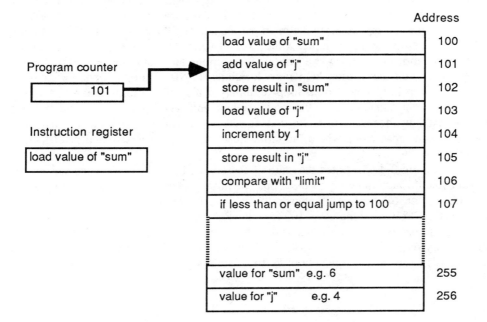

	Address
load value of "sum"	100
add value of "j"	101
store result in "sum"	102
load value of "j"	103
increment by 1	104
store result in "j"	105
compare with "limit"	106
if less than or equal jump to 100	107
value for "sum" e.g. 6	255
value for "j" e.g. 4	256

Program counter: 101

Instruction register: load value of "sum"

Instruction decoding first involves extraction of the op-code bits from the data now held in the instruction register. The op-code bits are examined and the timing and control circuits of the CPU establish the instruction as being a 'load'. 'Load' instructions require data; the remaining bits in the instruction word encode where to find the data. These operand description bits are passed to the address decoder circuits. Address decoding determines the data to be in the memory location with address 255. The execution phase of this instruction then involves obtaining the data value, that is, 6, from location 255 and copying it into the accumulator. The current machine status is shown in Figure 2-6.

Figure 2-6. Machine status on completion of decode and execute cycles

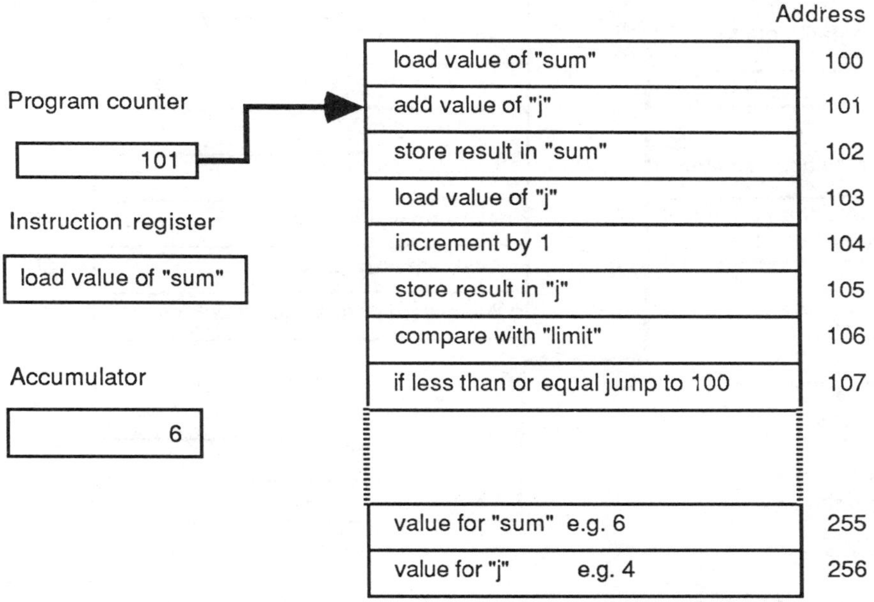

	Address
load value of "sum"	100
add value of "j"	101
store result in "sum"	102
load value of "j"	103
increment by 1	104
store result in "j"	105
compare with "limit"	106
if less than or equal jump to 100	107
value for "sum" e.g. 6	255
value for "j" e.g. 4	256

Program counter: 101

Instruction register: load value of "sum"

Accumulator: 6

The machine is now ready to commence the next instruction cycle. The fetch, decode, and execution stages of 'add value of "j"' and subsequent instructions proceed in exactly the same manner.

The only variation comes when the conditional 'jump' instruction, 'if less than or equal jump to 100', is obtained and the op-code part decoded. The machine status at this point is shown in Figure 2-7. Comparison instructions, like the one in location 106, clear or set bits in the flags register as appropriate to the result obtained by the comparison. Here, the 'less than' flag was set.

As this is a 'jump' instruction, the remaining bits in the instruction word are interpreted as representing an address and decoded, to yield in this case the value 100. Execution of a conditional jump instruction entails examination of the flags register to determine the setting of specified bits. For this instruction, a jump would be made if either the 'less than' or 'equal' bits were set. If the test on the flags is satisfied, a jump is made to the address determined in the decoding step; if the test is not satisfied, execution proceeds with the next instruction in sequence. Here, the test on flags is satisfied resulting in the program counter being reset to 100 (the start of the loop). With this step completed, the machine is again set to fetch the first instruction from the loop, the 'load value of "sum"' instruction.

Figure 2-7. Machine status after the conditional 'jump' instruction has been fetched and decoded

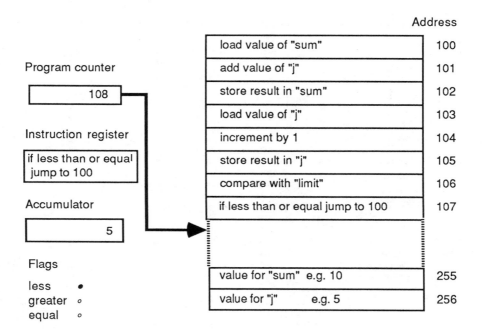

Calculations using machine addresses as data

Machine level code becomes rapidly more complex when more elaborate data structures are required. Access to arrays, records, and lists will require calculations of addresses. For example, the Pascal program:

```
program two;
var  a     : array[0..10] of integer;    j: integer;
begin
     for j:=0 to 10 do a[j]:=j;
end.
```

would correspond to the following code for the model machine:

```
        clear       "j"
        load        "constant 10"
        store       in "limit"
loop    load        value of "j"
        add         "address of the start of array a"
        store       in "temp"
        load        value of "j"
        store       in "location whose address is held in temp"
        increment by 1
        store       in "j"
        compare with "limit"
        if less or equal jump to "location identified by label loop"
        stop
```

Note how here it is necessary to calculate the address where the next data element is to be stored. For example, if the array 'a' has been allocated the addresses 180-190, then on the first cycle of the loop, when j=0, address 180 is required; on the second cycle, when j=1, address 181 is required, and so on. For this single-register machine, it is necessary to calculate the required address by adding the value of 'j' to a constant value (180), the address of the start of the array. The computed address must then be saved in 'temp'. The data value is again loaded from 'j' and stored in memory (in the location whose address is held in 'temp'). (A machine with an index register would permit a simpler set of instructions for accessing the array; however, the same address arithmetic operations would still be implicitly performed.)

Microcode: The 'computer within a computer'

As noted in Chapter 1, the timing and control circuits are really equivalent to a special computer executing a predefined *microprogram*. The Pascal code corresponding to a fetch instruction *microprocedure* would be something like:

```
microprocedure fetch;
type busoperation=(memoryread,memorywrite);
var     address    : integer;
        datum      : integer;
        busop      : busoperation;
begin
        address:=pc;
        busop:=memoryread;
        buscommand(busop,address,datum);
        ir:=datum;
        pc:=pc+1;
end;
```

Here, it is assumed that 'pc' and 'ir' are global variables, and that 'buscommand(b : busoperation; a : integer; var d : integer)' is a microcoded procedure that controls the bus.

The subsequent decoding and execution steps can also be described in terms of small microprocedures. A rather oversimplified decode and execute microprocedure would have something like the following form.

```
microprocedure doit;
type busoperation=(memoryread,memorywrite);
var   address   : integer;
      datum     : integer;
      opcode    : bitpattern;
      operand   : bitpattern;

begin
      { extract the bits representing opcode}
      opcode:=splitoutopcode(ir);
      { extract the operand bits }
      operand:=splitoutoperand(ir);
      case opcode of
          0000: { load }
              begin
              address:=decodeaddress(operand);
              busop:=memoryread;
              buscommand(busop,address,datum);
              acc:=datum;
              end;
          0001: { add }
              begin
              address:=decodeaddress(operand);
              busop:=memoryread;
              buscommand(busop,address,datum);
              acc:=adder(acc,datum);
              end;

              .
              .
              .

          0101: { less than or equal conditional jump }
              begin
              address:=decodeaddress(operand);
              if less_flag() or eq_flag() then
                  pc:=address;
              end;

              .
              .

          end;
end;
```

For simplicity, it has been assumed that, for all instructions, the decoding process is limited to extraction of op-code and operand bits (through microfunctions 'splitoutopcode' etc.). The op-code bit pattern is then used as a selector for a large case statement. Further, it has been assumed that the operand bits of the instructions like 'load' or 'add' will always encode the address of the data. Microfunction 'decodeaddress' interprets operand bits to yield the address. Microfunction 'adder' returns the sum of its two arguments.

Exercises

1. Recode the two examples of pseudo machine language so that the code representing the bodies of the loops is not traversed if the loop termination condition is satisfied prior to initial entry.

2. How would one compute the address of an array element 'a[j,k]' for an array declared as 'var a:array[0..11,0..5] of integer'?

3. What would the array accessing code be if the array declaration were 'var a: array[13..19,'a'..'n'] of integer'?

3

Bit manipulation

Most forms of data processing in machine language are identical to the kinds of data processing performed in high-level languages. Thus, one can process integers and floating point (real) numbers using instructions that perform standard arithmetic operations. All machines allow strings to be manipulated character by character; some have more powerful instructions that can copy complete strings, or can even search for characters in strings.

Simple bit patterns represent a data type used much more heavily in machine language programs than in programs written in higher level languages.

Some of the instructions available for bit manipulations are familiar. These are the *logical* operation instructions that correspond to the manipulation of sets in Pascal. Other bit manipulation instructions perform data transformations which do not have any analogies in high-level languages like Pascal and FORTRAN; these instructions include the various *rotates* and *shifts* of bit patterns.

The different forms of bit manipulation instruction are reviewed in this section. The logical operations are illustrated first. Examples are given showing both how these operations correspond to the set manipulations that can be performed in Pascal, and how these operations can sometimes allow for short cuts in special cases of data manipulation. Subsequently, the various rotates and shifts are illustrated. Most of the examples are concerned with 8-bit bit patterns.

Logical operations

There is one 1-input logical operation, 'complement' (or logical 'not'), and a few two-input operations including 'and', 'inclusive or', and 'exclusive or'. Machines generally have a 'complement' instruction, an 'and' instruction, and at least one form of 'or' instruction. Other logical operations (e.g. 'equivalence') can always be achieved by suitable combinations of these basic instructions.

The 'complement' instruction simply flips all the bits in the data element that it processes: all 1s become 0s and all 0s become 1s. The two-input logical instructions, such as 'and' and 'inclusive or', perform (in parallel) tandem processing on each bit position of the inputs. Thus, 'and' generates a result which has a 1 only in those positions where both inputs have a 1. The 'inclusive or' instruction yields a 1 at each position where either of the inputs have a 1; in contrast, the 'exclusive or' (or 'not equivalence') instruction produces a 1 in its output in those positions where either, but not both, of its inputs possesses a 1. These various bit manipulations are illustrated in Figure 3-1.

Figure 3-1. **Manipulation of, and combination of, 8-bit bit patterns**

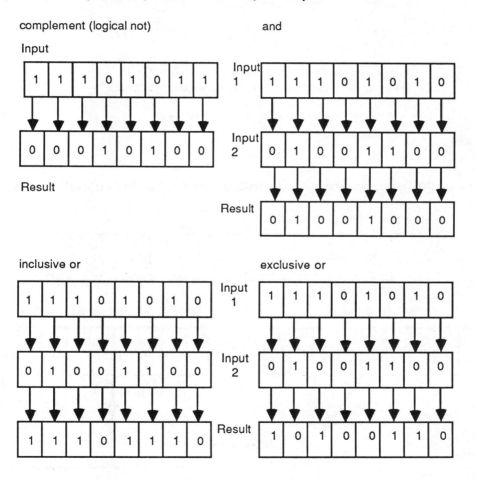

Bit patterns constitute the natural machine representation for Pascal set variables. The Pascal sets defined and used in the following program fragment could be represented in 8-bit bit patterns and manipulated as shown in Figure 3-2. The data manipulations require a 'complement' operation and a logical 'and'.

```
type days = (sun,mon,tues,wed,thur,fri,sat);
    daysets = set of days;
var week, labclasses, tv_movies,
    evening_lectures,watch_tv_movie : daysets;
begin
        .
        .
        .
        week:=[sun,mon,tues,wed,thur,fri,sat];
        labclasses:=[mon,wed];
        .
        tv_movies:=[sun,wed,fri];
        evening_lectures:=[tues,wed,thur];
        .
        { logical expression of set operation ...        }
        { watch_tv_movie:=tv_movies and (not evening_lectures); }
        { Pascal version ... }
        watch_tv_movie:=tv_movies -  evening_lectures;

end.
```

Figure 3-2.   Bit patterns constitute the natural representation for Pascal set variables

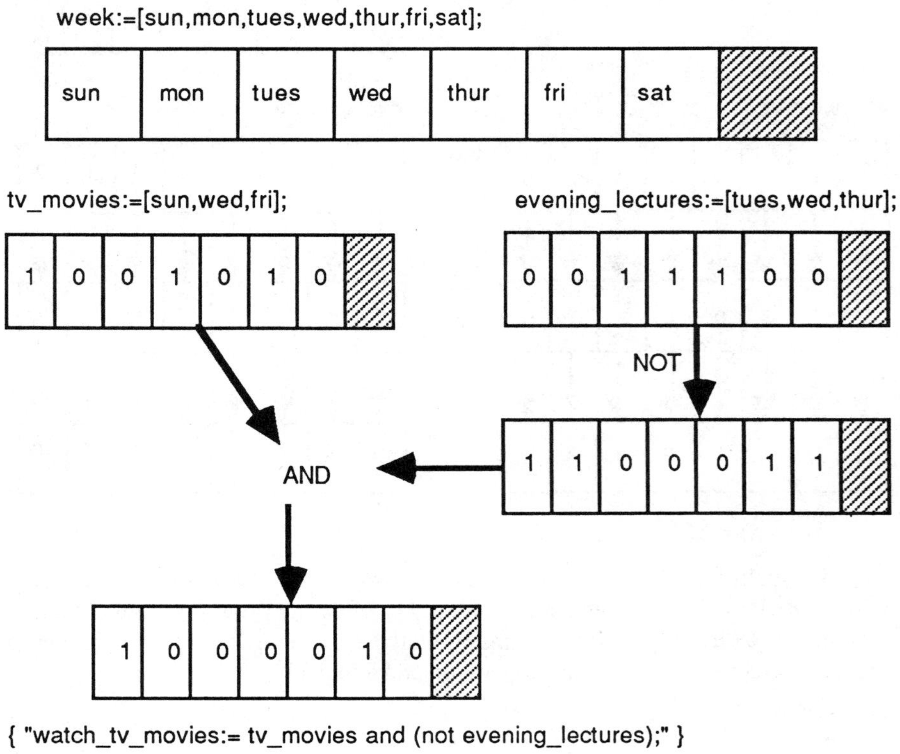

week:=[sun,mon,tues,wed,thur,fri,sat];

sun	mon	tues	wed	thur	fri	sat	

tv_movies:=[sun,wed,fri];

1	0	0	1	0	1	0	

evening_lectures:=[tues,wed,thur];

0	0	1	1	1	0	0	

NOT

1	1	0	0	0	1	1	

AND

1	0	0	0	0	1	0	

{ "watch_tv_movies:= tv_movies and (not evening_lectures);" }

There are many ways in which bit manipulation operations can be used to provide short cuts in various kinds of data manipulation. For example, if it were necessary to convert lower case letters into upper case letters then the typical Pascal code would be:

if ch **in** ['a'..'z'] **then** ch:=chr(ord(ch)+ord('A')-ord('a'));

Here, it is assumed that the ASCII (American Standards Code for Information Interchange) character code is being used so that these simple arithmetic steps will achieve the required conversion. The same conversion can be achieved more economically by appropriate bit manipulations. (The bit patterns conventionally used to represent characters are discussed in more detail in Chapter 4.) In ASCII code, corresponding upper case and lower case letters are represented by bit patterns that are identical in all but one position. The differences are illustrated in Figure 3-3. A bit masking operation can be used to change the case of a character; an appropriate bit pattern *mask* is shown.

Figure 3-3. Bit-masking operation to change the case of a character

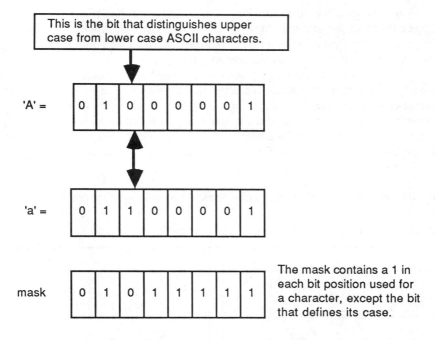

'And'ing together a bit pattern that represents a letter and the bit pattern shown as 'mask' will always yield the bit pattern that represents the upper case letter. The mask has been chosen to have 1s set in all those bit positions that need to be retained, and a 0 bit in the position where upper and lower case letters differ. 'And'ing the mask with the upper case letter representation produces no change; whereas, 'and'ing the mask against the lower case representation throws away just the one bit that distinguished it as being lower case. Rather than the elaborate test, function calls and arithmetic of the Pascal, one could perform the conversion with just three instructions, that is, 'load' value for character; 'and' with mask; and 'store' result in character.

The greater efficiency of well-chosen bit-manipulation-based data manipulations often so captivates the imagination of programmers that they will search for ways of using these instructions even at the expense of clarity of code. Such hackery is best avoided.

Rotate and shift operations

Most machines have a variety of 'rotate' and 'shift' instructions. These instructions allow the bits in a register to be moved about in various ways. Rotates move bits around within a register; a bit that moves out from one end of a register is copied in again at the other end. Thus, as shown in Figure 3-4, one can have a 'rotate left one place' in which each bit is moved leftwards one place, with the bit moved out of the left-most position being fed back in on the right. There is a corresponding 'rotate right' operation, also illustrated in Figure 3-4.

A simple machine might have instructions for one-place rotations; then, multiplace rotations are accomplished by having the 'rotate' instruction in a loop, or by several successive 'rotate' instructions. A more sophisticated machine would have instructions like 'rotate left five places' and so forth.

With shifts, the bits moving out from one end of a register are lost. (On some machines, there are arrangements whereby the last bit to have been shifted out of a register is saved in the carry bit in the flags register, or in some other CPU register.) The positions left vacant at the end of the register, because of bits shifted out, are usually filled with 0s. Thus, typically one has a 'shift left one place' and a corresponding 'shift right' (the 'logical shift right'), both of which are shown in Figure 3-5.

Figure 3-4. Rotate instructions move bits cyclically around in a register

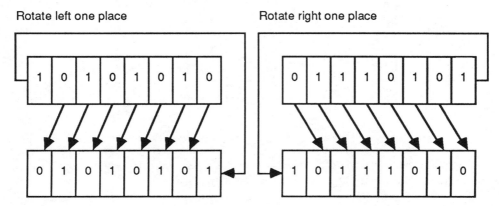

Figure 3-5. Shift instructions

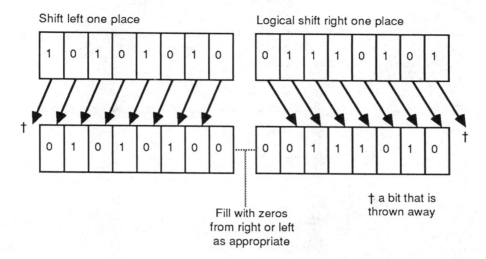

Fill with zeros
from right or left
as appropriate

† a bit that is
thrown away

However, there are usually two forms of the 'shift right' instruction. As well as the 'logical shift right' (which is the obvious inverse of a 'shift left') there is normally an 'arithmetic shift right', shown in Figure 3-6. In the arithmetic shift right, instead of filling from the left with 0s, the original left-most bit is duplicated. If, as in the example in Figure 3-6, the left-most bit was originally a 1, then the register is filled from the left with 1s; if the original left-most bit had been a 0, then the register would be filled from the left with 0s. This apparently esoteric operation is actually useful in some numeric applications; it makes it easier to code routines for performing multiplications and divisions on machines that don't have hardware circuits for these operations.

Figure 3-6. The 'arithmetic shift right '

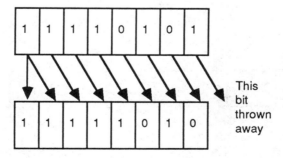

This bit thrown away

Shifts and rotates are both rather specialized data manipulation operations. An example of where they might be useful would be the handling of *packed data*. For instance, while working on a machine with a 16-bit word, one might find that one needs a large number of two-element records. For each of these records, one of the elements might require 7 bits, and the other 5. As shown in Figure 3-7, both elements of a record could be *packed* into a single word, so halving the overall storage requirement. However, it would usually be necessary to shift the 5-bit data element over to the right of the word before it could be used. Here, a 'shift' instruction would be helpful; if the 5-bit field were needed, the 16-bit data word would be copied from memory into a CPU register and then a 'seven place right shift' would be performed.

Figure 3-7. 'Shift', or 'rotate', operations are necessary to extract data from *packed* records

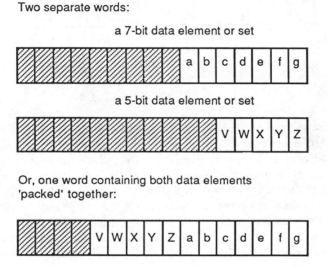

Exercises

1. Fill in the bit patterns that would result from the following sequences of bit manipulation operations:

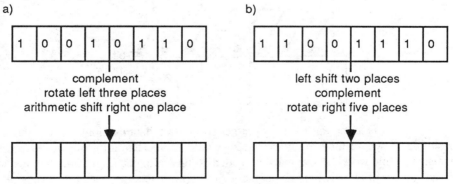

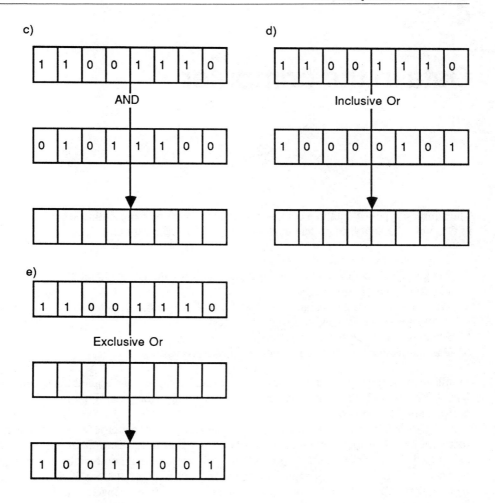

2. Using only 'and' and 'complement' instructions (and, also, 'load' and 'store' instructions for saving intermediate results) write a sequence of bit manipulation instructions that will derive the 'inclusive or' of two words of data.

4

Data in the computer

The simplest types of data in a computer are the bit patterns representing sets as described in Chapter 3. Other types of data that one may want to represent include:

1. Characters, as in message strings.
2. Integers (represented as binary numbers), both for integer arithmetic and for things like loop control variables.
3. Unsigned integers (a specialized simple form of integers).
4. Addresses (a special case of unsigned integers).
5. Floating-point numbers, for scientific calculations.
6. Packed-decimal numbers, for commercial data processing.

In this chapter, the representation of characters, and unsigned and signed binary numbers will be considered. Later, in Chapter 16, representations of floating-point and packed-decimal numbers will be reviewed briefly.

It is important to remember that all data are just bit patterns (as are the machine instructions). The interpretation of the data bit patterns is determined solely by the circuit(s) that process them. It is possible to build circuits that combine bit patterns in a manner consistent with their representing numbers in binary notation; other circuits can be built that will yield results consistent with an interpretation as encoded-decimal data. If data representing numbers in binary notation are sent to the decimal addition circuit then they will be processed; however, the results of such processing will no longer be meaningful for the application program. When working at the machine language level it is quite easy to make programming errors that, at run time, result in actions such as trying to execute, as an instruction, a value read from a memory location that actually holds the sum of data values. The resulting action would be unpredictable, and quite possibly unreproducible in different test runs of the program. Such opportunities for error add to the difficulty of programming at the machine level.

Character data

Characters are the simplest of the data types that must be considered. In order to represent characters, all that is required is some convention for determining the bit pattern that will be used internally for each possible character. Once the bit patterns have been agreed, electronic and electromechanical input devices can be designed to generate the correct bit pattern code for each character keyed-in or read from a card. Similarly, output devices can be designed to accept bit patterns and either electronically, or by electromechanical methods, proceed to generate the appropriate printed or displayed character representation.

Originally, most computers used a 6-bit bit pattern for representing characters. Six bits allow for 64 possible characters with representations from 000000 to 111111. Such codes could, for example, represent 'A' as 000001, 'Y' as 011001 and '=' as 111101. Various 8-bit codes are now more commonly employed. The 64-character limit of a 6-bit code meant that upper and lower case letters could not be separately represented and that relatively few special characters could be included.

There are a couple of different character codes in common use. EBCDIC is a code used mainly on IBM computers. ASCII (American Standards Code for Information Interchange) is a character-encoding scheme supported by most computer manufacturers (including IBM).

The basic ASCII code uses 7 bits to represent characters, so allowing for 128 different possible symbols. As well as printable characters such as the upper and lower case letters, the digits and the punctuation marks, the ASCII code includes also a number of standardized control characters. These control characters include standard formatting characters such as backspace, vertical and horizontal tabs, and newlines. Some of the characters, and their corresponding binary codes, are shown in Table 4-1 (a complete list of the ASCII character set and their octal equivalents is given in Appendix A).

Other control characters are passed between computers, or between a computer and peripherals. Usually, messages sent between machines are composed according to strict rules (or *protocols*) which specify that any data bytes in a message be preceded by a header and followed by a trailer, both composed of control characters (e.g. 'soh' *start of header*, or 'etx' *end of transmission*). Once one machine has sent a message it will normally await a response; the response might include the 'ack' (*acknowledge*) control character if the message was accepted by the recipient, or might be the 'nak' (*negative acknowledge*) control character if the message received appeared to be corrupt.

Table 4-1. Some example characters in 7-bit ASCII code

bs	0001000	backspace	(control character)
nak	0010101	negative acknowledge	(control)
sub	0011010	substitute	(control)
esc	0011011	escape	(control)
*	0101010	asterisk	(printable character)
7	0110111	digit 7	(printable)
H	1001000	letter H	(printable)
h	1101000	letter h	(printable)
~	1111110	tilde symbol	(printable)

Control characters such as 'sub' (*substitute*) and 'esc' (*escape*) allow terminals, plotters, and so forth to treat a number of subsequent characters in a special manner. For example, Tektronix™ storage display terminals allow pictures to be drawn as well as text to be displayed; these terminals can accept an 'esc <character>' combination as a command to be ready to draw a line or illuminate a point (the coordinates of the point or end of line would then follow in the next few characters).

Usually, an 8-bit version of the ASCII code is employed. The eighth bit carries *parity* information, information that is used to help detect errors when character data are transmitted over electronically noisy communications lines.

Characters being sent from a keyboard to a computer are normally transmitted bit by bit over twisted-pair cable, and possibly through modems and telephone lines. Ideally, the signal being transmitted would appear as square-wave voltage pulses. So, as illustrated in Figure 4-1, the signal for an ASCII 'A' (1000001) should have two voltage pulses (*ideal signal*). (Actually, there would be two or three additional *start/stop* bits transmitted; these are not shown in Figure 4-1.) Telephone lines and twisted cables can, however, pick up other signals and the signal received might have quite a lot of electronic noise imposed on the ideal signal (as shown by *actual signal*). As illustrated, a particularly large noise spike at some moment of time would cause the signal received to be interpreted as 1000101, that is as representing character 'E'.

Figure 4-1.   Transmission error: a noise spike has changed the ideal 1000001 signal into a 1000101 signal

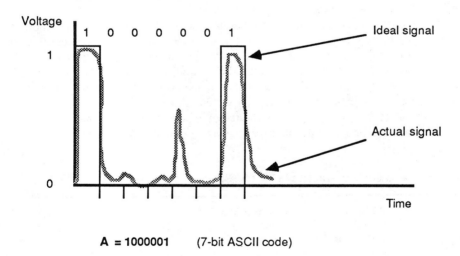

A = 1000001   (7-bit ASCII code)

If there were no way to check data, then the computer that received the erroneous 'E' would have to accept it as valid. The inclusion of a parity bit in the character representations provides the basis of a simple way to check data. In an *odd* parity code, the eighth or parity bit is set to make the total number of 1 bits in the 8-bit pattern an odd number. 'A' is represented in 7 bits as 1000001, and has only 2 bits set to 1. In order to have an 8-bit code with an odd number of 1s, the parity bit would have to be set to be a 1. The odd parity 8-bit representation of 'A' is, therefore, 1100001. The letter 'E' has the 7-bit code 1000101; this already has an odd number of bits set to 1 and therefore the extra parity bit should be a 0. The odd parity 8-bit representation of 'E' is therefore 01000101.

If the 'A' had been transmitted as 11000001 and the third from last bit were set to 1 by a noise spike, then the bit pattern received would be 11000101. A computer is then able to detect that the received character is faulty (the parity bit, the 1 in 11000101, is seen to be wrong because it gives an even number of 1s). Such limited data are not sufficient for the computer to be able to determine the exact nature of the error; but it can ask for the data to be retransmitted.

As well as odd parity codes, it is also possible to use *even* parity codes where the parity bit is chosen so an even number of bits are set to 1 in the overall 8-bit bit pattern.

Unsigned numbers

Internally, most computers use numbers in *binary* (base 2) rather than *decimal* (base 10). (Special decimal representations are implemented on many machines; but the circuits for manipulating numbers represented in decimal are more complex, more costly, and slower than those for handling binary numbers.) It is necessary to know a little about binary number representations; initially, consideration will be limited to unsigned integers because the representations of ± signs adds a little extra complexity.

Apart from being in binary rather than in decimal, the representations of integers in machines differ from more familiar representations in that the size of the machine word imposes a limit upon the largest integer that can be represented. (The examples that follow will use 8-bit representations of integers; consequently, the largest unsigned number will, as shown below, be equivalent to $255_{decimal}$.)

Unlike Roman numbers with their mix of I, II, III, IV, V, X, L, C etc., both binary and decimal notations are positional number systems. The position of each digit in a number determines its significance or weight; this weighting being some power of the base of the number system. Thus, the number $473_{decimal}$ has three sets of 10^0 ($10^0=1$), seven sets of 10^1 ($10^1=$ten), and four sets of 10^2 ($10^2=$hundred) and so represents four hundred and seventy three. The interpretation of a binary number is analogous; the positions of the digits in a number determine their significance, each being weighted as a power of 2 (the base for the binary number system). (Of course, in binary, there are only two possible digits, namely, 0 and 1.) A number 10101_b has one set of 2^0 ($2^0=$one), no sets of 2^1, one set of 2^2 ($2^2=$four), no sets of 2^3 and one set of 2^4 ($2^4=$sixteen); this binary number therefore corresponds to: 16+4+1, or $21_{decimal}$.

If integers are limited to an 8-bit representation, then one has the situation shown in Figure 4-2. The left-most of the 8 bits (0 or 1) will represent the number of 2^7s in the integer, the next bit will be the number of 2^6s, and so on, with the right-most bit determining the number of 2^0s. If all the bits are 0, then the number represented is zero; if all the bits are 1, then the number represented as 11111111_b is equal to two hundred and fifty five (128+64+32+16+8+4+2+1 = 255).

Figure 4-2. **Correspondence between bit positions in an 8-bit unsigned binary number and the powers of 2 that they represent**

2^7	2^6	2^5	2^4	2^3	2^2	2^1	2^0
(=128)	(=64)	(=32)	(=16)	(=8)	(=4)	(=2)	(=1)
0 / 1	0 / 1	0 / 1	0 / 1	0 / 1	0 / 1	0 / 1	0 / 1

An integer given in binary notation can be converted to decimal by simply listing out the number of each of the different powers of 2 that it contains, writing these values in decimal notation, and summing them. An example is shown in Figure 4-3.

Figure 4-3. **Conversion from unsigned binary to decimal number representation**

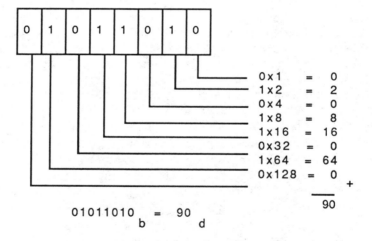

$$01011010_b = 90_d$$

A decimal number can be converted to binary by repeatedly dividing by two and recording the (0/1) remainders, as shown in Figure 4-4. These remainders constitute the binary representation.

Methods of addition and subtraction are the same in all positional number systems irrespective of the particular base they use. The sum of two numbers is obtained by adding the corresponding digits in the various positions, starting at the least significant (right-most) position. A *carry* into the next more significant digit column is generated when the sum of the digits in any particular column exceeds the base used for the number representation. In binary, $0 + 0 = 0$, $0 + 1 = 1$, $1 + 0 = 1$, and $1 + 1 = 10$, that is, 0 and carry of 1. Carries must be added onto the sum for the digits in the more significant position; this can result in carries being propagated. An addition, in binary, with carries, is shown in Figure 4-5.

Figure 4-4.   Conversion from decimal to unsigned binary number representation

$201_{decimal}$

201÷2	
100÷2	1 remainder
50÷2	0 remainder
25÷2	0 remainder
12÷2	1 remainder
6÷2	0 remainder
3÷2	0 remainder
1÷2	1 remainder
0	1 remainder

11001001_b

Figure 4-5.   Addition of unsigned binary numbers with propagating carries

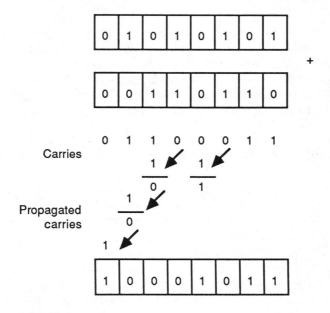

An extra problem with fixed-length representations for numbers is *overflow*. Sometimes, the result of an addition operation will be a number bigger than the largest that can be represented in the number of bits available. For example, 01010101_b + 11010110_b = $\underline{1}00101011_b$ ($85_{decimal}$ + $214_{decimal}$ = $299_{decimal}$). Although the two individual (unsigned) numbers can both be represented, their sum cannot be represented in 8 bits. The 8-bit result 00101011_b is equal to $43_{decimal}$ (43 = [299 modulo 256]). The generation of a number larger than that which can be represented results in an overflow condition. For example:

```
 01010101
 11010110
100101011
↑
```

In this case, there is a carry out at the left-most end of the number; this carry out would set the carry bit in the flags register (or, possibly, would complement the value in the flags carry bit). For these unsigned numbers, a carry out indicates the occurrence of overflow.

Although it is a bit more complex with signed numbers, the addition circuitry in a computer can still detect overflow conditions. Most computers have an overflow flag bit in their flags register which is set to indicate an error state whenever an arithmetic operation has generated a number that cannot be correctly represented.

Signed numbers

Any extension to allow for signed numbers requires a different way of interpreting the bit patterns. Unfortunately, machine representations of signed numbers often seem difficult and confusing. Problems arise with signed numbers both because there are several different ways in which they can be represented (each way having its own advantages and disadvantages), and because the more commonly used machine representations bear little resemblance to conventional representations of signed decimal numbers.

Sign and magnitude representation

It is possible to use a *sign and magnitude* representation for binary integers. This representation is analogous to conventional representations for signed decimal numbers; a number's sign (±) is given first and followed by its magnitude. In a computer, one bit of the machine word is reserved for the sign. A 0 in the sign bit designates a positive number; a 1 in the sign bit is used for negative numbers.

The remaining bits of the word represent the magnitude of the binary integer (in exactly the same manner as already discussed for unsigned numbers). Since one of the 8 bits is reserved for the sign, only 7 remain to represent the magnitude and the size of the largest number that can be represented has been halved. With sign and magnitude notation, numbers in the inclusive range $-127_{decimal}$ ... $+127_{decimal}$ can be represented in 8 bits. Figure 4-6 illustrates the use of sign and magnitude representation. (Note that there are two representations of 0, the 8-bit bit pattern 00000000 represents +0 whereas the pattern 10000000 represents -0.)

Figure 4-6. Sign and magnitude representation of signed numbers using 8 bits

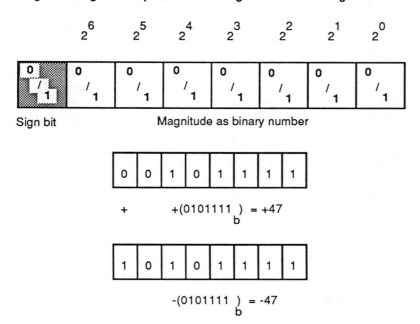

Although easy for mere humans to understand and interpret, sign and magnitude representations are not used much in computers. This representation is inconvenient because it requires additional circuitry in the various adders and subtracters of the arithmetic logic unit of the CPU.

Complement representations

Negative numbers are usually represented, inside computers, in some *complement* number system. A couple of different complement number systems can be defined for numbers in any base (or *radix*). These are known as the radix complement and the diminished radix complement. Both *two's complement* and *one's complement* representations exist for binary numbers and both representations are used in computers. Most machines use two's complement (as does the simulated machine in later practical exercises).

The bit pattern representing a positive integer in one's complement can be derived in the same manner described for unsigned numbers; however, the largest positive number that can be represented in n bits is now $2^{n-1}-1$ rather than 2^n-1 as for unsigned numbers. The left-most bit of the machine word must be a 0 for a positive number.

The bit pattern representing the corresponding negative number is obtained by flipping all the bits of the word (not just the left-most bit, as in sign and magnitude). For example:

```
00101111   =      +47
11010000   =      -47
```

Although a negative number is again identifiable by a 1 in the left-most bit, the remaining bits don't directly encode its value. (In this example, the bits set for -47 are those that would correspond to 2^6 and 2^4 in an unsigned or positive number.) One's complement representation again suffers from the disadvantage of two representations for 0; one has 00000000 for +0 and 11111111 for -0.

The alternative complement notation is two's complement. The representations of positive numbers in two's complement are identical to those in one's complement. The left-most bit of a positive number must again be a 0; the remaining bits encode its magnitude (in the same way as for unsigned numbers). If there are n bits available, and the left-most one is reserved to be 0, then there are n-1 bits available to represent a positive number; the largest positive number will again be equal to 2^{n-1}-1.

The bit pattern that represents a negative number in two's complement representation can be generated from the bit pattern of the corresponding positive number. Two steps are needed. First, the bit pattern is complemented (as was done to generate the one's complement representation). Second, 1 is added to the complemented pattern. As an example, +47 and -47 are represented in two's complement as:

```
00101111   =      +47
11010001   =      -47
```

The two's complement notation has only one representation for the value zero, 00000000. (If one tried to make -0, one would first complement the 00000000 (+0) bit pattern so obtaining the pattern 11111111, then add 1 to obtain 100000000 with a 1 carried out (the carry out bit can be discarded), so the final 8-bit representation is again 00000000.)

The two's complement notation exhibits one slight anomaly. In two's complement, the magnitude of the largest negative number that can be represented is one greater than the magnitude of the largest positive number. The range of numbers represented is from $-2^{n-1}...+2^{n-1}$-1 (in 8 bits, the range is -128...+127).

The following three examples illustrate that two's complement notation really does allow for correct arithmetic processing! As shown in the first example, complement representations of negative numbers make subtractor circuits unnecessary; it is possible to get by with just addition circuits (and the ability to generate a negative number representation by complementation and incrementation). In this first example, (10 - 3) is computed by adding the representations of (+10) and (-3). Note that the addition results in a carry out; unlike the case with unsigned numbers, this carry out does not indicate overflow. (The bit carried out would still be saved in the carry bit of a machine's flags register.) Overflow tests are more complex, for example, requiring checks that the addition of two positive numbers did not generate a result with a 1 in the left-most bit. Ignoring the carry, the result of this addition is 00000111, the correct representation of +7. The second example shows that adding the two's complement of a number to its positive value does indeed generate zero. (Again, there would be a carry out, but it has not been shown.) The third example illustrates the correct processing of negative values.

1. Decimal: 10 - 3
   = (10 + (-3)) = 7

   Two's complement binary:
10 decimal:	00001010,	10:	00001010
3 decimal:	00000011,	-3:	11111101
			00000111
		Carry out	1

   Result: 00000111   = 7

2. Decimal: (-9) + (+9) = 0

   Two's complement binary:
9 decimal:	00001001,	-9:	11110111
		+9:	00001001
			00000000

   Result: 00000000   = 0

3. Decimal: (-5) + (-12) = -17

   Two's complement binary:
5 decimal:	00000101,	-5:	11111011
12 decimal:	00001100,	-12:	11110100
			11101111

   Result: 11101111   = -(00010001)   = -17

It is not necessary for a programmer to be able to perform calculations in two's complement. Even the ability to convert from signed binary to signed decimal is scarcely ever required (most computer systems provide some debugging program which can perform such conversions). All that is really needed is the ability to tell at a glance whether a particular bit pattern represents a positive or negative number, and whether that number is large or small in magnitude.

Octal and hexadecimal notation

Binary representations of data may be acceptable to machines but they are ill-suited to human-machine interaction. Sometimes it is necessary to examine the contents of CPU registers or memory locations when debugging software (or even hardware); displays in binary are difficult for programmers to absorb. For example, was that number:

011000110111101000001101011110101

or was it:

0110000110111101000001101011110101?

A couple of alternative representations exist; both are readily converted to and from binary, and both allow for more compact and readily comprehensible presentations of data. These alternative notations are *octal* and *hexadecimal*. Each representation groups several 0/1 binary digits into a single symbol. In octal notation, each octal digit (0,1,2,3,4,5,6, and 7) combines data from three binary digits; the symbols of hexadecimal (hex) notation (0,1,2, 3,4,5,6,7,8,9,A,B,C,D,E,F) each represent data equivalent to that expressed in four binary digits. Figure 4-7 illustrates the correspondence of some binary data and the equivalent octal and hexadecimal representations. Equivalences between some binary bit patterns, octal, and hex notations are further detailed in Table 4-2.

Figure 4-7. Example data illustrated in binary, octal, and hexadecimal notations

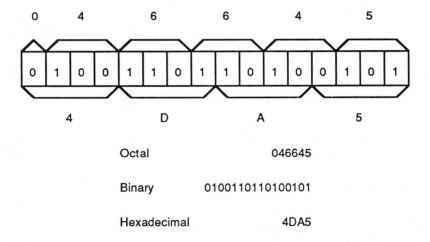

Octal   046645

Binary   0100110110100101

Hexadecimal   4DA5

Displays and printouts of the contents of registers and memory locations are usually given in hexadecimal. It is easy to determine the bit pattern that corresponds to any particular hex value; for example, the four digit hex pattern 3C3D corresponds to the 16-bit bit pattern 0011110000111101:

```
3      0011
 C         1100
  3             0011
   D                 1101
        0011 1100 0011 1101
```

Because of this easy conversion from hex to a bit pattern, it is simple to determine the settings of particular bits in a word. For example, on some machines the op-code might occupy the left-most 6 bits of a word; then the word 3C3D would incorporate op-code 001111 determinable by writing out the bit patterns that correspond to the hex digits.

Table 4-2. Data in binary, octal, and hexadecimal notation

binary	octal	hex	binary	octal	hex
00000	0	0	10000	20	10
00001	1	1	10001	21	11
00010	2	2	10010	22	12
00011	3	3	10011	23	13
00100	4	4	10100	24	14
00101	5	5	10101	25	15
00110	6	6	10110	26	16
00111	7	7	10111	27	17
01000	10	8	11000	30	18
01001	11	9	11001	31	19
01010	12	A	11010	32	1A
01011	13	B	11011	33	1B
01100	14	C	11100	34	1C
01101	15	D	11101	35	
01110	16	E	11110	.	.
01111	17	F	.	.	etc

octal	binary	hex	binary
0	000	0	0000
1	001	1	0001
2	010	2	0010
3	011	3	0011
4	100	4	0100
5	101	5	0101
6	110	6	0110
7	111	7	0111
		8	1000
		9	1001
		A	1010
		B	1011
		C	1100
		D	1101
		E	1110
		F	1111

Octal notation is used less than hex. However, it is the octal notation that will be used for all examples related to the simulated computer system. The contents of a 12-bit word used by the simulated computer can be represented either as three hex digits or as four octal digits. The second notation is more convenient because 3-bit groupings are significant in the machine, for example, the op-code requires 3 bits.

Octal and hexadecimal are also positional number systems with base (radix) 8 and 16 respectively, and calculations within these number systems are possible. Occasionally, the ability to add in hex is useful; for example, a debugging utility may be able to display, in hexadecimal, both the address of the start of an array and the value of an array index; given these data it is possible to calculate the address of a specific array element. In such a situation, it is more convenient to perform the additions in hexadecimal rather than convert into decimal, calculate, and then convert back to hex. But usually, the debugging utility is capable of performing such calculations. An ability to convert between octal and decimal will be useful in practical work on the simulator. The simulator system uses only octal notation; therefore, any constants needed in a program must be specified in octal. Conversion of a decimal number to octal is analogous to the method for converting to binary; one keeps dividing the decimal number by eight, noting down the remainders at each stage (these remainders define the octal representation). (If a negative constant is required then the octal constant corresponding to the two's complement binary representation of that number must be given.)

Exercises

1. Assuming a 12-bit word size, determine the binary patterns representing (as unsigned integers) the following decimal values:

Decimal value	Binary representation of unsigned number		Decimal value	Binary representation of unsigned number
76			376	
571			2046	
1204			3709	

2. With 12-bits, and two's complement conventions, what are the largest magnitude positive and negative numbers that can be represented?

Using 12 bits, and the two's complement conventions, determine the appropriate bit patterns that would represent the following signed decimal numbers:

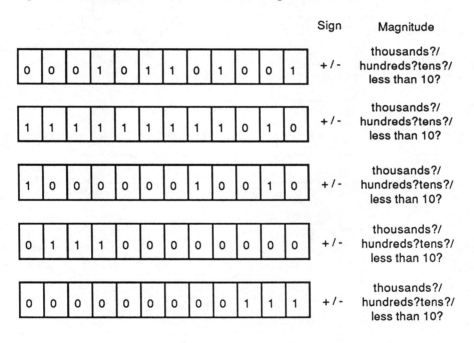

Decimal value	Two's complement number	Decimal value	Two's complement number
+35		-2001	
-48		-1	
+1966		257	

3. Assuming that the two's complement representation of positive/negative numbers is being used, determine whether the following 12-bit bit patterns represent positive or negative values, and estimate the decimal value represented:

												Sign	Magnitude
0	0	0	1	0	1	1	0	1	0	0	1	+ / -	thousands?/ hundreds?tens?/ less than 10?
1	1	1	1	1	1	1	1	1	0	1	0	+ / -	thousands?/ hundreds?tens?/ less than 10?
1	0	0	0	0	0	0	1	0	0	1	0	+ / -	thousands?/ hundreds?tens?/ less than 10?
0	1	1	1	0	0	0	0	0	0	0	0	+ / -	thousands?/ hundreds?tens?/ less than 10?
0	0	0	0	0	0	0	0	0	1	1	1	+ / -	thousands?/ hundreds?tens?/ less than 10?

4.   Transform the following binary and octal data representations:

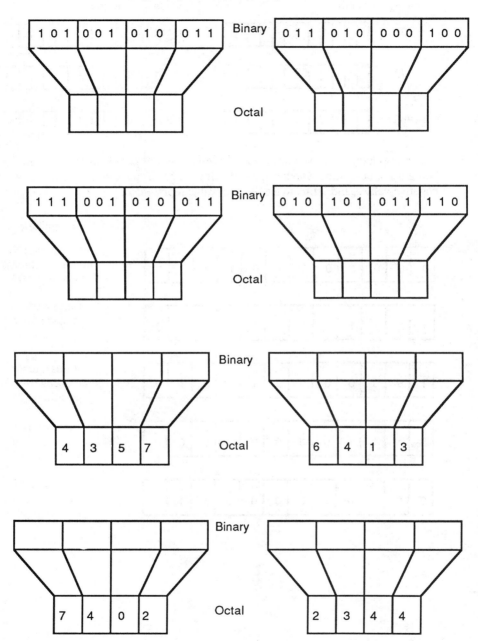

5. Convert the following four-digit octal constants to 12-bit bit patterns, then interpret these bit patterns as representing signed integers in two's complement notation, and derive the corresponding decimal values:

1750_{octal} = _ _ _ _ _ _ _ _ _ _ _ _ b = _ _ _ _ decimal

0144_{octal} = _ _ _ _ _ _ _ _ _ _ _ _ b = _ _ _ _ decimal

7200_{octal} = _ _ _ _ _ _ _ _ _ _ _ _ b = _ _ _ _ decimal

1777_{octal} = _ _ _ _ _ _ _ _ _ _ _ _ b = _ _ _ _ decimal

4000_{octal} = _ _ _ _ _ _ _ _ _ _ _ _ b = _ _ _ _ decimal

5000_{octal} = _ _ _ _ _ _ _ _ _ _ _ _ b = _ _ _ _ decimal

7777_{octal} = _ _ _ _ _ _ _ _ _ _ _ _ b = _ _ _ _ decimal

0040_{octal} = _ _ _ _ _ _ _ _ _ _ _ _ b = _ _ _ _ decimal

0400_{octal} = _ _ _ _ _ _ _ _ _ _ _ _ b = _ _ _ _ decimal

6. Which of the following are valid octal constants representing data that could fit into a 12-bit (or smaller) bit pattern?

1234	:	valid / invalid
7648	:	valid / invalid
1	:	valid / invalid
54321	:	valid / invalid
1A7	:	valid / invalid

7. Using the table in Appendix A, determine the bit patterns that would represent the string 'Hello world.' Assume a machine with a 16-bit word length, each word holding two bytes (or characters). Machines differ according to whether the first byte filled is the left- or right-hand byte; assume that the left-most byte is filled first.

Section II

The simulated machine

5

The simul8 simulator

The machine simulator for this course models an early (1965) laboratory computer (the Digital Equipment Corporation's PDP-8), a machine with a 12-bit word size and a basic memory of 4096 words. The machine was highly successful in its time, and a variant (the Decmate™ workstation) was still in manufacture as late as 1984. Figure 5-1 shows the complete system as modeled by the 'simul8' simulator: bus, CPU, memory, a keyboard, a Teletype™ (i.e. a slow-speed printing terminal), an analog-to-digital converter, a small disk, and a fixed-frequency clock.

Figure 5-1.   The computer system modeled in the simul8 simulator program

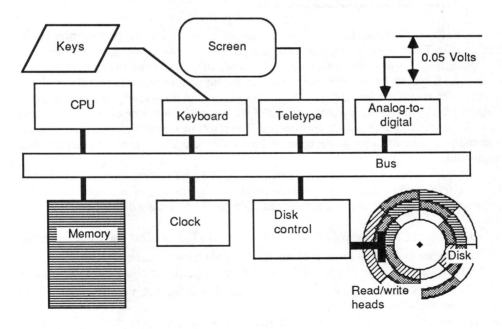

The CPU of the simulated machine is very restricted. As shown in Figure 5-2, it has only one data register, called the accumulator (acc). As well as the program counter and instruction register, there are two 1-bit flags in the timing and control unit. One of these, *interrupts-enabled*, conveys status information regarding how peripheral devices are being controlled. The other is the *link* bit. This link is a 1-bit register that serves both as a *carry* flag when performing calculations, and as a 1-bit extension to the accumulator when a bit pattern is being rotated.

Figure 5-2. The CPU of the simulated machine

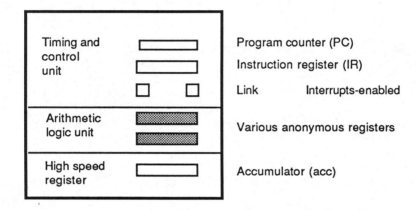

The arithmetic logic unit has a number of one-operand, data manipulation instructions. These instructions take as their input the value currently in the accumulator and place their result in the accumulator. For example, there is an instruction that can change all 0-bits to 1-bits (and vice versa) for the bit pattern in the accumulator. Other instructions rotate the bit pattern. There are only two two-operand, data combination instructions. Both take the current contents of the accumulator as one of their inputs, and combine these data with data from memory. The result of the operation is placed in the accumulator. One of these instructions performs a logical 'and', the other is an addition instruction.

All types of data are represented in single 12-bit words; therefore, each data transfer into, and out of, memory only requires the copying of a single word. The programming exercises on the simulated machine use the following data types:

1. Bit patterns, for example, 000001011111 (= 0137_{octal}), a bit mask that might be used when converting lower case ASCII characters to upper case.
2. Characters, for example, 000001111001 (= 0171_{octal}), the character 'y'. (Note that the use of a 12-bit word to store an 8-bit character means that the left-most 4 bits of the word are never used.)
3. Unsigned integers (usually for addresses), with the range $0\text{-}4095_{decimal}$ ($0\text{-}7777_{octal}$), for example, 001000010000 (=1020_{octal}) = $528_{decimal}$, 110000011110 (= 6036_{octal}) = $3102_{decimal}$.

4. Signed integers (two's complement notation), with the range -2048 ... +2047; for example, 001000010000 (= 1020_{octal}) = $+528_{decimal}$, 110000011110 (=6036_{octal}) = $-994_{decimal}$.

Instructions

The machine uses a 3-bit op-code. As illustrated in Figure 5-3, the left-most 3 bits of an instruction word define the type of instruction; the interpretation of the remaining 9 bits of the instruction word depend upon the instruction type. The 3 bits available for the op-code allow eight different bit patterns to be represented, and each is a basic instruction (see Table 5-1). These eight basic instructions fall into three categories: (1) the memory reference instructions, (2) an I/O class of instructions, and (3) the 'operate' instruction which subsumes both bit manipulation instructions and condition testing operations.

Figure 5-3. The format of the instruction word.

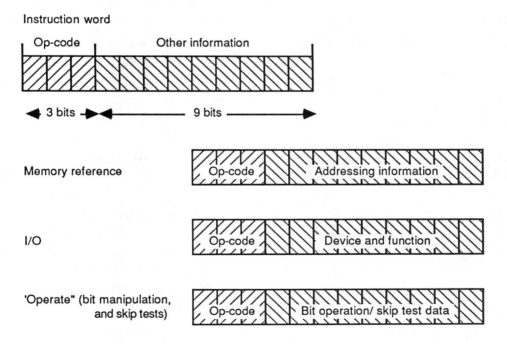

Memory reference instructions

The first six instructions, as listed in Table 5-1, have to *reference memory*: 'and' and 'tad' are both standard data combination instructions and require a memory location where the additional data are obtained; 'isz' will be examined in detail later; 'dca' is of the load/store type and needs a location for data storage; 'jmp' and 'jms' are used for program control and require the location where loops or subroutines and so forth start. In all these instructions, the remaining bits of an instruction word are used to encode the address of that memory location.

Table 5-1. The eight basic instructions of the machine

Op-code bit pattern	Name	Function
000	and	a data-combination instruction (it forms the logical 'and' of data from memory and data in the accumulator)
001	tad	another data-combination instruction (this one adds data from memory to the contents of the accumulator)
010	isz	'increment and skip if zero' (discussed later)
011	dca	this is a 'store' instruction (it copies data from the accumulator into some memory location, and then clears the accumulator)
100	jms	subroutine call instruction
101	jmp	jump ('goto') instruction
110	iot	this op-code identifies a set of I/O instructions
111	opr	this op-code combines two types of instruction; one of its subtypes involves data manipulation, the other subtype includes all kinds of tests

Input/output instructions

This machine controls its I/O peripheral devices through instructions that are device-specific; however, all these I/O instructions share the same op-code, 110 or 'iot' (I/O transfer). The remaining 9 bits of the instruction word encode both a device identification (6 bits of data) and a function to perform (the right-most 3 bits of the instruction word). These function bits encode messages that instruct particular device controllers to perform tasks such as reporting the status of a control-bit in a device status register, or transferring data from a device's buffer register into the accumulator.

'Operate' instructions

The most important criterion for the original design of the simulated machine was to save on bits, hence the short word length and short op-code. (In those days, the back-planes and buses of computers and all the magnetic cores of their memories were expensively wired by hand.) In order to reduce the number of bits that were required for an op-code, the machine combined its data manipulations and condition testing instructions into two subfamilies of a single instruction type, the operate ('opr') instruction type.

The 0/1 setting of the fourth bit of the instruction word is used to select the particular subfamily. If this bit is 0, then the instruction specifies the bit manipulation operations (e.g. 'cma' (complement accumulator, that is, the logical 'not' instruction), rotates, or special instructions such as those for clearing the accumulator or the link, or incrementing (i.e. adding one to) the contents of the accumulator).

The second subfamily of the operate instruction comprises a set of *skip tests*. The last few bits of the instruction word identify the particular skip test that is required. Skip test instructions test the value in the accumulator; tests include 'are the contents of the acc positive?', 'are the contents of the acc non-zero?', and so forth. If the value in the accumulator satisfies the test, then the program counter is incremented, causing the next instruction in sequence to be *skipped over*.

A skip test instruction is normally followed by an unconditional 'jmp' instruction. Together, the skip and jump instructions achieve the effect of any required conditional jump. On most machines, a conditional jump instruction will test the state of a bit in the flags register (as set by a preceding compare instruction). The simulated machine does not have a compare instruction; further, it does not have the normal set of 'equals', 'less than', etc. condition flags.

On this machine, instead of comparing two data elements and recording the 'equals', 'less than', or 'greater than' result in a flags register, a loop termination test (or other conditional test) involves two separate computational steps. First, the difference between two data elements (e.g. the loop count and a limit value) is calculated, with the result of the calculation left in the accumulator. Second, the result is tested by a skip instruction. If the skip test is satisfied, then the instruction immediately following the skip instruction is skipped over. The instruction following the skip will only be executed if the condition tested by the skip instruction is *not* satisfied; this instruction would normally be a jump back to the start of the loop. Typical coding of a loop construct, based on the use of a skip test instruction, is shown in Figure 5-4.

Figure 5-4. A loop construct using a 'skip test' instruction in the loop-termination test

```
cla              << First instruction of some loop

                 Instructions forming the body of
                 the loop

tad count
cia              Calculation needed for the loop-
                 termination test
tad lim

sza              The 'skip' instruction

jmp lp1          Jump back to the start of the loop

                 << Code following the loop
```

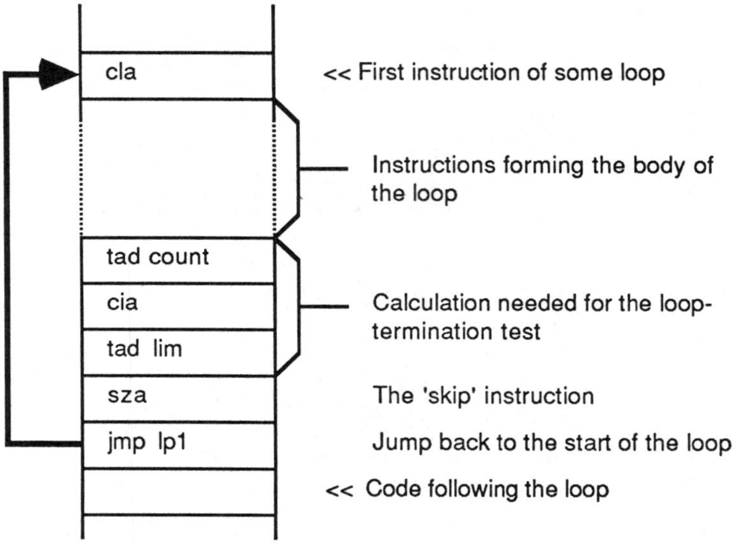

Is this a sufficient instruction set?

It might appear that the designers of this machine went too far in trying to economize on the number of bits in the word, and in the op-code that is within the word. There is no 'load' instruction, no 'subtract' (let alone 'divide' or 'multiply'), no 'compare', no proper 'store' instruction, and an 'and' but no 'or' instruction.

The instruction set was very carefully chosen. It is possible to get around the deficiencies with, in most cases, the use of two instructions instead of one. The design sacrificed speed and power for economy.

The handling of comparisons has already been discussed in relation to the skip test instructions. A 'compare' instruction implicitly uses subtraction when determining whether its first argument is greater, equal to or less than its second argument. On this simple machine, the subtraction must be explicitly programmed.

The missing 'load' is easily replaced by a two-instruction sequence; for example, 'load count' becomes:

```
cla
tad count
```

(i.e., clear [zero] the contents of the accumulator, then add in the value of 'count').

A subtraction is achieved by negating one argument (the *subtrahend*), then adding it to the other argument. So, for code like 'res:=a-b;', instead of 'load a'; 'subtract b'; 'store res'; the instruction sequence will be of the form 'load b'; 'negate'; 'add a'; 'store res'. The actual machine instructions are:

```
cla
tad b
cia
tad a
dca res
```

Here, the 'cla'; 'tad b' loads the value for 'b'. The 'cia' is one of the operate instructions, and complements and increments the contents of the accumulator. Complementing then incrementing is, of course, the way that one converts the sign of a number in two's complement notation. So after 'cia' the accumulator contains '-b'. Then the addition of 'a' ('tad a') gives the required result, which is stored in 'res' by means of the 'dca res' instruction.

The fact that the 'dca' (deposit and clear the accumulator) clears the accumulator after performing a store is often inconvenient. If one needs to both store a result and use it in further calculation then a two instruction sequence is needed: 'dca xx'; 'tad xx', that is, first deposit the value (in 'xx'), then load (add!) it back.

'Multiply', 'divide', 'ior', 'xor', and similar operations all require subroutines to be written. Some half dozen instructions are needed for the 'or's. Subroutines for the 'multiply' and 'divide' instruction operations would take around a hundred instructions and involve various loops; therefore, the machine might have to execute several thousand instructions just to multiply or to divide two numbers.

Although the instruction set is limited, it is quite adequate for the examples in the practical exercises. Most of the exercises are concerned more with how data are transferred between peripherals and the CPU than with elaborate data manipulations. It is also worth noting that the first version of the Unix™ operating system was implemented on the DEC PDP-7 computer, a machine quite similar to that simulated.

The 'increment and skip if zero' instruction

Although lacking many more obvious instructions, the instruction set of the machine contains an instruction, 'isz' (increment and skip if zero), which does not really fall into the standard categories of load/store, data manipulate, data combine, I/O, test, and program control. The 'isz' instruction is intended to help code the most common forms of iterative loop. As machines have evolved, increasing design attention has been focussed on the inclusion of instructions that make it easier to encode high-level language constructs. This simple machine has only its 'isz' instruction for the 'DO' loops of FORTRAN and similar iterative constructs. More elaborate machines have things such as special stack manipulation instructions that simplify the coding of Pascal procedure calls and returns.

The 'isz' instruction works as follows:

1. Decode the remaining bits of the instruction word to derive the address of a variable in memory.

2. Fetch the current value from the location with that address.
3. Add one to the value fetched
4. Test the updated value; if it equals zero then increment (add one to) the contents of the program counter (this change in the value of the PC will cause the next instruction in sequence to be skipped).
5. Store the updated value back into memory at the location whose address was determined in step 1.

The value brought from memory goes directly to the adder circuit, and the result is returned to memory; the accumulator is not affected by execution of the 'isz' instruction. Using this instruction, one can often encode a loop termination test in a single instruction (rather than the five or six instructions that might otherwise be needed).

Without the 'isz' instruction, the instructions needed for something like 'for j:=1 to 10 do ... { code for body of loop not using the value of loop control variable j } ...;' take the following form ('kten' is assumed to be a named location in memory containing value $10_{decimal}$; 'lim' is initialized to this value; 'j' (count of cycles completed) is initialized to zero):

```
/ initialize j and lim:
        cla
        tad   kten
        dca   lim
        dca   j
/ start of loop:
lp1,    cla
        .
        .
        .
/ code for body of loop
        .
        .
/ add one to j, another cycle is complete
        cla
        tad  j
        iac
        dca  j
/ prepare for test for termination, does (lim=j)?
/ i.e. is (lim-j)=0?
        tad  j
        cia
        tad  lim
/ skip test and jump back if appropriate
        sza
        jmp  lp1
/ code following the loop
```

With the 'isz' instruction, this code becomes:

```
/ initialize j:
        cla
        tad  kten
        cia                     / (negate)
        dca  j
/ start of loop:
lp1,    cla
        .
        .
        .
/ code for body of loop
        .
        .
        .
/ add one to j, another cycle is complete, test if the
/ value of j is now zero signifying that
/ sufficient cycles have been finished,
        isz  j
/ if not sufficient cycles, then jump back to start of loop
        jmp  lp1
/ code following the loop
```

Note how the value for the loop-control variable is initialized to minus the number of times the loop must be traversed. The loop-control variable is incremented on each cycle until it reaches zero and the iterations terminate.

The advantage of the second style of coding is less marked if the value of the loop control variable is needed within the body of the loop, for example, as in something like 'sum:=sum+a[j];'. Then, it would be necessary to keep both a loop cycle count variable (i.e. 'j'), and another counter variable used with the 'isz' instruction.

The 'isz' instruction treats the number on which it operates as an unsigned integer. If the current contents of 'j' is 3777_{octal} (the largest positive signed number), 'isz j' simply updates the value of 'j' to 4000_{octal} (a negative signed number) and tests if this updated value equals zero. Subsequent increments lead, eventually, to the value of j becoming 7777_{octal}; then, the next 'isz j' instruction changes it to zero and causes the skip to take place.

It is often useful to be able to add one to the contents of a memory location. The memory location might hold the count for the number of clock 'ticks' that have been detected, or the address of the next element of an array being processed in some iterative calculation. If it was essential to load a value into the CPU, then to add one to the contents of memory location 'ticks' would require code like 'cla'; 'tad ticks'; 'iac'; 'dca ticks'. An *increment store* instruction achieves the same result in a single step.

The 'isz' instruction can be used as this kind of increment store instruction. The appropriate code using 'isz' would be: 'isz ticks'; 'nop'. The 'nop' instruction following the 'isz' is an operate instruction that instructs the computer to '*do nothing for one CPU instruction cycle time*'. The 'nop' instruction is there to guard against the case where, by some mischance, the count being incremented reached zero, because in that case the 'isz' instruction would not only increment the count 'ticks' but would also cause the following instruction to be skipped. If the following instruction is really a part of the program code, rather than the 'nop', then the program would probably be lost.

Using the simulator

Although both the details of operation of many instructions, and the methods by which data addresses are encoded, are still to be covered, it is appropriate at this stage to start using the simul8 simulator program on the Macintosh (or other system).

The laboratory notes, in Appendix C, describe the use of the simulator in more detail. The disk with the simulator program contains also a number of examples of programs written for the simulator. The simplest of these examples is named 'exercise1'. The 'exercise1' file can be simply opened on the Macintosh; on other systems it should be opened and read with a text-editor program.

The assembly language program in file 'exercise1' is a variant on the Pascal program for summing the values of the integers in the range $1...10_{decimal}$. The code reads as follows:

```
1               cla  iac
2               dca      ndx            / set ndx to 1
3               dca      result         / and result to 0
4       loop,   tad      ndx
5               tad      result
6               dca      result         / accumulate sum
7               iac
8               tad      ndx
9               dca      ndx            / increment count
10              tad      ndx
11              cia
12              tad      dec10          / test against limit
13              sma cla
14              jmp      loop
15              hlt
16      dec10,  0012
```

Apart from these lines of code, the file 'exercise1' includes some comments, the declarations of the variables 'ndx' and 'result', and some *assembler directives*. Comments are introduced by '/' characters, everything after a '/' up to the end of a line is treated as being a part of a comment. The assembler directives in the example file include a couple of *origin* directives that are used to specify where in memory the code and data variables are to be placed. (An example in this file is '*200'. This directive places the first instruction of the code at the conventional starting address for this machine, 200_{octal} i.e. $128_{decimal}$.) All numeric constants must be given in octal, hence the constant representing the decimal value ten is given as 0012.

The layout of each line of the program has the form:

<optional label,> <instruction>

Labels are needed on those words that are to hold constants (e.g. 'dec10'), variables (e.g. 'ndx' and 'result'), or instructions that get referenced in jump instructions (e.g. 'loop' which is referenced in the 'jmp loop' instruction). (The line numbers are for subsequent reference, and are not in the file 'exercise1'.)

Although it does not appear as such, line 1 ('cla iac') represents a single instruction; there is a (nameless) operate instruction that combines the effects of clearing ('cla') and incrementing ('iac') the accumulator, that is, initializing the accumulator to hold the value 1. The instruction on line 2, 'dca ndx', causes this value 1 to be stored in 'ndx' and then clears (zeros) the accumulator; the next instruction, 'dca result', effectively zeros out the value of 'result'.

The iterative loop includes all instructions from lines 4 through to 14. At line 4, the current value of the variable 'ndx' is loaded into the accumulator (provided that the accumulator has already been cleared, this will constitute a 'load' operation). The next two lines have the instructions that add in the partial sum, as already held in 'result', and store the new partial sum back into 'result'. The 'dca' result instruction leaves the accumulator cleared and ready for subsequent calculations.

The next three instructions, on lines 7 through 9, add one to 'ndx'. The first instruction sets the accumulator to hold the value 1 (no clear is necessary as the accumulator is known to contain zero at this point), the current value for 'ndx' is added in, and the updated value stored back into memory (again leaving zero in the accumulator).

The loop termination test is here expressed as a check on whether the limit value 'dec10' minus the value of 'ndx' is negative ('dec10-ndx < 0' or 'dec10 < ndx'). The value of 'ndx' is loaded and two's complemented, the limit value is added in, and a test made for a minus number in the accumulator. The skip test instruction, 'sma' (<u>s</u>kip if <u>m</u>inus <u>a</u>ccumulator), is combined with an accumulator clearing operation (the accumulator is zeroed after its current contents have been tested). If the skip condition is not satisfied, a jump is executed back to the start of the loop and, since the accumulator has just been cleared as part of the skip test, the tad instruction at the beginning of the loop functions correctly as a load. When the value of 'ndx' exceeds the limit, a skip will occur and the next instruction will then be the 'hlt' at line 15. The 'hlt' is a special operate instruction that halts the computer.

The laboratory notes, in Appendix C, describe how this program should be assembled and run. Execution should then be followed in single-step mode. The simulator will maintain displays showing the results at each step of program execution. The arrangement of the displays depends on the version of the simul8 software used; Figure 5-5 illustrates the displays presented by the Macintosh version. The contents of the acc and pc registers are displayed in octal. The contents of the instruction register are shown as the source form of the instruction being executed. On the Macintosh, simul8 also updates a window in which it displays the text of the source program. Figure 5-5 illustrates the appearance of the display after the execution of the fourth instruction of program 'exercise1'.

By following the example program, from the file 'exercise1', in single-stepping mode, some feeling is obtained for the dynamics of program execution with data flowing from memory to CPU, manipulated, and results placed back into memory.

Figure 5-5. Displays of program execution as presented by the Macintosh Implementation of the simul8 system

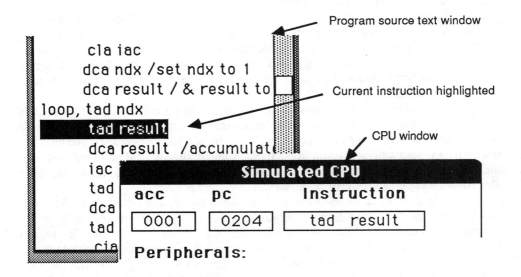

Exercises

1. Consider the following fragment of code:

```
          cla                 / clear acc
          dca     count       / and zero out count
lp1,      isz     count
          jmp     lp1
          hlt
count,    0
```

About how many instructions would be executed (from the first 'cla' to the final 'hlt')?

(a) Four?
(b) About 8200?
(c) ∞ (the machine would get stuck in the loop!)?

2. First, allow the example program from the file 'exercise1' to run to completion and end at the final 'hlt' instruction. Then, force one more instruction cycle by single-stepping again. Inspect the display to see what instruction was executed. Rationalize your observations.

3. Complete the following program and test it on the simulator:

```
        *200
/ compute "inclusive or" of the data in
/ "alpha" and "beta" storing result in "gamma"
/
/ uses "and" instruction and "cma" (complement)
/ instruction and stores temporary results in temp
        cla
        tad  alpha
        .
        .
        .
        dca gamma        / result now in gamma
        hlt
alpha,  0436             / octal for bit pattern    000100011110
beta,   4602             / octal for bit pattern    100110000010
gamma,  0                / here should get bits     100110011110
                         /  i.e. octal 4636
temp,   0                / place for temporary results during calculations
$
```

4. What would the final value in result be if the code of the example program read as follows:

```
1              cla  iac
2              dca     ndx        / set ndx to 1
3              dca     result     / and result to 0
4      loop,   tad     ndx
5              tad     result
6              dca     result     / accumulate sum
7              iac
8              tad     ndx
9              dca     ndx        / increment count
10             tad     ndx
11             cia
12             tad     dec10      / test against limit
13             sma
14             jmp     loop
15             hlt
16     dec10,  0012
```

5. Write a program that performs integer multiplication by repeated addition. In Pascal, this program would be:

```
program multiply;
var  a,b,product,count:integer;
begin
  { program to multiply by repeated addition }
  { form product of "a" and "b" and place in "product" }
  a:=5;  { first, pick some values for "a" and "b  }
  b:=7;
  product:=0;  { initialize 'product' to zero }
  { now, the repeated add loop, cycle the loop 'b' times on each }
  { iteration add  value of 'a' onto current value for 'product' }
  for count:=1 to b do
      product:=product+a;
end.
```

The framework of the program for the simulated machine is:

```
        *200
/ first instructions of program, initialize
/ count and zero out "prod"
                .
/ top of loop, add another instance of "a" onto
/ value for "prod"
                .
/ update count of number of times loop has been
/ cycled
                .
/ take difference of  cycle count and
/ limit (i.e. value of "b")
                .
/ skip test to see if sufficient cycles completed and
/ jump back to top of loop if necessary
                .
/ when product computed can halt
        hlt
a,      5                       / get the values of "a" and "b"
b,      7                       / set at "assembly time"
count,  0
prod,   0
$
```

(*Note*: This is *not* the best way to implement a multiply operation for a machine that does not have a hardware multiply instruction. There are standard algorithms (involving testing of individual bits and shifting of bit patterns) that form the basis of efficient methods for doing multiplication; there are also analogous methods for doing division. Such algorithms, coded to use the instructions available on a particular machine, are provided by machine manufacturers for those computers that don't have hardware multiply and divide circuits. These standard code fragments can be copied into user programs if required.)

6

Data manipulation and skip test instructions

Data manipulation instructions

The data manipulation instructions operate on the contents of the accumulator and the 1-bit link register. The basic repertoire of data manipulation instructions is shown in Table 6-1. (Note how the names for the instructions have been chosen to be mnemonic; the name of an instruction expresses what that instruction achieves.)

Table 6-1. The basic repertoire of data manipulation instructions

Name	Function
cla	clear accumulator
cll	clear link
cma	complement accumulator
cml	complement link
iac	increment (add 1 to) accumulator
ral	rotate accumulator (and link) left
rar	rotate accumulator (and link) right
rtl	rotate accumulator (and link) two places left
rtr	rotate accumulator (and link) two places right

The clear instructions set all the bits of a register (either the 12 bits of the accumulator (acc) register, or the single bit of the link register) to 0. The complement instructions flip the bits in the specified register, all 0s becoming 1s and all 1s becoming 0s. For example:

acc = 010000110001   = cma =>   101111001110

or, in octal:

acc = 2061   = cma =>   5716

The increment accumulator instruction is provided because often in program loops one needs to add one to a counter.

The machine lacks any 'shift' instructions, but it does have a set of four 'rotate' instructions. It is possible to rotate the contents of the accumulator left, or right, by one, or two places. As shown in Figure 6-1, the link and accumulator are treated as a single 13-bit register for rotate operations. Consequently, bits rotated in the accumulator must also pass through the link register. (Usually, the involvement of the link in the rotate operations is an inconvenience. Its presence is of value in various arithmetic operations, for example, in subroutines for multiplication and division, and in calculations on numbers requiring more than 12 bits. Apart from the 'cll', 'cml', and rotate instructions, the link bit can also be changed by addition instructions; if there is a carry out of the accumulator during a 'tad' instruction, then the link bit is complemented.)

Figure 6-1. The accumulator and link act as a single 13-bit register in rotate instructions

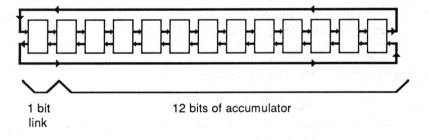

1 bit   12 bits of accumulator
link

The two examples in Figure 6-2 show the effects of 'rotate left one place' and 'rotate left two places' instructions on particular bit patterns (the octal representation, as would be displayed by the simulator, is shown as well).

Other data manipulation operations

The right-most bits of a data manipulation instruction word actually encode the particular operations required. One bit indicates if a clear accumulator operation is needed; another bit, if set, causes a complement accumulator operation. It is possible for more than one of these bits to be set in this part of the instruction, and consequently for more than one bit-manipulation operation to be performed by an instruction. There is a defined order in which the bits in the instruction word are checked and the corresponding operations performed; there are various restrictions on the operations that can be combined. Such details are unimportant.

The ability to combine certain of the basic bit-manipulation operations results in a few more instructions. Most of these do not have unique names, but must instead be specified by listing the basic bit-manipulation instructions that are being combined. The important combined instructions are listed in Table 6-2.

Figure 6-2.   Examples of rotates of data in accumulator and link registers

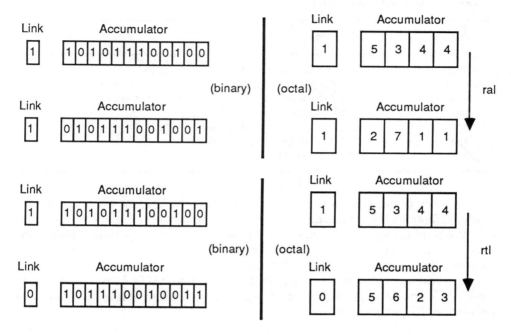

Table 6-2.   Useful combinations of the basic data manipulation instructions

Unique name	Combined instructions	Function
cia	cma iac	complement, then increment the accumulator (in effect, change the sign of the two's complement number held in the accumulator)
-	cla cma	clear, then complement the accumulator (set the acc to 7777, i.e. -1)
-	cla iac	clear, then increment the accumulator; (set the acc to 0001, i.e. +1)
-	cla cll	clear accumulator and clear link

Skip test instructions

The skip tests examine the contents of the accumulator (or the link register) and may increment the program counter; if the program counter is incremented, then the next instruction in sequence is skipped. The skip test instructions can also clear the accumulator after its contents have been examined. The basic repertoire of 'skip' instructions is shown in Table 6-3.

Table 6-3.   Skip test instructions

Name	Function
skp	(unconditionally) skip the next instruction
sma	skip if a minus (negative) number is in the accumulator
sna	skip if there are non-zero data in the accumulator
snl	skip if non-zero link
spa	skip if positive value in accumulator (≥ 0)
sza	skip if value zero in accumulator
szl	skip if zero link

Any of these instructions can be combined with 'cla'; for example, 'sma cla' would perform the test for a negative number in the accumulator (i.e. test for a 1 in the left-most bit of the accumulator, and if a 1 is present increment the program counter), and then clear the accumulator. Such combinations are convenient in that they allow temporary data to be cleared once they have been tested.

Just as with the bit manipulation instructions, skip instructions can be combined in limited ways creating are a few additional instructions (that don't have their own names). The important ones are:

sma sza	skip if contents of acc ≤ 0
spa sna	skip if contents of acc > 0

Other operate instructions

Two other operate instructions are implemented. These are:

hlt	halt the computer
nop	no operation (i.e. do nothing for one CPU cycle)

A 'hlt' instruction should be used at the end of a program (and, possibly, at other points such as where erroneous input has been detected). A 'nop' is most commonly used on this machine, in conjunction with 'isz' as illustrated in Chapter 5. The 'nop' instruction is sometimes useful in timing loops, where a particular number of instructions must be executed before the start of some operation. (On most machines, 'nop' instructions are used for curious purposes. For example, there was a range of machines with 60-bit words, each word could hold four 15-bit instructions; however, a restriction on those machines required that the first instruction of any loop be the first instruction in a 60-bit word.

Consequently, it was frequently necessary to have two or three 'nop' instructions immediately before the start of a loop so that things would be correctly aligned.)

The real DEC PDP-8 computer was produced in many different models which had minor variations in their repertoire of operate instructions. Though the simul8 system does not correspond to any particular model, it is closest to the earliest variants.

Exercises

1. Determine the bit patterns in accumulator and link that correspond to the initial octal values, and the bit patterns (and octal values) that result after the listed sequence of bit manipulation instructions has been performed:

a)

rtr
cml

b)

ral
cma
rtr
rtr

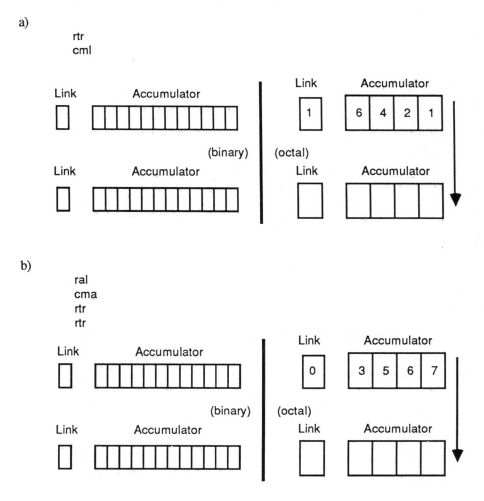

ut the contents of accumulator and link after the following sequences of bit
ation instructions have been performed:

a)

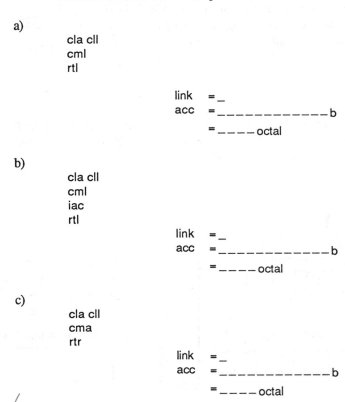

```
cla cll
cml
rtl
```

link   = _
acc   = _ _ _ _ _ _ _ _ _ _ _ _ b
        = _ _ _ _ octal

b)

```
cla cll
cml
iac
rtl
```

link   = _
acc   = _ _ _ _ _ _ _ _ _ _ _ _ b
        = _ _ _ _ octal

c)

```
cla cll
cma
rtr
```

link   = _
acc   = _ _ _ _ _ _ _ _ _ _ _ _ b
        = _ _ _ _ octal

Lab 4

3. Write a program that will count the number of binary 1s in a given word. A
framework for the program is as follows:

```
        *200
/ start of program, zero out count, copy
/ the given bit pattern into a temporary variable

        .
        .
        .

/ top of counting loop
/ pick up temp value

        .

/ if value is zero then finished so jump
/ to end

        .

/ clear link!

        .

/ rotate and isolate one bit in link
```

/ store rotated value back into memory

/ test link and increment count if appropriate

/ jump back to top of loop
end, hlt
thing,   4567 / the octal for the bit pattern 100101110111
count,   0   / the count of 1s,
/ count should be eight (0010 octal) when finished!
temp,   0
$

Why is it necessary to clear the link before doing the rotate? (This exercise does have practical value! For example, a program on a micro in a terminal might read 7-bit ASCII characters from a keyboard and need to convert these to 8-bit odd-parity ASCII for transmission to a host computer. Such a program would need to count the number of 1s in the character so as to determine the appropriate value for the parity bit.)

4. Write a program, making use of rotate left instructions, that will multiply a small integer by $10_{decimal}$. (A 'shift left one place' operation performed on a bit pattern that represents a number has the effect of multiplying that number by 2. So, if x is the original number, then y:= x << 1 (i.e. x left-shifted one place) = 2*x; z:= y << 2 (y left-shifted twice) = 2* 2* (2*x) = 8*x; y+z=10*x). There is no 'shift left' instruction but, if one is careful, the 'rotate left' can be used. Try running your program on the simulator. (Hint: if your program isn't producing the correct answers you have forgotten to clear the link bit before doing a 'rotate left' and so junk is being transferred into the low order bits of the numbers generated for 'y' and 'z').

7

Addressing

So far, the descriptions of the simulated machine have avoided any discussion of how the addresses of data elements might be encoded and represented in an instruction word.

The specification of data addresses has always been something of a problem for designers of computers because they have to find some trade-off between two totally opposing requirements:

1. One wants lots of address bits to be able to access lots of memory.
2. The other wants few address bits because larger address data make instructions longer (requiring either a larger word size or a multiword instruction format with several fetch cycles needed to collect all the words comprising an instruction).

There were two major constraints on the options available to the designers of the DEC PDP-8 machine. The first was a need to keep the word length short. The second was a requirement to keep the CPU logic simple (consequently, no multiword instruction formats). While working within these constraints, the designers had to devise an addressing mechanism that would be adequate for the small-scale scientific data acquisition and analysis tasks that the machine was to perform, and which might also be adequate for implemention of at least a subset of FORTRAN (which was then the major scientific programming language).

Any analysis of the type of programs that the machine was to run would reveal:

1. In most cases, referenced memory locations are *local*. For example. loops typically require a few dozen instructions; consequently, most jumps are over a dozen or so instructions, forward or backward. If jumps are likely to be local, then only a few bits will be needed to encode the number of words to be jumped; consequently, a short word length, with few address bits, should be practical.

    Further, the variables most used in any particular subroutine are usually those declared local to that subroutine; if local variables could be in local locations, that is, close to the instructions which use them, then again a limited number of bits would suffice for the address part of an instruction word.
2. A number of *global* variables are usually required. In addition to any local variables, most subroutines in a data-acquisition and analysis system make use of global data;

for example, there might be counts of the total number of analyzed samples, or records of the highest/lowest voltage readings on some analog signal input.

Similarly, in most FORTRAN programs there are usually a few global variables, such as those in a 'COMMON' area, used in many different subroutines.

It is obviously advantageous if some reasonable number of global variables could be readily accessible. The addressing scheme implemented must allow the addresses of these global variables to be encoded in a limited number of bits.

3.   Some *non-local* memory references are essential. Although the majority of data references in any subroutine are likely to be either to local variables or to global data elements, there will always be references to non-local data. In particular, large data arrays, requiring hundreds of words of storage, are normally placed in some part of memory remote from the code that uses them and they cannot be referenced through a local addressing scheme. The number of bits needed to specify an address anywhere in memory is determined by the total size of the memory on the machine; 10 to 12 bits are needed to define addresses on a machine with a few thousand words of memory, a memory of a few tens of thousands of words requires 15 or 16 address bits, while access to a million words is possible with 20 address bits.

As well as non-local references for data, some non-local references to instructions are needed. For example, non-local references frequently occur when calling subroutines. The code (and probably the local data) for the different subroutines would of course be placed in successive memory locations, beginning at some conventional starting address and filling up memory toward higher addresses. Inevitably, it is sometimes necessary to call a subroutine located at some remote address, several thousand words from the point of call. Unlike local jumps for program loops, it is not possible for the addresses in these calls to be encoded in a limited number of bits; again, it is necessary to allow as many bits as are required to define the total size of the memory on the machine.

Consequently, there have to be at least two different methods of accessing memory. One method can be restricted to using a small number of addressing bits, but is then limited to referencing local variables and, possibly, some limited set of globals. The other method, which allows the use of as many address bits as needed to specify any address (up to the maximum allowed on the machine), also has to be implemented. Since memory references requiring long addresses are less common, their implementation can be less efficient.

The addressing mechanisms implemented by the designers of the machine are *direct* and *indirect* memory references, with a further level of distinction for memory references to/via globals and to/via locals. These modes will be explained and illustrated in more detail below.

Briefly, a *direct* memory reference is made when an instruction accesses data held in either a local or a global variable (the address of this global/local variable is specified in a limited number of bits). *Indirect* memory references are made when the data are in some location whose specification requires a full 12 bits (12 bits being sufficient to represent any unsigned integer in the range $0...7777_{octal}$ ($0...4095_{decimal}$), and hence any address on this machine). An indirect memory reference must utilize a *pointer* variable to hold, as a 12-bit unsigned number, the full address of the required data. The pointer variable itself must be either a global or local variable.

Since 3 bits are required for the op-code of an instruction, the memory reference instructions on this machine have 9 bits available to encode a memory address. The use of these 9 bits is shown in Figure 7-1. One bit indicates whether the memory access is direct or indirect while a second bit provides the global/local distinction.

Figure 7-1.   Use of the 9 address bits in a memory reference instruction

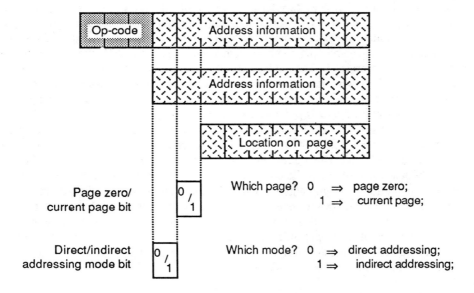

This global/local distinction is based on the concept of *paged-mode addressing*. Conceptually, the memory on the machine is divided up into fixed size pages, each page comprising 128 words. One page (page zero) is reserved for global variables. For any particular subroutine, the local variables will be found on the current page. The remaining 7 address bits specify the location of the variable on a page.

The term 'page' has, unfortunately, at least two slightly different interpretations in relation to computer architecture. A paged-mode addressing scheme, with a page for globals and a current page, is a feature present in many simple computers (however, most computers offer alternative modes). 'Page' is also used in the different context of *virtual memory systems* and *dynamic address translation* mechanisms. The issues of virtual memory and dynamic address translation are reviewed briefly in Chapter 21. These systems, implemented through a combination of extra hardware and software, provide the basis for schemes that allow an operating system to manage the use of machine's memory by user programs.

Direct paged-mode addressing

Direct paged-mode addressing (or, simply, *direct addressing*) is examined first because it is conceptually simpler as well as being more common. With direct addressing, the address incorporated into the instruction word is the location for the required data. This address is given as an explicit location on a page, with the page being defined implicitly. For an 'and' or 'tad' instruction, the address is the location containing the necessary data. In a 'dca' instruction, the address given is the storage location for the contents of the accumulator. For an 'isz' instruction, the address given is the memory location whose contents are to be incremented and tested for being zero. The address given in a 'jms' subroutine call instruction is the location of the start of the subroutine; while in a 'jmp' instruction, the address given is the location containing the next instruction to be executed.

The memory in the machine is, conceptually, divided up into 32 pages of 128 (or 0200_{octal}) words. These pages are numbered $0...37_{octal}$. The pages, their address ranges, and their conventional usage are summarized in Table 7-1. (On the real machine, the final page of memory might be implemented as read-only-memory (ROM) containing standard pieces of code such as a routine to load a program from a disk or cassette tape. On the simulator, the final page is just the same as any other page.) A program should be organized so that, on any particular page, there will be one or more subroutines. Each subroutine consists of a code section followed by its local variables and constants.

If, by some mechanism, the appropriate page is known, then to specify the address of a variable, on that page, requires only 7 bits. Since 7 bits can represent any unsigned number in the range 0 to 2^7-1 (=127), this unsigned number can define where, within the page, a particular variable is located.

Table 7-1. The pages, their address ranges, and typical use for the simulated machine

page #	address range	use
0	0000...0177	globals
1	0200...0377	main program
2	0400...0577	I/O subroutines
3	0600...0777	
4	1000...1177	pages 3...36 used for
5	1200...1377	subroutines or
.	.	data arrays as required
.	.	
.	.	
36	7400...7577	
37	7600...7777	(*loader* program etc.)

Reference to a page zero global

If the global/local bit is 0, then the reference is to a global variable (with an actual address in the range 0000...0177). As shown in Figure 7-2, for a direct memory reference to a global, the 7 address bits given in the instruction are filled out to make a 12-bit *effective address* by placing 0s in the 5 left-most bit positions. (An effective address is the address of the location containing the data used, it is obtained when all address decoding steps have been applied to the actual address as encoded in the instruction.)

Figure 7-2. Accessing globals on page zero

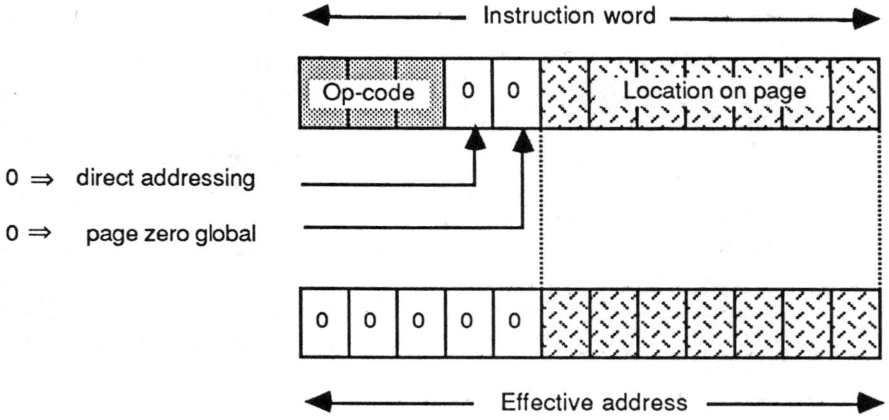

0 ⇒ direct addressing

0 ⇒ page zero global

Reference to a local variable on the 'current' page

Modern machines that employ some variant on paged-mode addressing, for example, the Motorola 6809, usually have a special CPU register (the *direct page register*) that identifies the page considered as the current page and, consequently, accessible using short paged-mode addressing. On the PDP-8 computer, there is no special register; instead, the current page is determined from the contents of the program counter.

The 5 left-most bits of the PC define the current page. If an instruction specifies a direct reference to a current page local variable, then these 5 bits from the PC are combined with the 7 'location on page' address bits from the instruction word to derive a full 12-bit effective address for the required data. The scheme is shown in Figure 7-3.

The following examples help illustrate the process. Suppose an instruction was executed at location 0242 (address 000010100010, that is, page 00001, location 0100010) and involved a reference to location 147 (1100111) on the current page, then the address of the data is 000011100111 or 0347 (the 5 left-most bits (underlined) come from the PC and the remaining bits are the page location taken from the instruction word). An instruction at address 2742 (address 010111100010), involving a reference to location 147 on its current page, yields the effective address 010111100111, that is, the address 2747 (again, the 5 left-most bits come from the PC and the rest from the instruction word).

Figure 7-3. Accessing locals on the current (PC-defined) page

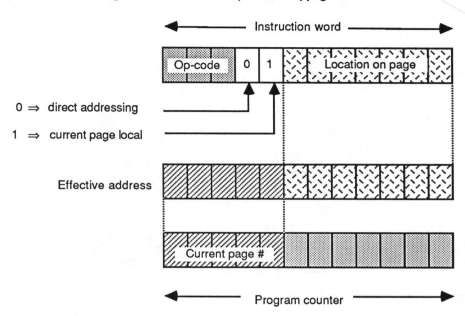

A further example of the instruction- and address-decoding processes is presented in Figure 7-4. The instruction word has the value 1340; the (updated) PC is 2620. The CPU's instruction decoding circuit extracts the op-code bits, 001, and hence identifies this as an addition instruction with the rest of the instruction word containing an address specification. The address decoding circuits extract the 7 low-order bits of the word. These bits, 1100000, define the 'location on page' of the datum to be added. The global/local page bit is checked and, as it is set, this is a reference to a local variable on the current page. As a current page reference, the 5 left-most bits of the effective address are filled with the current-page number (taken from the PC). The effective address thus generated is 010111100000 or 2740. Since the direct/indirect address mode bit is a 0, this instruction uses direct addressing and the process of address decoding is therefore completed.

A memory-read operation is then initiated. Data read from memory location 2740, and data from the accumulator, are then sent to the adder circuits.

Direct references to locals and globals in assembly language

In the written assembly-language source code, references to locals and globals take the form '<memory reference op-code> <name of local/global>'; some examples are: 'tad count' and 'dca result'. The assembler program that prepares executable code from assembly-language source programs differentiates between locals and globals, and therefore sets the global/local bit correctly in the instructions it generates.

Figure 7-4.   An example of address decoding for an instruction using direct addressing of a current page, local variable

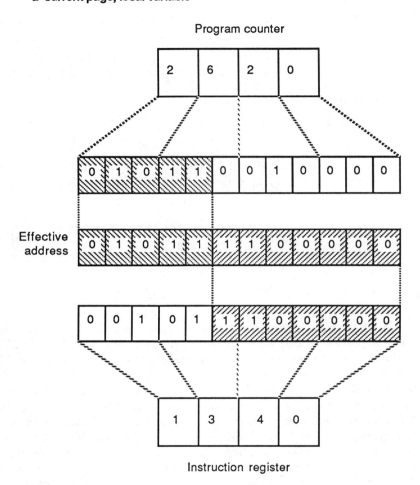

Instruction register

In all the program examples given so far, and also in those suggested as exercises, the data have been single word variables – either local variables or variables located on the global page. All these programs have also been sufficiently small, allowing their code to fit on one page. Consequently, only simple direct addressing modes have been required.

Minor restrictions on the use of page zero for globals

The example program in file 'exercise1' places its variables 'ndx' and 'result' on the global page, starting at location 0020 rather than at location 0. This reflects some additional restrictions on the use of page zero.

The first few locations, with addresses 0000...0007, are best left for data concerned with I/O (as described in Chapters 9-12). The next group of locations on page zero, those with addresses 0010...0017, are the so-called *auto-increment* locations. They have special attributes (of little interest for the examples and exercises of this course) and their use should be avoided. Because of these restrictions on the use of the first few locations, global variables located on page zero usually start at address 0020.

Indirect paged-mode addressing

Although convenient for accessing locals and globals, direct paged-mode addressing allows only 256 locations to be accessible from any point in the program (128 words on page zero and another 128 on the current page), but then, as illustrated in Figure 7-5, certain memory accesses are not possible. The subroutine on page 2 cannot be called directly from the main program on page 1, as its start address cannot be represented as a location within the main program's accessible pages (either current or global). Similarly, the subroutine is unable to access data in an array on page 15; again, the address of the data cannot be defined in terms of a location on either the current or the global page.

Figure 7-5. Some of the memory accesses that can and cannot be made using direct paged-mode addressing

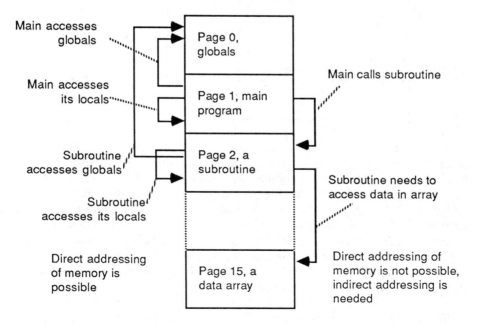

In cases such as these, a full 12 bits of address data are required to define where in memory the subroutine starts, or where the array element is located. Consequently, apart from the instruction word, another word in memory is required to hold address data.

This second word is commonly called a *pointer* because it points to the required data. When executing an instruction, the CPU will have to fetch the contents of this pointer in order to find the effective address of the program data. The instruction word has to specify the address of the pointer.

Consider, for example, the previous problem of the main program trying to call a subroutine on page 2. The situation is as shown in Figure 7-6, with the subroutine call instruction at location 0220 and the start of the subroutine at 0400. A pointer is used to hold the subroutine's start address, while the instruction must directly address the pointer. Therefore, the pointer can be either a page zero global or a local. Here, the pointer (named 'psub' because it points to sub) is a local, at address 0240. The subroutine call instruction contains a reference to 'psub', not 'sub', in its address field.

Figure 7-6. Use of a pointer in a call to a subroutine located on some other page

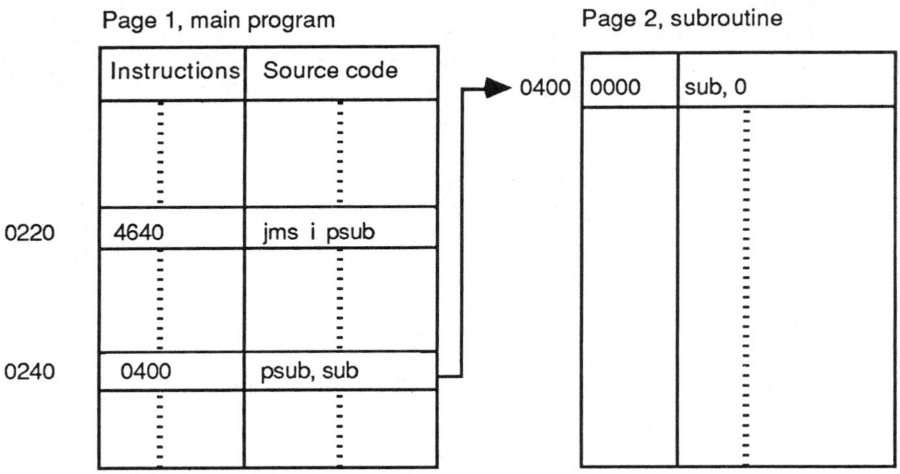

The address field in the 'jms' instruction word would have the indirect bit set causing an extra step to be carried out during the process of address decoding. The instruction- and address-decoding process is illustrated in Figure 7-7. The instruction-decoding circuitry of the CPU, having read the instruction 4640 and extracted the op-code, recognises it as a memory referencing 'jms' instruction. The initial phase of address decoding, determining the address of 'psub', is exactly the same as that illustrated in Figure 7-4 (the example using direct addressing). First, the 7 bits (0100000) that define the page location are isolated. The current-page bit is checked and, since it is a 1, the address is completed by taking the page-number bits from the PC yielding the address 000010100000, that is, 0240, the location of 'psub'.

The indirect bit is then checked and, since this time it is a 1, an additional address interpretation step takes place. The 12-bit address derived so far, that is, 0240, is taken to be the address of the location where the actual address of the required data is stored. So, a memory fetch is performed and a 12-bit address value is retrieved. In this example, the value retrieved is 0400 – the correct start address for the subroutine.

Figure 7-7. **An example of address decoding for an instruction using indirect addressing**

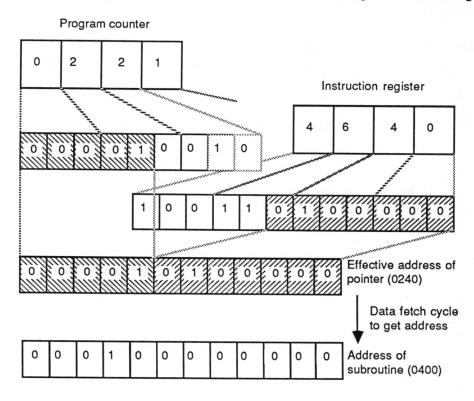

With indirect addressing, it is the address obtained from memory during the final stage of address decoding that is used for the next execution step.

Indirect references to locals and globals in assembly language

The programmer must determine when indirect references are required and then arrange for pointers to be defined. Instruction codes in assembly language must specifically indicate the use of indirect memory addressing and therefore are coded as '<memory reference opcode> i <name of global/local pointer>'; examples are 'jms i psub' and 'tad i ptr1'.

In the preceding subroutine call example, the value in the pointer 'psub' is a constant. After all, the location of subroutine 'sub' should not change during program execution; a value representing the address of 'sub' can be inserted into the location 'psub' when the program is prepared for execution.

More often, pointers are variables; they are used to point to various elements in data structures and, as different elements of the data structure are required, the values stored in the pointers are changed. The use of a pointer variable is illustrated in the next section.

Example use of indirect memory reference: sequencing through a data array

The following program provides an example of the use of a pointer variable. The program computes the sum of a set of data elements stored in memory starting at address 1000. These data elements represent small positive integers while a zero value marks the end of the data. The program code is:

address	contents	code
		*200
		/ copy, into "ptr", the address
		/ of where the data are stored
0200	7200	cla
0201	1214	tad addr
0202	3215	dca ptr
		/ zero out "sum"
0203	3216	dca sum
		/ top of loop, pick up next array
		/ element and test if zero
0204	1615	lp, tad i ptr
0205	7450	sna
		/ if zero, then halt
0206	7402	hlt
		/ otherwise, add in to partial sum
0207	1216	tad sum
		/ store back new value
0210	3216	dca sum
		/ increment "ptr" so that it
		/ points to next array element
0211	2215	isz ptr
0212	7000	nop
		/ jump back to top of loop
0213	5204	jmp lp
		/ - - - - - - - - - - -
		/ constants and variables:
		/ constant address of start of data
0214	1000	addr, datab
0215	0	ptr, 0 / pointer variable
0216	0	sum, 0 / sum
		*1000
1000	0123	datab, 0123 / data elements as
1001	0012	0012 / octal constants
1002	0001	0001
1003	0000	0000
	$	

In this program listing, the addresses and the contents of the words used are presented along with the actual program source statements. (All these data are given in octal.) This is a standard *assembly listing* such as produced by the assembler program while it prepares a program for execution.

The first three instructions initialize the pointer variable 'ptr' to the address of the first array element. Of course, direct addressing is used in this first reference to 'ptr' (location 0202) as the value in the accumulator is to be placed in the location labeled as 'ptr', that is, in location 0215. The state of the memory of the machine, after these initialization instructions have been executed, is shown in Figure 7-8.

Figure 7-8. State of the memory of the machine after completion of the instructions that initialize the pointer variable

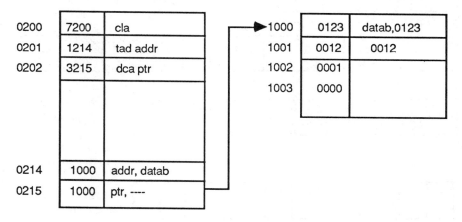

After 'sum' is explicitly zeroed, the first instruction in the loop (the instruction in location with address '0204') loads the next array element to be processed. (A correct 'load' operation will be performed since the program ensures that the accumulator will always contain zero before this 'add' instruction is executed.) This instruction, 'tad i ptr' (i.e. 'add, to the current contents of the accumulator, the contents of that memory location whose address is held in the variable ptr') uses indirect addressing. The address interpretation steps are summarized in Figure 7-9.

The instruction 1615 is read, decoded, and identified as a memory referencing 'add' instruction. The low-order 7 bits, giving page location, are extracted; the current-page/page-zero bit is checked and, since it is a 1, the address reference is to a current page variable. The address is completed by taking the 5-bit page number from the PC combined with the 7-bit page location, giving the address of 'ptr', that is, 0215. Since the indirect bit is set in this instruction, the contents (1000) of location 0215 are obtained and then interpreted as the address of the data required.

The execution phase of this 'add' instruction therefore involves a fetch from address 1000. The value 0123 found there is added to the (zero) contents of the accumulator. Therefore, by using indirect addressing via 'ptr', it is possible to access the required array element.

The next few instructions of the loop check for the terminating zero and add any non-zero data values to the partial sum.

Figure 7-9. Indirect access to an element of a data array

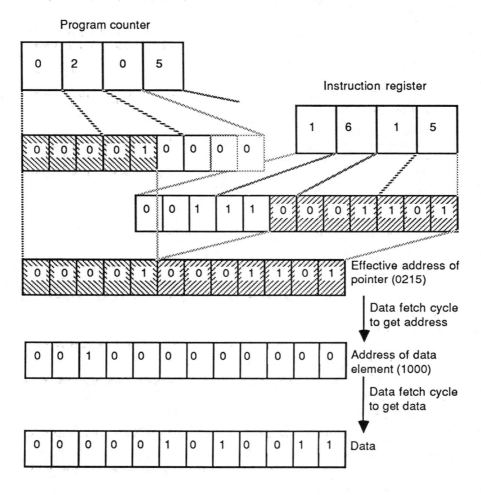

The pointer variable must then be updated to point to the next array element. An 'isz' instruction can be used to increment 'ptr' without requiring separate instructions to first load the accumulator and then store back into memory. The state of memory following execution of the 'isz ptr' instruction is shown in Figure 7-10.

After the jump back to the top of the loop, the 'tad i ptr' instruction is again executed, only on this second iteration it results in the contents (0012) of address 1001 being loaded into the accumulator.

This method of using indirect addressing, and updating a pointer variable, allows successive elements of an array to be processed in sequence. Access to any selected array element can also be achieved by the use of indirect addressing and pointer variables.

Figure 7-10. State of the memory of the machine after completion of the instructions that update the pointer variable

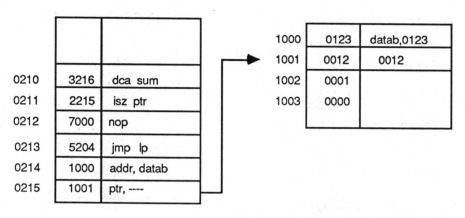

For example, suppose it was required to load the jth element of an array 'buff1'. This could be achieved by the following code:

```
        cla
        tad  addrb              / load address of start of array "buff1"
        tad  j                  / add on index value
/ acc now holds address of "buff1[j]"
/ save this address in a pointer
        dca  ptrx
/ now can load required data element by using indirect
/ referencing via pointer ptrx
        tad i ptrx

        .
        .
        .
addrb,  buff1                   / address constant holding address of buff1
        .
        .
/ here is the start of the array known as buff1
buff1,     0
```

An address constant, here 'addrb', can be used to hold the address of the start (zeroth element) of the data array ('buff1'). (The start address of the array is referred to as its *base address*.) An index value, specifying which word in the array is required, is added to the base address of the array. This addition gives the address of the data element required and this computed address is stored in a pointer variable. The data fetch from the array then works by indirect addressing via this pointer.

Exercises

1. Determine whether indirect addressing is needed for the following data accesses:

Address of instruction	Address of required data	Mode
0230	0074	direct / indirect
0240	0334	direct / indirect
0250	1074	direct / indirect
0334	0110	direct / indirect
0446	0377	direct / indirect
0447	0577	direct / indirect
1234	1376	direct / indirect

2. For the following instructions, represented in octal, determine their 12-bit bit patterns and identify whether they involve direct/indirect addressing, on/via page-zero/current-page.

Instruction (octal)	Bits	Mode	Page
4342	_____	direct/indirect	page-0/current
1020	_____	direct/indirect	page-0/current
0000	_____	direct/indirect	page-0/current
0100	_____	direct/indirect	page-0/current
1577	_____	direct/indirect	page-0/current
2375	_____	direct/indirect	page-0/current
3020	_____	direct/indirect	page-0/current
1640	_____	direct/indirect	page-0/current
3421	_____	direct/indirect	page-0/current

3. Write a program that will find the largest of a set of small positive integers (these integers are to be defined in the assembly language source program). The program is to loop, examining integers stored in successive memory elements until an integer representing a negative value is found. The program is to halt with the accumulator containing the largest of the positive values, or the value zero if no positive values are found before the negative end-of-data marker. Test the program on the simulator. A framework for the program is:

    ```
        *200
    / initialize pointer to start of data area, and
    / max (largest element) to some appropriate value.

            .
            .
            .
    / top of loop, get next data element and test for -ve datum
            .
            .
            .
    ```

```
/ if negative jump to code to finish up, i.e. getting max
/ into acc etc and halting
        .
        .
/ otherwise, "compare" next data element with largest so far
        .
        .
        .
/ if needed, replace value of max
        .
        .
/ update pointer so that will get next data element
        .
        .
/ jump back to top of loop
        .
/ code for finishing up
        .
        hlt
/ constants and variables
/ - - - - - - - - - -
/ the predefined data
        *1300
datav,  0001 / some test data values
        0044
        0043
        0100
        0076
        7777                    / this one's negative
$
```

4. As noted earlier (Chapter 4), in the discussion of even/odd parity bits in an 8-bit ASCII code, data transmission lines are often noisy. Noise on the lines can garble messages sent between computers. Usually, to combat problems of data loss, some form of message protocol is used. These protocols require that each message sent from one computer to another be composed of a *header, data bytes, check data, end-marker*. The header will include special characters (e.g. stx or soh) and maybe information specifying the number of data bytes in the message. The data bytes will follow, each having an appropriate parity encoding (so allowing for some error checking). After the data bytes, some additional check data will be provided, usually including a checksum byte(s). The final end-marker will use some special character (e.g. etx).

    Although parity bits on individual characters allow some data corruption (single bits being flipped) to be detected, such checks are rarely sufficient. Line noise frequently occurs in bursts, several bits changing within a single byte. For example, if two bits were flipped during transmission of an (odd-parity) ASCII letter 'S' (11010011) over a noisy line, then it is possible for an apparently correct (odd-parity) ASCII letter 'V' (11010110) to be received.

Since error checks on individual characters are inadequate, a checksum is often used to provide some check on the complete message. A checksum is calculated by adding together the bit patterns representing the characters of a message (a character bit pattern can always be interpreted as an unsigned number). The checksum is reduced modulo 64 (or maybe modulo 128, or some other number), giving a final checksum value that can be transmitted as a single byte. (Rather than actually computing a sum then calculating its value modulo 64, one can simply mask the partial sum, after each addition step, keeping the low-order 6 bits.)

Example: computing the checksum for the message 'STOP':

Character   7-bit ASCII(octal)

S	123
T	124
O	117
P	<u>120</u>
sum =	506
sum 'and' 077 =	06

checksum character   06.

If this message was transmitted over a noisy line, and the 'S' did get changed to a 'V', then the message received would be:

Character   7-bit ASCII(octal)

V	126
T	124
O	117
P	<u>120</u>
sum =	511
sum 'and' 077 =	11

checksum character   11.

The receiving computer could check the characters it received, calculate their checksum, and compare this with the checksum character that it was sent. If, as in this example, the checksum characters did not match, then a request could be made for the message to be re-transmitted.

Write a program to compute the modulo-64 checksum for a sequence of characters. The program to be written will have the following form:

```
        *200
/ initalize, setting a pointer to first of the characters
/ to be processed, zeroing out checksum etc
```

/ top of loop, fetch next character, a zero character marks
/ the end of the message whose checksum byte is being
/ calculated

.

.

/ test for termination, and jump to finish up code

.

.

/ add new character into checksum value and mask down to
/ six bits, store updated checksum

.

/ increment pointer so as to point to next character of
/ message

.

.

/ go back to top of loop

.

/ code to finish up

.

       hlt
/ - - - - - - - - - - -
/ constants and variables:
mask6,   0077 / mask to pick off six low order bits
addra,   chars / address constant specifying where data located
ptr,   0   / pointer variable used when accessing data
 chksum,   0 / checksum mod 64 (&77)
        *400
/ here are characters for message, as octal values, one per word
/ terminated by a zero
chars,   0110   / H
        0145   / e
        0154   / l
        0160   / p
        0   / end mark for data
$

8

Subroutines

There are two main issues in subroutine call mechanisms:

1.   How is *subroutine linkage* achieved?
2.   How are data passed to, and retrieved from, subroutines and functions?

The problem of subroutine linkage is to find a mechanism by which a calling program can cause a jump to the code of a subroutine while at the same time saving the address following the subroutine call instruction as a *return address*, allowing execution of the main program to be resumed after the work of the subroutine is complete.

The problems of passing arguments and results relate to where these data should be held. Some data can be passed to a subroutine in the CPU registers (on the simulated machine, there is only the accumulator, so only one item of data can be passed this way). Other data can be stored in global variables, accessible both to a main program and to a called subroutine. Similarly, results being passed back by a subroutine may be stored in CPU registers or global variables. However, there are many cases where it is undesirable to use global variables and where there are too many arguments to use solely the CPU registers. Consequently, other methods of passing data are always needed.

Subroutine linkage

The requirement for some linkage mechanism is illustrated through the following fragment of code. (This code is taken from 'tstmsk', one of the example programs provided on the disk with the simulator.) This code fragment comes from a group of routines used to provide a printout of a 12-bit bit pattern as a sequence of four octal digits.

The problem of printing a 12-bit bit pattern can be broken down into the subproblems of (1) isolating each 3-bit bit pattern in sequence, and (2) converting a 3-bit bit pattern into the appropriate printable character (i.e.'0' for 000_b, '1' for 001_b, ..., '7' for 111_b). (The bit patterns representing the required printable ASCII characters are 0110000 for '0', 0110001 for '1' etc.; they can be obtained by adding 0110000 to the given 3-bit bit patterns.)

Obviously, the same code is needed to convert each 3-bit bit pattern into a character. Rather than duplicate this code in four places within the program, the code should be written as a separate subroutine. This subroutine would isolate the 3 bits at the right-hand end of the accumulator and convert them into the bit pattern for the appropriate printable character.

Then, the main routine has only to rotate the original bit pattern in order that each of the four different 3-bit groups are processed in turn by the subroutine. This code therefore has the general form:

.

.

rotate left-most three bits to right end of acc
call subroutine
rotate next three bits to right end
call subroutine
rotate next three
call subroutine
get the original three right-most bits
call subroutine

.

.

The actual code of the routine reads, in part, as follows:

Address	Instruction	Assembly language	
0440	1260	tad oval	/ pick up value
0441	7006	rtl	/ rotate most significant bits
0442	7006	rtl	/ into place
0443	4261	jms oput	/ call subroutine
0444	1260	tad oval	/ now get bit pattern
0445	7012	rtr	/ and rotate next
0446	7012	rtr	/ three bits into place
0447	7012	rtr	
0450	4261	jms oput	/ call subroutine
0451	1260	tad oval	
.	.	.	

The first subroutine call is at location 0443; when the subroutine 'oput' is completed the appropriate return address is 0444. For the second call, at 0450, the appropriate return address is 0451. It is these different return addresses that must be saved before the subroutine is executed.

There is of course a problem as to *where* this return address should be saved. Many machines use a CPU register; then part of the execution phase of a subroutine call instruction involves copying the current value of the PC into this register before making a jump to the start of the subroutine. Some machines have a specific *subroutine linkage register*. More commonly, on a multiregister machine, the programmer must encode, into each subroutine call instruction, a specification of the particular CPU register that will be used for subroutine linkage. (Although a machine design may allow any register to be used, there are frequently programming conventions that limit the programmer's choice.)

On the simulated machine, there are no CPU registers that could be used for subroutine linkage. Consequently, the return address must be placed somewhere in memory.

The location used to store the return address must have an address that is known to both the calling routine and the called subroutine. There is only one possible location: the first word of the subroutine. (A subroutine must know its own starting address and, once address decoding is complete, the starting address is also known at the point of call.)

The subroutine call instruction is, in consequence, implemented in the following manner (this fragment of pseudo Pascal represents the micro-code in the CPU):

```
.
sub_address:=decodeadress(operand);
{ sub_address represents the actual address of the    }
{ start of the subroutine after all address decoding  }
{ (including, if necessary, any indirection step)     }
memory[sub_address]:=pc; { save pc in that location   }
pc:=sub_address+1; { jump to first instruction of sub. }
.
```

Figures 8-1 and 8-2 illustrate the entire process for a specific case. Figure 8-1 shows the state of the machine at the point where a subroutine call instruction has been read (from location 0443) and decoded. The PC was incremented (as part of the fetch step), and holds the value 0444 (the address of the instruction following the subroutine call). The address decoding is also completed and the start address of the subroutine identified as 0461.

The execution step of the subroutine call instruction stores the value 0444 from the program counter into location 0461, and then sets the address 0462 into the program counter. The machine state is now as shown in Figure 8-2.

Now the machine is ready for the next instruction. This fetch reads the first instruction of the subroutine. The subroutine does a masking operation ('and seven') to select the 3 right-most bits, adds in the constant 060 (i.e. 0110000) ('tad zeroch') to convert to the bit pattern for an ASCII character, and then calls a further subroutine to print the character ('jms put').

The complete code for the subroutine 'oput' is:

Address	Instruction	Assembly language
0461	0000	oput, 0
0462	0266	and seven
0463	1267	tad zeroch
0464	4216	jms put
0465	5661	jmp i oput

Figure 8-1. State of machine after reading and decoding the subroutine call instruction

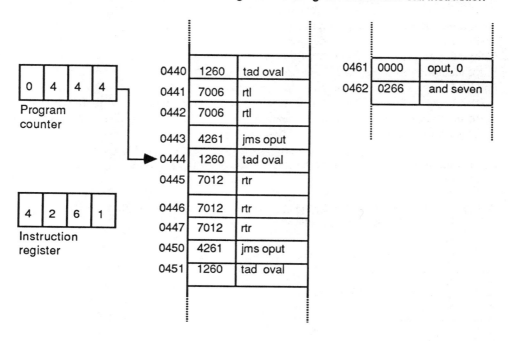

Figure 8-2. State of machine after completion of the subroutine call instruction

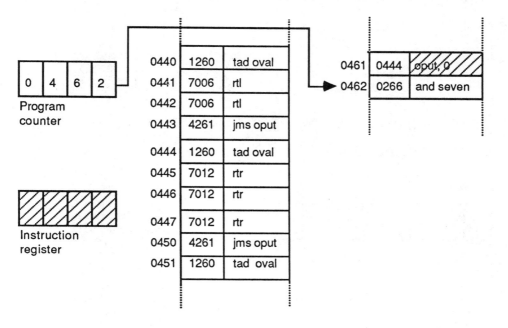

The return from subroutine 'oput' is achieved by the instruction 'jmp i oput' at address 0465. The full 12-bit return address is stored at location 'oput' (the start address for the subroutine; an indirect jump via this location makes it possible to return to the point of call). The process of address decoding is shown in Figure 8-3. Address decoding is identical with previous examples of indirect addressing (illustrated in Chapter 7). The 7 bits containing the page location are extracted. The page-zero/current-page bit is checked, and as it is a 1, the current page bits are taken from the PC yielding the address 000100110001 (0461). The indirect bit is checked and, as it is set, an indirect cycle is performed with data obtained from location 0461. The data, 0444, constitute the actual destination address for the jump instruction.

      The execution phase of the jump instruction involves copying the final decoded address into the PC. The machine state is now as shown in Figure 8-4.

Figure 8-3. Address decoding for the indirect jump to return the program from subroutine 'oput' to the calling routine

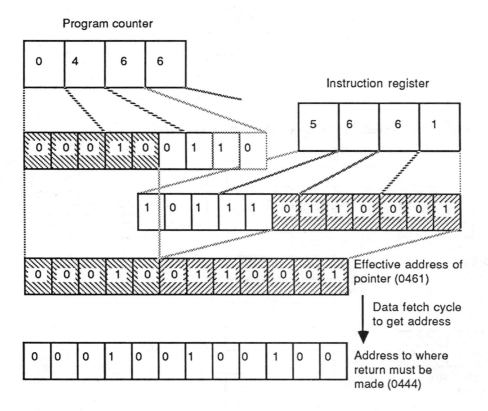

Figure 8-4. The state of the machine on completion of the jump instruction for the return from subroutine 'oput'

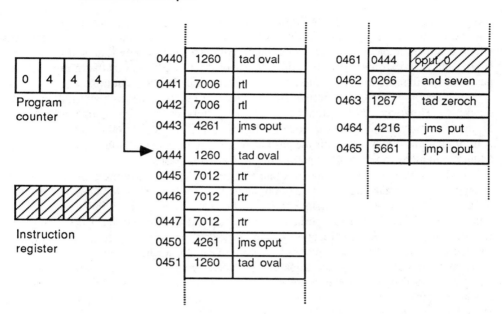

Summarizing the subroutine linkage method used on the simulated machine

This subroutine call mechanism requires a word, for storage of the return address, to be reserved at the start of every subroutine. The first executable instruction in a subroutine is in the next word. (The contents of the linkage word can be defined in the assembly source program as 0, as in the examples, or maybe as a halt instruction (a halt instruction catches errors where, by mistake, the code specifies a jump to the start of the subroutine, 'jmp' instruction, instead of a subroutine call, 'jms' instruction).)

The subroutine call instruction uses the effective address, derived by the address-decoding process (including, if necessary, any indirect references), to identify the location where the contents of the PC are to be stored. The subroutine call then causes a jump to the following location.

Return from a subroutine requires an indirect jump via the location holding the return address (stored by the subroutine call instruction).

It is not possible to have recursive subroutine calls. (A recursive call causes the original return address to be overwritten, by the return needed for the recursive call.) Apart from this restriction, there are no problems with regard to subroutines calling other subroutines. (*Note*: code written for a machine using a special subroutine-linkage register has to explicitly store, in memory, the return address of a subroutine before that subroutine can call another routine.)

Passing data to and from subroutines

In all the examples and exercises for the practical component of this course, subroutines will work either by using global variables or by having just one argument (and/or result) which can then be passed via the accumulator. (In those cases where it is necessary for a subroutine to work on a data array, the address of the first element of that array will be passed, in a global or in the accumulator, as the argument for the subroutine.)

Passing data to subroutines in the CPU registers is generally preferred on most machines. However, if the number of CPU registers is insufficient to hold all the arguments then some must be located in memory. Again, there is a problem of communication – how can both the calling routine and the called subroutine know the addresses in memory where these argument data have been stored?

The use of a *stack* data structure represents the generally preferred method of passing data. (A stack data structure is implemented as a large reserved area in memory, usually located in that part of memory with the highest addresses accessible to a program. One, or more, CPU registers point into the stack: these registers hold the addresses identifying the next unused location in the stack and, possibly, where in the stack are located data associated with a particular subroutine.) On machines with a stack pointer register in the CPU, data on the stack can be located relative to the address held in the stack pointer. The calling routine places argument values on the stack and adjusts the stack pointer; the called routine then finds these data via the stack pointer. These stack-based methods of passing data are reviewed in Chapter 15.

The simulated machine has no stack pointer register. On this machine it is necessary to use some other method of locating arguments in memory at addresses known to both calling and called routines.

The actual method used for argument passing has a number of disadvantages. One of these is that this method forces the intermingling of instructions and data elements. Any intermingling of code and data introduces opportunities for programming errors that are often particularly difficult to diagnose and correct. The following discussion of argument passing on the simulated machine is included only for completeness. There should be no need to use these techniques in actual examples.

Consider, for example, a sort routine that is called from different points in a program to sort different arrays. Since it is to work with different arrays, neither the number of elements nor the address of a particular array can be coded into the sort routine. Instead, both the address of the array and the number of elements in that array must be passed as arguments; the values of these arguments differing on each call.

A program using this subroutine will have the general form:

```
/ compute data for array 'a'
        .
        .
        .
/ place address of array 'a' and count of its elements in
/ locations accessible to subroutine
        .
        .
/ call sort subroutine
```

```
        jms sort
            .
/ compute data for array 'b'
            .
/ place address of array 'b' and count of its elements in
/ locations accessible to subroutine
            .
/ call sort subroutine
        jms sort
            .
        hlt
/ - - - - - - - - - - - - - - - - - - - - -
/  sort routine
sort,   0                           / return linkage
/ pick up arguments
            .
/ do the sort
            .
/ return
        jmp i sort
```

Subroutine 'sort' has to find the different argument values appropriate to each call. Its only link back to the caller is the return address, saved in its first linkage word. The argument values must, therefore, be capable of location by means of this return address.

The argument data, such as the number of elements and the address of the array, can be stored in the locations immediately following the subroutine call:

```
/ place address of array 'a' and count of its elements in
/ locations accessible to subroutine
        tad numa                / copy count into argument word
        dca nval
        tad addra               / copy address into argument word
        dca adrval
/ call sort subroutine
        jms sort
nval,   0   / an empty location to hold number of elements
adrval, 0   / an empty location to hold address of array
/ now get first instruction for execution on return from
/ subroutine sort ---
```

The state of the machine after filling in values for the arguments and completing the subroutine call instruction is illustrated in Figure 8-5.

Subroutine 'sort' can be written to fetch its arguments using its return address as a pointer. Its first argument, the count of elements in the array, is located by the instruction 'tad i sort'. The return address is incremented ('isz sort'; 'nop'); then, another 'tad i sort ' instruction will fetch the address of the array. Again, the return address has to be incremented ('isz sort'; 'nop') to point back to the first executable instruction following the subroutine call and the arguments. The state of the machine after the arguments have been obtained is shown in Figure 8-6.

Figure 8-5.   The state of the machine after setting argument values and completion of the subroutine call instruction

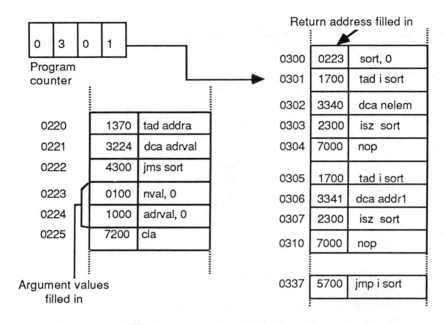

Figure 8-6.   The state of the machine after arguments have been copied into local variables and the return address has been updated

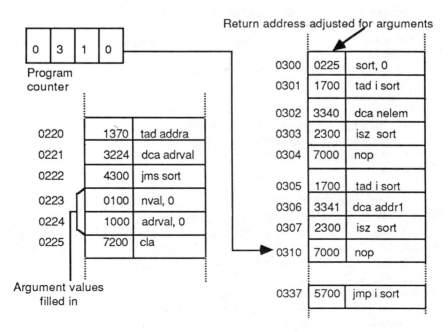

If return address pointers etc. are correctly updated, then when the final return instruction of the subroutine is executed, the jump will be back to the instruction after all the subroutine's arguments, as illustrated in Figure 8-7.

Although the scheme can be made to work, there exists considerable opportunity for error. For example, if one forgets to increment the return address pointer after fetching an argument then, on return from the subroutine, the value of that argument is going to be read and interpreted as an instruction.

Figure 8-7. The state of the machine on completion of the return from the 'sort' subroutine

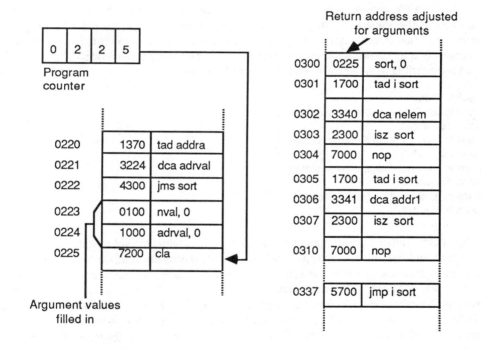

'Multiple returns' from a subroutine

A very common requirement in programs is for a subroutine to be called to perform some task and provide a *status* or *return code*. A return code indicates the subroutine's success (or failure) in its task, or encodes other control data. This return code is then tested in the calling program and, based on the results of the test(s), jumps are made to appropriate parts of the program depending on the different reported status values. Thus, code of the following form is common:

```
call subroutine
load status
compare with status_value_1
```

```
if equal then jump to do_state_1
compare with status_value_2
if equal then jump to do_state_2
compare with status_value_3
if equal then jump to do_state_3
jump to do_default
```

Quite often, such code involves considerable redundancy. The subroutine carries out a series of tests in order to determine the correct value for its status or return code; then, on return to the calling program, another sequence of tests is performed on the returned status to select a destination address for a jump.

Multiple returns from subroutines can sometimes permit a more economic expression of the same program requirements. (Caution: although the use of multiple returns does often lead to shorter programs, and fewer instructions executed at run time, this economy may come at the cost of more obscure and error-prone code.) If multiple returns are possible then the above code fragment becomes:

```
call subroutine
/ return to next location if status=status_1
jump to do_state1
/ return to next location if status=status_2
jump to do_state2
/ return to next location if status=status_3
jump to do_state3
/ return to next location in all other cases
goto do_default
```

In this scheme, rather than compute a value for a return status, the subroutine adjusts its own return address. In the example code fragment, the return address would be left unaltered in those cases where the subroutine needed to indicate 'status=status_1'. If the situation was that the subroutine returned 'status=status_2', then it would have to increment the value for its return address prior to performing any 'return from subroutine' (or indirect jump) instruction. In the remaining cases, the return address would have to be incremented twice (for 'status=status_3'), or incremented three times (for the final 'default' choice).

Exercises

1.   Write a subroutine that will perform an 'inclusive or' operation on two 12-bit bit patterns. (The inclusive or can be derived using the available 'and' and complement instructions.) The bit patterns are to be passed in the global variables 'alpha' and 'beta', and the result is to be returned in the accumulator. Write a driver program that uses the routine to compute inclusive ors of three different pairs of bit patterns. Try arranging the code so that (1) both the main program and the subroutine are on page 1, and (2) the main program is on page 1 and the subroutine is on page 2 (an indirect reference will be necessary in the actual subroutine call instruction).

2. Write a subroutine to compute the number of binary 1s contained in a value ʃ as an argument in the accumulator. This count is to be returned in the accumulator. Write a driver program that will call this subroutine to process in turn each data value held in an array. The counts are to be stored in a second array.

Lab 8

3. Using the subroutine developed for question 2, write a subroutine that will convert 7-bit ASCII characters to an 8-bit odd parity representation. Write a driver program that will call the subroutine to process, in turn, each character in some predefined message string. Note: characters in the message string must be defined as octal constants; for example, the message 'Stop' will have to be represented in the source code as:

```
/ message Stop
msg,    0123
        0164
        0157
        0160
        0
```

The characters are held one per word, with a zero word terminating the message. The 8-bit odd-parity characters are to be stored in an array in memory.

4. Write a subroutine to find the largest positive number in an array. The subroutine is to take, as arguments, the address of the first (zeroth) element of the array and the number of array elements; these arguments are to be passed as page zero globals (this example could use arguments passed in locations following the subroutine call). The result, the value of the largest element, is to be returned in the accumulator.

5. Write a subroutine to determine whether or not a character passed as an argument in the accumulator represents a lower case letter. (The subroutine can be coded so as to pass back a boolean (0 = false, 1 = true), or may be coded to use a multiple return.) Write a driver program that uses this subroutine to count the number of lower case letters in a predefined message.

Section III

Input and output

9

Wait loops for input and output

There has been one major limitation in all the examples and programs considered so far – they have neither inputs nor outputs. Of course, all real programs must read data from some input device(s) and produce results on appropriate output device(s). This chapter, and all subsequent chapters relating to the simulated machine, focus on aspects of how it performs data input and output. The exercises relating to input/output (I/O) handling are more valuable and informative than those earlier exercises concerned solely with data manipulations.

High-level languages, like Pascal and FORTRAN, combine with the operating system running on a computer to completely hide the complexities of input and output. A language system provides run-time support routines that convert numbers to, and from, character strings, and perform any formatting of the output, then call on the operating system to transfer the actual characters to/from peripheral devices.

The real complexities in I/O come at the operating system level. An operating system must be capable of handling different types of device. Different devices require different handling. For example, the keyboards and terminals on a computer work on a character by character basis, therefore the operating system must arrange to accept/send single characters. In contrast, tapes and disks work with blocks of several hundred characters; the operating system must read these blocks and pass the data on to the user program, character by character, as requested. One function of an operating system is to arrange appropriate handling of data to enable a user program to take its data from a terminal or, on other occasions, from a disk file (without any changes being required in the user program).

At a still more detailed level, the operating system program running on the computer must control that computer's peripheral devices. Each type of peripheral device has its own unique controls. A simple device like a terminal needs only to be told (1) to display a particular character, and (2) to report when it has done so. A more complex device like a disk unit has many controls. A disk control unit must be directed to move to the appropriate spot on the disk where data transfers are to occur; it may have to be told how much data to transfer, whether it is to transfer data from disk to memory or vice versa, and where the data are to be found in memory. As with the terminal, the disk control unit must also have a mechanism by which it can report the completion of its tasks.

A major objective of an operating system is to have many different peripheral devices working simultaneously while the CPU is used, most of the time, for executing the data processing code of the user's programs. The various simultaneous activities of peripherals and CPU must be coordinated. A large part of the code of an operating system is concerned with this coordination. The coordination of activities on a computer depends on the various signals that are generated when I/O tasks are completed by peripheral devices.

Methods for switching the CPU between different pieces of code in response to signals from devices are considered in Chapter 12. The first examples of I/O handling will, however, focus on a much simpler approach to the problems of coordinating concurrent activities.

The first method of handling I/O avoids all the tiresome and difficult coordination problems – by the simple expedient of ensuring that the computer system never attempts to proceed with more than one thing at a time. (However, one consequence of this simple approach to I/O is that, in the end, the CPU spends most of its time doing nothing, waiting for devices to complete their data transfers.)

In this section, the examples will use solely keyboard input and terminal output. Consequently, these initial examples have two major simplifications: (1) all data transfers will be of single characters, (2) the simplest approach to I/O (wait loops for individual peripheral devices) will be used.

Wait loops to coordinate the CPU and a peripheral device

A program that prints a message serves as the first example of I/O handling and illustrates the use of *wait loops* for coordination of CPU and device activity. The example program works through an array of character data held in memory, printing each character on the output terminal (the 'tty' or 'Teletype' of the simulator). A zero word marks the last of the character data, and the program stops when this is encountered.

Each character must be individually brought from memory into the accumulator. Its bit pattern is then copied, from the low-order 8-bits of the accumulator register, and sent to a data register in the terminal controller.

The terminal controller sends these bits, as a slow sequence of voltage pulses, to the device. In the device, the sequence of voltage pulses are, by electronic (or electro-mechanical) means, used to select the character to be displayed or printed. The device might be capable of dealing with 100 characters per second (if an electronic video terminal) or maybe as few as 10 characters per second (if a slow electromechanical printing terminal). The device controller has to send the bit data at a suitably slow rate.

The code for the mainline program takes the following form (the 'put' routine, which actually outputs the character, remains to be coded):

```
/ Message printing program
      *200
      cla                              / copy address of message into a pointer
      tad       addrm
```

```
            dca       ptr
/  main loop,
/  get next character from memory,
/  test for  zero word end marker
lp,         cla
            tad  i    ptr
            sna
            jmp       done              / if have hit end marker then can finish.
/ have a character,
/ call subroutine to print it
            jms       put
/ update ptr
            isz       ptr
            nop
/ now loop back and test for more characters
            jmp lp
/ all data printed, can stop
done,       hlt
/ - - - - - - - - - -
addrm,      chars                       / address of array of characters
ptr,        0                           / pointer into 'chars'
/ - - - - - - - - - -
/ subroutine to print a character.
put,        0                           / for return linkage.
            ?
            ?
            jmp i put                   / return from subroutine
/ - - - - - - - - - -
            *400
/ - - - - - - - - - -
chars, 124            / T
       145            / e
       163            / s
       164            / t
       0              / end mark
$
```

The simple machine, as modeled in the simulator, used special purpose I/O instructions. These instructions had the general form shown in Figure 9-1. Each device controller had its own device identifier number, which was coded in the middle 6 bits. The last 3 bits coded the function that the CPU required the device controller to perform.

One of the functions that the terminal controller (device identifier # = 04_{octal}) could perform was to *print character*. The print character instruction (function code #4_{octal}) had the mnemonic name 'tpc' (teletype print character). When executed by the CPU, this instruction caused the low order 8 bits of the accumulator to be copied into the terminal controller's data register, and initiated the process whereby the controller sent these bits to the actual terminal device.

This 'tpc' instruction forms the basis for a 'put' routine required in the message printing program.

Figure 9-1. Format of the I/O instructions of the simulated machine

| 1 | 1 | 0 | Device identification # | Function |

'iot' op-code

The simplest (but incorrect) coding for the 'put' routine is:

```
put,    0                    / for return linkage
        tpc                  / send the character
        cla                  / no longer need copy in acc
        jmp  i  put          / return from subroutine
```

If the program is run with this encoding of 'put', then:

1. The first character of the message ('T' in the example) is read from memory.
2. The 'put' routine copies the bit pattern 01010100 from the accumulator to the data register in the terminal controller, and the terminal controller immediately starts to send the bits to the actual terminal.
3. The 'put' subroutine is exited, and the jump back to the top of the loop performed.
4. The next character ('e') is read from memory into the accumulator.
5. The 'put' subroutine is again called.

This second call to 'put' therefore occurs about 10 instruction cycles after the first character was sent to the terminal controller.

The time taken by individual instructions depends on the number of memory cycles involved and various other intrinsic factors. An average of about 3 microseconds per instruction is reasonable for the real machine executing these 10 instructions. Consequently, the CPU is ready to execute the second 'tpc' instruction some 30 microseconds after the first.

Meantime, the terminal controller works at a much slower speed. If driving a 100 character per second terminal, it expects to handle about 800 bits per second, allowing about 1000 microseconds for each bit sent as a voltage pulse to the actual terminal device. In 30 microseconds, it would not have completed the transmission of a single bit from the first character.

The effect of a second 'tpc' instruction, only 30 microseconds after the first, is to replace the original bit pattern with the new value (or, depending on the design of the controller, it might cause the two bit patterns to be 'or'ed).

The program continues to run and, within about 150 microseconds, sends all the characters to the terminal controller, and the CPU then halts. Some 1000 microseconds or so later, the controller finishes sending a character to the device. Only a single character is printed.

For this message printing routine to work, the CPU has to be 'slowed down', to coordinate its sending of characters with the character handling actions of the terminal controller. The CPU must not send any additional data until the controller has indicated it is ready.

The terminal controller incorporates a 1-bit flag register (in addition to the data register where the character bit pattern is held). The circuitry in the controller sets this *ready flag* to 1 when the 8 bits of a character have all been transmitted to the device. (When the machine is started, or *reset*, all such device status flags are set to 0.)

In addition to the 'tpc' instruction for copying data from the accumulator to the terminal controller's data register, there were other instructions that allowed the testing and/or resetting of the device controller's ready status flag. One of these additional instructions was 'tsf' (teletype skip flag). This instruction tested the current state of the terminal controller's ready flag. If the flag was set, then the instruction caused the program counter to be incremented and, consequently, the next instruction to be skipped.

A more complete (though still not yet quite correct) version of the 'put' subroutine can be constructed using the 'tsf' instruction:

```
put,    0                   / for return linkage
        tpc                 / send character
        cla
putl,   tsf                 / wait for its safe delivery
        jmp     putl        / to be flagged.
        jmp i   put         / now, its been delivered, return from subroutine
```

With this coding, the first time subroutine 'put' is called, the character is sent to the terminal controller (as before) but now, rather than immediately returning, the CPU is made to wait in the subroutine.

The two-instruction wait loop, 'putl, tsf'; 'jmp putl', forces the CPU to wait until the terminal controller sets its flag indicating safe delivery of the character just given. If the flag is not set, then there is no skip and consequently the jump back instruction is executed. When the flag is finally set, the 'jmp putl' instruction is skipped and the CPU carries on with the remaining program instructions.

Once the first character ('T') of the message is flagged as delivered, the return from the 'put' subroutine is performed. The next character ('e') is loaded into the accumulator and 'put' again called. After sending the character by the execution of the 'tpc' instruction, the code for the wait loop is entered again.

However, the test on the terminal controller's flag is satisfied immediately, since the flag is still set to a 1 (indicating the successful delivery of the 'T'). There is no delay in the wait loop and the program again fails to perform properly.

For the program to work correctly, the CPU must clear the flag in the terminal controller at an appropriate time. Another instruction, 'tcf' (teletype clear flag), wh executed by the CPU, causes a signal to be sent via the bus to the terminal controller, and on receipt the terminal controller resets its flag to 0 (it doesn't matter if the flag was already 0; in that case the controller does nothing).

A workable version of the 'put' routine is as follows:

```
put,    0                   / for return linkage
        tcf                 / clear the flag
```

```
            tpc                     / send the character
            cla                     / get rid of copy in acc
putl,       tsf                     / wait for delivery of character
            jmp     putl
            jmp  i  put             / return from subroutine
```

This code clears the ready flag, sends the character, and waits for the ready flag to again be set. Thus, the CPU will always wait until each character is delivered before continuing with any other work. In this way, the CPU slows down to a speed comparable to that of its peripherals.

The combination 'tcf'; 'tpc' is so common that these two operations are put together in another single instruction, 'tls' (teletype load and send). The 'tls' instruction clears the ready flag (if set), copies the character from the accumulator to the controller's data register, and then starts the print process.

Using 'tls', the 'put' subroutine becomes:

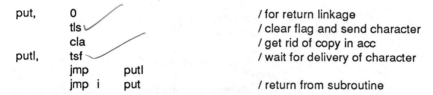

```
put,        0                       / for return linkage
            tls                     / clear flag and send character
            cla                     / get rid of copy in acc
putl,       tsf                     / wait for delivery of character
            jmp     putl
            jmp  i  put             / return from subroutine
```

(A different way of encoding the routine is considered as one of the exercises at the end of this chapter.)

Copying characters from keyboard to terminal

The same wait loop methods for handling I/O are used in this second example program. This program simply displays characters as they are typed.

The route followed by each character typed in at the keyboard is from keyboard to keyboard controller's data register; to accumulator in the CPU; to data register in the terminal controller and hence eventually to the output terminal. The events involved are, in principle, as follows:

1. Keystroke.
2. Keyboard hardware sends encoded form of character, as a series of voltage pulses, to the keyboard controller.
3. The keyboard controller collects these pulses and assembles the appropriate bit pattern in its data register.
4. When the keyboard controller has collected all 8 bits that comprise a character, it sets its flag register to 1. This 1 in the flag indicates the keyboard has provided data that are now ready for transfer to the CPU.
5. At its own convenience, the CPU checks the status of the keyboard controller. When the keyboard-ready flag is detected as set, the CPU knows that character input data are available; again, a skip test on the setting of a device flag permits a conditional

transfer either to the code dealing with a ready device, or to the code that continues a wait loop.

6. The CPU reads the 8-bit bit-pattern representing the character; that is, the bit-pattern is copied from the keyboard controller's data buffer, and transferred along the bus into the accumulator in the CPU.

7. The CPU directs the keyboard controller to clear its ready flag (because the data, previously flagged, have been collected).

8. The CPU copies the contents of the low order 8 bits of the accumulator, transferring these data over the bus to the terminal controller to be loaded into the terminal controller's data register (the terminal controller's ready flag is cleared, if by chance already set, at the same time as the data are loaded into the data register).

9. The terminal controller sends an appropriate sequence of voltage pulses to the circuitry of the output terminal. There, by electronic or electromechanical means, these voltage pulses select the character to be displayed or printed.

10. The CPU is, in the meantime, executing a program loop in which the ready flag of the terminal controller is tested; the loop is cycled repeatedly until this flag is set.

11. After the terminal controller has sent the last of the 8 bits to the actual output device, it sets its ready flag, thereby indicating the successful delivery of one character and its readiness to accept another.

12. The CPU breaks out of the program loop where it has been waiting for the output of the last character to be completed.

13. The code of the program causes the CPU to jump back to the loop where the input data are awaited. The CPU repeatedly cycles through a program loop, testing the keyboard's ready flag; execution of this loop continues until another key is struck and the entire process is repeated.

Typically, keyboard input data rates are about 10 characters per second; printing terminals usually manage 30 characters, or more, per second, while video display terminals can handle 100 characters per second. Consequently, the CPU spends most of its time executing the instructions of the wait loop where it waits for data to arrive from the keyboard. Code for this character-copying program is as follows:

```
        *200
        cla
/ wait until user types a character:
kwt,    ksf
        jmp     kwt
        krb                     / read the character that has just arrived
        tls                     / send it to terminal
        cla
/ wait for character to be delivered:
twt,    tsf
        jmp     twt
/ that last character has been delivered,
/ loop back to get another
        jmp     kwt
$
```

ındling of keyboard and terminal are similar. There is a minor difference: the
ter initiates the data transfer on the terminal and waits for it to be completed; the
~~~,~ter must wait for the user to start the keyboard operations.

All those wasted hours!

It is instructive to consider how many times the CPU cycles around one of those wait
loops. Suppose, for example, that the printing device can print 100 characters per second.
Then, from the moment a character is loaded into the printer controller's buffer, the CPU
has to wait one hundredth of a second before the ready flag sets again. Now, the two
instructions:

```
twait,  tsf
        jmp  twait
```

might together take ≤5 microseconds on a real computer. Therefore, the number of cycles
through that wait loop is:

$$\frac{(1/100)}{(5/1000000)} = \frac{10000}{5} = 2000$$

If the machine is waiting for input from a 10 character per second keyboard, then the
corresponding wait loop is cycled something like 20,000 times for each character entered.

Computer peripherals are very much slower than CPUs. If computers are
programmed to control their peripheral devices by means of these simple wait loops, then
the vast majority of the CPU cycles are expended idling – that is, just waiting for devices
to set flags indicating their readiness to accept or supply another data element.

(The relative speeds of CPU and peripherals have been distorted on the
simulator used in practical exercises. (The peripherals are very fast.) Although wait loops
are still required when reading data from keyboard and printing data on the teletype, these
loops typically get cycled only a few dozen times rather than many hundreds or thousands
of times. This speeding up of the peripherals allows exercises, involving wait loop I/O
handling, to be run in display modes without requiring excessive run times.)

Exercises

1. Write a program to read characters from the keyboard, echo them to the terminal, and
'buffer' them (i.e. store them in an array in memory). The program is to stop after
storing the third carriage-return character (ASCII value = 015_{octal}).

2. Write a (trivial) encrypting program. Characters read from the keyboard are to be
encrypted by looking up their (fixed) substitutions (e.g. 'a' → 'x', 'b' → 'n', etc.) in an

array, and the substitute characters are to be echoed to the terminal. The program is to terminate after processing 50 characters of input data.

3. Write a subroutine that will print the binary representation (i.e. 12 '0/1' characters) of a value passed in the accumulator; the printout is to be followed by a carriage return. Write a main program loop that causes the subroutine to print out, as binary numbers, representations of all the instructions in the program.

4. Write a program that reads characters from the keyboard; any that correspond to octal digits are echoed to the terminal and all other characters are ignored; the program is to terminate after printing ten output characters.

5. Write a program that reads octal numbers. The program is to terminate on reading the value 0. (The input data are to be typed in on the keyboard as sequences of the characters '0'...'7', with spaces separating different octal values (e.g. '7 111 1234 01 7767 0 ').) The values read are to be stored in an array in memory. The program then prints out the message 'The largest positive number was ', followed by the largest number (printed as an octal value).

6. The example routines for sending characters to the 'teletype' have used code of the form:

```
/ send character, passed as argument in acc, to 'teletype'
put,        0                  / return linkage
            tls                / send the character (and clear tty flag if set)
            cla                / no need to retain character in acc
/ now wait for tty flag to set and indicate
/ safe delivery of this character
twait,      tsf
            jmp     twait
            jmp  i  put
```

Sometimes, you will find the code re-arranged as follows:

```
put,        0                          / return linkage
/ wait, if necessary, for previous character to be delivered
twait,      tsf
            jmp     twait
/ now, start this character going
            tls                / send the character (and clear tty flag if set)
            cla                / no need to retain character in acc
            jmp  i  put
```

What is the main advantage of the rearranged code? What additional initialization step is required to make the rearranged code work?

7. Write a program that emulates an 'intelligent terminal' with capabilities for local editing of input data.

Background description:

Many terminals incorporate a simple microprocessor comparable in computational power with the PDP-8 mini-computer modeled by the simulator. The microprocessor, in this kind of 'intelligent terminal', is used to perform local editing tasks as well as managing the transmission of information to and from the main computer. Such a microprocessor normally possesses a small amount of read/write memory as well as a program probably held in read-only memory. Characters typed in by the user are temporarily buffered in the microprocessor's memory prior to transmission to the main computer.

The program in the microprocessor provides limited editing facilities that can change the characters held in the buffer. For example, the microprocessor might interpret a special cancel key as a request to delete all currently buffered data, and interpret some other control key as a request to delete the immediately preceding character.

When data entry is complete, and a carriage-return or enter key typed, the micro- processor packages the complete set of characters and transmits them over a communications line to the main computer. As discussed in previous examples on handling character data, there will be some relatively elaborate line-protocol that defines how a set of characters is to be packaged; packaging usually includes making all data bytes have the same parity, prepending a header with a byte count, and appending a trailer with checksum.

Program:

The program written should:

a) Read characters typed at the 'keyboard' up to and including a period ('.') character; convert each to an 8-bit odd-parity representation.

b) Store (*buffer*) these (odd-parity) characters, one per word, in an array in memory. (All messages are assumed to have fewer than 64 characters; the program is not required to check for excessive length.)

c) Maintain counts both of the total number of characters entered and the number currently buffered. The count of buffered characters must be updated when editing operations are performed.

d) Compute a checksum. The checksum is to be calculated by adding all the buffered characters after data entry has been completed (i.e. the period character has been read). At each addition, the checksum is to be masked so that only the 6 least significant bits are preserved (i.e. the checksum is computed modulo 64).

e) Allow the '@' character to be used to delete all preceding input.

f) Allow the back-slash ('\') character to be used to delete the immediately preceding character.

g) Print the complete message, subsequent to all editing operations, when the terminating period is read. (Characters sent to the 'tty' should be masked back to 7 bits.)

Test the program on an example input string that exercises the various input and editing options. An example of final test input data is:

ltwo@i\\\lt wooks\\\rks, and about time too.

A *dump* printout is useful when checking whether the characters have been stored correctly and whether or not the correct checksum has been computed. Simpler sets of test data should be chosen when testing the individual parts of the program – for example, the checksum routine will need to be hand-checked on some simple data like 'ab'.

10

Peripheral devices

Figure 10-1 illustrates a basic division of peripheral devices (and their controllers) into two main classes. First, there are simple devices whose operation involves the transfer of a single character, or other datum, between a CPU register and a data register in the controller. Second, there are devices that transfer large blocks of data in any one operation with the data transferred direct from device to memory.

Figure 10-1.   The two main classes of peripheral device

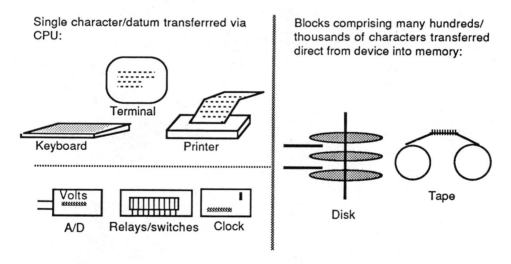

The keyboard and terminal, as described in Chapter 9, are good examples of the simpler type of peripherals, as are most printers. A number of other devices are controlled in a similar way. For example, a programmable clock has a data register which is loaded with a *tick-count* (corresponding to some required time interval), and a *ready flag* which is set when the time interval has expired. (An initial value for this tick-count is loaded with data copied from a CPU register.) An analog-to-digital (A/D) input device will have a controller with a data register that holds a numeric value representing a measured voltage, and a flag register that is set when a measurement has been taken. When this ready flag is set, data can be read from the A/D controller's register into a CPU register. Relays and switches can be monitored via a controller which has a multi-bit data register, with individual bits representing the on/off state of individual switches, and a flag register that is set when one of the switches changes its setting. Again, information transfer involves copying data from the controller's register into a CPU register.

Control of the block transfer devices is more elaborate. The device controllers have a number of internal registers that are used to hold information that describes the particular data transfer in progress. These control registers for the device are normally loaded with information copied from CPU registers. Control information might include the number of bytes to transfer, the address in memory where the data are to be transferred, and the location on the device where the data are located. In addition, the controllers have the usual complement of status flags: ready flags, error flags, and so on. With these devices, the actual data transfer will almost always entail moving information from/to memory, over the bus, via the controller and to/from the device. This type of data transfer is said to work by *direct memory access*. Disks are the most important device in this class. Tape units also work in this manner as do certain types of video display. (Direct memory access circuitry is relatively expensive. Cheap disk and tape controllers that require data be routed via the CPU are available; however disks working through such controllers have a poor performance.)

This section provides brief descriptions of some of these devices and some programs for their control. First, the simple devices are considered; examples are given of programming for the clock and A/D as implemented in simul8. Then, direct memory access is illustrated in more detail. Both tapes and disks are used for the storage of data files; the descriptions of these devices extend to include some consideration of how files are arranged and accessed. A simple disk-handler routine, for reading/writing chosen blocks of simul8's disk, is also illustrated.

The simple devices

The simple devices have controllers with the prototypical form shown in Figure 10-2. Typical features are: (1) connection to the bus of the computer system; (2) circuitry that can interpret the control and address lines of the bus (a controller must recognise when a message on the bus is one to which it should respond); (3) a data register (the number of bits in this register depends upon the type of device being controlled); (4) a status register (in most cases, just a 1-bit ready flag); (5) circuitry to convert the external representation of data into the bit-pattern that goes into the data register; (6) connection to the device that it controls by two or more external data lines.

For devices such as keyboards there are usually only two wires connecting the controller to the device. Data, such as the bit pattern encoding a character, are sent as a series of short voltage pulses (e.g. a voltage difference of 1 volt between the two input lines could encode a 1 bit, while a 0 bit could be encoded by having the input lines at the same voltage). Such interfaces between controller and device are said to be *serial* interfaces (because the data transfer involves sending a *series* of 1-bit data signals).

Figure 10-2. Prototypical controller for a simple input or output device

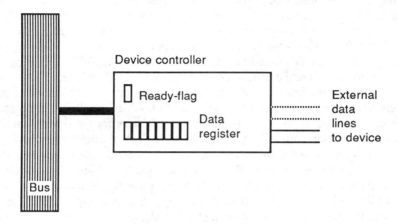

In other cases, there will be as many external data paths as there are bits in the controller's data register (plus at least one common ground so that voltages on the lines can be measured). A printer controller might be connected to its printer through eight data lines allowing all the bits in a character to be transmitted at the same time. This represents an example of a *parallel* interface. Though usually more costly, parallel interfaces allow for higher rates of data transfer.

Simple devices are controlled by the CPU, issuing instructions such as:

Input	*Output*
a) read data from controller register into CPU register;	a) copy data from CPU register into controller register;
b) initiate input operation;	b) initiate output operation;
c) test for input ready;	c) test for output-completion/readiness to accept further output;
d) clear/reset controller's status flags.	d) clear/reset controller's status flags.

The CPU does not always have complete control over an input device. A device may work with complete autonomy from the CPU, as is the case for most keyboards on which operations are initiated solely by the user. Therefore, frequently, there will be no 'initiate input' instruction. However, an 'initiate input' instruction is sometimes appropriate, for example, on those keyboards that lock after a character has been typed, and then must be explicitly re-enabled.

The use of wait loops for device control has already been illustrated in examples using the keyboard and terminal. For an input device, a wait loop requires an 'initiate input' instruction (if required for the particular input device), a 'test input ready' instruction (in a loop cycled until the test is satisfied), a 'read data into CPU' instruction, and a 'clear ready flag' instruction. One approach to handling an output device is to use the sequence of a 'clear ready flag' instruction, a 'load device controller's data register with data from CPU' instruction, a 'start output' operation, and, in some appropriate loop, a 'test ready flag' instruction.

Simple I/O for clocks

There are two different kinds of clock that can be interfaced to a computer: *fixed-frequency* and *programmable*. At their simplest, these clocks simply correspond to controllers with one 1-bit ready flag set when some time interval has elapsed. Control of such a clock involves just a few instructions: an instruction that tests the current setting of the flag and an instruction that clears the flag. (There will also be an instruction to start the clock, and another instruction that stops it.) Often, a fixed frequency clock on a simple computer uses the line frequency of the mains voltage supply, that is, 60 Hz ('60 ticks per second') or 50 Hz; clocks with other preset frequencies can be obtained.

A programmable clock has a data register that is loaded with a tick-count. This count is decremented, at some constant rate, by the circuitry of the clock, and the ready flag is set when the count reaches zero. (An extra instruction for loading the clock's count register is then required.)

The simplest use of a clock is in code that delays the CPU's progress through a program for a specified time period. If a clock is monitored continuously, it can be used (1) to establish a time-of-day record for the computer, and/or (2) to schedule operations that must be performed at particular time intervals or at specified times. (How this continuous monitoring might be done should become clearer after later discussions of more elaborate methods of I/O control, in particular *interrupts*, as discussed in Chapter 12.)

Simple I/O on analog-to-digital converters (ADCs) and via switches and relays

Apart from character-oriented I/O, computers must also be capable of monitoring and controlling industrial machinery and scientific experiments. Two kinds of data are involved: voltage levels (represented in the computer as binary numbers) and data defining the on/off status of each switch in a set of switches (represented as set bit patterns in the computer). These data must be manipulated both as inputs (in monitoring tasks) and as outputs (in control tasks).

The input voltages that must be measured may represent the outputs of thermocouples (and hence temperatures), pressure transducers, photomultipliers (light intensities), or any one of a number of other analog data inputs. An ADC incorporates circuitry to measure (analog) voltages and convert these data into binary numbers that can then be processed by a computer.

Usually, an ADC must be instructed to start taking a sample. The actual measurement of a voltage, and subsequent conversion of its value to a binary number, takes some small amount of time (equivalent to a few tens of instructions). The ADC sets its ready flag when the measurement process is complete.

An ADC and its controller have a data register with a particular number of bits which determines the largest binary number that can be represented, and consequently defines a limit on the accuracy with which voltages can be measured. (For example, an ADC, with a 10-bit data register, might be used to measure a voltage v in the range $0 \leq v < 1$ volt. Ten-bits allow (unsigned) numbers in the range $0...1023$ to be represented. The value 1023 can be used to represent an input voltage v of approximately 1 volt. The actual voltage value is then measured to an accuracy of about $^1/_{1000}$ volt. If, however, the voltages are measured on the range $0...5$volts then the value 1023 represents about 5 volts and the voltage values are accurate only to $^5/_{1000}$ volt.)

An ADC is typically *multiplexed*, that is, it can measure several different inputs. The CPU instructs it as to which input is to be used. An ADC is also normally capable of measuring over different voltage ranges, such as $0...1$ volt, $0...5$ volts, and $-5...5$ volts; again, the CPU instructs the controller which range is appropriate.

Analogous output devices are also required. These are *digital-to-analog* converters. They have a data register, loaded by the CPU with a binary number, and this number is converted to an output voltage. (Again, the number of bits in this data register determines the accuracy with which an output voltage can be set.) This voltage can be used to determine the electric power to be supplied to a heater, compressor motor, or whatever.

An interface and controller for monitoring the settings of individual switches has individual bits in its data register wired to corresponding switches. By simply reading this n-bit data register, the CPU can determine the settings of n different switches. (In an actual industrial application, these switches might be open/closed valves in some reactor, locked/unlocked gates, and so forth.) The controller might be wired to set its ready flag whenever there is a change to any bit in its data register.

Switch-register-type output devices are also required. With these, the CPU places a bit pattern in the controller's data register, the 0/1 settings of the individual bits representing the required off/on settings of the corresponding switches. The circuitry of the controller and the device interfacing then make any necessary changes to the settings of the actual switches, valves, locks, or other machine controls.

The clock and analog-to-digital peripherals of simul8

Simul8 incorporates a fixed-frequency clock. This is controlled by three instructions: 'clkt', 'clksf', and 'clkcf'. The instruction 'clkt' acts as an on-off 'toggle' and starts the clock running, or stops it, as may be appropriate; 'clksf' is for testing whether the clock's ready flag is set; and 'clkcf' clears the flag and starts the clock counting again.

A simple subroutine that delays a program for a given number of clock ticks has the form:

```
/ subroutine to cause a delay,
/ value in acc on entry  is number of 'ticks' of delay required.
delay,    0
          cia                          / negate argument
          dca      countl              / store in counter
```

```
/ start clock
        clkt
/ main delay loop starts here
/ it incorporates the usual two instruction wait loop:
dellp,   clksf
        jmp     dellp
/ clear the flag, causing clock to resume
        clkcf
/ update count of ticks and, if appropriate,
/ go back to await next tick
        isz     countl
        jmp     dellp
/ stop the clock, return from subroutine
        clkt
        jmp  i  delay
/ - - - - - - - - - - -
countl, 0               / used when counting clock ticks
```

In this subroutine, after the clock is started there is a double loop; the inner loop being the wait for the next clock 'tick', and the outer loop being the count of the ticks. When the delay requirement is satisfied, the clock is stopped and the delay routine is exited.

The analog-to-digitial (A/D) device for the simulated machine is again a rather simplified version of a real ADC. It is operated through the instructions 'adstrt', 'adsf', and 'adcrb': 'adstrt' starts the sampling process; 'adsf' tests the ready flag, while 'adcrb' (analog-to-ditital clear-flag and read buffer) reads the contents of the A/D controller's data register into the accumulator as well as clearing the ready flag.

The code required to read one sample from the A/D is:

```
/ start a-to-d's measurement process
        adstrt
/ wait for flag to set,
/ this occurs when data are ready
adlp,    adsf
        jmp     adlp
/ read data and clear the flag
        adcrb
```

A more elaborate example is shown below. This code illustrates how the simul8 computer could acquire 128 readings from the A/D, with successive samples being taken at successive clock ticks, and the data stored in memory. (It is assumed that the time taken for the data-sampling steps is only a small fraction of the time between successive clock ticks, as would normally be the case in such an application.) This type of data-acquisition process is typical of many scientific applications; very commonly, a set of data must be acquired and then subjected to further mathematical transforms, for example, a Fourier transform, that yield the information required from the experiment.

```
/ initialize pointers and counters;
/ 'counts' holds (as -ve value) the number of samples still to be acquired
/ 'ptr' is an address pointer identifying where the next datum is to be stored.
/ Therefore, 'counts' is initialized to -(number of samples)
/ 'ptr' initialized to start of array 'x
        cla
        tad     numsmp
        cia
        dca     counts
        tad     addrx
        dca     ptr
/ start the clock
        clkt
/ main loop here:
/ at start of loop have the wait for next clock 'tick'
mainl,  clksf
        jmp     mainl
/ when clock 'ticks' clear its flag and set it counting again
        clkcf
/ read the sample
        adstrt
adwt,   adsf
        jmp     adwt
        adcrb
/ store the sample
        dca i   ptr
/ update ptr
        isz     ptr
        nop
/ now test for termination of loop:
        isz     counts
        jmp     mainl
/ stop the clock
        clkt
/ now go off and process the data
        .
        .
        .
/ - - - - - - - - - - - - -
numsmp,   0200              / 128 (decimal) samples needed
addrx,    x                 / address of array
counts,   0                 / counter used for loop control
ptr,      0                 / address pointer used for array access
        .
        .
/ - - - - - -
        *6000
x,     0                    / start of array
        *6200
/ - - - - - -
```

Direct memory access

The example just given for the A/D illustrates how blocks of data can be read in from a device and loaded into memory. The approach demonstrated is for each individual data element to be explicitly and individually read by an I/O instruction. Each data element is copied into the CPU, from where it is stored into memory. Further, the CPU executes instructions to update a memory pointer and counter.

Disks and tapes (and video displays) need to transfer blocks of data to/from memory. In principle, it is possible for most such data transfers to use the same I/O methods already illustrated. However, this represents an inconvenient approach; and, in some cases, timing constraints of particular devices render the method unfeasible.

The timing problems are easily illustrated. Data on disks and tapes are stored in blocks of hundreds, or thousands of characters. Although there can be quite substantial delays while blocks of data are found, and even significant delays between blocks when sequences of successive blocks are being transferred, the actual transfer of the successive individual bytes comprising each block is fast. High performance tapes and disks can easily deliver the bytes from a block at a rate equivalent to 500,000 characters per second. Even if the transfer rate was only 100,000 characters per second, that leaves the CPU only 10 microseconds to deal with each character. The number of instructions that can be executed in a given time depends largely on the memory cycle-speed and the number of memory cycles required by each instruction; in 10 microseconds, a machine like that simulated would complete only three or four instructions. The CPU simply could not keep up with the data transfer if it has to fetch and execute an I/O instruction, a store instruction, an update pointer instruction, an update and test count instruction, and a jump instruction.

Of course, the updating of counts and address pointers can be performed fast enough provided control data are stored in high speed registers and special purpose circuits are used.

If the CPU can be relieved from the task of transferring the individual bytes in a block, then it can proceed with other work. Once the CPU has started the transfer of, for example, a block of 1024 bytes, then, at a transfer rate of about 100,000 characters per second, about one hundredth of a second will elapse before the transfer is complete. Provided that external circuitry attends to the details of the data transfer, the CPU can proceed with some other work during this period. Eventually, the CPU will require the data and, at that point, it can wait on a flag indicating the completion of the data transfer.

The extra circuitry needed is relatively simple. A suitable controller would incorporate adders (or decrementers) to update counts and address pointers, and also a couple of extra registers: one to hold the address for the next datum, the other to hold the count of the number of data elements still to be transferred. The prototypical form for a direct memory access (DMA) controller is shown in Figure 10-3.

Before the data transfer is started, the CPU loads the *address register* in the controller with the address for the first data element; the *count register* may also be set (often, the device will transfer blocks of a specific size, in which case the initial value for the count may not be set explicitly, because the count value can be built into the controller's circuitry).

Figure 10-3. **Prototypical controller for a device that utilises direct memory access data transfers**

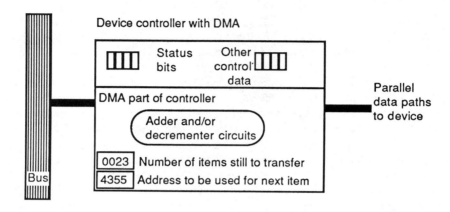

Once a data transfer is in progress, it is the controller that keeps track of the appropriate address for each data element, maintains the count, terminates the transfer when the count reaches zero, and then sets a *transfer complete* flag in its status register.

The connection between the controller and the bus has to be more elaborate if the controller is to use DMA. Whenever the controller receives a data element from its device, it has to claim the bus. Once it gains control of the bus, it places (1) the contents of its address register on the bus's address lines, (2) the value of the datum, just received from its device, on the bus's data lines, and (3) a write to memory 'instruction' on the bus's control lines.

As illustrated in Figure 10-4, each datum in a block of data moves from the device, through an interface and the controller, along the bus and directly into memory.

The bus, the CPU/bus interface, and the interfaces between the bus and those controllers using DMA, all have to be more elaborate for this scheme to work. There has to be a *bus arbitration* system that can choose which of several possible requests for the bus is honored next. An example request sequence for the bus is shown in Table 10-1.

The DMA device controllers normally take priority over the CPU. While a controller does a data transfer using DMA, the CPU may slow down slightly because, sometimes, it has to wait for access to the bus, when it tries to fetch its next instruction or program data element. (On simul8, the DMA cycles are indicated on the CPU-display by DMA flashing every time a bus- and memory-cycle is 'stolen' by the disk. The disk DMA transfers use every third memory cycle; this is atypically fast.)

The code for the control of a DMA-type block transfer device is simpler than the code, illustrated earlier, to transfer 128 words from the A/D. A basic framework for code to read a block of several hundred data values is:

```
{ load CPU register with count
I/O instruction to copy count into device's counter register }
load CPU register with address
I/O instruction to copy address into device's address register
```

Figure 10-4. Transfer of data using direct memory access

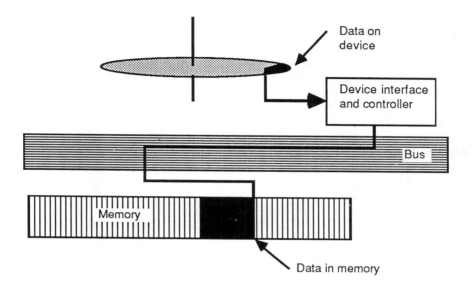

Table 10-1. Example trace of activity on a computer's bus (asterisks indicate the completion of a bus activity)

Requestor	Request	Response	Activity
CPU *	memory read	bus granted	instruction fetch
disk control	memory write	bus granted	DMA
CPU *	memory read	delay	attempt data fetch
		bus granted to CPU	data fetch
CPU *	memory read	bus granted	instruction fetch
CPU *	memory write	bus granted	data write
disk-control	memory write	bus granted	DMA
CPU *	memory read	delay	attempt instruction fetch
		bus granted to CPU	instruction fetch

I/O instruction to start the transfer

{ possibly, get on with some other work not needing the data
 now being transferred }
.

I/O instruction+branch instruction forming a wait loop that
waits for completion of the transfer
I/O instruction to clear the transfer complete flag
.

{ code using data transferred }

As noted above, some devices have implicit 'count' values, avoiding the need for a count
to be loaded. Although the CPU can continue with some other work while the transfer
proceeds, frequently, there will be no useful work to do, so, in the simplest schemes for
I/O handling, the wait for the transfer complete flag immediately follows the start transfer
instruction.

Tapes and disks

Disks and, to a much lesser extent, tapes provide the file storage for a computer system.
'Industry compatible' computer tape-drive units are just larger, more specialized versions
of reel-to-reel magnetic tape recorders; tapes are mounted on the drives as needed. Disks
can either be permanently mounted ('fixed') or use detachable disk packs that are mounted
on drives when needed.

        The actual data capacity of a tape depends markedly on how the data are
organized; maximum data capacities of several tens of millions of bytes (tens of
megabytes) are possible. The capacities of detachable disks vary from the 100,000 bytes
(100 kilobytes) or so of small floppy disks, to the several hundred megabytes of large
detachable disk packs. Fixed disks typically store from 1 to 100 megabytes. These fixed
disks generally have higher performance than detachable disks, with faster rates of data
transfer to/from memory and shorter *seek* times. (As explained later, a disk unit must first
find ('seek') a block of data and then set up the transfer.)

        The disks are used to store both system's and users' data files. Files for heavily
used utility programs (like editors and compilers) are typically located on the higher
performance fixed disks. Users' files are placed on either shared or private detachable disk
packs. Apart from data reads/writes to interactive terminals, most program I/O is to disk
files. Even when a program generates output for printing, these data usually go first to a
file on disk, from where they are eventually read and sent to the printer.

        There are two main uses for tapes: archival storage and data exchange. For a
relatively low cost, say $10, tapes can store 10-20 megabytes of data; this low cost
makes it practical to store large quantities of data for which there are no longer any
immediate demands but which might be required later. Increasingly, this archival role is
being taken on by detachable disk packs (the introduction of permanent optical disk
storage will accentuate this trend). The advantage of tapes for data exchange is that there
are standards for the physical recording of data on tape, and standards for organizing data

into files. These standards are accepted by different manufacturers; consequently, data files written on one machine are readable on completely different machines. (Detachable disks usually have recording and formatting conventions unique to their manufacturer and therefore unreadable by different machines.) In the longer term, even the data exchange role of tapes is likely to be reduced; increasingly, file exchange will exploit computer-computer communications links via telephone networks.

Files ⇔ data blocks

A programmer wants to envisage data storage on disks and tapes in terms of *files* that can be referenced by name, and which have a coherent structure that relates to the application in which they are used. Data storage is actually in terms of blocks of bytes; these blocks are usually a fixed size dictated by the hardware but, in some circumstances, can have sizes that are selected by the user. The hardware devices and their controllers can only perform tasks such as 'move to block xxx' and 'read/write block'. A 'read-file' request by a user program implicitly entails operations such as (1) determine which block is needed, (2) find that block on the device, and (3) do the data transfer. The detailed steps involved in determining the block number and finding the block are largely hidden from the programmer. Subroutines in a computer's operating system perform the necessary translation from the programmer's file-oriented model to the hardware's data- block representation.

The remainder of this section provides an overview of how data are stored on disks and tapes, and illustrates some of the simpler ways in which conceptual file structures can be mapped onto physical storage structures. Tapes are considered first because they are simpler; the discussion of tapes also introduces the ideas of *logical/ physical record* and *blocking of records*.

Tapes

An 'industry compatible' tape unit uses $1/2$ inch wide plastic tape containing a magnetic oxide. Typical tape lengths range between 600 feet and 2400 feet. The tape moves, from reel to reel, at high speed over a set of read/write heads. Speeds as high as 100 inches per second are employed while recording or playing back. Elaborate tape-tensioning mechanisms accommodate the abrupt starts and stops of the tape reel drive motors.

The read/write heads incorporate a set of 9 individual units which transfer data to 9 parallel tracks on the tape. (Other timing and control signals can also be recorded along the tape.) A set of 9 bits written across the tape usually represents an 8-bit data byte and an extra parity bit generated by hardware inside the tape unit. The 0/1 bits are distinguished by differing magnetic polarity. Each set of 9 bits is recorded in a 'frame'. The bits in a 'frame' are transferred in parallel, via the read/write heads, between tape and a temporary data register in the tape unit. Frames are written close together along the length of the tape. Their density along the tape is determined by the quality of the read/write heads (but is also limited by the tape quality). These physical arrangements of data bits are illustrated in Figure 10-5.

Figure 10-5.   Physical arrangement of data bits into frames on a nine-track tape

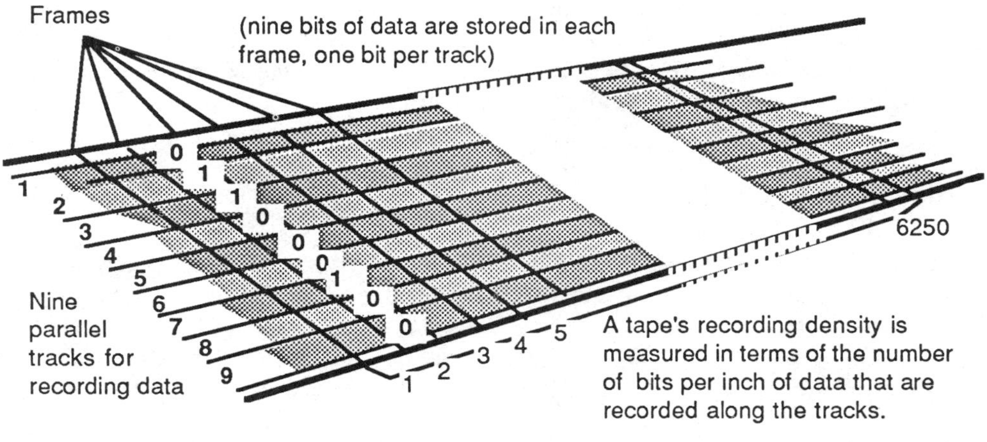

Frames   (nine bits of data are stored in each frame, one bit per track)

Nine parallel tracks for recording data

6250

A tape's recording density is measured in terms of the number of bits per inch of data that are recorded along the tracks.

Tapes are normally written with about 1600 frames-per-inch, or, equivalently, bits-per-inch (bpi), along the track; other common densities are 800 and 6250 bpi. If data were recorded continuously, then there could be 6000+ characters on one inch of tape. However, data are stored in blocks, *physical records*, of *n* bytes; successive blocks are separated by *interrecord gaps* (IRG), as illustrated in Figure 10-6. (The structure of a real data block is somewhat more elaborate than shown in this diagram. There may be checksum data, generated by the hardware of the tape unit. There are special *preamble* and *postamble* magnetic patterns written on the tape just before and just after the data; these special patterns are used by the tape drive hardware to check that the tape is moving at the correct speed before a 'read' operation is attempted.)

Interrecord gaps need sufficient length (about half an inch) to allow a tape, stopped after reading a record, to reach the correct speed for a 'read' operation before the next block passes under the read/write heads. These gaps, where no data are stored, have to be considered when estimating how much data can be recorded on a tape and how fast those data can be transferred.

A typical *logical* unit of data is one *card-image*, that is, 80 bytes. If this is the size of the physical data records written to a tape, then the layout is: 80 bytes data, IRG, 80-bytes data, IRG, 80 bytes data, and so on. On a 1600-bpi tape, an 80-byte data record fits in $1/20$ inch. Consequently, $1/20$ inch of tape used for data is followed by $1/2$ inch of unused interrecord gap, leading to only about one eleventh of the potential storage capacity of the tape being used. Further, the data transfer rate is also reduced.

Such problems require data on a tape be written in larger physical records. The *logical* records (records meaningful to the application program) are grouped, or *blocked*, into *physical* records (records of a size suitable for recording on the tape device). Figure 10-7 provides an illustration of unblocked and blocked data. If the physical records contained ten logical records, then (on a 1600-bpi tape) one has an 800-byte data record (using $1/2$ inch of tape) followed by the $1/2$ inch interrecord gap. Now, half the tape is used for data storage.

Figure 10-6. Data on tape are organized into physical records separated by inter-record gaps

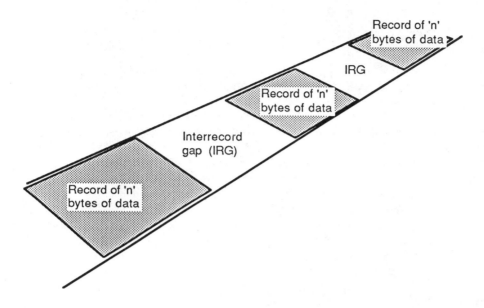

Figure 10-7. Blocked and unblocked data

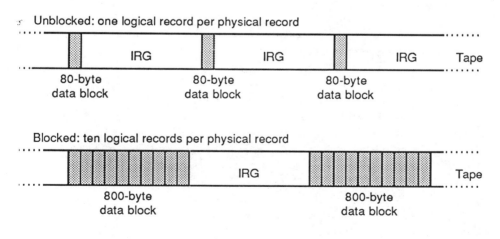

The advantages of *data blocking* include:

1. Better use of potential storage capacity of tape.
2. Fewer 'read' operations needed to transfer the same total amount of data from tape to memory.

But, there are costs, including:

1. More CPU time is used to block, or unblock, data being written to, or read from, tape.
2. More memory is used to hold the large physical records.

Therefore, the choice of an appropriate blocking factor represents a compromise. A computer system usually allows programmers to select appropriate block sizes for data being written to tape.

Apart from the data, the interrecord gaps, the extra checksums, and so forth, additional special magnetic patterns are recorded. These include *tape marks* used to help delimit files.

A file on tape is represented as a sequence of physical records (almost invariably, all the records in a tape file have the same size). A tape mark can act as a file separator. The tape unit can recognize tape marks, and thereby find the starts/ends of files. Figure 10-8 illustrates a typical tape organization. The tape starts with a special *labels* file containing an assigned tape name and other management data. Data files follow; the files are separated by tape marks and each consists of a sequence of physical records separated by interrecord gaps.

Files on this type of tape are written/read sequentially. When reading, the correct file is found by repeatedly 'skipping to tape mark' until the file is reached. The successive blocks (physical records) of data in the file are then read. Files are written by moving to the end of the used portion of tape (possibly indicated by two successive tape marks) and then writing data blocks. Normally, it will not be possible to overwrite a file *in situ*; a new copy of the file must be written at the end of the tape.

Figure 10-8. Organization of files on a tape

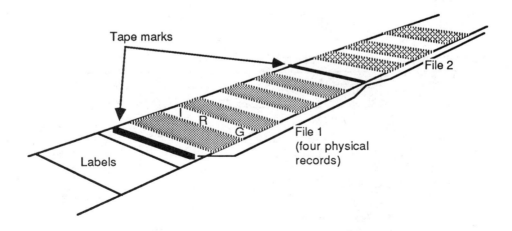

Disks

Moving-head disk packs represent the most important variant of disk storage devices. These disk packs, which may be either fixed or removable units, comprise a set of platters mounted on a common central spindle. The diameters of these disk platters vary from 14 inches down to 3 inches; they are about $1/20$ inch (or less) thick and covered with a very thin film of magnetic oxide.

An assembly of read/write heads can be moved, by a precise stepping motor, between the surfaces of the disk platters (see Figure 10-9). The various arms of this assembly move in conjunction, with all the different read/write heads always having the same instantaneous distance from the central spindle. On each arm of this assembly, there is one read/write head for accessing the disk surface above the arm, and another read/write head for accessing the surface below. The read/write heads fly very close to the recording surfaces (the gap between surface and head is a few microns).

Figure 10-9. Arrangement of disk recording surfaces and the read/write mechanism

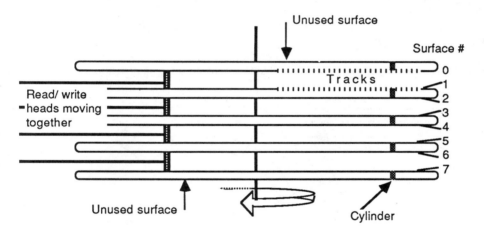

The parts of the disk surface closest to the spindle are unused. The rest of the disk surface is divided up into *tracks* onto which data can be written/read. Looking down on a disk surface, one would see the tracks as a set of concentric rings; maybe as many as 200 on a large disk. Data are stored, as sequences of bits, around these tracks (the 0/1 bits being stored as regions of different magnetic polarity). On most disks, the bit capacity of the different tracks is constant; since the outermost tracks are longer, the bits-per-inch density is lower on these than on the innermost tracks. Therefore, the number of bits per track is determined by the maximum density of bits written on the innermost track. (Some of the newer disks have variable speed motors that rotate more slowly when the heads are on an outer track; this allows bits to be written at a higher density on those outer tracks, and consequently increases the storage capacity.)

There are a number of different ways in which the storage capacity of a track is used. It is possible to work in terms of the tracks themselves. A track has some maximum capacity (e.g. about 17 kilobytes); the programmer can choose to divide this up into blocks whose size is selected as a multiple of the logical record size of the application. Various control data are stored between each block on a track, and there are small gaps between blocks. These overheads slightly reduce the data capacity of the track. The programmer might organize a track to hold one 17-kilobyte block, or sixteen 1-kilobyte blocks, or thirty 512-byte blocks. This approach to the use of disk storage is advantageous if large files, with a specialized internal structure, are held on private-volume disks. Since space must be allocated in units of complete tracks, this method can be wasteful of storage if only small files are required.

In an alternative approach, the data capacity of a track is split up into fixed sized blocks (this division may be effected by the hardware of the disk unit or may simply be a convention enforced by the operating system). Then, each track holds a fixed number of blocks (512 bytes is a typical block size). These blocks are the unit of space allocation.

It is this second model, illustrated in Figure 10-10, that is used in subsequent discussions. Space on a disk is assumed to be available as fixed-size blocks. Each block is usually specified in terms of block #/track # ; this is its *disk address*. If the disk has multiple platters, then the address will also include a specification of the disk surface. Sometimes, it is more convenient to think in terms of a continuous sequence of block numbers for all the blocks on a disk surface. Then blocks 0...15 are those in track 0 of surface 0, blocks 16...31 are those in track 1, and so on. The seventh block in track 3, of surface 0, would be numbered 55.

Figure 10-10.   Arrangement of tracks and data blocks on a single disk surface

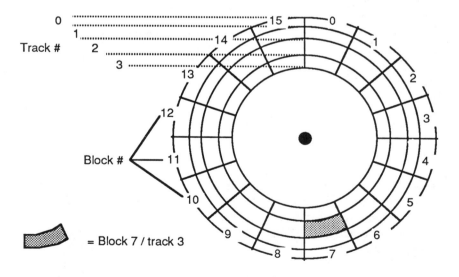

A stepping motor moves the read/write heads in and out across the surface of the disk, locating the heads precisely over a desired track. A disk unit must move the heads to the required track prior to any 'read/write' operation (see Figure 10-11). This movement takes a relatively long time (i.e. $\geq 1/10$ second to move from outermost to innermost track). This *seek time* represents the main component of any delay in transferring data from a disk.

Figure 10-11.   Reading or writing a disk block

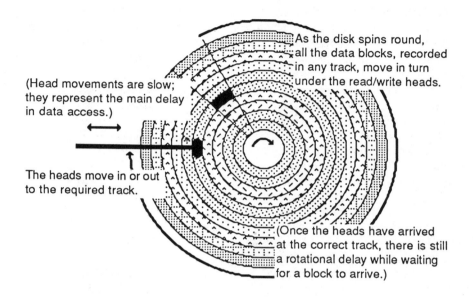

As the disk spins round, all the data blocks, recorded in any track, move in turn under the read/write heads.

(Head movements are slow; they represent the main delay in data access.)

The heads move in or out to the required track.

(Once the heads have arrived at the correct track, there is still a rotational delay while waiting for a block to arrive.)

Once the read/write heads are positioned on the required track, it is still necessary to wait for the disk to rotate and bring the needed block under the read/write heads. (How long this takes determines the disk's *rotational latency* time.) The hardware of the disk unit determines which block is passing under the heads. (There are various ways in which this can be done. One way is to record the block number, or maybe a kind of search key/identifier, in the control data that frames each block on a track; these control data are read by the disk unit's internal circuitry thereby allowing the required block to be recognized and data transfers to be initiated at the right time.) Delays, while waiting for disk rotations, have to be taken into account when modeling the performance of a disk system and when, in special circumstances, attempting to optimize the arrangement of blocks around a track. Usually though, these delays may be ignored.

On large systems, for example, mainframe IBM machines, the programmer is permitted quite detailed control over the arrangement of data on disk files. As well as being able to specify the arrangement of data blocks within tracks, such systems permit the user to request particular groups of tracks. One useful grouping is the set of tracks, on the different surfaces, that all have the same track number. (This set is called a *cylinder* – make a model if you need to see why this name is appropriate.) A file requiring many tracks would have its first few blocks on say track 30 of surface 0, the next few on track 30 of surface 1, and so forth. The advantage of such an arrangement is that no head movements are necessary when reading/writing successive blocks. Of course, this advantage only pertains to private-volume disks. If the disk is shared, then another program may have had a chance to execute and cause the disk heads to move, while the first program worked, intermittently, with data already read; the next 'read' operation would again require head movements.

Such detailed control over disk usage is less appropriate if the disk is to be shared. Attempts to optimize file organizations for particular application programs often conflict with the policies employed by the operating system – policies that are intended to provide for equitable sharing. Complex and varied space allocation schemes add to the size of the operating system, and often make the task of the casual user somewhat more difficult.

At the lowest level, all I/O to disks involves the CPU in specifying the track and block number, as well as the address in memory where data transfer is to occur. (This is the *disk-handler* level, explored in the practical exercises at the end of this chapter.)

A disk controller has a *disk address register* that is loaded by the CPU with the appropriate block number (or block #/track # combination). The CPU then uses an I/O instruction to issue a 'seek' command to the disk controller. In response, the controller moves the heads to the required track. When the heads are correctly positioned the 'seek' flag, in the controller's status flags register, is set. The CPU waits on this flag.

The CPU loads the memory address register (and maybe count) into the DMA part of the disk controller and instructs the controller to initiate a 'read' or 'write' operation from/to the desired block. The controller then, using DMA, performs the data transfer. Once the transfer is complete, a 'transfer' flag is set in the controller's status register.

Just as with data blocks on tape, those on disk have checksums. As transfers are made, the hardware of the disk controller and interface checks if the data read from disk appear correct. A controller usually makes more than one attempt to read a block; if all attempts fail, a hard error is signalled in some error bit in the controller's status register.

Simple coding for a disk-handler is along the following lines:

```
load acc with block and track number
I/O instruction loading disk-address register from acc
I/O instruction to start seek

wait loop, waiting for seek flag to set

load acc with memory address
I/O instruction loading disk controller's memory register from acc

if 'reading' then I/O instruction start_read
else I/O instruction start_write

wait loop, waiting for transfer flag to set

(check for error flag)

return from disk-handler
```

A computer's operating system has to translate file-oriented I/O operations down to this track/block level and then use its disk-handler routines to effect the actual data transfers.

There are a number of different ways of mapping from files onto tracks and blocks. In the next subsection, a couple of the simpler methods of mapping files onto physical blocks on disk are considered (again, attention will be focussed on systems which allocate space in fixed sized blocks, as opposed to systems that allow allocations of tracks or cylinders for holding user defined blocks).

Arranging data files on disk

Arranging and accessing files on a disk is a much more complex process than that required for reading/writing files on a magnetic tape. Programmers are usually not responsible for choosing where/how a file is actually placed on the disk. Instead, this task is performed by the operating system that runs on the computer. The operating system requires methods (1) for selecting the blocks that are to be allocated to a file, and (2) for recording this selection.

Contiguous file allocation

The simplest policy is to allocate *contiguous* sequences of blocks on disk, recording these allocations in a simple, fixed-size *file directory*. For example, the first four blocks of a disk can be reserved for a file directory; the remaining blocks of disk space are allocated to files as these are created. Figure 10-12 illustrates the disk usage after the allocation of space for first a 6-block file, then, a 7-block file, and then, two different 9-block files.

The recording of space allocated to files is simple. It is only necessary to record the first block number and number of blocks in each file. These data form a part of the entry for a file in the file directory kept by the system. The file directory is an array of records of the following form:

```
type  directory_entry = record
            fname :  array[1..8] of char;
            start,length : integer;
            end;
var files : array[1..NFILES] of directory_entry;
```

The operating system has a number of subroutines through which user programs access these files. One of these routines allows a user program to 'open' a named file. The operating system finds the file, by searching for the name in the directory blocks (which are read into memory; since the directory is at a known location on the disk, its reading requires just straightforward 'read' calls to the disk-handler). The 'open' routine creates a *file descriptor* data record containing the location on disk of the file's first block of the file and, also, its length.

Another routine in the operating system is a 'file_read' subroutine. The user program specifies, explicitly or implicitly, a logical block number, for example, 'file_read(4th block of my file)' (additional arguments to 'file_read' would identify an array into which the data block was to be read, and would also identify the file to be read by providing a pointer to the file descriptor made by the 'open' subroutine). The operating

Figure 10-12. Correspondence between disk blocks and files in a system using contiguous allocation

Files:

1

2

3

4

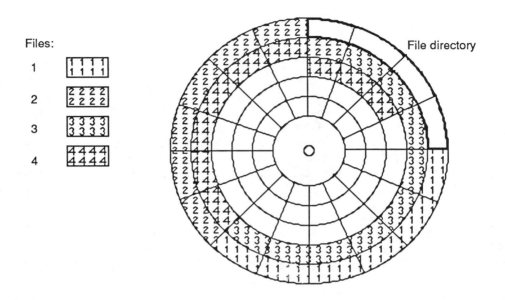

File directory

system checks the request against the known length of the file and then, if it is a valid request, determines the actual physical block number for the required logical block. For example, if the first logical block of the user's file is known, to the operating system, to be block 10 of track 1, then the fourth block of that file is block 13 of track 1. The operating system's 'file_read' subroutine passes this disk address to the disk-handler which performs the actual 'read' operation.

A user program can obviously process the data in a file in a sequential manner by requesting successive logical blocks in its calls to the 'file_read' operating system subroutine. It is also possible for the logical blocks of the file to be processed in a random order. There is no difficulty in taking blocks out of sequence because the operating system's routines can apply the same checks against limit length and the same mapping using the known location of the first logical block. Therefore, this simple contiguous file allocation allows for both sequential and random access to data.

The operating system provides an analogous 'file_write' subroutine. Again, the user program calls the routine passing as an argument a logical block number together with the address of a block/array of data that is to be written to disk. A similar check against limit length and mapping relative to a known start of the file is used to find the required physical block. The 'file_write' subroutine passes this disk address, and the address of the data array, to the actual disk-handler. Data can be written in sequence or in a random order.

The 'file_write' routine's checks against length and its use of a known starting location for a file presume that space is allocated for a file prior to that file being written. The operating system would incorporate a 'create' subroutine that takes, as arguments, a file name and a specification of the number of disk blocks required, and which returns a file descriptor with starting block number and length limit. The 'create' routine also has to make an entry in the file directory. As well as 'create', there would be a 'delete' operating system routine that removes the directory entry and frees the space of a file that is no longer needed.

In addition to manipulating entries in the file directory disk blocks, 'create' and 'delete' need to maintain some map-like data structure in which details of the allocations of physical disk blocks are recorded. (This map might be no more than a large set variable with one bit for each physical block on the disk, the 0/1 bit values indicating whether particular blocks were allocated or free.) Initially, all the entries for disk blocks, other than directory blocks, are marked as free. As 'create' calls are made, the next group of as yet unallocated blocks is assigned to the new file, and appropriately marked in the map.

When files are deleted, gaps of free space are opened up between other allocated files. For example, if file 2 of the example, shown in Figure 10-12, is deleted, then there is now a gap of seven free blocks (from block 10/track 0 to block 0/track 1). The next 'create' request for a file of seven, or fewer, blocks could make use of all or some of this free space.

Although a simple and quite useful approach to space allocation, this contiguous allocation scheme does have problems. One problem is that the (maximum) size of a file has to be specified when that file is first created. Often, this is a considerable inconvenience because the correct file size may not be known at creation time.

Another problem can be illustrated by considering the state of the disk after an extensive sequence of 'create' and 'delete' calls. The data in Table 10-2 show the use of various disk blocks after such a sequence of 'create' and 'delete' calls. (The disk blocks are assumed to be numbered sequentially from the start; blocks 0-15 are in track 0, blocks 16-31 in track 1, and so on.)

The next 'create' call might request the allocation of space for an 8-block file; this request has to be rejected, and the requesting program stopped. Although there are some 15 blocks of disk space free, this free space has been *fragmented* into small non-contiguous areas; none of which is of sufficient size for the new file. This fragmentation of free space is a major disadvantage of the contiguous allocation policy. Frequently, it will be necessary to rearrange the files on disk to gather together the separate areas of free space. In this rearrangement, or *compaction* process, files that are located after free areas are simply copied into the free blocks and then their directory entries are adjusted; the data in Table 10-3 illustrate the results of a compaction process as applied to the files detailed in Table 10-2. Compaction can take some minutes on a large disk.

This simple form of contiguous allocation is limited to use in single user computer systems because of the disadvantages of (1) the need to specify file size (or, by default, getting the largest region of free space), and (2) the need to compact files.

Table 10-2. Disk block allocation after many 'creates' and 'deletes' in a system using contiguous allocation

Blocks	Use	Blocks	Use
0-3	file-directory	4-9	file-1
10-12	file-19	13-16	free
17-25	file-3	26-34	file-4
35-38	free	39-45	file-6
46-51	file-7	52-53	file-8
54	free	55-57	file-10
58-61	file-11	62-64	free
65-66	file-18	67-72	file-14
73	file-15	74-76	file-17
77-79	free		

Table 10-3. Disk block allocation after compaction of fragmented free areas

Blocks	Use	Blocks	Use
0-3	file-directory	4-9	file-1
10-12	file-19	13-21	file-3
22-30	file-4	31-37	file-6
38-43	file-7	44-45	file-8
46-48	file-10	49-52	file-11
53-54	file-18	55-60	file-14
61	file-15	62-64	file-17
65-79	free		

Linked file allocation

One alternative way of selecting and recording the physical disk blocks of a file is based on single-linked list structures. The contents of an allocated disk block are mainly user data, but a couple of bytes at the end of each block is reserved to hold the disk address of the next logical block in the file. The scheme is illustrated in Figure 10-13.

Initially, all the non-directory blocks of the disk are placed in a free list. When a new file is created, a directory entry is made and the first block on the free list is taken and allocated for the file. Subsequently, when data are written to the file, additional blocks are taken from the free list as required. Thus, after the first 510 bytes of data have been generated, a new block is allocated. The disk address of this new block is inserted at the

Figure 10-13. Linked file allocation

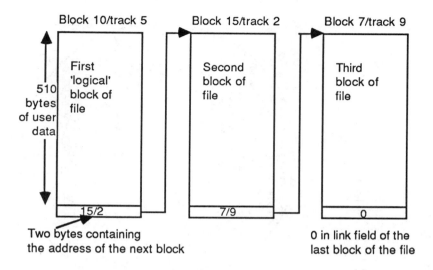

Two bytes containing
the address of the next block

0 in link field of the
last block of the file

end of the 510 bytes of data and the completed 512-byte data block is be written to disk. This process is repeated as each additional block of data is generated. A 'close' call is used to write any last partially filled data block to disk and to modify a directory entry to record the actual file length.

The 'create' routine no longer needs to have the file size specified in advance; a file can be extended, as necessary, while it is being written. Instead of a map of free blocks, the space-allocation procedures may simply keep a pointer to the first free disk block (before this block can be allocated it has to be read to obtain its link to the next free block), or a list data structure in memory may be used to identify free blocks. The 'delete' routine then simply appends a file onto this free list.

Since the disk blocks allocated to a file do not have to be contiguous, any free space can be used. Files can be created and extended as long as free disk blocks are available. After a long period of use, with many 'creates' and 'deletes' on files of different sizes, the use of the disk might be as shown in Figure 10-14.

As illustrated, individual files tend to be scattered around the disk. This scattering slows down access to data. If a program is trying to read a file sequentially, the disk heads may have to move in and out to get at succcessive logical blocks located on different tracks. Although this allocation scheme removes the requirement for regular compaction of free space, it is still advantageous to rearrange files on the disk so that they are allocated contiguous blocks. A disk-tidying program will typically be run every week or so on a system that uses this approach to file allocation.

The linked-list approach has one disadvantage: random access to the different logical blocks of a disk file is no longer possible. The physical disk blocks comprising a file are scattered, and the only record of the blocks used is stored in the blocks themselves. In order to find any particular logical block in a file it is always necessary to start reading that file from the first block and follow the links.

Figure 10-14. Linked file system after long period of use

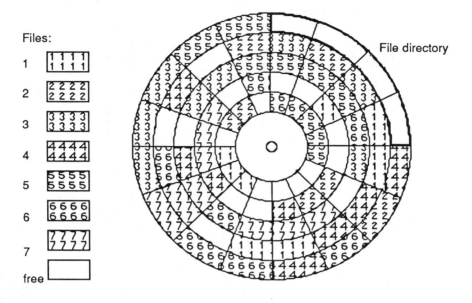

Files:

1

2

3

4

5

6

7

free

File directory

Other file allocation schemes

Other file allocation schemes are used in more sophisticated computer systems. These schemes organize the files so that (1) data can be accessed randomly as well as sequentially, (2) the file size does not have to be specified at create time, and (3) all free space on the disk can be used for files.

These goals can be met if the identities of the physical disk blocks that comprise a file can be recorded in some form of *map*. At its simplest, this map could be represented as an array. This array would be indexed by logical block number; the information recorded in each entry of the array would be the disk address of the block.

If the array size is small, that is, if the maximum size of any file is limited to a few disk blocks, then this file map can be stored in the directory entry for the file. Alternatively, the file map can be stored in some extra disk block(s) associated with the file (but which are not used to hold user data).

Since the disk address is recorded explicitly for each logical block of a file, any free disk blocks can be used to extend a file; so it is possible to gain all the benefits of the linked list scheme. Once a file map is in memory, the operating system's 'read/write' routines can look up the disk address of any required logical block, and so random access is possible.

Handling simul8's disk

A disk is included in the set of peripherals in simul8 to allow some practice in the lowest level operations involved in disk-handling. This disk is small! It has 16 tracks; each track holding only a single 128 word block. Data transfers to or from disk use DMA. The disk controller has a memory-address register and a disk-block register.

One group of I/O instructions is used to cause the disk to find a required block (i.e. track on this little disk). These are:

Name	Function
dlsk	load disk controller's block register and start a seek
dssf	skip if disk's seek flag has set
dscf	clear disk's seek flag

The instruction 'dlsk' copies the contents of the accumulator into the disk controller's block register and causes the disk to start a 'seek' to the required track. The block number given should be in the range 0..17. Initially, the disk heads are located at track 0; the time taken to find a required track depends linearly on the number of tracks over which the heads must move.

The code to find a block has the form:

```
        cla                     / load desired block number, 'sought'
        tad     sought
        dlsk                    / copy into disk controller and start seek
        cla                     / dispose of block number, no longer required
/ now a wait loop where CPU waits until disk has found
dwait,  dssf
        jmp     dwait
/ the block is found, clear the wait flag
        dscf
```

The second group of instructions arranges the data transfer. These instructions are:

Name	Function
dlma	load the disk's memory address register with the address of the first word of the buffer (array) being transferred
drd	start a 'read from disk' operation
dwrt	start a 'write to disk' operation
dtsf	skip if 'transmit' flag is set
dtcf	clear the 'transmit' flag.

The 'dlma' instruction loads the disk controller's memory address register with the address in memory where the data transfer is to start. There is no need to load a count of words to be transferred as the controller will always transfer 128 words. Once the address has been loaded, one or other of the instructions 'drd' or 'dwrt' must be used to start the actual data transfer. The instruction 'drd' reads a block from disk into memory and 'dwrt' writes data to disk. When the transfer is complete, the disk controller's transmit flag is set (there is no error flag as this disk never fails). The two instructions 'dtsf' and 'dtcf' can be used in the standard wait loop.

Code to start reading a block, once it has been found, is:

```
/ load address where data are to go
        cla
        tad     adrbuf
/ load into disk controller
        dlma
/ clear acc
        cla
/ start the read operation
        drd
/ wait for the transmit flag to set
/ (indicating that the read is finished)
twait,  dtsf
        jmp     twait
/ clear the flag
        dtcf
```

A complete disk-handler routine has to take arguments specifying (1) the disk block, (2) the memory address, and (3) an indicator saying 'read' or 'write'. Since the routine has multiple arguments, these use page zero globals. One possible encoding for a complete disk-handler is:

```
        *20
rwflag,  0              / flag to indicate if read (=1) or write (=0)
addrb,   0              / variable holding memory address where data
                       / are to be transferred
blknum,  0              / block number
         .
         .
         *400
/ - - - - - - - - - -
/ disk-handler routine
/ - - - - - - - - - -
dhndl,   0
/ start seeking
         cla
         tad     blknum
         dlsk
```

```
          cla
dhl1,     dssf
          jmp       dhl1
          dscf
/ have found, now set up transfer
          tad       addrb
          dlma
          cla
/ check for read or write
          tad       rwflag
          sna cla
          jmp       writes
/ the flag was non-zero, interpret as a read request
          drd
/ jump on to wait loop
          jmp       dhl2
/ if flag was zero, then a write request
writes,   dwrt
/ now wait for transfer to complete
dhl2,     dtsf
          jmp       dhl2
/ clear the flag
          dtcf
/ return from subroutine
          jmp i     dhndl
```

Exercises

1. Write a program that will (a) read an octal number in the range $0..17_{octal}$ (entered as two characters typed at the keyboard), (b) read that block from the disk into memory, and (c) print the contents of that block on the terminal.

2. Write a program that will read 128 values from the A/D into an array in memory, and then write these data to block 0 of the disk.

3. Features of the Macintosh MFS file system include:

   • A file can be opened for input and then the point of access can be moved to any required location in that file prior to each successive read operation (or one can simply read the file from its start).
   • Although the operating system does provide a mechanism for pre-allocating a contiguous block of space for an output file, it is not necessary to call this allocate routine when creating a new output file.
   • Existing files can be extended as and when necessary.

With this information, explain the type of method that must be used to organize the Macintosh's disk blocks into files (justify your claims regarding file organizations by showing how they serve to explain the known properties of the Macintosh's files).

If it is not necessary to pre-allocate space when creating a file, why was the *allocate* facility provided?

4. 'The Macintosh computer's disk does not have DMA circuitry'.
   What is DMA?
   How are data transfers performed on a disk with DMA?
   How will the Macintosh's disk work?
   Explain how the Macintosh's lack of disk DMA might be related to restrictions on the maximum speed of character input on the Macintosh's other input/output ports.

5. A library recorded details of its stock of 1,270,000 books on standard 1600 bpi 2400-foot magnetic tapes (their tape drives required half-inch inter-record gaps). Each book was represented by four card images (4x80-bytes) of data. Unfortunately, they did not know about *blocking*, and they recorded the card images as separate records separated by inter-record gaps. Approximately how many tapes did they require? How many would they have needed if they had blocked ten cards/record? How many if one hundred cards/record?

The following exercises require the use of a Pascal compiler.

6. Write a Pascal program that models the running of a file allocation scheme that uses contiguous allocation.

   The program should allow for up to 10 different files to be held on a disk with a total of 100 blocks of space available for files. A fixed-size 'file directory', containing data that identify those blocks which are allocated to particular files, will need to be maintained, as will some other record structure that contains data identifying those disk blocks that are free.

   Use a random number generator to produce 'create' and 'delete' requests. A 'create' operation will add another entry to the file directory; a 'delete' operation will remove an existing entry, (after a 'delete' the data in the directory are to be rearranged so that the current n ($n<10$) files are always defined by data in the first n elements of the file directory array).

   A 'create' request will specify a (randomly chosen) number of blocks in the range 1...20. The file allocation routine should reject 'create' requests that would result in more than 10 files being in existence, or requests that require more new blocks than the total number that are free. The 'create' function is to search through the data structure wherein block allocations are recorded; the first sufficiently large group of contiguous free blocks is to be used for the new file. (Unless, by chance, the request asks for exactly as many blocks as were in this contiguous free area, this will result in a smaller group of contiguous free blocks being left.)

A 'delete' request will specify a randomly chosen number i, $1 \leq i \leq n$ where n is the number of files then in existence. The file corresponding to file directory entry i is then to be deleted and its disk blocks are to be marked as free.

The files should be compacted whenever this is necessary to satisfy a 'create' request.

Run a simulation until a total of 150 'create' and 'delete' requests have been completed. Print out details of the 'create' and 'delete' requests, showing how 'create's were satisfied by particular block allocations and identifying those occasions on which file compaction was necessary.

7. Modify the program of question 6 to explore different schemes for selecting the particular set of free blocks that is used to satisfy a 'create' request. Investigate the following schemes:

   a) Rather than searching from the beginning of the disk for the first sufficiently large area of free space, make each successive 'create' request start a search that begins after the point where the last file was created (but which also goes back to search from the beginning of the disk when necessary).

   b) Instead of taking the first free area into which the request can be fitted, find that free area which best fits with the request (if there are no free areas equal in size to the request, but there are several that are larger, then choose the smallest of these).

   c) Always allocate space from the largest free region.

   Determine which of these policies works best for the data in the simulation (i.e. which is the policy that results in the least number of file compactions).

8. Implement a Pascal program that simulates a linked file allocation scheme. The requirements will be similar to those of question 6. There will have to be 'create_and_write' requests that build a new file needing a randomly chosen number of blocks, and a 'delete' request that removes a file. A limit of 10 files should again apply. Of course, compaction will not be necessary. Pascal list structures should be used to model the free list and the lists of blocks comprising each file. 'create_and_write' calls needing j blocks should take the first j blocks from the free list; 'delete' operations should place the blocks of the deleted file at the head of the free list.

   Run the system until 150 'create' and 'delete' requests have been completed. Then, compute a measure of how scattered the files have become. For each file then in existence, add up the 'distances' between its successive blocks. For example:

File	= #9	– #31	– #15	– #92	– #93	– #40.
Distance		22	16	77	1	53

   This file would contribute 169 to the total measure of scattering for all the files.

   Without going to the extent of sorting the free list after each file deletion, find ways of improving the allocation scheme to reduce the scattering effect.

11

More elaborate input/output handling

Input/output methods, as described so far, have utilized the very simple wait-loop approach to the problem of coordinating CPU and peripheral activity. The advantage of this simple approach is that it is easy to program and (almost) infallible. I/O handling using wait loops is quite appropriate if there is nothing better for the CPU to do (i.e. if the 'wasted' CPU cycles have no cost). In such circumstances, simple, easily developed and reliable programs are preferable to programs that use the computer efficiently but which have much higher development costs.

Often though, it is necessary to achieve better overall utilization of the machine. It is necessary for the work of peripherals and CPU to be overlapped in time, with all components in a computer system proceeding simultaneously with their own subtasks. For example, one may want a single-user computer to be able to print out listings of programs while the programmer continues with a compilation. (The printer is then in use, the user's terminal is in use, the disk is used when parts of files are written or read, and the CPU is busy looking after all these devices as well as executing the compilation.) In more elaborate computer systems, there may be many simultaneous would-be users; their individual instantaneous demands for CPU power are mostly small and a single powerful CPU can serve them all, provided it has some mechanisms that let it switch attention among users and which guarantee that the CPU will not ignore any peripheral device that needs help to transfer its data.

If printers need continuously fed data, if responses must be made to keyboards with data, and if disk transfers must be handled simultaneously, then the CPU must execute device-handling code whenever devices are ready. With many devices running, problems of coordinating CPU and peripheral activity become more marked. While some devices can safely idle if the CPU does not respond to them immediately, other peripherals may have to be served within certain critical time periods if data are not to be lost or corrupted.

In the general case, peripherals need an ability to interrupt the work of the CPU. Whenever a peripheral needs CPU assistance (e.g. to hand over a character or to be told the memory address for the transfer of a block of data), it must be able to force the CPU to suspend its current work and execute an appropriate piece of device-handling code.

The interrupt mechanism is relatively complex, and will be treated in Chapter 12. First, some of the simpler problems of concurrent peripheral and CPU activities are considered. This chapter examines *buffering* techniques, and *polling loop* methods for controlling multiple simultaneously operating I/O devices.

Buffering is concerned with the problems of transferring data into the memory of the computer before these data are required for processing. Ideally, an input device will transfer one block of data into the computer's memory while, at the same time, the CPU executes code to process a previously read block of data. Analogous principles apply to output; an output device can consume one block of data while the CPU executes the code that creates another block of data for output.

Polling loops represent a generalization of the wait-loop approach to device-handling. Polling loops are most useful in applications where a computer system is really just copying data from various input devices to appropriate output devices, with very little processing of these data being performed. The code for such applications is really a sequence of device-handler subroutines invoked from the polling loop as and when the various devices need attention.

Double buffering

Table 11-1 contains data that illustrate the run-time behaviour of a system running disk-I/O and using the programming methods considered so far. Much of the time the CPU is idling as it waits for transfers (points marked by 'I' in Table 11-1). The disk is idle when the CPU is processing a block of data (points marked by '!'). The CPU and disk work at alternate times; while one works the other idles.

A DMA disk, like that on simul8, does not need continuous attention by the CPU. It can be left to work autonomously once it has started on a 'read' or 'write' operation. Once the operation is complete the disk will set its transfer flag, but this flag does not necessarily have to be cleared immediately. If the CPU is busy on other work, the transfer flag will just remain set. When the CPU finally requires the data, it will check the flag; and, if it finds the flag set, it proceeds to process the newly read data. The CPU, having been programmed to wait for the transfer flag to set, allows processing to remain coordinated with input even if, on some data, the CPU proceeds faster than the input.

This feature of a DMA disk can be exploited in schemes that allow both CPU and disk to work concurrently. Overlap of CPU and disk activity requires that the CPU has some data already in memory for it to process while the disk is used to transfer subsequent data into memory (or transfer already processed data from memory). As shown in Figure 11-1, two different areas of memory are used. One area in memory holds the block of data currently being processed by the CPU; a second memory area is used for the concurrent data transfer from disk.

These two memory areas, or *buffers*, are used alternately by the CPU and the disk. First, data are read into buffer A, with the CPU waiting for this initial transfer. Then, the disk is set to read into buffer B, while the CPU processes the data already read into buffer A. Once the first buffer full of data is processed, the CPU checks the disk's transfer flag; if this is not yet set, it waits. When the transfer flag is set, indicating that

Table 11-1. A trace of system activity for a system using unbuffered disk I/O

CPU	Disk
start a seek (for 1st block)	
|	seeking
|wait loop for seek	
|	set seek flag
initiate read	
|	reading (1st block)
|wait loop for transfer	
|	set transfer flag
process data from	
1st block	!-
start a seek (for 2nd block)	
|	seeking
|wait loop for seek	
|	set seek flag
initiate read	
|	reading (2nd block)
|wait loop for transfer	
|	set transfer flag
process data from	
2nd block	!-
start a seek (for 3rd block)	
|	seeking
|wait loop for seek	
|	set seek flag
initiate read	
|	reading (3rd block)
|wait loop for transfer	
|	set transfer flag
process data from	
3rd block	!-

the second block of data was read into buffer B, the CPU initiates the next data transfer. This involves the disk reading a third block of data into buffer A (overwriting data that are already processed). While this third disk transfer proceeds, the CPU continues with the processing of the second block of data in buffer B. These activities of CPU and disk are summarized in Table 11-2.

The simple approach, with unbuffered I/O, has a loop in which each successive block of a file is read into a fixed area of memory and, after each 'read' operation, the contents of this single buffer are processed. The code has the following form:

```
for i:=1 to Numblocks do begin
        seek_block(i);
```

Figure 11-1. **The use of double-buffered I/O (computations proceed concurrently with data transfers)**

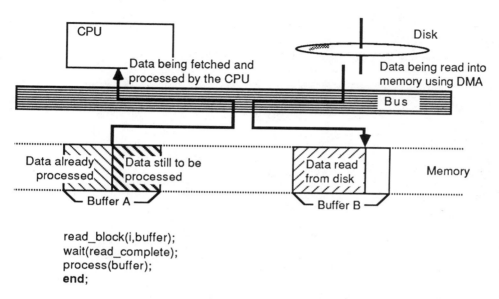

```
read_block(i,buffer);
wait(read_complete);
process(buffer);
end;
```

Coding to exploit the possibility of overlap of disk and CPU activities is slightly more complex. The double-buffering scheme requires an initiating step, where the first block is read:

```
{ initiate, get first block }
i:=1;
bufferR:=bufferA;
bufferP:=bufferB;
seek_block(i);
read_block(i,bufferR);
```

Pointer variables are used to identify which particular buffer is available for the next 'read' operation ('bufferR') or process operation ('bufferP'). The values in these pointers are the addresses of the two buffer areas. After each block is read, these values are swapped.

The main loop must start with a wait for the most recent disk transfer to complete. Buffer pointers can then be swapped and, if appropriate, the subsequent disk transfer can be started. While the next disk transfer proceeds, the contents of the full buffer are processed:

```
{ main loop }
repeat
        wait(read_complete);
        { switch buffer pointers }
        temp:=bufferP;
        bufferP:=bufferR;
        bufferR:=temp;
```

Table 11-2.   A trace of system activity for a system using double-buffered disk input

CPU	Disk
start a seek (for 1st block)	
|	seeking
|wait loop for seek	
|	set seek flag
initiate read	
|	reading (1st block)
|wait loop for transfer	
|	set transfer flag
start a seek (for 2nd block)	
|	seeking
|wait loop for seek	
|	set seek flag
initiate read	
process data from	
1st block	reading (2nd block)
	set transfer flag
finish processing (1st block)	
|wait loop for transfer	
start a seek (for 3rd block)	
|	seeking
|wait loop for seek	
|	set seek flag
initiate read	
process data (from	
2nd block)	reading (3rd block)
	set transfer flag
finish processing (2nd block)	

```
            { if appropriate, start another transfer }
            i:=i+1;
            if i≤Numblocks then begin
                    seek_block(i);
                    read_block(i,bufferR);
                    end;
            { process contents of buffer }
            process(bufferP);
   until (i>Numblocks);
```

On a computer with an operating system, double buffering is widely used. When a file is opened for sequential reading (or writing), the operating system attempts to arrange some form of double-buffered scheme. Buffering can be automatically arranged on behalf of user programs; the applications programmer does not need to be concerned with this level of operation. The system allocates space for the buffers, and copies data, from buffer to user program space as needed. (Some elaborate operating systems permit user control over buffering, and can arrange to avoid the copying operations. On the whole, details of buffering are best hidden from users.) The operating system tries to read a file ahead of the read requests made by the user program. If all disk transfer requests are made sufficiently in advance, required data are always in memory when needed by user program. This minimizes the amount of time during which a user program idly occupies memory waiting for data and so improves overall machine use.

Another problem – another buffering solution

Many applications involve copying characters from an input device to an output device. In the examples considered so far, such applications are coded in the form:

```
loop,
          wait for input device to flag arrival of character
          read character from input device
          write character to output device
          wait for output device to flag safe delivery of character
          goto loop
```

This coding is fine provided the output device always consumes characters faster than they can be produced by the input. Although this code forces the CPU to wait for the output device to finish with a character, the CPU will still be back, waiting for more input, before the next character is produced.

Obviously, in the long run output must be faster than input (otherwise, data would be lost or the computer's memory would slowly fill to capacity with data produced, processed and still waiting for output). Problems arise in many applications because while the output may be faster overall, it runs at a constant speed whereas the input may come in bursts. For brief periods, the input device may try to provide characters at a much higher rate than they can be accepted by the output.

For example, one might have a small computer acting as controller for a dot-matrix printer connected to a mainframe machine by a telephone connection. The printer might run at 100 characters per second, while the phone connection might be rated at 4800 bits per second. Allowing for various overheads (stop bits, start bits, and so forth), this is equivalent to about 400 characters per second. It is normally advantageous for a mainframe computer to send data at full speed down the line; therefore, data composed into messages of 50 to 100 characters would be sent at the 400 character per second rate. The small computer has to accept characters at this rate even though it cannot immediately print them. The characters received have to be queued for later printing.

After any message, there might be some time before the main machine again sends data. The small computer is always able to limit overall data transfer to the speed of its printer. Once it accepts a message, the small computer sends a reply indicating that no more data are to be sent by the mainframe. When the small machine can again accept data, another message is sent to the mainframe indicating that further data can be sent.

Buffering techniques are used to allow data to be saved either for later processing or for subsequent output. Double-buffered techniques are appropriate for block-transfer devices like disks and tapes, but are not too useful for character devices like keyboards, terminals, and serial communications lines. What is needed is some form of queue data structure. While data elements arrive faster than they can be disposed of, the queue grows as new entries are appended. When input runs slowly (or has been suspended), the queue shortens as elements are removed from the front and disposed of. If the queue is empty, then the output device idles.

A *circular buffer* represents a commonly used implementation of a queue for such I/O tasks. An array with some number of elements, for example, eight, is used to represent the buffer. As each element of this array can hold one character, characters in the buffer represent the queue of data that awaits processing. There are a couple of pointers into the array: one identifies the element that is filled when the *producer* next delivers a character; the second identifies the element from which the *consumer* next takes a character. (In the example, the producer corresponds to code that 'listens' to the phone line and reads characters from the mainframe machine; the consumer corresponds to code that takes characters from memory and sends them to the printer.) The pointers work cyclically around the array, that is, after the producer fills in the seventh element, the zeroth element is the next filled.

Initially, these pointers point to the same element. The consumer idles while the producer waits. Eventually, data arrive for the producer and, in the general case, are stored in memory. The consumer might have to be 'woken up'; when it starts, it takes the first character from the buffer and updates its pointer.

While the consumer works on the first data element, other data might arrive for the producer and be placed into the queue. Figure 11-2 illustrates the state of the data structures at a point where several data elements have arrived; one ('0') has been processed and the consumer is about to fetch the next ('1'). Here, the queue has grown to six elements. If the producer is too far ahead of the consumer, its pointer catches up with the consumer's pointer. If this occurs, the producer must suspend its activities.

Eventually the consumer catches up with any backlog of data. The producer is allowed to resume when space is again available in the buffer. When all the data are both produced and consumed, the buffer is again left empty, with both pointers equal, the consumer again idling, and the producer running/waiting.

There are many subtle problems relating to the management of such a bounded buffer. The steps for updating the pointers and the tests that determine whether to suspend, or restart, the producer (and similar tests on the consumer), have to be robust against values being changed at inconvenient moments. These problems are studied in courses on operating systems where the bounded-buffer problem is commonly used as a first example to illustrate problems of *concurrent processes*.

Figure 11-2. A circular buffer data structure with the producer running ahead of the consumer

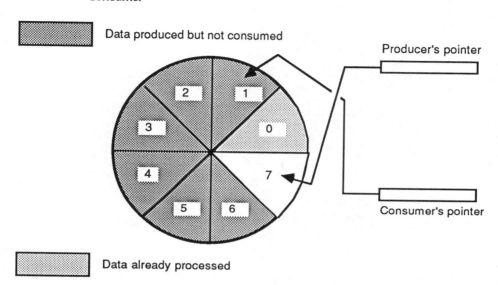

Data produced but not consumed

Producer's pointer

Consumer's pointer

Data already processed

Here, the focus is on the implementation of such a buffering scheme. Some simplifying assumptions are made to eliminate the more complex problems. In particular, it is assumed that the buffer is sufficiently large to prevent the producer from ever filling the entire buffer and catching up with the consumer. Consequently, there is no need to stop the producer. The other major simplification relates to the way in which pointers are updated. Since this first example does not use interrupts, there is no possibility of pointers being left in an inconsistent state while a test is made.

The following illustrative code fragments are based on the example of a small computer with a serial input line and a printer. The serial input line delivers characters in bursts; these characters are queued for the printer which prints continuously while data are available. In the long run, the printer speed is faster than the rate at which characters are received via the serial line. The computer has sufficient memory for a large circular buffer data structure capable of holding all characters queued for the printer. The system is shown in Figure 11-3.

Both the serial line and printer interfaces have data registers that hold single characters and flag registers. These interfaces are similar to the keyboard and terminal interfaces of earlier examples. The serial input interface's flag is set when a character arrives. The CPU must read the character into the accumulator; from there it must be stored into the circular buffer in memory. When the printer sets its flag, it is ready to accept another character; so then the CPU should execute code that causes a character to be read from memory into the accumulator, and from there copied to the data register in the printer controller.

The code for the main program being executed on the small computer consists of a loop in which the ready flags of the two devices are repeatedly checked. When a device sets its flag, an appropriate device-handling routine is invoked. The main loop has

Figure 11-3. An example system that uses circular buffered I/O

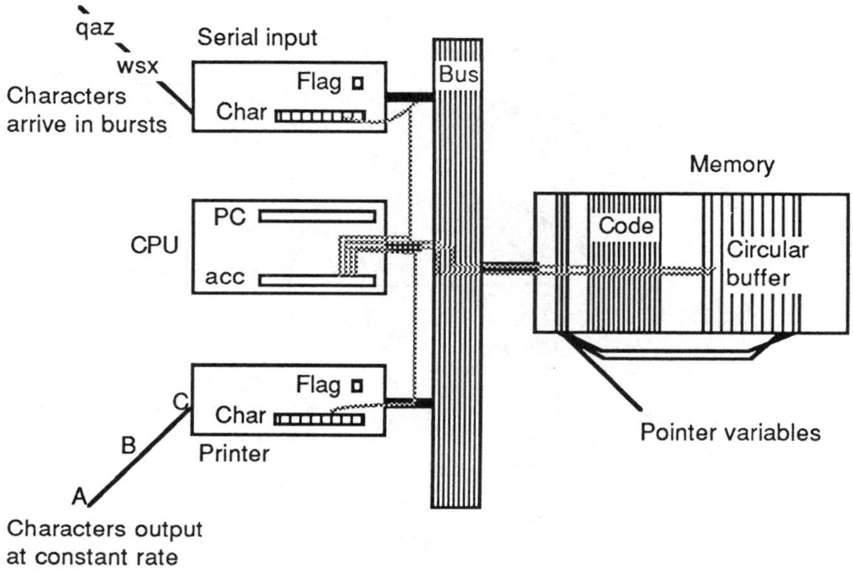

the following form:

```
loop,    skip_if_serial_line_flag_set
         skp
         jmp shndl  / jump to serial_line_handler
         skip_if_printer_flag_set
         skp
         jmp phndl  / jump to printer_handler
         jmp loop
```

Flags might be set as fast as 500 times per second (100 characters per second from the printer, and 400 characters per second from input line). The code to respond to a device might involve ≤30 instructions being executed (e.g. for the printer: the flag has to be cleared, the next character found in memory, read, and sent to the printer). Therefore, less than 15,000 instructions per second are utilized in handling the devices. The CPU can execute about 400,000 instructions per second. Most of the time the CPU is executing the instructions of the main loop, repeatedly finding that neither device is yet ready.

The 'serial_line_handler' code must first read the character into the accumulator and clear the serial input flag. There are two possible subsequent courses of action. If the printer is running, and characters are queued, then the newly arrived character must be appended to the queue in the circular buffer in memory. If the printer is idle, then the newly arrived character can be sent immediately. The case where the incoming character must be queued in the circular buffer is considered first.

In the computer's memory, a circular buffer is just an array. The code for using such a buffer is simplest if access is made using an index and a base address that defines the start of the buffer. The index moves cyclically by being incremented modulo the length of the buffer. The code that the producer ('serial_line_handler') uses to access the circular buffer is:

```
acc:=read_serial();
memaddress:=base+input_index;
store[memaddress]:=acc;
input_index:=(input_index+1) mod buffer_length;
```

Usually, the buffer length is chosen to be equal to a power of two; then, the modulo operation degenerates to an 'and'ing operation. The assembly language code for reading and storing a character in a buffer of 128 words is:

```
shndl,  read_serial_input              / read data, clear flag
        dca    inchar                  / save temporarily
/ CODE HERE TO DETERMINE IF NEED TO SAVE IN MEMORY OR CAN
/ SEND IMMEDIATELY TO PRINTER

        .
        .
        .

/ - - - - save in circular buffer for later printing - - - -
/ compute address by adding index (inndx) to array base (addrb)
        cla
        tad    addrb
        tad    inndx
        dca    inptr
/ store character into buffer
        tad    inchar
        dca i  inptr
/ update index
        cla iac
        tad    inndx
/ take modulo 128 by masking operation
        and    k177
        dca    inndx
/ - - - - - have finished queuing character, return to main loop
        jmp    loop
/ - - - - - - - - -
addrb, buffer           / address of start of buffer
k177,  0177             / mask to cut to 7-bits (i.e. value 0-128 decimal)
inptr,  0               / pointer when accessing buffer array
inchar, 0               / place to store character
inndx,  0               / (cyclic) index into buffer
```

Note again, there is no test for a full buffer; it is assumed that the input is never too far ahead of output.

The 'printer_handler' routine uses the same method for accessing the buffer when it needs to fetch another character for printing. The 'printer_handler' routine is executed whenever the printer sets its flag indicating that the last character has been safely delivered. After clearing this flag, a check must be made to determine whether there are any further characters queued in the circular buffer.

This check can be made by comparing indices into the circular buffer array. The array indices used by the two handler routines define the producer and consumer pointers. The index for the 'serial_line_handler' (producer) defines where the next incoming character will be stored. The index for the 'printer_handler' (consumer) identifies the buffer location from where the next character will be read. If these two index values are equal, then the printer must have caught up with the incoming data. In that case, after clearing the printer flag, the 'printer_handler' should record that the printer is idle. If the indices are not equal, then there are data queued for output and the next character should be sent.

The 'printer_handler' code has the form:

```
clear_print_flag();
if output_index=input_index then begin
          { no data queued }
          idle:=true
          end
else begin
          { fetch next datum }
          memaddress:=base+output_index;
          acc:=store[memaddress];
          print_character();
          { update index }
          output_index:=(output_index+1) mod buffer_length;
          end;
```

Here, an explicit boolean flag is used to indicate whether or not the printer is idle; this is not strictly necessary, but it does somewhat simplify the coding.

There is no explicit wait loop checking on the delivery of the character to the printer; the necessary wait is implicit in the control structure of the main program. This 'printer_handler' code is only executed when the printer has set its flag indicating that it is indeed ready to accept another character. Consequently, no wait is necessary before the 'print_character' instruction. Further, a wait following that instruction (as has been used in most of the earlier examples on terminal output) is now no longer appropriate. Here, there is other work to be done while the character is printed. (For this example, this 'other work' is just the monitoring of the input serial line.)

Details of the assembly language coding follow:

```
phndl,  clear_print_flag
/ test the indices for equality ---
        cla
        tad     inndx
        cia
        tad     outndx
        sza cla
```

```
        jmp     fetchd
/ the indices were equal, no data queued
        iac
        dca     idle            / mark 'idle' as true (non zero)
        jmp     loop
/ - - - - - - - - -
/ if indices unequal, then there are data queued
/ so fetch character, send character, and update index
fetchd, tad     addrb
        tad     outndx
        dca     outptr          / address of next character,
        tad  i  outptr          / next character
        print_character         / send to printer
        cla  iac
        tad     outndx
        and     k177
        dca     outndx
        jmp     loop
/ - - - - -
outptr, 0                       / pointer for accessing buffer
outndx, 0                       / index into buffer
idle,   0                       / flag indicating printer idle
```

The code for the input line handler can now be completed. Once a character is read and stored temporarily, the first check should be on the boolean variable 'idle'. If the printer is shown as being idle, then the input character can be sent immediately without needing to be stored in the memory buffer, and the printer should be marked as being active. If another input character arrives before the first is printed, then this second character is stored in the buffer and the buffer indices ('pointers') are updated; but if no other input characters are received, then the buffer indices remain the same, and the response to the setting of the printer flag again causes it to be marked as idle. Initially, when the program first starts, the printer is recorded as being idle.

The complete 'serial_line_handler' is:

```
in_char:=read_serial();
if idle then begin
            acc:=in_char;
            print_character();
            idle:=false
        end
else begin
            memaddress:=base+input_index;
            store[memaddress]:=acc;
            input_index:=(input_index+1) mod buffer_length
        end;
```

A complete program in the assembly language of simul8 is as follows. (Since simul8 doesn't have appropriate peripherals, there are no mnemonics for the printer and serial line device, and this example cannot be run.)

```
/ complete demonstration program for serial-line=>printer example
/ using circular buffer (and simple polling loop)
        *200
/ initialization
        cla   iac
        dca     idle            / printer idle
        dca     inndx           / both indices are zero
        dca     outndx
/ poll loop,
/ wait for a device (serial line) to set a flag and start activities
/
/ just keep asking devices ('polling') until one says its ready
loop,   skip_if_serial_line_flag_set
        skp
        jmp     shndl           / jump to serial handler
        skip_if_printer_flag_set
        skp
        jmp     phndl           / jump to printer handler
        jmp     loop
/ - - - - - - - - - - - - - - - - - - -
/ Serial_line_handler:
/ get character,
/ if printer idle then { send character; marker printer busy }
/ else save character in queue in circular buffer
shndl,  read_serial_input       / read character, clear flag
        dca     inchar
        tad     idle
        sna   cla
        jmp     saved
/ printer was idle, send character immediately
        tad     inchar
        print_character
        cla
        dca     idle            / mark 'idle' as false (zero)
        jmp     loop
/ - - - - - - save in circular buffer for later printing
saved,  cla
        tad     addrb
        tad     inndx
        dca     inptr
/ store character into buffer
        tad     inchar
        dca   i inptr
/ update index
        cla   iac
        tad     inndx
        and     k177
        dca     inndx
        jmp     loop
/ - - - - -
```

```
/ Printer_handler:
/       clear flag;
/ if characters in buffer (unequal pointers) then
/               { get next character; send; update index }
/       else mark printer as idle;
phndl,  clear_print_flag
/ test the indices for equality ---
        cla
        tad     inndx
        cia
        tad     outndx
        sza cla
        jmp     fetchd
/ the indices were equal, no data queued
        iac
        dca     idle            / mark 'idle' as true (non zero)
        jmp     loop
/ - - - - - - - - -
/ if indices unequal, then there are data queued
/ so fetch character, send character, and update index
fetchd, tad     addrb
        tad     outndx
        dca     outptr          / address of next character,
        tad i   outptr          / next character
        print_character         / send to printer
        cla iac
        tad     outndx
        and     k177
        dca     outndx
        jmp     loop
/ - - - - -
addrb,  buffer                  / address of start of buffer
k177,   0177                    / mask to cut to 7-bits
inptr,  0                       / pointer for accessing buffer
inchar, 0                       / character just read
inndx,  0                       / (cyclic) index into buffer
outptr, 0                       / pointer for accessing buffer
outndx, 0                       / (cyclic) index into buffer
idle,   0                       / flag indicating printer idle
        *400
/ - - - - - - -
/ here is the 128 word buffer
buffer, 0
        *600
$
```

Polling loops

The preceding example involves a simple *polling loop*. Its main program is a continuously cycled loop in which the CPU asks each device in turn whether it needs assistance. (The term *polling* is used to describe this process of checking on devices.) Frequently, polling loops serve as the basic structure for applications programs that need to control many simultaneously operating peripheral devices. These tend to be applications where data are read from some input, are subjected to a few minor transformations, and forwarded to an output device.

There are limitations to polling. The approach is not practical if any of the peripheral devices have very demanding requirements for the speed of CPU response to their setting of a flag. There are general limits on the amount of processing permitted when handling any *event*, that is, any setting of a device's ready or error flag(s). The CPU must always cycle around the main loop in time to check the flags and deal with incoming data. If too long a time elapses following the setting of a flag, then data may be lost. But, if these limitations are not relevant to the application, then a polling loop is often the best choice for a control structure. Coding is almost as simple as wait loops for individual devices, and yet allow for a number of concurrent activities on CPU and peripherals.

A polling-loop program involves:

1. An initiating phase where software flags are set (e.g. the 'idle' flag in the preceding example), and where any necessary buffer data structures are defined.
2. Possibly, some initiating input/output steps to start the various peripheral devices.
3. A main polling loop where the devices are checked in turn and, if any needs CPU assistance, a jump (or subroutine call) is made to the appropriate device-handler code.
4. A set of device-handlers. There will be a device-handler for each device used by the application program. Each handler is responsible for clearing the device flag and performing other device specific actions as needed. These actions may involve the reading and buffering of data, dequeuing and transmission of output data and, possibly, the setting of various software flags.
5. A set of data buffering routines and a number of data buffers in memory.

Most polling loop applications need some form of data buffering or queuing (because temporary fluctuations in rates of input and output have to be accommodated). Circular buffering techniques are common, but other buffering schemes may be appropriate. For example, in some applications it might be simplest to work entirely in terms of 'printer lines' with length ≤ 130 characters. Cards read from a card reader yield partly filled 'printer lines'; messages to and from another computer use the same 'printer lines'. The program can now use a large set of fixed size 'printer line' buffers queued for the various devices. List structures, with pointers to the 'printer line' buffers, are used to maintain the various queues.

Software flags can be utilized in a polling loop structure. After input/output instructions that check all the device flags, the main polling loop continues with checks on software flags (i.e. true/false settings of boolean variables). This can improve program organization when various special purpose processing has to be performed in response to particular events. For example, when the last character on a card has been read, it might be necessary (1) to compose a message from the data on the card with appropriate additional header, trailer, and checksum data, and (2) to queue this message for a serial-output line. Such special processing should not form part of the card reader's handler code. The card handler should be restricted to reading and storing characters, and setting a software flag when an end-of-card is detected. The setting of this software flag is then checked in the main loop and the special processing routines are invoked from there.

There are many minor variations on the basic structure of the polling loop. It can be arranged so that all devices are checked on each cycle of a loop. If one device needs CPU attention then its device-handler code is invoked as a subroutine. When completed, this subroutine causes a return to the next point in the polling loop, where the next device is checked. Alternatively, once a device has been served, a jump may be made back to the start of the loop. If, in the loop, the devices are checked in order of their urgency, then this second structure reduces the chance that data might be lost (because only one device-handling routine will ever be executed before checks are again made on devices that require reasonably fast CPU response).

A polling loop might be appropriate in an application like a simple *remote job entry* (RJE) controller or a *terminal multiplexor* with some small number of terminals. These applications use a small computer connected through phone lines to some main-frame machine. An RJE would have printer(s), plotter(s), and cassette-tape/card reader(s). Input data are read and composed into messages that are transmitted to the main machine where they are queued for later processing. Simultaneously, the main machine transmits results from previous jobs to the printers and plotters. A terminal multiplexor might have a printer and several terminals that must share a common connection to a main machine. Inputs from individual terminals are collected, composed into messages (which would include some terminal identifier), and transmitted to the main machine. The main machine then responds with messages directed to specific terminals and, possibly, with messages containing data to be printed.

An RJE example program would be organized, in the computer's memory, as (1) a main polling loop, (2) a set of device-handlers, (3) a set of special routines for composing/validating messages, queuing and releasing buffers, and (4) buffers that could be used to queue characters for the various devices. Circular buffers might be used, but list-structured queues of fixed-size message buffers are more appropriate. Since an RJE system works with fixed format messages that must be composed for transmission and checked on reception, it is simplest if a message is equivalent to a buffer full of data. So, associated with each of the devices, there could be a queue of message buffers. These buffers, and initial queues, have to be created by special purpose initialization routines.

The RJE program has as its main loop:

```
loop,    if print_flag then serve_printer
         if card_flag then serve_card_reader
         if serial_in_flag then serve_serial_in
         if serial_out_flag then serve_serial_out
         if plot_flag then serve_plotter
         checks on software flags for special cases

         goto loop
```

The printer handler code, for example, clears the print flag and then checks in the current printer buffer for any additional character(s). If data are present, then the next character is read and sent. If the buffer is empty, then the printer handler could check its queue of subsequent buffers and, if any existed, switch to the next buffer from which data could be taken.

Extending the polling loop approach

The polling loop approach is mainly used when dealing with *external events* such as a key being pressed on the keyboard, a mouse-button being clicked, or a disk being inserted into a drive. Sometimes, the loop may be extended to cater for software flags that indicate the occurrence of special cases in the I/O handling, like 'card-complete'. More general *internal events* can also be simulated and integrated into a polling-loop scheme. Thus, by software, it is possible to represent such events as a change of content of, or the activation of, a display window on a video terminal. These program initiated events may necessitate the execution of particular routines that redraw window displays. The main program can still be organized around a polling loop. Some of the flags tested will be program variables, set by software, rather than registers in device controllers. This approach can often simplify the coding of interactive programs that must present a user with a choice of many different processing options. The various processing functions that are invoked in response to the user's selection of an option typically involve only limited processing, for example, the insertion of a character into an array or a check on the parts of a document that are still visible after some adjustment to the size of a window. After a few hundred instructions for the subroutines, the CPU will again cycle through the same control loop.

Applications programs on the Macintosh computer are based upon such a polling loop organization. A software-based event queue is used to store data about events to which the program is to respond. Actual external events, such as keystrokes and mouse-clicks, are dealt with at a lower interrupt-based level which presents them to the applications' programmer as events in this event queue. The software events are mainly concerned with updates of the windows on the Macintosh screen; but, there are other defined event types that relate to handling of special types of I/O, for example, events relating to the local area network communication links that can be used with these computers.

Exercises

1. Take the code of the example 'tstmsk' program (which should be on the simul8 disk) and modify it to use double-buffered disk input. (The tstmsk program reads data blocks from disk and searches for particular bit patterns in the data words; details are printed of the block number and word number of those words with the required pattern. As constructed, the program loops – reading a block, then processing the block.) The reconstructed program should read block 0, and then start the transfer of

block 1 from the disk into memory; while this second transfer is in progress, the processing of the first block read should be started. When both the processing of block 0 and the transfer of block 1 are complete, buffers should be swapped so that processing of block 1 can commence simultaneously with the transfer of block 2 from disk. The program is to read and process the contents of blocks 0...3 of the disk.

2. Write a program that will sample the A/D and produce, on the teletype output device, a histogram showing the data read. The program is to use a polling loop technique with the loop monitoring the teletype, the A/D, and the clock. Characters generated for the teletype are to be queued in a circular buffer. Data sampling is to be coordinated with the clock; every third 'tick' of the clock should initiate a data sampling from the A/D. The data values read from the A/D are in the range $0...777_{octal}$. The histogram produced for the data readings 107, 223, 005, 674, 067 and 555 should appear as:

```
|*
|**
|
|******
|
|*****
```

That is, for each reading, print a vertical bar, followed by a number of asterisks, followed by a newline – the number of asterisks is determined by the high-order octal digit of the A/D value read. The program is to take 20 readings and to complete the display of these data.

12

Interrupts

Why interrupts?

An analysis of a remote-job-entry system or a terminal multiplexor system, as described in Chapter 11 to illustrate polling loop I/O, reveals that most of the time the CPU is not doing any useful work. Most CPU cycles are expended simply checking devices that are not yet ready to transfer data.

Consider, for example, a terminal multiplexor with four terminals and a printer connected, via serial lines, to a mainframe. At any moment, it is likely that three of the four terminals are transmitting data (at 10 characters per second typing speed) while the fourth terminal and the printer receive data at 100 characters per second. Each of the 250 characters or so, being input or output each second, must also be either transmitted to, or received from, the mainframe; so the serial lines will contribute, in effect, about another 250 characters that must be handled. Doubling the total (for safety in estimating loading of CPU and to allow for bursty rates of data transfer) means that maybe 1000 characters are handled each second. Even if it took 100 instructions to deal with each character (and it should take much less on average), only 100,000 instructions are really used in any second. The CPU of the small computer in the multiplexor could execute anything from 300,000 to 1,000,000 instructions per second (depending on the type of machine and the memory cycle-speed). At least two-thirds, if not nine-tenths, of the CPU's time is spent unnecessarily traversing the polling loop.

Given so many leftover CPU cycles, it is tempting to extend the usage of the small computer in such a system. For example, rather than do all the data processing on the remote mainframe, one could allow the terminals either to connect through to the remote mainframe or to run BASIC programs that are interpreted on the CPU within the multiplexor.

Setting up such a scheme is reasonably practical. A BASIC interpreter and its workspace could be fitted into memory, and software flags used to indicate whether data coming from a particular terminal were to be packaged for transfer to a mainframe or passed to the interpreter. Characters passed to the interpreter are collected until a carriage return is entered, at which point the input line is interpreted.

The scheme works to a limited extent. On 'desk calculator'-type inputs (e.g. 'PRINT 5*(13+X)') the processing necessary to interpret and perform the command could be completed in a few hundred instructions. For such inputs, the BASIC interpreter routine is called from the main polling loop and returns, in sufficient time, for the CPU to again be testing flags before any new data arrives from terminals or the serial input line.

However, the system will eventually fail. Inputs to the BASIC interpreter exist that require large amounts of processing time (e.g. the 'RUN' command given after typing in the text of a program to find the thousandth prime). If the interpreter is called from the main poll loop with such input, then the CPU simply continues to execute the code of the BASIC interpreter for many seconds and does not return to the poll loop.

Meanwhile, the peripheral devices continue to run. The serial input interface collects the bits of the next incoming character and, when all 8 bits have arrived, the interface places the bits in its data register and sets its flag. Similarly, though much more slowly, the terminal controllers continue to receive bits from their terminals. But, if the CPU is still executing the code of the BASIC interpreter, no response is given to the flags that are set.

The mainframe computer sends the next character over the serial line; the bits are collected by the serial input interface and, some $1/400$ second after the serial input's flag is first set, the content of its data register is replaced by the next character. The incoming message is now corrupted.

The output peripherals similarly complete their current character transfers, set their ready flags and then hang, waiting for more data.

When (if?) the CPU ever returns from its compute bound task, it re-enters the polling loop and finds flags set, but then it is too late. An indeterminate amount of input data has been lost. Further, a lack of CPU response to certain peripherals can even cause mechanical failures (card readers have been known to tear up cards just to spite an unresponsive computer); most mechanical input and output devices have difficulties with start/stop operations and are best kept running at constant speed.

The problem, as illustrated in this example, is really a consequence of a peripheral controller raising its flag and then waiting meekly for the CPU to respond. But, there is no response, no coordination between CPU and peripherals; the CPU continues busily with its computations.

The working of peripherals is too subservient to the CPU. Peripherals need to be able to signal the CPU: *'I don't care what you are doing now, you must come at once and help me deal with these data!'* If peripherals are able to *interrupt* any compute-bound work of the CPU, then one obtains a workable system.

If peripherals have the ability to interrupt the CPU, and thereby force the execution of device-handler code, coordination of peripherals and CPU activities is again achieved. But with interrupts, it is also possible for the CPU to undertake long computational tasks without any risk of data loss. Whenever data arrive, or whenever data must again be fed to an output device, the data processing work of the CPU is temporarily suspended while the necessary device-handling code is executed.

The structure of a program has to change quite radically if peripherals are able to interrupt the CPU. In general, a program will have quite distinct peripheral handlers, buffering schemes, control code of some form, all in addition to the data processing routines that really do the work required by the application. The particular piece of code (handler, control, data processing) executed by the CPU at any moment is determined largely in response to the activities of peripheral devices.

Peripheral-device-handler code deals with the data transfers, buffering data and setting software flags. A main control program selects among various compute-bound tasks, such as the interpretation of a BASIC program, according to whether or not necessary data are available for these tasks (this selection uses information in the software flags set by the device-handlers). The main program may also, in response to software flags, invoke small routines that allocate and queue buffers, and perform similar housekeeping tasks.

Special code is also required to cause the CPU to switch between appropriate device-handlers, main-line code, analysis routines etc. *This switching cannot be done by software alone.* It has to be coordinated by, and forced by, the activities of the peripherals. This requires additional hardware both in peripherals and in the timing and control circuitry of the CPU.

Handling peripheral devices using interrupts

The intent of an interrupt mechanism is to allow a device, that needs CPU assistance, to force the CPU to suspend its current work, execute appropriate device-handling code and then resume the interrupted work. This overall process requires that:

1.   Peripheral devices must be able to signal their need for CPU assistance.
2.   The hardware of the CPU must be capable of responding to such signals.
3.   The CPU's hardware response to such an *interrupt signal* must save some record of the address of the next instruction to be executed (had there been no interrupt), and then the CPU must change the value in its PC so that code appropriate to dealing with an interrupting device is executed.
4.   Other data, held in CPU registers, is also saved.
5.   The device causing all this fuss must be identified.
6.   The appropriate device-handling routine must be executed.
7.   Data, saved from the CPU registers in step 4, must be restored.
8.   Using the address that was saved in step 3, the CPU must return to the code whose execution was interrupted.

An interrupt mechanism is only useful if it is possible to guarantee that the occurrence of the interrupt will not change the results of an interrupted data-processing calculation. Thus, it is essential to save the state of a computation before executing device-handling code and then to restore the state of the computation.

It is undesirable for one interrupting device to be further interrupted by a second device. Here, the simplest solution is to rescind permission for devices to cause interrupts, from the time the CPU starts dealing with the first interrupt until the interrupted task has again been resumed.

There is a quite definite change in the mode in which the CPU is working. The CPU changes from a mode where it is executing the data-processing instructions of a user program (with interrupts enabled) to an interrupt-handling mode where it executes special device-handling code (with further interrupts temporarily disabled). On sophisticated machines, this switch in execution mode can be quite elaborate. For example, it might entail the use of a different set of data registers (some machines have multiple sets of registers in their CPUs).

Hardware and software for handling interrupts

Some of the steps involved in the interrupt-based methods for handling peripherals are performed automatically by the hardware. The rest must be accomplished by the execution of interrupt-handling code. Figure 12-1 illustrates a possible division of the various steps between hardware and software. The various extra pieces of hardware, and software routines, are described in the following subsections.

Figure 12-1. **A possible division, between hardware and software, of the steps involved in handling an interrupt from a peripheral device**

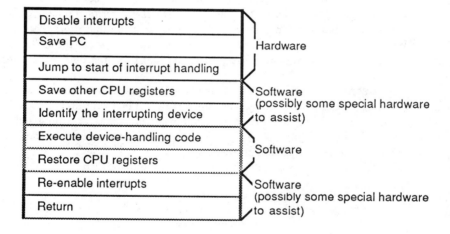

An 'interrupts-enabled/disabled' switch

The first extra hardware requirement for the handling of interrupts is a form of switch, or flag, in the CPU that indicates whether the interrupt mechanism is to be used. After all, for simple programs it is actually best not to use interrupts; wait loops or polling schemes suffice. The entire interrupt mechanism should be optional, something that can be switched on for those more sophisticated programs that have been designed to use this more elaborate approach to device-handling.

Consequently, there will be a 1-bit register in the CPU acting as an interrupts-enabled/disabled flag. If the machine has a proper flags register in its CPU, then this interrupt flag is represented by one bit of the flags register. By default, when a machine is started, the interrupt flag is set with interrupts disabled; the machine expects to control peripheral devices by the simpler means considered in previous chapters.

There will be an 'interrupts enable' instruction which, when executed, changes the flag and gives peripherals permission to interrupt the CPU whenever they need assistance. A program written to use interrupts will have some initiating phase where buffers and software flags are set up for the device-handlers and, if needed, certain peripherals are explicitly started. When this initiation is complete, the 'interrupts enable' instruction is executed and the main control program loop is started.

The interrupts flag is reset to disabled at various subsequent stages in the processing. As described in more detail later, this is done automatically as part of the hardware's response to any device causing an interrupt. Sometimes, it is also necessary for a program to request that interrupts be temporarily disabled. There will an 'interrupts disable' instruction to switch the mechanism off. The interrupt mechanism must be explicitly re-enabled after it has been disabled.

An 'interrupt line'

The second requirement is for a signal line into the timing and control circuitry of the CPU. If set, this signal line indicates that one (or more) of the peripheral devices is trying to attract the CPU's attention (i.e. a device is trying to cause an interrupt). This interrupt line can be gated through the interrupts-enabled/disabled flag; so, if the CPU does not want to be interrupted it can simply disconnect the interrupt line by setting interrupts disabled.

The interrupt line must be set whenever any device sets its ready flag (or error flag, transfer flag, or other status flag). The simplest model is a wire that threads through all the appropriate flag registers of the devices and then passes into the timing and control circuitry in the CPU (see Figure 12-2). The line is set whenever a device sets a flag (and the line remains set until all flags are cleared).

The signal on the interrupt line illustrated in Figure 12-2 is:

```
interrupt:= disk_seek_flag or disk_transfer_flag or
            disk_error_flag or keyboard_ready_flag
                    or terminal_ready_flag or ...;
```

'Microcode' in the CPU that controls response to interrupts

The microcode in the CPU, that is, the controlling circuitry that determines how instructions are executed, needs elaboration. The main loop of the CPU's microcode is the basic fetch-decode-execute loop:

```
while running do begin
        fetchinstruction();
        decodeinstruction();
        executeinstruction();
        end;
```

Figure 12-2. The interrupt signal line

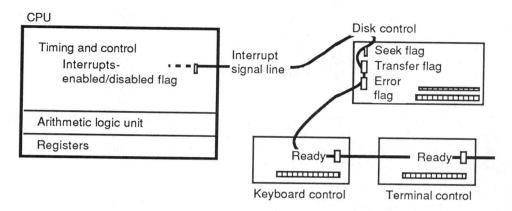

If interrupts are to be used to control devices then, after each instruction has been interpreted by the hardware, a check is made to see if any of the devices has set the interrupt line:

```
while running do begin
          fetchinstruction();
          decodeinstruction();
          executeinstruction();
          if interrupts_enabled and
                    interrupt_line_set then begin
                              { switch to interrupt-handling mode! }
                              .
                              .
                              .
                              end
          end;
```

The first step in the handling of an interrupt is to disable further interrupts; this allows the CPU to finish at least one thing before it is again disturbed.

The PC at this point, contains the address of the instruction that normally would have been executed next. This value must be saved somewhere in memory before the PC is changed to hold the address of the first instruction of the interrupt-handling code.

On the simple simul8 machine, a fixed memory address is used to hold the value saved from the PC on interrupt. Location 0 is used. So, the next step in the microcode is to cause a memory write operation, to location 0:

```
while running do begin
          fetchinstruction();
          decodeinstruction();
          executeinstruction();
```

```
if interrupts_enabled and
            interrupt_line_set then begin
                        { switch to interrupt-handling mode! }
                        disable_interrupts();
                        store[0]:=pc;

            end
end;
```

Again, on this simple CPU, the address of the start of the code for handling interrupts is hardwired into the CPU. The first instruction of the interrupt-handler code must be held in location 1; therefore, the value in the PC is changed to 1. Thus, the complete microcode is:

```
while running do begin
            fetchinstruction();
            decodeinstruction();
            executeinstruction();
            if interrupts_enabled and
                        interrupt_line_set then begin
                                    { switch to interrupt-handling mode! }
                                    disable_interrupts();
                                    store[0]:=pc;
                                    pc:=1;
                                    end
end;
```

The next instruction fetch cycle collects the instruction that is stored in location 1; this will be a jump to the start of the interrupt-handling code at some location in memory chosen by the programmer.

The sequence 'disable_interrupts()'; 'save pc in location 0'; 'change pc to 1'; represents the entire hardware response to an interrupt on the simulated machine. All the rest of the work must be done by programmed code. More sophisticated machines use additional hardware to perform tasks analogous to those performed by software on simul8, and described in the following subsections.

Saving the state of the computation

The first instructions of the main interrupt-handler code save the state of the computation. The process of handling an interrupt involves data transfers to/from device registers and possibly changes to software flags. Such data manipulations require the use of CPU data registers. The minimal hardware response to an interrupt saves only the PC. The values in the other CPU data registers must also be saved before the registers are used. The interrupt-handling code starts with some register store instructions.

This is simple on the simulated machine as there are only two other CPU registers whose values must be saved. Fixed memory locations are used to hold the values of the accumulator, and also the link register, while the interrupt-handling is completed.

```
/ prototypical interrupt-handling code for simul8
          *0
          0                    / location to save the program counter
          jmp  i  pints        / (indirect) jump to main interrupt-handler
pints,    ints                 / address constant, address of interrupt-handler
accsav,   0                    / place to save acc
lnksav,   0                    / place to save link
          .
          .
          .
          *400
/- - - - - - - - - - - - - - - - - - - - -
/ start of interrupt-handling code;
/ save state of computation:
ints,     dca     accsav       / save value in acc
          ral                  / get link bit into acc
          dca     lnksav       / and save it
```

Identifying the device

The next step is to identify the device that caused the interrupt. The setting of the interrupt line established that a device needs assistance, but the identity of the particular device is not yet known. Of course, the interrupting device has its ready flag (or transfer, seek, or error flag) set. Consequently, it is possible to find the device.

On the simple simul8 machine, the only means by which the interrupting device can be identified is to test, in turn, the flags in each device. Code for performing such testing is known as a *skip chain.* (The reason for the name will be obvious from the following example code.) Successive I/O skip-test instructions check the settings of flags and are used to select conditional jumps to appropriate device-handling code. Prototypical code for simul8 is:

```
/ prototypical interrupt-handling code for simul8
          *0
          0                    / location to save the program counter
          jmp  i  pints        / (indirect) jump to main interrupt-handler
pints,    ints                 / address constant, address of interrupt-handler
accsav,   0                    / place to save acc
lnksav,   0                    / place to save link
          .
          .
          .
          *400
/- - - - - - - - - - - - - - - - - - - - -
/ start of interrupt-handling code;
/ save state of computation:
ints,     dca     accsav       / save value in acc
          ral                  / get link bit into acc
          dca     lnksav       / and save it
```

```
/ - - - - - - - -
/ skip chain: ask each device in turn whether it has flags set and
/ is therefore the culprit who interrupted
            dtsf                    / disk transfer?
            skp
            jmp     diskt           / go and handle a completion of a disk transfer
            dssf                    / disk seek?
            skp
            jmp     disksk          / handle a seek, i.e. start the transfer
            tsf                     / teletype?
            skp
            jmp     ttyhnd          / handle a tty request (feed it another character)
            ksf                     / keyboard?
            skp
            jmp     keyhnd          / handle keyboard (eat another character)
             .
/ - - - - - -
/ have tried all known devices, something is amiss, best stop!
            hlt
```

It is best to terminate the skip chain with a halt. Sometimes, it is possible to get unexpected interrupts from devices that are not supposed to be working. If there isn't an appropriate device-handler, no mechanism exists to clear the device's flag and so the interrupt line remains set. The device does not then go away; it pesters the CPU with continual interrupts and prevents any further work being done. (On the simulator, a halt from an unexpected interrupt is usually due to an error in a program causing a jump to location 0 and hence entry to the interrupt-handling code when none of the device flags is actually set.)

Handling the device

Code for device-handling is obviously specialized. Basically, each device-handler clears its flag, but the rest of its actions depend on the type of device (and flag):

1. If it is something like a clock, then update a count.
2. If it is a character-input device, then accept the input character, store it in a buffer (and, if necessary, set software flags to say that the buffer now contains data).
3. If it is a character-output device, then look in the output buffer and if there are data there, read the next datum and forward it to the output device; otherwise maybe set a software flag to indicate that the output device is 'idle'.
4. If it is a disk seek, then complete arrangements and start a transfer.
5. If it is a disk transfer, then update the software flags that indicate whether data buffers have been read/written.

The clearing of the device flag acts as an acknowledgment to the device, an indication that the CPU is making some response. It also clears the interrupt line (unless several devices have flags set).

Data transfers using interrupts are inevitably buffered. Input data arrive as and when they will, and are stored until the CPU executes code to consume those data. Output data are generated, buffered, and then released to the output devices at speeds they can manage. As well as any necessary data transfers, most of the device-handler code consists of updating counters, adjusting pointers into buffers, and setting software flags that encode the status of each different data buffer.

Restoring the state of the interrupted program

Eventually, the device-handling is completed. At the end of each device-handler routine is a jump to the *return-from-interrupt* code. This code comprises instructions that restore the CPU state to what it was before the interrupt, re-enable the interrupts, and jump back to the instruction that that was previously the next to be executed.

The return-from-interrupt code is really a reversal of the save-state code. Saved values are read from memory and reloaded into the CPU registers. On simul8, the following instruction sequence is used:

```
/ 'exiting' from interrupt-handling,
/ restore the CPU registers
xit,      cla  cll
          tad      lnksav         / get link bit back in place
          rar
          cla
          tad      accsav         / and re-load accumulator
```

On most machines, there is an explicit 'return from interrupt' instruction that both re-enables interrupts and causes a jump back to the saved address. The simple simul8 machine does not have such an instruction and so two instructions must be executed:

```
/ 'exiting' from interrupt-handling,
/ restore the CPU registers
xit,      cla  cll
          tad      lnksav         / get link bit back in place
          rar
          cla
          tad      accsav         / and re-load accumulator
/ re-enable interrupts (delayed by one instruction)
          ion
/ jump back to instruction whose address has been saved
/ (saved address is in location zero, so this is an indirect
/ jump via location zero)
          jmp  i  0               / return from interrupt
```

(The actual re-enabling of the interrupts is delayed for one instruction so that the jump that does the return is executed before interrupts are again permitted. This is essential for the scheme to work; try to determine why this is so.)

Organizing the interrupt-handling code

Interrupt-handling code is arranged as shown in Figure 12-3. These details are specific to the simul8 machine, but other machines use similar organizations for their code. A few locations with lowest address values have either hard-wired uses, for example, locations 0 and 1 for the stored PC and the jump to the first instruction of the interrupt-handler. On simul8 a couple more low-address locations are used for saving registers.

The main code of the interrupt-handler starts with the instructions necessary to save the state of the CPU; this is followed by the device identification code and jumps to device-handlers. The return from interrupt code terminates the main component of the interrupt-handler. The various device-handler routines are organized in succeeding locations in memory.

Figure 12-3. Organization of interrupt-handling code for the simul8 machine

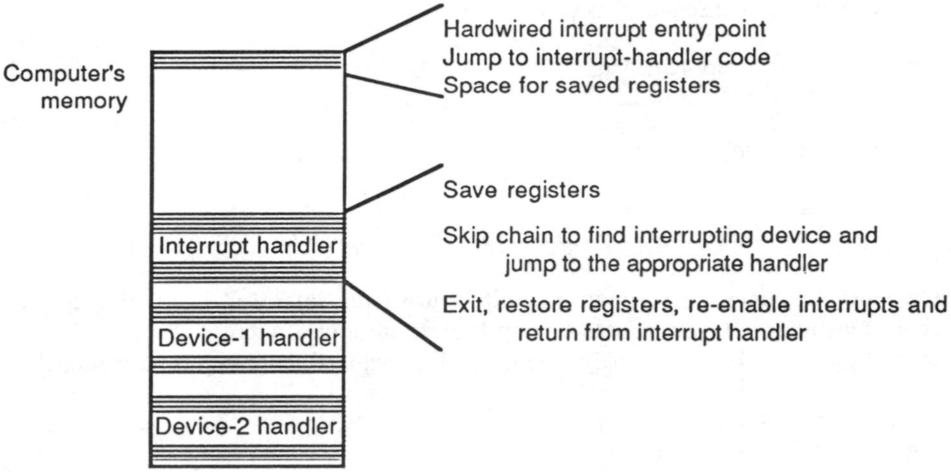

Computer's memory

Hardwired interrupt entry point
Jump to interrupt-handler code
Space for saved registers

Save registers

Interrupt handler

Skip chain to find interrupting device and jump to the appropriate handler

Device-1 handler

Exit, restore registers, re-enable interrupts and return from interrupt handler

Device-2 handler

A first example interrupt-driven program

The following is a complete, though very simple, example of an interrupt-driven program for simul8; this is program 'ints1' on the simul8 disk. The program uses the interrupt mechanism to monitor the clock. Meanwhile it proceeds with a 'compute-bound' task, multiplication of two numbers (by the inefficient method of repeated additions).

The first few locations on page zero are reserved for the save-location for the PC, for the jump to the interrupt-handler, and for holding the accumulator and link. The program uses one global, a count of clock ticks, at location with address 020.

```
/ 1st interrupt driven demonstration program:
/
/ it uses the interrupt mechanism to monitor 'clock ticks' while it
/ performs some computations.
/
/ (the computations involve a multiplication done by repeated addition )
                *0
                0                               / for storing pc on interrupt
                jmp i       pints               / jump to interrupt-handler
pints,          ints                            / pointer to interrupt-handler code
accsav,         0                               / somewhere to store acc
lnksav,         0                               / somwhere to store link
                *20
ticks,          0                               / counter for clock ticks
```

Initialization is simple for this program. The count 'ticks' must be zeroed, the clock started, and interrupts enabled.

```
                *200
                cla
                dca         ticks
                clkt                            / start the clock
                ion                             / enable interrupts
```

The main loop of the program is equivalent to the code:

```
cntr:=-a;
prdct:=0;
repeat
        prdct:=prdct+b;
        cntr:=cntr+1;
until (cntr=0);
```

Execution of this code is suspended whenever the clock sets its flag; the clock-handler code is then executed and the computation loop resumed. When the loop is complete, the clock is stopped, interrupts are disabled, and the program terminates.

```
/ - - - - - - - - -
/ The following represents the 'main line' code that will be interrupted
/ for clock ticks.
/ now start the multiplies, its for unsigned small values 'a' and  'b'
/ a*b = (b+b+b+ ... ) i.e. add b the necessary number of times
/ (it's assumed that product will fit in 12 bits)
                cla
                tad         a
                cia
                dca         cntr
                dca         prdct
loop,           tad         prdct
```

```
        tad     b
        dca     prdct
        isz     cntr
        jmp     loop
/ - - - - - - - - - - - -
/ when multiply is done then finished, stop the clock
        clkt
/ disable interrupts
        iof
/ and halt
        hlt
/ - - - - - -
a,      0076
b,      0017
cntr,   0
prdct,  0
```

The interrupt-handler code is standard. Registers are saved. A skip chain is used to identify the device; since only the clock is supposed to be running, an interrupt from any other device will cause the program to halt. The return from interrupt code restores registers, re-enables interrupts, and jumps back to the interrupted computation.

```
/ - - - - - - - - - - - - - - - - - - - - - - - - - -
            *400
/ interrupt-handler
/ - - - - save state of calculation - - -
ints,   dca     accsav          / save acc
        ral
        dca     lnksav          / save link
/ - - - - identify device - - - -
        clksf                   / was it clock
        skp
        jmp     clksrv
/ - - - - unknown device, best stop
        hlt
/ - - - - return from interrupt
xit,    cla cll
        tad     lnksav
        rar
        tad     accsav
        ion
        jmp i   0
```

Handling the clock is simple. Its flag must be cleared. (This also starts it counting down again to cause another interrupt later.) A count is then updated and then a jump made back to the exit from interrupt code.

```
/ - - - - - -  device-handlers
clksrv,     clkcf                    / clear flag
            isz       ticks          / update count
            nop
            jmp       xit
$
```

Figure 12-4 presents a graphic trace of the activities of the system during execution of the 'ints1' program on simul8. The first clock tick occurs when about 80 instructions have been completed. At the moment when the clock interrupts, the PC will (probably) contain address 0212 (the 'tad b' instruction), and the accumulator then contains 0322. The value from the PC is written into location 0 and the interrupt- handling code started. The second clock interrupt occurs after about 160 instructions; this time coming when the PC (probably) contains 0215 and the accumulator contains 0.

The 'ints1' program should be executed, in visual step-step mode, on simul8. Stepping through execution should clarify the steps involved in handling interrupts. After observing execution of the program in step-step mode, try setting breakpoints at entry to and exit from the interrupt-handling code and use the single-step mode to follow execution in more detail. (This is one of the advantages of a simulated machine – time can be made to stand still while breakpoints are adjusted, memory locations inspected, and so forth; subsequent interrupts and data are not lost. It is less easy on a real machine.)

Figure 12-4. A visual trace of CPU activity during execution of the 'ints1' program on simul8

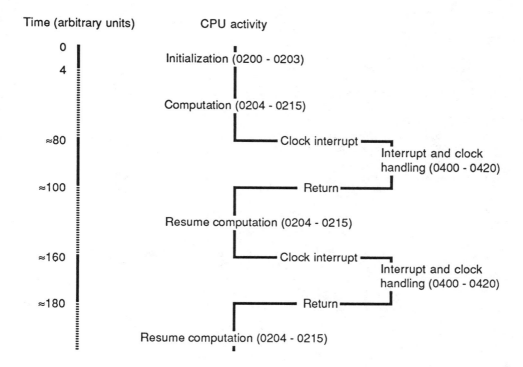

A second example interrupt-driven program

A second example interrupt-driven program ('intsin' on the simul8 disk) uses the interrupt mechanism to read characters and to monitor the clock. Characters read are stored in a circular buffer.

The data-processing task consists of reading and analyzing characters from the circular buffer. Characters that don't represent digits are discarded. When digits are found in the input, a character-to-number conversion routine is invoked. This routine interprets the digit characters as representing a decimal number, and performs the conversion; numbers are terminated by any non-digit character. After conversion, the numeric values are stored in memory and added into a cumulative total. The program terminates when this total exceeds one thousand.

The interrupt-handling code is standardized. There is the usual sequence of register saves, a skip chain to identify the device (clock or keyboard), and jumps to appropriate handler routines. The exit from interrupt code performs the restores, re-enabling of interrupts, and the jump back to the interrupted code.

```
        *400
/ Here is the interrupt-handler
inthnd,  dca      accsav
         rar
         dca      lnksav
/ saves completed, now skip chain
         clksf
         skp
         jmp      clksrv
         ksf
         skp
         jmp      keysrv
         hlt                           / unknown interrupt
/ here, have return from interrupt
xit,     cla  cll
/ restore registers
         tad      lnksav
         ral
         tad      accsav
/ re-enable interrupts
         ion
/ do return
         jmp i    0
```

The clock-handler clears the clock flag, updates a count, and exits from the interrupt:

```
/ clock service routine
clksrv,  clkcf                         / clear clock flag
         isz      ticks
         nop
         jmp      xit
```

The keyboard device-handler has first to read in the character (and, simultaneously, clear the device flag), and then place this character in a circular buffer. Buffer access is done using the base address of the buffer and a cyclic index value to determine the address of the next buffer location to be filled. The character is copied into this location. (The code assumes that there is no possibility of the buffer ever being full of previously read but not yet processed data.) The cyclic index, 'pptr', is updated modulo the length of the buffer (which is 128 words long).

```
/ keyboard service routine
keysrv,    krb
           dca      temp1
/ need to index into array
           tad      inbuff        / base address
           tad      pptr          / + index
           dca      temp2         / = required address
           tad      temp1
           dca  i   temp2         / character stored in 'inbuff[pptr]
           tad      pptr
           iac
/ here we cheat a little, use a masking operation
/ to force pptr to stay in range 0-177 octal
           and      m177
           dca      pptr
           jmp      xit
m177,      '0177
temp1,     0
temp2,     0
```

The speed at which characters are processed varies considerably with character type. Sequences of non-digits are rapidly disposed of and the buffer is emptied. Digits are processed much more slowly because the number-input routine requires multiplications. While digits are being processed, the buffer tends to fill with subsequently arriving characters.

The processing routines call a subroutine 'nxtch' to retrieve the next buffered character whenever one is required. Subroutine 'nxtch' compares two pointers into this buffer in order to determine whether any data are available. These pointers are 'pptr', the pointer used by the 'producer' (i.e. the keyboard-handler routine), and 'cptr', the pointer used by the 'consumer' (i.e. 'nxtch' itself). If these pointers are equal, then there are no data.

Subroutine 'nxtch' acts as a wait loop when data have not arrived. The loop is based on the comparisons of the two pointers and will only be terminated when characters arrive, are buffered by the keyboard-handler routines, and 'pptr' is appropriately updated.

If data are available ('pptr≠cptr'), then the next character is read from the buffer. (The usual indexing steps apply using the value of 'cptr' and the start address of the buffer to determine where the next character is located.) The character is stored in a global, 'nchar', and the 'consumer pointer' 'cptr' is updated appropriately.

```
/ - - - - - - - - - - - - - - - - - - - - - - - - - - - - - - -
          *600
nxtch,    0
/ wait till there are characters, this applies only when the buffer
/ has been emptied completely, usually there will be characters already
/ queued up and awaiting processing and then there will be no wait in this
/ loop
nxtl,     cla  cll
          tad       cptr
          cia
          tad       pptr
          sna cla
          jmp       nxtl                    / if pointers are equal then no characters yet
/ when character arrives, pptr will be changed; then can break out of
/ loop and collect the  next character.
/ need to index into array
          tad       inbuff          / base address
          tad       cptr            / + index
          dca       ntemp2          / = required address
          tad  i    ntemp2
          dca       nchar
          tad       cptr
          iac
/ here we cheat a little, use a masking operation
/  to force pptr to stay in range 0-177 octal
          and       nm177
          dca       cptr
          jmp  i    nxtch
nm177,    0177
```

It is again worth running this example in step-step visual mode on the simulator; breakpoints and 'dumps' are also helpful with this example because these can provide printouts of the contents of buffers at various points in the computations. On an input sequence such as 'a123 xyz', the processing would be approximately as shown in Table 12-1.

Disabling of interrupts

The hardware response to an interrupt on the simul8 machine disables the interrupt mechanism. Interrupts are not re-enabled until completion of the return from the interrupt-handler (the 'ion'; 'jmp i 0' instructions). This complete disabling of further interrupts is necessary because of the way the machine uses a fixed location to store the return address.

If interrupts are not automatically disabled, then it is possible for the return address to be corrupted. For example, the CPU might be executing data-processing code at about 0220 when interrupted by the keyboard; the next address, 0221, is saved in location zero. Keyboard-handling code at about 450 might then be executed when the printer

Table 12-1. Trace of processing and interrupts during execution of the 'intsin' demonstration program

initialization	
wait in nxtch for data	
keyboard interrupt	
	keyboard-handling (a)
checking if character was a digit	
clock interrupt	
	clock-handling
wait in nxtch for data	
keyboard interrupt	
	keyboard-handling (1)
checking if character was a digit	
call to readnumber routine	
clock interrupt	
	clock-handling
wait in nxtch (called by readnumber)	
keyboard interrupt	
	keyboard-handling (2)
checking for digit	
clock interrupt	
	clock-handling
starting multiplication (1x10)	
keyboard interrupt	
	keyboard-handling (3)
resume multiplication (1x10)	
clock interrupt	
	clock-handling
resume multiplication (1x10)	
keyboard interrupt	
	keyboard-handling( )
resume multiplication (1x10)	
clock interrupt	
	clock-handling
resume multiplication (1x10)	
keyboard interrupt	
	keyboard-handling(x)
finish multiply (1x10)	
call to nxtch, fetch buffered character	
check for digit	
start multiplication (12x10)	
clock interrupt.	
.	
.	
and so on	

interrupts. Location 0 is then overwritten with the value 0451 and the printer-handling code is executed.

When the printer is dealt with, a return takes the CPU back to keyboard-handling code. But, when an attempt is made to return from the keyboard-handling, the CPU is again directed back to somewhere in the keyboard routine. There is no way to return to the original program.

In Chapter 18, more elaborate machine architectures with multiple levels of interrupts are considered. On such machines, devices like disks can interrupt the code that deals with interrupts from slower devices like terminals.

Problems associated with interrupts

Interrupts are an essential mechanism for achieving full use of a single CPU. It is through the interrupt mechanism that it is possible to allow overlap of computation and peripheral operations while still guaranteeing correct coordination of CPU and device activities. However, the interrupt mechanism does introduce a whole host of new problems. A whole new breed of *timing-dependent bugs* (see Figure 12-5) is spawned by this mechanism. These bugs are peculiarly difficult to diagnose and correct.

The problem is that the machine is no longer fully deterministic. Before the introduction of interrupts, given the code of the program (and the data it works with), it is possible to analyze in advance the exact sequence of instructions that is executed, and then to trace that sequence during execution. With interrupts that occur at totally random times dictated by external events, this is no longer possible. Between any pair of data-processing instructions, it is now possible for the CPU to divert in some wild foray through interrupt-handler and device-handler code. Since this code will inevitably change some variables, the state of the machine is no longer the same on return from interrupt.

Figure 12-5. A graphic reminder: the interrupt mechanism introduces the possibility of timing-dependent bugs

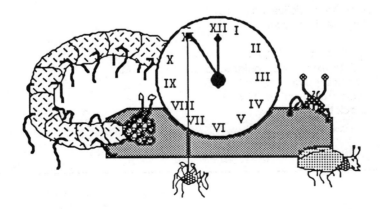

Although the CPU state may be correctly saved and restored, changes to variables in memory may disrupt the correct processing of a program. The following example illustrates the kind of problem that can arise.

This example buggy code was produced by a student for one of the standard exercises involving a circular buffer:

Main line	Interrupt and device-handler code
/ get next character	/ read character
/ from buffer 'b'	krb
cla	/ store temporarily
tad cindx	dca nchar
tad addrb	/ now find place in buffer
dca ptr	tad pindx
tad i ptr	tad addrb
dca nxtch	dca ptr
/ update index circularly	/ store character
.	tad nchar
.	dca i ptr
.	/ update 'pindx'
.	cla iac
.	tad pindx
.	

Considered individually, these fragments of code are correct. However, they have a fatal interaction. Remember the main-line code can be interrupted between any pair of instructions.

For example, a keyboard interrupt might occur just as the CPU is executing the 'dca ptr' instruction in the main-line. The value stored into location 'ptr' could be 1021 for a buffer starting at 1000 and a 'cindx' value of 021. This store instruction is completed and then the interrupt-handling code is invoked.

Since this is a keyboard interrupt, the keyboard-handler is executed, and the new character read and stored temporarily. The address of the appropriate buffer location is then computed and the address might be 1033 for the same buffer starting at 1000 and a 'pindx' value of 033. This address 1033 is then stored in 'ptr', overwriting the 1021 that was there previously. The newly read character is correctly stored in location 1033 and a return made from the interrupt.

The main-line code resumes with the instruction 'tad i ptr' and therefore reads the character in location 1033 rather than the desired character in location 1021. The program proceeds with the wrong data.

The problem is the common variable, 'ptr', that is updated and used at two different places in the code. Further, execution of these two separate pieces of code can be overlapped in time. The value of 'ptr' may be changed at any arbitrary moment during execution of main-line code.

Whether or not the program appears to work depends on the particular chance times data arrive. When initially testing the code, one may be fortunate and never have an interrupt between that crucial pair of instructions in the main line (or one may not notice one erroneous character). However, when the program is used for its intended application, the intermittent occurrence of errors will eventually be detected. Finding such timing-dependent bugs is extremely difficult; most debugging techniques are irrelevant or inapplicable.

The difficulties with this example program are totally self-inflicted. There is no need for any variable to be changed and used in both components of the code. The program works if the interrupt-handler simply uses a different temporary pointer variable, a 'ptr1' instead of 'ptr'.

Unfortunately, it is not always possible to make different parts of the code completely disjoint. Sometimes, common variables must be tested, updated, or used in two different sections of code whose execution may be overlapped in time.

For example, consider the code needed for outputting characters to the teletype of simul8. (This type of problem has been discussed already in relation to one of the polling loop examples.) This code is somewhat analogous to the character-input routines of the 'intsin' program illustrated earlier. A subroutine called from the main line queues a character for eventual printing (analogous to the 'nxtch' subroutine used for reading a character), and a teletype-handler routine deals with teletype interrupts (analogous to routine 'keyser', the keyboard-handler routine of 'intsin').

The teletype-handler first clears the teletype flag and then checks if data characters are still buffered. This check is based on a comparison of a couple of cyclic indices into the output data buffer. If these indices are equal, then there are no data queued and the handler sets a boolean variable to show that the printer is idling and then exits. If the indices are unequal, then there are characters queued, the next can be read, and the index used by the teletype-handler updated.

The character queuing routine usually just enters the character into the buffer and updates its own index.

A problem arises when the teletype has already consumed all previously sent characters. The teletype flag is cleared when dispatch of the last character is acknowledged. The teletype is idle, and the buffer is empty. If the character queuing routine simply inserted the next character into the buffer, then nothing starts its transfer to the teletype. The character, and all subsequent characters, just fills the buffer.

The character-queuing routine must determine if the teletype is idle when it is called. If the teletype is idle, then rather than queue the character in the buffer, the queuing routine should arrange that the character be directly transmitted to the teletype.

In pseudo-Pascal, the code for character queuing routine and the teletype-handler would be something like:

```
const len=128;
var buff : array[0..(len-1)] of char;
    qptr,optr : integer;
    idle:boolean;
    .
    .
    .
```

```
procedure queue(ch:char)              interrupt_handler ttyhndl;
                                      var temp:ch;
begin                                     begin
  { if teletype idle then send   }         clear_tty_flag();
  { character, otherwise place }           If qptr≠optr then begin
  { in buffer }                              temp:=buff[optr];
  if idle then      begin                    print(temp);
        print(ch);                           optr:=(optr+1) mod len;
        idle:=false                        end
    end                                    else idle:=true;
  else begin                            end;
        buff[qptr]:=ch;
        qptr:=(qptr+1) mod len;
    end
end;
```

As usual, the examples are simplified by ignoring the possibility of the buffer being already full when data need to be inserted. Note, that here there is a variable 'idle' that is changed in both interrupt-handler and queuing routine, and which is tested in the queuing routine. (The variable 'idle' is presumably set to true during some general initialization step, that also sets both 'qptr' and 'optr' to 0.)

This common variable cannot be avoided. Furthermore, execution of the testing code may overlap in time with execution of the updating code. Inevitably, such a common variable is the source of timing-dependent errors. The following scenario leads to disaster:

1. A few characters are generated, buffered, and mostly printed.
2. The last character has already been collected from say location 9 in the buffer and sent to the teletype, but not yet acknowledged; 'idle' is false, both 'qptr' and 'optr' contain the value 10, the index of the next buffer location to be used.
3. The main-line program generates another character and invokes procedure 'queue'.
4. The variable 'idle' is tested; since it is false, the 'else' clause of the 'if... then ... else' starts to be executed. The character is placed into the buffer at the location determined by the index value 'qptr'.
5. The teletype causes an interrupt.
6. The teletype flag is cleared; the test on the index values 'qptr' and 'optr' is made. Since these indices are equal, there are no characters queued; 'idle' is set to true. The return from interrupt is made.
7. Execution of procedure 'queue' continues; the value of 'qptr' is updated. Procedure 'queue' terminates, and execution of the main-line program continues.

Now, the character that was queued is sitting in location 10 of the buffer, where it will remain. Eventually, another character will be generated by the main-line program and passed to procedure 'queue'.

8. The 'idle' flag will be found to be true, so this new character will be sent directly to the teletype.

9. Eventually, the teletype will interrupt, the indices checked, found unequal, and the character that has been sitting in the buffer will be collected and sent.

Unfortunately, although the character will eventually be sent, the overall message has been scrambled. The main-line program may have generated output 'ABC' but this will have been printed as 'ACB'.

Rearranging the code can transform this problem, but it cannot be eliminated. There is an inherent need to test a variable that is changed in another part of the code, with the possibility of tests and changes becoming interleaved in time.

There is a solution!

Procedure 'queue' has to temporarily disable interrupts while it manipulates 'idle' and 'qptr'. Then there is no possibility of interleaved execution. Processing is again simple and deterministic. So, procedure 'queue' would start with an 'interrupts off' instruction, and re-enable interrupts, with an 'interrupts on' instruction, just before it returned to the calling main-line program.

Disabling interrupts is a somewhat crude expedient. It is not always going to be permissible. It is not always going to be sufficient. But, for simple uniprocessor machines, the ability to disable/re-enable interrupts provides a workable approach to dealing with this type of timing-dependent problem.

Exercises

1. Write a program that monitors readings from the A/D converter, printing warning messages when 'excessive' values are detected.

    The program should take an A/D sample after each clock tick. The samples from the A/D are to be queued for subsequent processing; a one page circular buffer should be used for this queue. A count, 'ndx', is to be maintained of the number of sample values processed. The processing routine is to compare each value read from the A/D with a constant representing 450_{decimal}. If a sample value exceeds this limit, then the current 'ndx' count is to be printed along with the sample value read. The two values are to be printed, in octal, separated by a '/' and followed by a newline character.

    Output to the teletype is to use the interrupt system. A teletype-handler routine must be written. This routine is to send the next character to the teletype when the teletype-flag is set following successful transmission of the preceding character. Characters are to be queued, in a circular buffer, awaiting printing. The circular buffer used for storing characters should not exceed one-half page in length.

    Processing is to be terminated when either 15 samples have been read from the A/D or when two excessive readings have been reported. The printing of any second warning must be completed before interrupts are turned off and the program is terminated.

2. Modify, to use interrupt driven I/O, your solution to Exercise 2 from Chapter 11. (This is the example where A/D values were taken every third clock tick and printed in histogram form.)

3. Write a program using interrupt driven output for the following task:

```
program tables(input,output);
const T=9;
var j,k:integer;
begin
     writeln(T,' times table');
     for j:=1 to 12 do begin
        k:=T*j;
        writeln(j,' x ',T,' = ',k);
        end
end.
```

Characters generated by the message and number output routines (the equivalents to the Pascal 'writeln's) are to be queued in a circular buffer for printing. Output of queued characters is to proceed concurrently with subsequent computations. The multiplication should be done by a simple repeated addition loop (or, a proper shift and add routine can be taken from one of the example programs). The decimal output routines should be taken from the 'fndmax' demonstration program.

4. Write a program to simultaneously:

    a) Read character data from blocks 0, 1, 2, ... of the disk and print these characters on the teletype.
    b) Read characters from the keyboard and store them one per word in blocks of 128 words in memory. When filled with characters, these blocks are to be written to disk starting at block 5 of the disk.

The program is to be terminated when two blocks have been written to disk. Thus, while data from the keyboard fill up the disk using blocks 5 and 6, the teletype is emptying the disk, taking block 0, then block 1 and so forth. Both keyboard-to-disk input, and disk-to-teletype output are to use 'double buffering'. Therefore, there will be four buffer areas in memory. Each buffer should be 128 words long, the same size as one disk block.

5. Explain the principles of the following I/O methods and suggest applications where their use is appropriate:

    a) wait loops for individual I/O devices,
    b) polling loops controlling several I/O devices, and
    c) interrupts.

Section IV

Assembly languages and high-level languages

13

Assemblers and loaders I

This chapter introduces methods for converting an assembly language source program into an executable program in the memory of the computer. As illustrated in Figure 13-1, two tasks must be performed in this overall process. First, the assembly language program must be translated into *object code*. Second, this object code must be loaded into memory.

The translation from assembly language source to object code is performed by an *assembler*. Since this translation step is the more complex task, before discussing assemblers some details of object code and loaders are given.

Figure 13-1. Conversion of assembly language source code into object code and loading of code to create an executable program

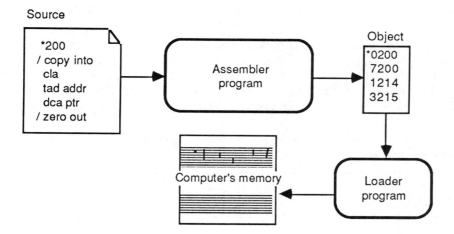

Object code and loaders

The hardware of a computer interprets programs represented as specific bit patterns stored in particular memory locations. Before a program can be executed, it must be converted into this form in memory.

A program must, at the final stage of its preparation, be explicitly or implicitly represented as a set of pairs of binary data. The first element of each pair is a bit pattern representing, as an unsigned integer, the *address of a memory location*. The second element of the pair represents, by a bit pattern, the instruction or datum that is the *contents of that location*. (Often, it is possible to represent implicitly many of the addresses; this allows for a more compact representation of the program, but does not change any principles.) This representation, as pairs of bit patterns, is the *object code* form of a program.

In the earliest computer systems, composing the program in this form was the responsibility of the programmer. An example program in object code form is:

Location address	Location content
000010000000	111010000000
000010000001	001010001100
000010000010	011010001101
000010000011	011010001110
000010000100	001110001101
000010000101	111100101000
000010000110	111100000010
.	.
.	.
.	.

Prior to the development of assemblers, programmers wrote programs in this form (it is actually the program used in Chapter 7 to illustrate array access). Of course, the programmer normally did the coding in octal or hexadecimal notation and left conversion to binary as the last step; but even if octal, or hex is used, the coding is not much simpler. For example, in octal, the code corresponding to the above reads as follows:

Location address	Location content
0200	7200
0201	1214
0202	3215
.	.

Once a program exists in object code form then it must be loaded into the memory of the computer. On the earliest systems, the binary data of the object code might be entered into the computer by a set of switches on the computer's control panel. More commonly, these binary data were punched on cards, or paper tape, and then read into the computer's memory by a simple *loader* program. The simple 'absolute' loader needed to process such data was only one or two dozen instructions long, and occupied the last few words of the memory of the machine. The term 'absolute loader' describes a loader program for object code containing explicit location addresses.

The loading process involves reading the (location address, location content) pairs. A simple loader for the simulated machine could be coded along the following lines. (This example assumes that the object code data are represented as characters on cassette or paper tape, with 6 bits of each character used to represent object code data.)

```
loop,      read_character
           check for special end mark character
           if end mark, jump to default start address
/          if not end mark, this character is part of
/          an address data element
           mask out six bits
           shift to left half of word
           save in temp
           read_character
           mask out six bits
           add in previously saved value from temp
           store in pointer
/          now read, as two characters, the contents
/          of the address just defined
           read_character
           mask out six bits
           shift to left half of word
           save in temp
           read_character
           mask out six bits
           add in previously saved value from temp
           store indirect pointer
           jump to loop
```

The role of an assembler

The manual composition of an object file, with its addresses and its machine code instructions, is an extremely tedius and error prone procedure. However, most of the individual processing steps involved are fairly mechanical and repetitious. These tasks are themselves fairly easy to program. Very soon after the original development of computers, assembly languages and their assemblers were invented. An assembler performed the more mechanical tasks of generating the correct binary code and therefore simplified this aspect of programming.

With an assembler, the program preparation procedure involves more steps. As represented in Figure 13-2, the programmer writes a program in assembly language. The program document is prepared on punched cards or paper tape. The assembler program, available as a file of object code, is loaded into the machine and started (1). It then reads the assembly language source code from cards or tape (2), and produces an object file as its output (3). After successful assembly, the object file of the user's program is then loaded into memory (4), using the standard loader program for a second time.

Figure 13-2. The program preparation process using an assembler and a loader

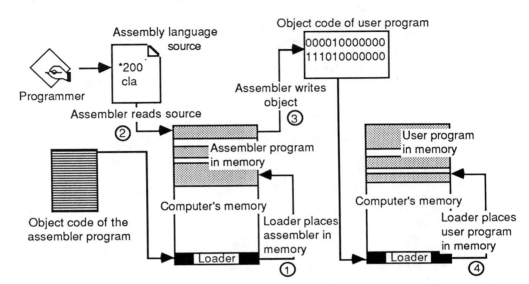

The assembly language of simul8 has been introduced, informally, through the examples in the preceding chapters and in the appendixes. Although restricted in many ways, it typifies simple assembly languages. As shown through the examples, the assembly language of simul8 allows for (1) mnemonic names for the instructions, (2) specification of constants, (3) declaration of variables, (4) directives that specify where particular instructions and/or data elements are to be located, and (5) comments. Each statement in this assembly language specifies a particular instruction to be executed.

The specific form of any assembly language is determined mainly by the structure of its target machine, that is by the particular instruction formats and addressing modes available. The form of a language is further restricted by the way the corresponding assembler program is written. For example, in simul8, the restriction that all numeric constants be represented as unsigned octal numbers is a consequence of a design decision made when implementing the assembler; a more sophisticated assembler for the same machine might permit signed decimal as an alternative data representation.

Although there may be a simple one-to-one correspondence between the program statements written in an assembly language and the executable instructions in memory, some *translation* of the program code is still necessary:

1. The assembler must make explicit all those addresses that the programmer has left implicit.
2. The assembler must construct each instruction word by filling in the appropriate bit patterns for the op-code field, the address mode field, and address field.

The 'hand assembly' process

It is informative to 'hand assemble' a fragment of program, because features required in an assembler program can then be perceived by the performance of various processing steps. The following example uses the program previously used to illustrate how to access an element of an array. Here, the program code is first expressed informally, as it might be composed by a programmer for a computer without a defined assembly language and assembler. 'Comments' are shown in italics; instructions are described by their desired effects.

code is to start at 0200
    clear accumulator
    add value held in address constant that defines where array located
    store in a pointer variable
    clear a variable for sum
main loop starts here
    add the data element pointed to by pointer variable
    test and skip if non-zero value
    halt
    add in partial sum from summation variable
    store in sum variable
    increment the pointer
    do a nop, just in case got skip
    jump back to start of loop
now have some constants and variables
    address constant with address of the array
    pointer variable
    sum variable

Encoding operate and input/output instructions

The appropriate bit patterns for a few of the instructions in the program could be determined immediately by simply looking up their values in the instruction reference table in the programmers' handbook for the machine. Thus, both the 'clear accumulator' and the 'halt' instruction are standard operate instructions whose bit-pattern representations would be listed in the machine manual.

If the instructions are accorded standardized names, then their encoding involves just simple table look-up techniques (i.e. the name of an instruction keys into a table of instruction names and bit patterns). It is obviously advantageous for an instruction name to describe its function, for this makes it easier to remember. By combining these two ideas, a program processed by an assembler will have the instructions specified by their mnemonic names, rather than by descriptions.

For this example the first coding step is simple and yields:

Location address	Location contents	Name	Function
000010000000	111010000000	(cla)	clear accumulator

Encoding memory reference instructions

The encoding of a memory reference instruction is, however, a bit more complex. Consider the instruction 'add value held in address constant that defines where array located'. The op-code part is simple enough. Since it is an 'add' instruction, the first 3 bits of the word must be 001 (determinable by looking up the instruction mnemonic name in a look-up table). It is obviously a direct memory reference, so the indirect bit in the generated instruction must be a 0. However, the remaining bits of the address cannot be filled in; the address of the location that will be used to hold the required address constant is not yet known when this instruction is first encountered.

Location address	Location contents	Name	Function
000010000000	111010000000	(cla)	clear accumulator
000010000001	0010????????	(tad ---)	add value held in address constant that defines where array located

In fact, *two* readings through the text of the program are needed in order to generate the code. On the first reading (*pass*) through the program text, the programmer seeks solely to determine the locations used for each instruction, constant, and variable. Only on the second pass, when the addresses are known, does code generation proceed.

Calculation of addresses in the first pass

The calculation of the addresses, in the first pass, is simple. The start (*origin*) for any piece of code is known. Each instruction, variable, and constant occupies one word. A counter is set to the address of the first location in a piece of code, and updated by 1 for each line of code processed. The value of this *location counter* is noted for each line.

Location counter in binary	Function
000010000000	clear accumulator
000010000001	add value held in address constant that defines where array located
000010000010	store in a pointer variable
000010000011	clear a variable for sum
	main loop starts here
000010000100	add the data element pointed to by pointer variable
000010000101	test and skip if non-zero value
000010000110	halt
000010000111	add in partial sum from summation variable
000010001000	store in sum variable
000010001001	increment the pointer
000010001010	do a nop, just in case got skip
000010001011	jump back to start of loop
	now have some constants and variables
000010001100	address constant with address of the array
000010001101	pointer variable
000010001110	sum variable

Generating the object code in the second pass

When the addresses are determined, the encoding of the memory reference instructions is performed. When an address of some location is needed in an instruction, it is possible to scan through the code to find that location and its assigned address. With the address data shown above, it is possible to continue the translation to yield:

Location address	Location	Name contents	Function
000010000000	111010000000	(cla)	clear accumulator
000010000001	001010001100	(tad addr)	add value held in address constant that defines where array located
000010000010	011010001101	(dca ptr)	store in a pointer variable
.	.	.	
	.		
	.	.	

Using symbolic labels

It is, of course, easier if some scheme for naming or labeling particular locations is used. Then, a table of user-defined names and their addresses can be set up:

Name	Variable	Address
addr	address constant with address of the array	0214
ptr	pointer variable	0215
sum	sum variable	0216

If these symbolic user names are employed when referencing variables in instructions, then the coding of the address part can again be reduced to what is basically a look-up operation in a table.

It is slightly more complex in practice. There must be checks (for illegal cross-page references, page zero references, and current page references) made on the basis of address values: the address value in the table for the referenced symbol, and the value of the location counter at the point where the instruction is being built (assembled). If the programmer performing a manual assembly finds a cross-page reference, then he or she knows that the program is erroneous and redesigns it. The distinction between page zero and current page allows the corresponding bit in the generated instruction word to be correctly set. Once the page-zero/current-page bit is set, the remainder of an address is encoded by taking the low order 7 bits of the address retrieved from the table.

So, in the second pass through the program code, both instruction and address encoding can be reduced to looking up names in various tables and retrieving the values.

The symbol table

It is actually simpler to have a single look-up table with each entry characterized by name, symbol type, and value. The symbol types are 'memref' instruction, 'input/ output' instruction, 'operate' instruction, and user 'label'. The values for mnemonic instruction symbols are the (octal) values of the bit patterns that represent the actual executable instructions. The values for the user symbols are the addresses of the corresponding locations.

The programmer performing a hand assembly builds up the symbol table during the first pass through the text of the program. The symbol table is initialized to contain all the standard instruction mnemonics, types, and values. The code of the program is read and addresses determined for each instruction/datum. Whenever a program label is encountered, it is inserted into the symbol table along with its appropriate address. Now, during the second pass, this single symbol table can be used for all look-up operations, and appropriate object code generated using the values retrieved.

Syntactic checks in the second pass

Second pass processing entails a number of simple syntactic checks prior to the actual code generation step. For example, I/O instructions shouldn't have any operands; if an operand is found following an 'iot' class instruction, then the program must be faulty. Similarly, the only thing that should appear in the operand part of a memory reference instruction is the name of a user label (optionally preceded by a symbol to indicate indirect addressing). These simple syntax checks are in addition to checks made for violations of addressing limitations.

'Tokens' in the assembly language source program

The assembly process involves:

1. A first pass, in which the addresses for each instruction and data element are determined and in which the user labels are added to predefined standard data in the symbol table.
2. A second pass, in which the source code is checked for syntactic correctness and the actual object code is generated.

In pass 1, an assembler (human or program) has to recognize: directives that define the origins for sections of code; instructions; constant data elements; comments; and labels. The processing performed depends on the nature of the *token* just read. Origin directives are used to establish an initial value for the location counter. Instructions and constants can be discarded once the location counter is appropriately incremented to allow for their presence. Comments should be totally ignored, and labels put in the symbol table.

In pass 2, the same tokens must be recognized; though a somewhat finer distinction is usually necessary to discriminate memory-reference from I/O instructions. The processing is more complex in that the sequences of tokens read from the source program must be checked for compliance with allowed syntactic patterns. Subsequently, the object code can be produced by suitable combination of the various token values for the component parts of each instruction.

This analysis of tokens in the input program requires that the actual characters of the program text be grouped together and recognized as constituting particular types of token. The term *lexical analysis* is applied to the processing of characters to derive tokens.

Of course, if the text of the source program is made more regular, more restricted, then the task of token recognition is simplified. Assembly languages usually have very restricted formats devised to make processing simpler.

For example, assembly languages originally devised for computers using card input frequently define fixed fields on a card; each field is used for one particular type of token. For example, the first six columns of the card can be used for a label; columns 8-15 for an op-code and operands, and other data in all columns after column 16 to represent comments. In such a scheme, recognition of tokens relies in part on determining their position on the card. (Although fixed formats are convenient if a program is prepared on cards, they are less practical with a machine that has cassette or paper tape input. Alternative ways of distinguishing label field and instruction field are devised, like the comma used in the assembler on the simulator.)

For the most part though, the recognition of tokens depends on the use of rules that define the token types – rules such as:

1. Octal constants are composed of from 1 - 4 octal digits.
2. Octal digits are represented by the characters '0', '1', ..., '7'.

In an assembler program, the rules that define how to recognize tokens must be expressed in code and/or in data structures. These rules are used in the routine that reads the assembly language source text and returns successive tokens. This token-reading routine is called during both pass 1 and pass 2. Pass 1 is concerned mainly with the origin directive tokens and the label tokens. Pass 2 must identify all the tokens on a line, verify that the particular combination of tokens found does represent a correct pattern for an instruction, and, if all is well, generate the code.

An assembler program

An automatic assembler program requires (1) a lexical analyzer or token-recognition procedure, (2) a symbol-table building procedure, (3) a symbol-table look-up procedure, (4) syntax check routine(s) that verify whether instructions are correctly expressed, and (5) code generation routines that output the bit patterns representing instructions.

The workings of an assembler are illustrated here by examining parts of the code for 'smap', a version of the assembler incorporated in the simul8 system. The complete code for this assembler is given in Appendix B.

This assembler is a standard two-pass assembler. It initializes its symbol table by reading the predefined op-codes from a file.

The first pass

The code for this first pass is:

```
procedure pass1;
begin
     reset(source); { Get ready to read file with source code. }
     where:=0;     { Initialize origin for code/data. }
     ended:=false;  { Mark not yet at end of source text. }
     numchars:=0;
     passno:=1;
     posn:=1;
```

```
      while not (ended or error) do begin
          case nextsym of
                  comment:              skipline;
                  origin:               where:=newval;
                  labels:               insertsymbol;
                  ending:               ended:=true;
                  octal,identifier:     begin
                                        where:=where+1;
                                        skipline;
                                        end;

              null,errors:
              end { case } ;
          end { while};
  end;
```

Processing of tokens in pass 1

This 'pass1' routine depends upon a lexical analysis routine, 'nextsym', to identify the next token in the input stream. The token types recognized are: 'comment', 'origin', 'labels', 'ending', 'octal', 'identifier', 'null', and 'errors'. A 'null' token is returned at end of line. An 'errors' token is returned if the lexical analyzer has encountered a problem, for example, the character '8' in an octal number. An 'ending' token corresponds to end-of-file or terminating '$' character. A 'comment' token is returned when a '/' character is encountered. The routine 'skipline', used in processing comments, causes any data remaining on an input line to be skipped.

The tokens that require significant processing are 'origin', 'labels', 'octal', and 'identifier'. An 'origin' token requires that the assembler's location counter (in 'smap', the location counter is represented by the variable 'where') be reset to the value read ('newval'), as part of the processing of the origin token.

If either an octal constant or an identifier, for example, an instruction name, is encountered, then the value of the location counter is incremented and the rest of that input line discarded.

Symbol-table manipulations

The 'insertsymbol' routine is used to process 'labels'. The symbol table organization in 'smap' is primitive. It is suitable for small symbol tables with few initial entries and only a limited number of additions. Symbols in this table are kept in alphabetic order. New symbols are inserted in place, after all alphabetically later symbols have been moved down to make room. The code of 'insertsymbol' is as follows:

```
procedure insertsymbol;
  var sposn: integer;   { Position where symbol should go in table }
      n   : integer;
  begin
          sposn:=findposn; { Find where it should go }
          if newsym=symtab[sposn].name then { doubly defined symbol }
                              errs(dd,passno)
```

```
else begin      { Insert a new symbol in sequence }
                        n:=numsym;
                        while n>=sposn do begin
                                        symtab[n+1]:=symtab[n];
                                        n:=n-1
                                        end;
                        symtab[sposn].name:=newsym;
                        symtab[sposn].stype:=label8;
                        symtab[sposn].value:=where;
                        numsym:=numsym+1
        end;
end;
```

First, the routine 'findposn' is used to find where the symbol, defined by the label, should be inserted. The routine 'findposn' uses a simple binary search. If the symbol is already defined, then the entry at this point in the table will have the same name as the new symbol ('newsym', created by the lexical analyzer routine as it identifies an identifier or label token). This represents an error and an error report of *doubly defined symbol* is generated. Otherwise, the symbol is inserted in place, characterized as being a user label, with a value that is determined by the current value in the location counter 'where'.

The coding of the 'pass1' routine is simplified by having all the more detailed character manipulations performed in the token-returning, lexical analysis routine 'nextsym'.

The lexical analyzer 'nextsym'

The main tokens that 'nextsym' must process are:

1. 'Comments' – These can be identified if the first symbol read (other than spaces) is a '/'.
2. 'Origin' – An origin token is indicated if the first symbol read is a '*'; this should then be followed by an octal number.
3. 'Octal' – If the first symbol is an octal digit then the next token is probably an octal number, and should include all successive octal digits, and be terminated by a space or newline.
4. 'Identifier' – This is suggested whenever the first symbol read is a letter; the letter should be followed by at most five letters or digits, and should terminate with a space or newline.
5. 'Label' – If an identifier is found to be terminated by a comma, then it should be reinterpreted as a label.

The routine 'nextsym' is an example of a *finite-state-machine*-based lexical analyzer. It works in terms of *states* and *transitions between states* that are induced by, and depend on, the next character read from the source text of the assembly language program. Its scheme for dealing with the defined types of tokens is as shown in Figure 13-3.

Figure 13-3. State transitions in 'nextsym'

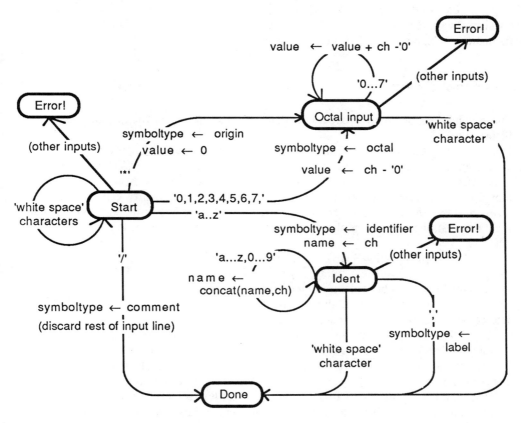

Each time it is invoked, 'nextsym' begins in its 'start' state (see Figure 13-3) reading characters from the source code of the assembly language program being processed. Leading white space characters ('space', 'tab', 'newline') are ignored; consequently, there is a loop transition which specifies that any leading white space characters be consumed without causing a state change.

If a '/' is encountered, then 'nextsym' immediately makes a transition to the 'done' state with the 'symboltype' set to 'comment'. A '*' symbol read when in the 'start' state causes the 'symboltype' to be specified as 'origin' and makes the current state 'octal input'. The 'octal input' state is also entered if an octal digit is encountered when in 'start'; in that case the 'symboltype' is 'octal' and the value of the symbol is initialized according to the character read. The 'nextsym' routine remains in 'octal input' consuming all subsequent octal digits (and updating 'value' appropriately). The 'octal input' state is successfully terminated by a white space character that causes a transition to 'done'. If any character other than white space or digit is encountered when in 'octal input' state an error has occurred; an error report is generated and 'symboltype' is set to 'errors'.

A similar analysis of 'ident', the identifier reading state, shows that it reads all alphanumeric characters building up a name. There are two valid exits from the 'ident' state. If a white space character is encountered, then an identifier is recognized. If a comma is found as the terminating character, the 'symboltype' is reset to label.

Extra detail in the code of 'nextsym', beyond that shown in the diagram, is concerned with restrictions like the limit of four digits in an octal number or the limit of six characters on a name (see listing in Appendix B).

The second pass

The second pass of 'smap' produces two output files: the object file and the assembly listing file.

An assembly listing is the document an assembly-language programmer needs as reference when checking and debugging a program. The listing starts with the symbol table: this gives the addresses of the locations used for each labeled instruction and data element in the user program (this portion of the listing is actually generated at the termination of the first pass). The main part of the listing shows the address of each location used, the contents of that location, and the source statement that yielded these data.

The information provided through this listing (1) helps the programmer determine where to set breakpoints, (2) assists in the examination of 'dumps' (octal or hexadecimal printouts of contents of memory) when overwritten code must be found, and (3) provides the addresses of data elements, which may be needed when using an interactive debugger to inspect particular locations.

The object file contains the code that 'smap' generates for running on the simulator. A generated object file has data printed in octal (rather than economically represented as binary data); this output is meant to be readable by humans as well as by the computer. Most addresses are represented implicitly, and as each datum in the file is printed on a line by itself, the first character on that line is used to distinguish between location address data (a leading '*') and location contents data (a leading space character). (The end of the object code is marked by a '$' character.) An example of part of an object file is:

```
*0200
 7200
 1214
 3215
 3216
   .
   .
   .
*1000
 0123
 0001
$
```

A copy of the symbol table is appended to the code in these object files. Such data are often provided with an object file so that symbolic debugging techniques can be used. If the symbol table is present, an interactive debugging program can allow reference to named variables. On the simulator, the symbol-table data are also required, at run time, to allow the display of the instruction register to show the (disassembled) source form of the instruction. Most computer systems provide special loaders and debuggers capable of dealing with a symbol table as well as loading code.

The syntax-checking and code generation loop

The code for the main loop in the second pass in 'smap' is as follows:

```
while not (ended or error) do begin
            printval:=0;
            case xnextsym of
                    xcomment: begin tab(20);
                                        dumpline;
                                        skipline; { skip over comments }
                            end;
                    xorigin: begin
                                    { want to output equivalent of an }
                                    { origin directive for the loader }
                                    write(object,'*');
                                    octwrite(newval,4,object);
                                    writeln(object);
                                    where:=newval;
                                    tab(20);
                                    dumpline;
                                    if xnextsym <> xnull then errs(sx,passno)
                            end;
                    xoctal,xvariable: begin
                                    { just copy octal constants to output }
                                    writecode(newval,xnextsym)
                            end;
                    xmriopcode: memrefs;
                    xiotopcode: iots;
                    xopropcode: operate;
                    xending: ended:=true;
                    xnull,xerrors,xlab8: { do nothing }
                    end
    end;
```

The main loop involves processing tokens, read from the assembly language source code, until either an error is detected or all data are consumed. Routine 'xnextsym' is a token-returning one and is merely a slight elaboration of 'nextsym'. Rather than return the token 'identifier', 'xnextsym' distinguishes among variables, memory reference instructions, I/O instruction, indirect symbol, and operate instruction. Routine 'xnextsym' calls 'nextsym' to perform the basic token analysis. If an 'identifier' token is returned, by 'nextsym', it is looked up in the symbol table and its type is determined; this type then defines the token type returned by 'xnetsym'.

The token returned by 'xnextsym' is used in a case statement to select an appropriate processing routine. Given the simple nature of this assembly language, *ad hoc* methods are used for organizing the processing of the different token types.

If a 'comment' is returned then the appropriate processing routine is 'dumpline', a routine that copies the comment from the input source file to the listing file being generated. An 'origin' token requires (1) that an address record be output to the object file, (2) that the location counter, 'where', be reset so that the appropriate addresses are printed in the listing file, and (3) that the origin directive is echoed to the listing file. There should be no other data on a line with an 'origin', hence a check that the token following the 'origin' is 'null'. 'Octal' or 'variable' tokens, as the sole data elements on a line, should represent numerical or address constants. For these the processing is simple; their values are sent to the object file and the input line echoed to the listing file. (An octal constant defines its own value, while the values of identifiers correspond to their address values recorded in the symbol table.) The processing of labels having been completed in pass 1, can be ignored during pass 2.

Slightly more elaborate processing is required when instructions are found. Since each instruction type has a unique syntax, three special purpose routines are used. These routines check for valid sequences of tokens. For example, in a memory reference instruction, two sequences are valid:

```
xmriopcode    xvariable
xmriopcode    xindirect    xvariable
```

The 'memrefs' procedure checks that the sequence of tokens is correct and generates the appropriate bit pattern for the instruction. This bit pattern is assembled from the value for the op-code, the value for the indirect bit if needed, and the page bit, plus 7 location-on-page bits. Checks for illegal memory references are made during the encoding of these address bits.

Exercises

1. Examine the 'exercise1' example program given in Chapter 5. This program could be assembled in a single pass. Identify the characteristic of this program that makes a one pass assembly possible.

2. Implement a simple model loader for the simulated machine. The loader is to be implemented as a standard program starting at 0200, and reading characters from the keyboard. The low order 6 bits of each character should represent binary data to be processed. The loader is to read (location address, location content) pairs and should construct the appropriate instruction sequence in the correct memory locations. (Each such pair will be represented by four characters of keyboard input.) The end of data is to be marked by some suitably chosen terminating character. Test the program on data chosen to represent the object code for a four or five instruction program located at 0400. (There are limitations on the characters that can be read from the Macintosh keyboard; for example, it is not possible to type in an ASCII 'null' character (0000000). Instead, it is necessary to type in '@' for 000000, A for '0000001', 'B' for 000010, ... etc.; note that it will not be possible to enter data representing 111111.)

The following exercises require the use of a Pascal compiler/interpreter, and presume that a standard data structures course has been/is being studied.

3. Investigate the relative efficiency of two or three different symbol table organizations. Write a Pascal program that reads a file containing a large number of 'names', that is short alphanumeric strings, and keeps a 'symbol table' into which each new name is entered when first encountered. The names are to be printed as they are read; a tag character is also to be printed with each name. This tag character should indicate whether that name was new to the symbol table or whether it was a repeat of a previous entry. (Each name should contain at most six characters; names should be separated by 'white space' characters. The input data should be in random order, with each distinct name being repeated many times.)

    The different symbol table organizations used could include the following:

    a) An unordered array or list of names; a linear look-up algorithm being used to check for a name just read; new names being placed at the end of the list or array.

    b) An ordered array; with a binary search algorithm to find an existing name or place to insert a name; insertion in order with existing data being moved.

    c) A scheme employing a hashing technique.

    d) A scheme using a tree structure.

    Compare the processing times of the different schemes that you implement on several sets of input data. The first two data sets should contain some 60 data elements: (i) five distinct names repeated about 12 times each, and (ii) 30 names, each repeated a couple of times. Other data sets used to test the algorithms should be much larger. Try to determine empirically a limit to the size of the data sets for which the simpler methods, (a) and (b), are adequate.

4. Take the code of the assembler, listed in Appendix B, and recode and simplify the 'nextsym' routine. (You could consider classifying each input character into one of a defined set of types, for example, 'letter', 'octdig', 'star', ..., 'other', and then using 'case' statements, rather than 'if...then...else if...then else...', for selecting an appropriate processing routine.)

5. It is not essential to use two passes in an assembler. Some assemblers work with a single pass. In these one-pass systems, the code for most instructions is generated as they are read. The addresses of all known variables and other program labels can be simply filled in. Special processing is only required for *forward references*, that is, for references to variables and labeled-instructions that have not yet been encountered. Then a one-pass assembler makes a note of the place where, in the generated object code, an address is still to be inserted. When the appropriate label is finally processed, and the address for the corresponding location is determined, the assembler goes back through the previously generated code filling in omitted addresses.

    Write a 'one-pass assembler' capable of processing the same input assembly language, and producing the same object file output, as the example assembler.

14

Assemblers and loaders II

Most students go on to do some programming using assembly language on systems that are more elaborate than the simul8 model. The assemblers and loaders for these systems incorporate features not present on simul8:

1. The assembler program will be somewhat more powerful. It will have more directives for controlling how code and data are organized. It will have additional facilities that can simplify the declaration of constants, for example, messages might be defined as text strings in the assembly language source program. It may have some facility for *conditional assembly* .

2. The overall program development system may include a *macro-preprocessor* in addition to the normal assembler program. 'Macros' can simplify the task of the assembler programmer by providing a short-cut method for specifying frequently employed, standardized fragments of code. A macro-preprocessor (which may be a distinct program, or which may form an extra preliminary pass in an assembler) can expand macros to the appropriate full sequence of instructions in the standard assembly language.

3. Large programs are normally composed of many separately assembled parts. These separate parts have to be threaded, joined, or *linked* together in some final *linking-loading* step. Separate assembly requires that the assembler program be extended to allow for references to variables, subroutine entry-points, and so forth that are not defined in the particular source code file (or *module*) being processed (otherwise, such references result in 'undefined label' errors). Further, the object file/module produced by the assembler has a more elaborate structure. As well as data defining the bit patterns of instructions, the object module will include information that identifies where gaps remain; these gaps are filled in with address data when the relevant addresses are known. (As well as dealing with separately assembled user modules, a linking program must also permit the use of libraries of object code for standard subroutines and functions.)

4. It is atypical for the applications programmer to know where in memory a program is located on any computer with an operating system that runs multiple tasks. The addresses occupied by a program are instead determined by the operating system when that program is loaded. On successive runs, a program may be located in different

parts of memory. To achieve this flexibility, the assembly language code must be written with all addresses implicitly defined relative to some arbitrary starting address (usually 0). Of course, many instructions do not require address data; in others the address may be already relative (e.g. 'branch back 20 bytes'); in yet other cases (as in a reference to a 'location on current page') the 'address' (given as part of an instruction) is not absolute, that is, not an actual address value. But there are going to be address constants; and, the correct values for these constants are not known until the program is loaded. Then, the values in these address constants will be adjusted or *relocated*. The CPU may provide some hardware support that simplifies relocation, but if there is no such hardware relocation, then addresses are adjusted by the loader once the start address for the program has been decided. The object modules must contain additional relocation information that identifies those address values embedded in the object code that require adjustment.

Additional features of typical assemblers

All assembly languages have the same basic structure of separate instruction lines with fields for a label, an instruction op-code, operands, and comments. Minor details differ; tabs or spaces may separate a label from an op-code (instead of the comma as on simul8); asterisks may introduce comments (instead of the '/' character). The operand fields are inevitably more complex than those in simul8 because, on more elaborate machines, it is necessary to identify the registers used in instructions, the addressing modes used for accessing data, and so forth.

More instruction formats are possible. Instead of the three or four in simul8 (direct and indirect memory reference, I/O, and operate) there may be a dozen formats. Some instructions require no operands; others require a single operand, two operands, or more. On the DEC VAX computers there are even instructions that require five or six different operands. The syntax of the assembly language becomes more complex to accomodate the various different instruction formats.

Some other features common to assembler programs are summarized below.

Numbers in different bases

Most assemblers allow numeric data to be specified in decimal, octal, or hexadecimal (and, maybe, even binary). Further, signed numbers may be permitted (at least, signed decimal data). Common conventions are that octal numbers begin with a leading zero and hexadecimal numbers have a leading '$' character.

Additional directives

The common repertoire of assembler directives includes:

Directive name	Alternative name
extern	
entry	
align	
define constant	(data)
define storage	(reserve)
equate	(define)
origin	

The *extern* and *entry* directives are used to identify variables and subroutine entry-points that need to be known in the linking-loading steps. These directives are discussed later in the section on the linking and loading of relocatable code.

Align directives may be necessary on machines where there are restrictions on the addresses of data elements and/or instructions. Most machines address individual bytes (rather than 2-byte or 4-byte words). However, there are frequently restrictions on the addresses used in instructions. For example, a load of a 2-byte integer may require that the integer be located beginning at a byte address divisible by two; similarly, 8-byte floating point numbers may be required to start at a byte address divisible by eight. Since data elements can occupy variously single bytes, 2-byte words, long-words, and so on, it is quite easy for a particular data element, defined among many others, to have the wrong *alignment*. For example, a 17-byte text string followed in the assembly language source by an 8-byte floating-point number would not yield the correct alignment for that number. In such a situation, the assembler should leave a few unused bytes and thereby arrange that the address assigned to the number is indeed divisible by eight. Many assembler programs need assistance in recognizing such restrictions on the location of data. An align directive, just before a constant or storage declaration, identifies any necessary restrictions. For example, the directive 'align 8' instructs the assembler to leave some number of unused bytes so that the next constant/variable is located at an address divisible by eight. (Sometimes, there are analogous restrictions on where instructions may be located; then there will be another directive, similar to align, that places some number of 'nop' instructions to satisfy any restriction on the address on the next instruction.)

Origin directives are as illustrated for simul8.

Equate directives are similar to 'const' declarations in a Pascal program. It is not good programming practice to represent limits for loop counts, test values, and so forth, as numeric constants hidden away in the middle of the code. Instead, such control values should be given symbolic names, and the correspondence of names and values defined at the start of the program. For example, a program might start with equate directives like 'newl equ 015', 'linlen equ 80' (the '=' symbol may be used instead of equ) that define the 'newline' value to be octal 15 and a 'line length' to be 80. A subsequent change so that the program could work on a different terminal, with some other line length and newline code, requires just alteration of the equate directives rather than a search through the code to find particular numeric values.

Define storage directives provide a generalization of the simple 'name,0' variable declarations of simul8. Define storage directives specify the number of bytes, words, or long-words that are to be reserved for a variable. Such directives also serve to define a variable in the assembler's symbol table (with a value equal to the start address of the area of storage reserved). Typical define storage directives might be:

counts	ds.l	128	an array of 128 long integers
sum	ds.w	1	a short integer for a checksum
inline	ds.b	80	an 80-byte input buffer

(The variants 'ds.b', 'ds.w', and 'ds.l' specify whether storage is being reserved in units of bytes, words, or long-words.)

Define constant directives generalize on simul8's 'cname,cval' statements. Like define storage directives, define constant directives can work in units of bytes, words, or long-words. Typical define constant directives might be:

scale	dc.l	12877649	a long integer constant
es	dc.w	1,4,5,6,7,8	a table of short integer constants
offset	dc.w	buf0-buf1	a constant representing an address offset
msg	dc.b	'Hello world',0	a message

As illustrated here, many assemblers can perform simple arithmetic operations when determining values for constants.

Conditional assembly

Conditional assembly facilities allow parts of programs to be included, or omitted, in accord with conditions that can be tested at assemble time. Typically, there are a couple of directives (commonly, these are 'if' and 'endif') which bracket any code to be conditionally assembled:

```
if  <cond>
        .
        conditionally assembled code
        .
endif
```

The '<cond>' facility specifies a simple test, usually a test on the value of a symbol defined by an earlier equate directive.

Conditional assembly can be used to include debugging code in trial versions of a program; when the program appears to work, the debugging code can be eliminated by simply changing the value in an equate directive.

The other common use of conditional assembly is to help deal with situations where several variants of an application program are developed for slightly different hardware configurations. Most of the code in these variants is common, with just minor changes in particular instruction sequences. It is undesirable to have to maintain several separate copies of the application source; instead, a single copy can contain the common code together with a number of conditionally assembled fragments that define the special-case code for the different hardware configurations. Then, after some update of the common code, new object modules can be generated for each hardware system by simply redefining an equate value and reassembling the code.

Macros

Sometimes, a program requires the same sequence of instructions at many different points. These instructions sequences may be identical, or they may differ in that the same instruction sequence is used, but reference is made to different variables. Such patterns of frequent use of similar instruction sequences usually reflect a deficiency in the instruction repertoire used. For example, the IBM-370 instruction set is not ideal for code generated for a recursive stack-based language. Since the 370 doesn't make direct provision for references to stacks, standard sequences of two or three instructions must be used whenever a stack reference is desired.

The simul8 machine is another example of a machine with a deficient instruction set. Thus, every reference to an array requires a standard sequence of five instructions namely 'cla', 'tad <base address>', 'tad <index value>', 'dca <pointer>', 'tad i <pointer>'.

It is tedious for the programmer to repeatedly encode such standard sequences (and such repetitive coding can become a source of errors). Macros provide a way of avoiding the need for the programmer to spell out an instruction sequence every time it is needed.

There are two steps to using macros. First, the standard instruction sequences must be defined and named. Second, *macro calls* should be used at all points in the source code of an assembly language program where these standard instruction sequences are required.

As illustrated in Figure 14-1, a macro-preprocessor takes the definitions of the macros, and the source text of a program with macro calls, and produces an output file in which the calls are expanded to the required instruction sequences. Macro definitions may be unique to a particular program, in which case they normally come at the start of the source text of that program. But, often, the same macros are needed in many different programs. A standard set of macros, defining array accessing, an 'or' instruction, and so forth, is obviously of value for all programs being prepared for simul8. Standard macros can be held in separate files which are read by the macro-preprocessor before the source text of the program containing macro calls.

The definitions of standard instruction sequences for a macro can accommodate *parameters*. For example, the sequence of instructions for simul8's array reference needs as parameters, (1) the name of an address constant that holds the base address of the array, (2) the name of a variable with the index value, and (3) the name of a temporary pointer variable. In the definition, the places where variable names are required are occupied by formal tokens. The actual variable names are specified in the macro call.

Figure 14-1. Inputs to and output from a macro-preprocessor

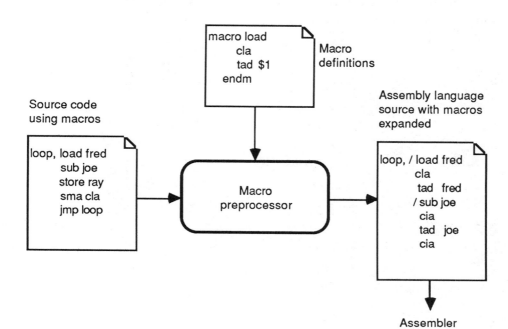

Some example macro definitions that would be useful on simul8 are shown in Table 14-1. The exact format of a macro definition depends on the macro-preprocessor being used but these examples are typical. The tokens 'macro' and 'endm' delimit the macro definition; the 'macro' token is followed (or preceded) by a name for the instruction sequence. In the body of the macro, the various parameters are designated by tokens like the $i 's of these examples.

The following example code illustrates calls to these macros. In the macro call, the macro name is specified and followed by an ordered list of arguments to be substituted for the formal $i 's in its definition. Thus, in the call to the macro 'array' shown below, 'buffb' is to be substituted for $1, 'incntr' for $2, and 'ptr1' for $3.

```
/ get next character from buffer b
        array       buffb,incntr,ptr1
        store       nchar
/ if same as last then increment duplicate count
        sub         ochar
        sna cla
        isz         dupls
/ now take new character and ...
        load        nchar
```

Table 14-1.   Examples of macros that would be useful if available on the simul8 system

```
/ macro definition of a load instruction
macro    load
         cla
         tad $1
endm
/ macro definition of a store instruction
macro    store
         dca $1
         tad $1
endm
/ macro definition of a subtract instruction, (acc-data)
macro    sub
         cia
         tad $1
         cia
endm
/ macro definition of an array access,
macro    array
         cla
         tad $1
         tad $2
         dca $3
         tad i $3
endm
```

The processing performed by the macro-preprocessor is really no more than sophisticated editing. Input source text that does not involve any macros is simply copied to the output. Where macro calls occur, the macro calls themselves are copied to the ouptut as comments and are followed by the appropriate instruction sequence with the actual parameters substituted for the formal parameters of the definitions.

The output produced for the example would be:

Input	Output with macros expanded
/ get next character from buffer b	/ get next character from ..
array buffb,incntr,ptr1	/ array buffb,incntr,ptr1
	cla
	tad buffb
	tad incntr
	dca ptr1
	tad i ptr1
store nchar	/ store nchar
	dca nchar
	tad nchar

Input	Output with macros expanded
/ if same as last then increment duplicate count	/ if same as last then ...
sub ochar	/ sub ochar
	cia
	tad ochar
	cia
sna cla	sna cla
isz dupls	isz dupls

Sophisticated macro-preprocessors include many more capabilities than those suggested by these examples. Thus, macros may invoke other macros; or, macros may be needed to define special loops, in which case a label will be needed in the macro body, but, each different call of the macro will, of course, require a different label name. A good macro preprocessor is capable of generating unique label names as required.

Although macros are generally helpful they do have some disadvantages. If the macro-preprocessor is separate from the assembler, then an extra program preparation step is required. Further, any error messages from the assembler will include references to lines in the macro expanded code, and it is not always easy to trace these errors back to lines in the original source.

The generation, linking and loading of relocatable object code

It is unwise, and usually impractical, to try to develop an applications program as a monolithic entity. The various subroutines and functions required for an application are best grouped, according to role, into separate modules. The source of each module should be kept in a separate file that can then be edited, compiled, and assembled individually. The assemblers and loaders on a computer must possess the capability of processing and combining separate modules.

A requirement for separate assembly introduces a number of new problems. Within any individual module there will inevitably be references to subroutines and variables that are defined in other modules. The addresses of these variables will not be known. Inherently, the assembly process must be incomplete; the object modules generated will have 'gaps' where address data must be filled in during the subsequent linking-loading steps.

It is possible, in fact probable, that none of the addresses will be known! Then, a gap is left wherever an absolute address is required in the object code. Even if the origin address for the main program was known, the origins for the code in other separately assembled modules would not be known. The main module (comprising the main program, some subroutines, and some variables) occupies an unknown number of memory locations. It is only when the main module is assembled that the lowest address for the origin of the code in the second of a set of modules is found. It would be extremely inconvenient if an assembler required the separate modules to be processed in sequence, with address data derived from one assembly hand edited into the next module to be assembled.

An assembler that works with separately assembled source modules needs additional data in each source module; these additional data define how a particular module relates to the other modules of a complete program.

The assembler generates, as illustrated in Figure 14-2, an object module containing two distinct types of data. The object module first contains the bit patterns for the instructions and constants (as already noted, this part of the object file has gaps where addresses are to go). The second type of data in the object module comprises information needed when the missing addresses are determined and are to be filled into these gaps. These *relocation data* include (1) a form of map, identifying each point in the code where an address must be inserted (and specifying which variable's address is to be inserted), (2) information defining the names (and positions relative to the start of the module) of variables whose existence and addresses are to be known by other modules, and (3) names of those variables whose definitions should occur in other modules but which are referenced in this module (together with details of where in the code such references are made).

The assembler directives 'extern' and 'entry' are used to define the interfaces between modules. (These directives usually appear at the start of the source code in the module, following any equate directives.)

The 'extern' directive names those *external* variables, subroutine entry points, constants, and so forth that are referenced, but not declared, in the module. The assembler adds these names to its symbol table marking them as being external. Subsequent references to these names are accepted even though their address values are not known. All external variables are accorded special processing when the relocation data of the object file are produced.

Figure 14-2.   A relocatable object module with code and relocation data

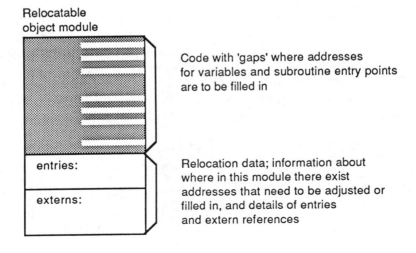

Relocatable
object module

Code with 'gaps' where addresses
for variables and subroutine entry points
are to be filled in

entries:

externs:

Relocation data; information about
where in this module there exist
addresses that need to be adjusted or
filled in, and details of entries
and extern references

The 'entry' directive names variables and subroutines that are defined in the current module and which will be referenced in other modules. More data have to be passed to the linking loaders for those variables declared as entries than for other purely local variables. The 'entry' directive tells the assembler which variables require this special processing in the final stages of the generation of the object file.

Following its initial processing of 'entry' and 'extern' directives, the assembler continues with essentially the normal two-pass processing. There are changes because, if origins are not defined, all addresses determined in the first pass are specified relative to the start of the module.

The example modules in Figure 14-3 illustrate the processes. The example program is presumed to comprise at least three modules, with the main module and one of the other modules being shown. The main module's 'entry' directive identifies a subroutine 'sub1' and a couple of variables, 'alpha' and 'count', that are declared in this module and which are referenced elsewhere. The two subroutines, 'sub2' and 'sub3', are declared as 'extern' as shown (several 'entry' and 'extern' directives may occur in the same module). The main module contains some local variables, for example, 'beta', as well as those named in the 'entry' directive. The first pass of the assembly process deals with the 'entry' and 'extern' directives, and defines the addresses for the local variables. These addresses are defined relative to the start of the module. These details are summarized in Figure 14-4. Correspondingly, in the sub2 module, 'sub2' is identified as an 'entry', 'sub1' and 'alpha' are 'extern's, and again there are some local variables. The 'jsr' subroutine call instructions in the modules illustrate actual references to externals, as does the 'move...alpha' instruction in 'sub2'.

Figure 14-3.   **Example modules for the discussion of the handling of 'extern' and 'entry'
directives and for the description of the linking-loading process**

Main module

```
enough equ 1000

entry sub1, alpha,
count
     .
extern sub2, sub3
     .
* 68000 program to ...
main  move.l beta,sp
     .
     jsr sub2
     .
sub1
     .
beta .
alpha .
```

Sub2 module

```
entry sub2
extern sub1, alpha
* 68000 subprogram to ...
sub2  clr.b d1
      moveq #7,d3
     .
     .
     jsr sub1
     .
     move.l d0,alpha
     .
     rts
temp1 ds.l 1
```

Figure 14-4. The first pass of the assembly process for a relocatable module

Main module

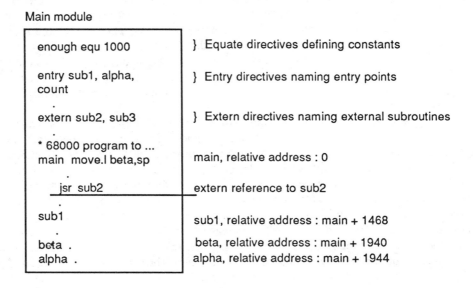

enough equ 1000	} Equate directives defining constants
entry sub1, alpha, count	} Entry directives naming entry points
.	
extern sub2, sub3	} Extern directives naming external subroutines
.	
* 68000 program to ... main move.l beta,sp	main, relative address : 0
. jsr sub2	extern reference to sub2
.	
sub1	sub1, relative address : main + 1468
.	
beta .	beta, relative address : main + 1940
alpha .	alpha, relative address : main + 1944

After the 'extern' and 'entry' directives have been processed, the first pass of the assembly is completed and relative addresses are assigned to all labels defined in the module.

The code for the corresponding object module and the relocation data are generated in the next pass. There are many different methods for recording relocation data. Figure 14-5 suggests a rather over-simplified approach, but one that will serve to illustrate the principles. On completion of the second pass of the assembler, an object module is generated. The code will have gaps for addresses. Relocation data identifies where addresses need to be entered or changed, where entries are located, and where externals are referenced. These relocation data are held in tables appended to the object code.

The correct values for the absolute addresses of locally defined variables are not known; only their offsets relative to the start of the module are known. When a starting address for the module is decided, for example, 'main' to be located at 20000, then the correct absolute addresses for all locals can be determined by adding their known offsets to this start address. (So, 'beta' becomes 21940, 'sub1' becomes '21468', and so forth.) Meantime, the assembler provides the relative offset of each local variable, and a list of those locations in the code where it is referenced. Once a variable's address is known, then this value is placed into those locations in the correct form for all absolute addresses used in either instructions or address constants. (Details of the names of local variables need not be kept in the object module; however, such data are often preserved because they can be of value when debugging programs.)

The names, and relative offsets within the module, of all entry variables must be recorded in an appropriate table. The names in this table are checked when 'extern' references in other modules are being processed.

Figure 14-5. The second pass of the assembly process for a relocatable module

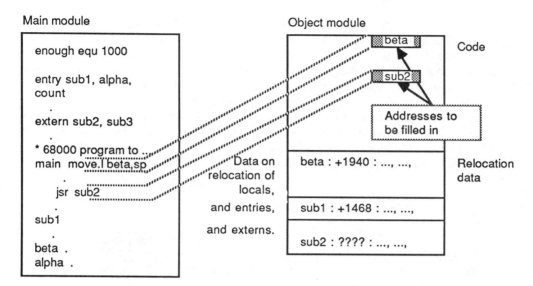

The names of any 'extern's referenced in the module are listed in another table in the relocation data, together with details of where in the module's code the addresses of these externals should eventually be inserted.

The work of combining the separately assembled modules is performed by the *linker* part of a *linking-loader*. The determination of final addresses and all the necessary relocations of variables are done by the *loader* part. The linker and loader are sometimes organized as separate programs, but it is simplest to envisage a single program combining these tasks.

As shown in Figure 14-6, the linking-loader takes as inputs the starting address in memory for the complete program, the constituent relocatable object modules, and, optionally, one or more libraries of standard subroutines. (Almost all programs will require the library with the standard I/O formatting subroutines. Maths routines, graphics routines etc., are usually kept in separate specialized libraries which are scanned only on request.)

The example linking-loader starts by placing the code for 'main' and other subroutines from the main module into memory beginning at the given starting address. The relocation data for the locals and entries in this module are used, together with the known starting address, to fill in addresses. The final address used by this module, for example, 21947, establishes the start address (21948) for the next module loaded. When the 'sub2' module is loaded into memory, the address of 'sub2' is known and therefore now used to resolve the outstanding external references left in the main module. References in 'sub2' to 'sub1' and 'alpha' are resolved against the entry table, now containing actual addresses. (A real linking-loader might require more than one pass through the various object modules in order to resolve all the 'extern's and 'entry's, and would typically first produce an image of the final code on a disk file and only copy this into memory in a later step.)

Any 'extern' directives that cannot be resolved by an 'entry' from the various input relocatable object modules are assumed to refer to routines in the libraries. Once all relocatable modules have been processed, the linking-loader scans the libraries and attempts to find routines that resolve the outstanding 'extern' directives with a suitable 'entry'. The example in Figure 14-6 shows a 'sort' routine taken from the library, presumably to resolve an 'extern' reference in either the main module or the sub2 module. It is only when all libraries have been scanned that any missing routines can be identified. If the example program did actually reference 'sub3' (declared as being an 'extern' in the main module), then this reference is eventually reported as an error, because this routine is apparently neither in the relocatable modules provided, nor in the library.

Figure 14-6. The linking and loading process

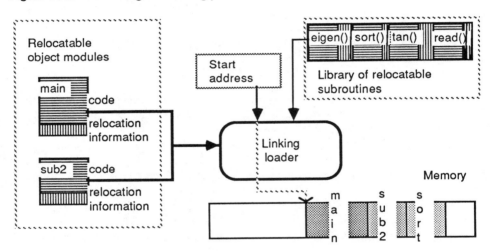

15

High-level languages

As programming languages have evolved, differing patterns of memory usage and access have appeared. Machine designers have exploited analyses of how existing machines execute programs to identify possible new machine architectures that might prove more effective. Before proceeding with a review of extensions to simul8's simple architecture, it is appropriate to consider, briefly, some of the requirements of compiled high-level languages. The following two subsections review the requirements of FORTRAN and the languages in the ALGOL family. FORTRAN is undemanding; its needs can be satisfied by a machine architecture little more elaborate than that of the simul8 model. (Of course, a FORTRAN compiler can exploit all the power of a more sophisticated architecture.) The ALGOL languages are less readily satisfied. The use by these languages of stack-based schemes for procedure invocation and memory allocation has had a profound influence on machine design.

FORTRAN

The FORTRAN language was originally designed around 1956. An extended version of the language was standardized by 1966. A subsequent standard, in 1977, extended the allowed data types and provided a new set of control structures. The 1977 control structures, for example, the 'BLOCK IF' (i.e. IF...THEN...ELSE...ENDIF) construct, are the major advantage of this revision. The older style FORTRAN control structures could easily be misused, resulting in the introduction of errors (these older style controls, such as the 'assigned GOTO' and the 'arithmetic IF', were preserved to allow program compatibility).

The FORTRAN language is limited. Its data types are just real and integer numbers (with some use of character data in later variants). Its data structures are restricted to arrays. Its programming constructs focus on iterative calculations. FORTRAN does not allow for recursive subroutines or functions. The standard does not provide for any dynamic storage management facilities, as are required for the 'new()' and 'free()' record allocation primitives of Pascal. Although these restrictions limit the types of algorithm that can be expressed in the language, FORTRAN can be very effective for calculations such as matrix multiplication and inversion, and eigenvalue determination. Such computations require, simply, efficient access to static array structures, and deeply nested iterative loops. Variants of FORTRAN have dominated scientific and engineering data processing for some 30 years.

The simul8 machine represents a scaled down version of the scientific computers that were built in the early days of FORTRAN's dominance of scientific data processing. A FORTRAN machine can be created by scaling simul8 back up to size. A recipe for a primitive FORTRAN machine could be as follows:

1. Take the simul8 machine.
2. Extend the word length to, at least, 24 bits; provide 64K words of 24-bit memory (16-bit address space).
3. Provide (a) a 16-bit program counter, (b) a 24-bit instruction register, (c) a 24-bit integer accumulator, (d) at least one other 24-bit integer register (that can be used as an index register), and (e) a 48-bit 'floating-point accumulator'.
4. Allocate a few extra bits to the op-code, permitting more instructions, for example, integer load/store/subtract, and also a set of floating-point load, add, subtract, multiply, divide, and store instructions.
5. Abolish the paged-mode addressing (which exists on simul8 to economize on address bits in an instruction); provide both direct/indirect addressing (as in simul8) and an indexed addressing mode.

As illustrated in Figure 15-1, the memory of such a computer would be shared between a simple operating system and the user's compiled FORTRAN program. The operating system handles the low-level aspects of I/O (i.e. the device-handling and data buffering). The user's program comprises both the compiled user code, and a set of run-time support routines taken from library files and linked in.

The run-time support routines include all the special mathematical functions, format interpretation routines, and I/O number conversion routines. The I/O support routines call on the underlying operating system routines to perform the actual I/O data transfers (on the earliest of systems, there was no separate operating system; instead, the run-time routines were extended to include the lowest level of I/O handling).

The restrictions of the FORTRAN language permit the compiler writer to generate assembly-language code with a simple structure, just like all the example simul8 programs. Since there is no recursion and no facilities for dynamic record structure allocation, and since array sizes must be determined at compilation time, it is possible to allocate statically all the space required for data structures. Memory locations can be reserved (by 'define storage' and 'define constant' directives in the assembly language produced by the compiler). These locations can then be allocated at linking-load time. In the code, these static variables can be referenced using their absolute addresses. (The FORTRAN language definition does not require such a static allocation; the compiler writer can choose to employ more elaborate schemes; the 1977 standard favors implementations similar to those discussed later for the ALGOL languages.)

FORTRAN's subroutines and functions can be compiled separately. Each subroutine compiles to a sequence of assembly-language instructions, and storage-allocation directives for both the explicitly and implicitly defined local variables of that routine. FORTRAN has a mechanism, the 'DATA' statement, for initializing local

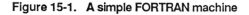

Figure 15-1.   A simple FORTRAN machine

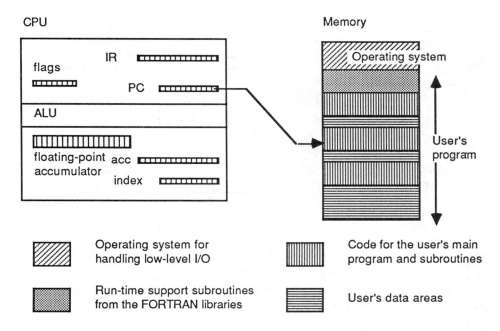

variables. When compiled, a 'DATA' statement results in the initial values being specifed in the 'define storage' directives for the corresponding variables. Then, when the program is loaded, the initial values are placed into the storage locations allocated to the variables.

FORTRAN allows for shared data areas through its 'COMMON' and 'COMMON/<blockname>/' constructs. References to 'COMMON' variables are treated in a manner somewhat analogous to 'extern' directives. Allocation of addresses to 'COMMON' variables is postponed until all modules have been processed and the sizes of the various common areas are known. FORTRAN allows for aliasing; the same 'COMMON' variables may be accorded different names in different subroutines. Consequently, the references to 'external' 'COMMON' variables work in terms of the name of the 'COMMON' area, and relative location within that area, rather than in terms of the variable names themselves.

If the object code modules for the main program, subroutines, and functions are linked together, without any further rearrangements of code and data areas, then a program's organization in memory is as shown in Figure 15-2. Each section of code is followed by its local constants and variables; 'COMMON' variables are grouped together after the last of the subroutines. (This diagram illustrates how the program was actually organized by early FORTRAN systems; modern compilers tend to separate all variables from code, combining the space for the locals of the various routines and the space for all 'COMMON' areas into a single large data area.)

FORTRAN passes arguments to subroutines by reference; that is, it passes the addresses where each argument can be found. The subroutine saves the various addresses in

Figure 15-2. Organization of a FORTRAN program in a computer's memory

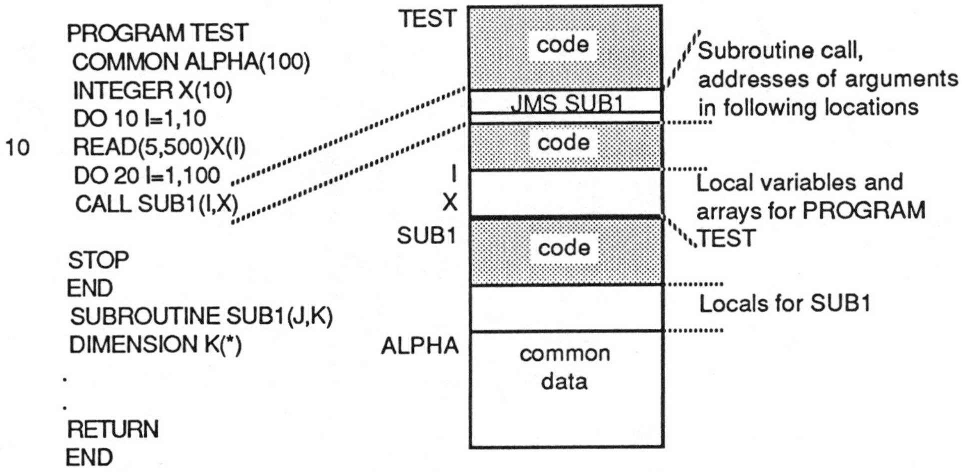

```
                                    TEST  ┌───────────────┐
       PROGRAM TEST                       │░░░░░░░░░░░░░░░│        Subroutine call,
       COMMON ALPHA(100)                  │░░░░  code  ░░░│        addresses of arguments
       INTEGER X(10)                      ├───────────────┤        in following locations
       DO 10 I=1,10                       │   JMS SUB1    │
  10   READ(5,500)X(I)                    │░░░░  code  ░░░│
       DO 20 I=1,100                      ├───────────────┤        Local variables and
       CALL SUB1(I,X)                I    │               │        arrays for PROGRAM
                                     X    ├───────────────┤        TEST
       STOP                        SUB1   │░░░░  code  ░░░│
       END                                ├───────────────┤
       SUBROUTINE SUB1(J,K)               │               │        Locals for SUB1
       DIMENSION K(*)              ALPHA  ├───────────────┤
          .                               │    common     │
          .                               │     data      │
                                          └───────────────┘
       RETURN
       END
```

address pointers (possibly in memory, but in CPU registers if these are available), and accesses data indirectly via these pointers. (The 'dummy arguments' named in the subroutine statement serve as the pointers.) Results can similarly be written back using indirect addressing via pointers.

If possible, the addresses of the arguments are held in CPU registers when a subroutine is called. In other cases, the subroutine is passed a pointer to a table in memory which holds the addresses of its arguments. A commonly used technique was to hold the addresses of the arguments in the locations immediately following the subroutine call instruction, the return address of the subroutine serving as a pointer to this 'table' of argument addresses. (This same technique was noted in relation to subroutine calls on simul8.) Figure 15-2 illustrates the approach; the two locations following the subroutine call hold the address of the index variable 'I' and the address of the start of the array 'X'. Often, as in this case, the addresses for the arguments are constants; the values are filled in during the linking-loading steps once static addresses are assigned to these variables. However, not all addresses passed as arguments are constant. A call like 'COS(A(J))', made from within a loop that changes 'J', involves a different element of the array 'A', and therefore a different address, on each invocation. The program has to include code, within the loop, to compute the appropriate address and then store this computed address in the location following the function call. It is this need to store values into the code portion of a program that represents the major disadvantage of schemes for passing arguments in the locations following a subroutine call. Factors such as improved error control and sharability all confer advantage on systems where code is effectively *read only*. It is safer if any table of argument addresses is built in a separate data area, rather than in the locations following the call instruction.

FORTRAN code, as compiled for arithmetic expressions, provides for effective register usage; the number of loads and stores of data from memory are minimal. The compiler allocates extra (anonymous) locations in the data area associated with each subroutine if temporary data values have to be saved from the CPU registers. For example, a compiler for a machine with a single floating-point CPU register converts the FORTRAN code 'RES=(U+V)*(T+(W+X)/(Y+Z))' into a sequence of instructions like 'FLOAD U', 'FADD V', 'FSTORE TEMP1', 'FLOAD Y', 'FADD Z', 'FSTORE TEMP2', 'FLOAD W', 'FADD X', 'FDIV TEMP2', 'FADD T', 'FMPY TEMP1', 'FSTORE RES'. (The 'FLOAD's, 'FSTORE's, etc. are the instructions for loading and storing data from the floating-point accumulator; on a 24-bit word machine, these instructions manipulate the contents of 48-bit 'double words' . The floating-point number for 'V' is held in the location labeled 'V', and the immediately following location. Addressing can be assumed to be absolute; the static addresses of the data values are specified in the instructions.) Here, the compiler has to invent a few extra temporary variables which are added to the locals for the subroutine.

The machine requirements of FORTRAN are met simply. The lack of recursion makes it practical to use a simple subroutine call instruction that saves the return address in a CPU register (or, if really necessary, in memory). Local and common data can be accessed using absolute addressing modes. Arguments that are passed to subroutines can be accessed using indirect addressing. The major additional requirement, beyond the facilities in simul8, is indexing. FORTRAN programs make heavy use of one- and two-dimensional arrays (higher dimensional arrays occur, but are infrequent). The calculation of addresses of array elements, as done in simul8, represents an intolerable overhead. At the very least, hardware-supported single indexing is required. (Double indexing for a two dimensional array is advantageous but not so commonly provided by hardware.)

Access to an array element needs to be achieved in a single instruction cycle. Source code like 'T12=ALPHA(N)' should utilize an index register in the array-address computations. This index register can be any integer register in the CPU of a general-purpose-register machine, or some specially designated CPU register used solely for indexing. The instruction holds the absolute address of the base of the array, and indicates indexing through the addressing mode bits. The address decoding step takes the base address from the instruction word, adds the contents of the specified index register, deriving the actual address of the data. The data fetch from the correct address is made when the address decoding is complete. Compilation of the source statement 'T12=ALPHA(N)' should lead to an instruction sequence like:

```
LOADX    N                / load index register,
FLOAD    ALPHA(X)         / load floating point number from array
FSTORE   T12
```

(Obviously, the exact syntax of the indexing mode depends on the target machine and its assembler.) The index value 'N' might be maintained in the index register to avoid the load index register instruction. An index register can also be used as an address pointer (to avoid indirect addressing through memory); an instruction like 'LOAD 0(X)' loads an integer into the accumulator from the memory location whose address is held in the X index register.

FORTRAN's 'logical ifs' map simply into a comparison test and a jump. The computed 'GOTO' statement, for example, 'GOTO (105,210,330,470),I' (which causes a jump to the FORTRAN statement labeled 105 if I=1 etc.), translates simply into an indirect jump using a table of label addresses. 'DO'-loops map onto the type of code illustrated for simul8. The prevalence of 'DO'-loops makes it worthwhile for machines to provide specially tailored loop instructions. Such instructions require that a CPU register be reserved to hold the loop index; when executed, these instructions (1) decrement (increment) the contents of the register, (2) test whether its adjusted value is zero and, if not zero, (3) cause a branch back over a number of instructions to the head of the loop.

The ALGOL-family

ALGOL-60 (developed about 1960) was the first of a now quite extensive family of languages for scientific programming, systems programming, and teaching. The original ALGOL-60 language emphasized power of algorithm expression rather than computational efficiency. The language permitted general recursive algorithms to be defined, removing the limitation to iterative computations of FORTRAN.

The implementation of the full ALGOL-60 language was practical, though difficult; the language received some use, though nothing commensurate with that of FORTRAN. More work has been done with derivatives of ALGOL. These derivatives usually exclude some features of the original ALGOL language, both to simplify compilation and improve the efficiency of the code generated.

Developments of ALGOL have proceeded in a number of directions. One major thrust was the development, largely due to Wirth, of ALGOL variants now widely used for teaching. The languages ALGOLW (developed about 1966) and Pascal (dating from about 1970) focussed on improvements to the syntax of ALGOL-60 and the structure of programs, and on the incorporation of extensions such as simple record structures. Another line of development led, via the abortive CPL language, to the system programming languages BCPL and then C. ALGOL has also influenced a number of other languages including Simula, ALGOL68, Modula, Ada, and even PL/1.

Features of Pascal and C will be used to illustrate some of the ways in which the ALGOL-family languages utilize a computer and why additional memory-addressing capabilities are required of the CPU for efficient execution of these languages.

The same three levels identified for a FORTRAN system are also present in Pascal and C systems: (1) there will be some underlying operating system routines that perform low-level I/O, (2) there will be a set of run-time support routines that link to the compiled user-written code, and (3) there will be the compiled user code. The major difference from FORTRAN relates to how the compiled user code makes use of memory for its data structures.

Recursion ⇒ use of a stack

An approach to storage management, more elaborate than required by FORTRAN, is inherent in the ALGOL-family's requirement that recursive subroutines and functions be permitted. The evaluation of recursive functions requires a stack. Introduced out of necessity, a stack proves advantageous in other aspects of the computational task.

Recursion is essential in the evaluation of certain mathematical functions; some data-structure manipulations are also inherently recursive. Unfortunately, realistic examples of the value of recursion are usually complex. So, recursion is illustrated here through an example (printing the value of a positive number as a sequence of decimal digits) that might be better solved through an iterative algorithm.

A simple example recursive procedure

Given a positive number, of arbitrary magnitude, it is possible to determine the low order decimal digit by dividing that number by 10. The division gives a quotient and a remainder; it is the remainder that gives the value for the low-order digit. This can be converted immediately to a printable character. Of course, the low-order digit should be printed last. Therefore, the number printing routine must first print that number represented by the quotient, before it prints the character just determined. Thus, one has a naturally recursive algorithm for printing numbers that can be expressed in Pascal:

```
procedure printposnum(num : integer);
var   ch              : char;
      temp1,temp2   : integer;
begin
      temp1:= num mod 10;
      temp2 := num div 10;
      ch:=chr(ord('0')+temp1);
      if temp2>0 then printposnum(temp2);
      write(ch);
end;
```

The interesting problem here is how should the compiler allocate memory locations for 'num', 'c', 'temp1', and 'temp2'. It is obviously wrong to use static allocation, as in 'temp2 ds.l 1, temp1 ds.w 1, ch ds.b 1'. For example, suppose that the routine was called to print a number whose value was 19, then (1) the first call sets 'ch' to '9', (2) the recursive call occurs, (3) 'ch' is set to '1', (4) this value is printed, (5) return is made to the previous level of recursion, and (6) 'ch' is again printed. Hence, the value printed is '11'.

A different set of memory locations *must* be used for the local variables and arguments generated by each recursive call of this procedure. A stack can be used to hold the temporary data appropriate to each level of recursion, with each recursive call building another data *frame* – another level onto the growing stack.

If the language allocates space for arguments and local variables on a stack, then each recursive call is allocated its own unique location. Consequently, there is no problem with data appropriate to one level of recursion being overwritten by information for another level.

The use of a stack by routine 'printposnum', while processing the example value of 19, is illustrated in Figure 15-3.

Figure 15-3. Use of a stack for storing the local variables associated with each recursive call to the procedure 'printposnum'

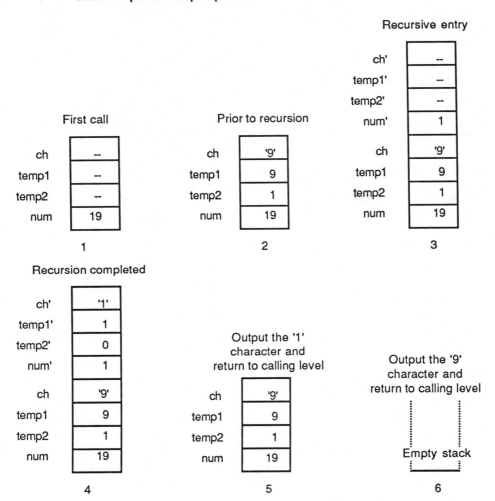

At step 1, the value for the argument is placed on the stack and space for the three local variables is claimed. By step 2, the values of 'ch' etc. for this call have been determined; since 'temp2>0' another recursive call is necessary. Thus, situation 3 is reached, where a new *stack-frame* has been built to hold the new argument value 'num' and for new instances of 'temp1' etc. At step 4, recursion completes (or 'bottoms out'); 'temp2=0' so further recursion is not required. The value ('1') of the current instance of 'ch' is printed and a return is made to the calling level. This level proceeds to print the value of its own version of 'ch' (which held the '9' character since step 2).

Organizing the use of a stack

The stack is simply a large area of successive memory locations in the data area of a program; it is just a big vector. This area is used to hold the data in the stack-frames associated with each call of a procedure. Procedures (both recursive and non-recursive) are executed in a last-in-first-out (LIFO) order; that is, if procedure A calls procedure B, then B must be completed before execution of A is resumed. This LIFO order of execution matches the use of a stack; as each procedure is entered a new frame is built on the top of the stack, deeply nested procedure invocations continue to build up the stack, then, as procedures are completed and exited, these frames are discarded last on, first off.

The code generated for a recursive procedure or function must make provision for use of a stack data structure. The local variables and arguments of procedures have to be found in the stack; therefore, in the instructions generated, the addresses of variables are specified relative to a pointer into the stack. The 'subroutine return links' are also held in this stack. When a recursive subroutine/procedure is called, its return address must be placed on the stack (in the current stack-frame); if there is then a subsequent recursive call, the next return address is saved somewhere else on the stack in the next stack-frame. One register in the CPU must be reserved to act as a pointer to the *top of stack*.

Stack usage is simpler if at least two CPU registers are available for holding pointers into the stack. Apart from the *stack pointer* (that holds the address of the top of stack), it is helpful to have at least one *stack-frame pointer* register. The stack-frame pointer holds the address of the start of the current stack-frame (i.e. the collection of arguments, return addresses etc., and local variables pertaining to the current call). These two pointers are just extra CPU registers, like the index register already introduced for the FORTRAN machine. (Again, it is possible to use any two integer CPU registers on a general register machine; however, it is very common to have a specially designated stack pointer register which is used by special hardware instructions.)

The CPU and a program's organization of its memory space both become a little more complex. The CPU has a few extra registers, and both additional instructions and additional address-decoding circuits to make full use of these registers. A part of the memory space allocated to a program must be reserved for its stack data-structure. Figure 15-4 illustrates a primitive ALGOL machine for comparison with the primitive FORTRAN machine of Figure 15-1.

Conventionally, the stack starts at the highest memory address available to a program and expands down toward the locations containing program code. (The top of stack is therefore the lowest numbered address occupied by a stacked datum. Subsequently stacked data are higher on the stack, but have lower addresses.)

A stack-frame contains arguments, a return address, a place for the previous value of the stack-frame pointer, a save area for CPU registers, and space for local variables. The frame is extended if the procedure needs temporary workspace when evaluating expressions. The exact form of a stack-frame is defined partly by the particular stack manipulation instructions of the machine hardware, and partly by the conventions of the compiler for the stack-based language. Figure 15-5 shows the nature of a stack-frame as might be created by a particular call of the recursive 'printposnum' procedure used in earlier examples.

Figure 15-4.   A simple ALGOL machine

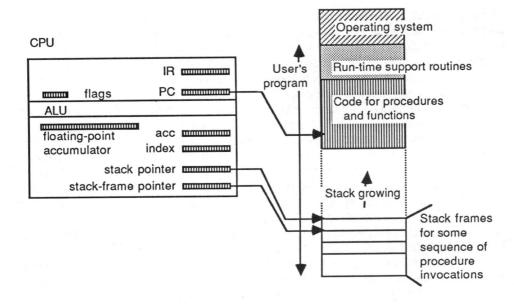

Figure 15-5.   The structure of a prototypical stack-frame

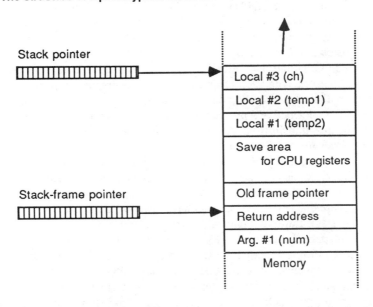

A register-save area is suggested as a part of the stack-frame. Typically, there will be a convention that either all CPU registers, or a subset of CPU registers, are saved on entry to a procedure. This makes it possible for procedures to use registers to hold data like loop indices, without any worry that an index might be corrupted by a call made from within the loop to another function or procedure.

The stack pointer always contains the address of the top element of the stack (the lowest address used). The value in the stack pointer usually changes during the execution of any procedure as temporary data are *pushed* onto the stack for saving, and then *popped* off the stack as required.

The stack-frame pointer contains the 'start address' for the current stack-frame. In Figure 15-5, this 'start address of the frame' is set to the location that holds the return address; this is solely an example, the conventions of a particular compiler determine the real 'start of frame'. The addresses of arguments and local variables can all be specified in terms of *offsets* relative to the value in the stack-frame pointer. Assuming for simplicity a word-addressed machine, then, in Figure 15-5, a reference to the first argument for the procedure would cite the address 1(sfp) (i.e. the address is one word above the address given in the stack-frame pointer (sfp) register). If say four registers, in addition to the frame pointer, are saved, then the address of local #1 is -6(sfp), and local #3 is at -8(sfp). Such *based addressing* is a variant on indexed-mode addressing.

The stack-frame pointer is mostly used in data loads and stores. It provides the base of the current stack-frame from which the instruction provides a fixed offset appropriate to the particular data element required. The base from the register and offset from the instruction are combined to give the address in the stack for the data.

The stack pointer is used mainly in instructions that push data onto the stack or pop data off. These data might be temporary information for use during expression evaluation or might be argument or results being prepared for or retrieved from procedures. Pushing something onto the stack requires that the stack pointer first be decremented (so as to point to the first free stack location); then the datum must be stored in the address specified by the contents of the (updated) stack pointer. Popping something off the stack requires that the datum be read from the address specified by the stack pointer, and then the stack pointer incremented. If there is no hardware assistance, then these operations each require at least two instructions (a load or store, and an updating of the stack pointer register). Pushes and pops are sufficiently common that it is worth having hardware circuits that can do the updating as an integral part of the store/load (push/pop) operation.

Stack manipulations during a procedure call and return

For Pascal, the instruction sequence for any procedure calling another is something like:

1. A sequence of pushes places arguments on the stack. Arguments go in reverse order; the last argument is pushed first. Pascal has 'value' parameters and 'var' (reference) parameters. Values are pushed on the stack for 'value' parameters and addresses are pushed on the stack for 'var' parameters.
2. The subroutine call instruction is executed. If possible, the hardware saves the return address on the stack. If this is not done by hardware, then a standard sequence of instructions, at the begining of each procedure, must get and then push the return address onto the stack.

3.   The stack-frame pointer must be pushed on the stack; since it holds the address of the stack-frame of the calling procedure, it must hold that same value when the called procedure finally returns. Meanwhile, this pointer is needed to hold the start address of the new stack-frame being built for the called procedure.

4.   A new value of the stack-frame pointer must be set from the contents of the stack pointer.

5.   Other CPU registers are, if necessary, pushed onto the stack.

6.   The stack pointer should be adjusted to leave space for locals.

Then, the code of the newly called procedure can be executed. When it is completed:

1.   The stack pointer is adjusted back down the stack (to higher address), freeing the space used by locals.

2.   Saved register values are popped off the stack into the registers.

3.   The stack-frame pointer is restored to point to the frame of the calling procedure.

4.   A jump is made back to the return address saved on the stack.

5.   The old arguments are popped off the stack, moving the stack pointer back to where it was before the call sequence started.

Use of the stack for non-recursive routines

Stack-based allocation is only required for the arguments, local variables, and return links of recursive routines. It is possible for a compiler to recognize (or be told) that routines are not recursive. Space for local variables of non-recursive routines can be allocated statically, just like the locals of FORTRAN.

   Language systems differ as to whether recursive and non-recursive routines are handled in the same manner. Some languages take advantage of the ability to use static memory allocation; these languages allocate static data areas and use instructions with absolute addressing modes. For example, PL/1 has to be specifically informed that a routine is to be compiled to allow recursion; otherwise, a PL/1 compiler normally uses a static memory allocation scheme for the locals of that routine. Both BCPL and C have facilities whereby the programmer can declare variables static, instead of letting them default to dynamic stack variables. (Statics in C and BCPL are mainly used for globals, in a manner similar to the use of 'COMMON' storage in FORTRAN.) In contrast, most implementations of Pascal store all variables in the stack.

   Consistent use of stack space for local variables has advantages other than uniformity of code and simplification of the compiler. (The compiler is inevitably simpler if it has to generate only the one kind of code.) Statics take up space in memory throughout the duration of the program, although they are only used within the routine where they are declared (and, possibly, by other routines and functions which it calls). A program comprising a dozen or so non-recursive routines each using 10 kilobytes of local variables needs >100 kilobytes of statically allocated space. All 100 kilobytes of space are not used simultaneously unless there is a call sequence that caused all the routines to be active (having been called from one another). The actual maximum depth of nested procedure calls might depend on the data being processed, but will typically be six deep or fewer. If the maximum depth were six, then a 60 kilobyte stack would suffice (i.e. 10 kilobytes in each of six stack-frames). Stack variables only take up space while they are needed; therefore, a stack serves as the basis for a convenient method for reusing the same memory space for different data as required.

The stack as store for temporary data

The discussions on FORTRAN noted how a compiler might frequently have to save data temporarily. During the evaluation of expressions, partial results may be computed which cannot be saved in CPU registers because these are needed for subsequent calculations. The partial results will be again required before the final result is determined. Consequently, partial results must be saved in memory. It was noted that the FORTRAN compiler invents extra local variables, for a subroutine, to hold such temporary data.

The stack represents a much more convenient place for holding temporary data. If a stack is used then the compiler can specify instructions that simply push data onto the stack whenever CPU registers need to be reused, and later pop the same data off the stack. Then, the compiler does not need to keep track of the number of temporary variables it has invented for the current routine, and whether those already invented are in use or free (and so reusable) at any particular point in the code. Of course, in a recursive routine, temporaries go on the stack anyway.

Scope rules add some additional complexities

The examples so far have suggested that use of a stack requires just a stack pointer and one frame pointer. These two pointers allow access to temporary data pushed onto and popped from the stack (via the stack pointer), and access to the local variables and arguments of the current procedure (via the frame pointer). This is almost sufficient for BCPL and C, but not for Pascal.

The scope rules of BCPL and C, and the absence of nested procedure declarations in C, mean that in any procedure one can only access the arguments, the procedure's own dynamic variables on the stack, and some set of statics. In these languages, some statics serve much the same role as 'COMMON' variables in FORTRAN: they are allocated separately from all the routines; they have fixed addresses and their absolute addresses can be link edited into the code of the routines at linking-load time. Other statics are more akin to the local variables in FORTRAN subroutines. They exist throughout the entire run time of the program but the compiler guarantees that they are referenced only from the procedures where they are declared. C and BCPL work through the use of statics, and a stack with a stack pointer and one frame pointer.

Pascal's scope rules are more complex and necessitate multiple frame pointers into the stack. (It is easy to have multiple frame pointers if there are enough spare CPU registers; enough is about eight because there are usually restrictions imposed by the compiler anyway. Provision of extra pointers is more involved if use of CPU registers is impractical.) Nested declarations of Pascal procedures are possible and the scope rules allow a nested procedure access to variables defined within an enclosing procedure. The following example code is used to illustrate those variables accessible at different points in the program:

```
program test;
var t1,t2:integer;
    procedure A1;
    var a1,a2:integer;
    begin
        { body of A1 }
    end;
    procedure B2;
    var b1,b2:integer;
        procedure C3;
        var c1,c2:integer;
        begin
            { body of C3 }
        end;
    begin
        { body of B2 }
    end;
begin
    { body of test, the main program }
end.
```

Within the body of 'test', only the 'global' variables are accessible; these are the variables of 'test's own stack-frame. Procedure 'A1' can access these 'globals' as well as any arguments and its own locals from its stack-frame. If 'A1' is called directly from the main program of 'test', then two frames are on the stack: that for 'test' and that for 'A1'. Both should be accessible, so two frame pointers are needed. A call of 'B2' from within the main program, followed by a call to 'C3' from within 'B2', would lead to three frames on the stack (those of 'test', 'B2', and 'C3'). The code of 'C3' could contain references to variables held in any one of these stack-frames, and so three stack-frame pointers would be needed. If C3 were recursive, additional frames would be built on the stack, but, as illustrated in Figure 15-6, one wouldn't need any more pointers. (The frame pointer for 'C3' always points to the frame associated with the current call to the procedure.)

As an extra complexity, 'C3' could then invoke procedure 'A1'. While 'A1' is executed, five frames are on the stack, but, as shown in Figure 15-7, only two are accessible. (The scope rules require that 'A1' have access just to its own locals and arguments in its frame, and the 'globals' of 'test'.)

The code that a Pascal compiler must generate to allow accesses to the variables of enclosing procedures is obviously fairly involved. Commonly, the locals and arguments of the current procedure are referenced relative to a stack-frame pointer; all other data references may require chasing through a chain of indirect links. Pointers are placed in each stack-frame that identify those other frames to which access is allowed. Maintenance and use of such links can represent a significant run-time overhead. This was why BCPL and C changed the scope rules and eliminated the opportunity for such references. These languages are used for writing the heavily used parts of operating systems and utility programs, and, therefore, require compilation into efficient code.

Figure 15-6. An illustration of the stack-frames that would exist, and would be accessible, at various stages in the execution of 'program test'

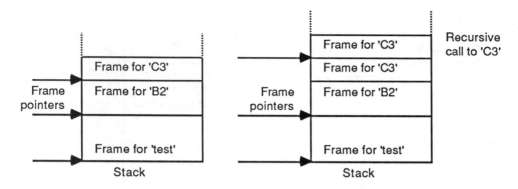

Figure 15-7. If in 'program test' procedure 'A1' is invoked from within 'C3', then only the frames for 'A1' and 'test' are active

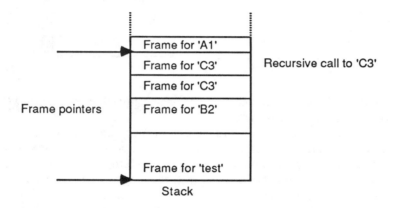

For contrast with the FORTRAN model presented in Figure 15-2, the corresponding Pascal program is shown in Figure 15-8. Figure 15-8 shows the state of the stack at the moment the procedure call is about to be executed. The frame for the main program is on the stack and contains 'alpha', 'x', and 'i'. The procedure call consists of instructions to push the addresses of the 'var' parameters 'x' and 'i' onto the stack and the subroutine call instruction itself. A new frame, for 'p1', is then built on the stack and the stack-frame pointer is reset. A link, back to the stack-frame for the main program, is left to allow access to the array 'alpha'.

The 'heap'

In addition to statics (in C and BCPL) and dynamic stack variables, the languages Pascal, C, and BCPL all utilize another memory allocation system – the *heap*. The heap is used

Figure 15-8. Organization of a Pascal program in a computer's memory

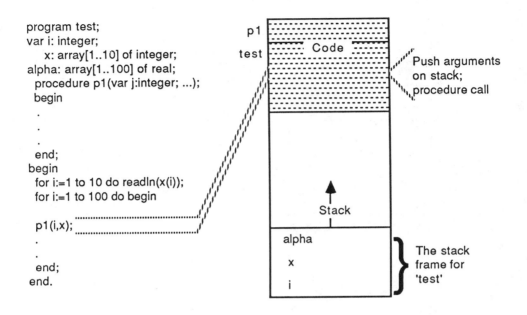

```
program test;
var i: integer;
    x: array[1..10] of integer;
alpha: array[1..100] of real;
  procedure p1(var j:integer; ...);
  begin
  .

  .

  .
  end;
begin
  for i:=1 to 10 do readln(x(i));
  for i:=1 to 100 do begin

  p1(i,x);
  .

  .
  end;
end.
```

for those dynamic record structures created and destroyed by Pascal's 'new()' and 'free()' functions (C's 'alloc()' and 'free()').

The heap is another reserved area of memory. Space in this area is managed by run-time support routines. When a user routine requests a block of memory, a search is made through the heap zone to find a region from which this block can be allocated. The address of the start of this block is returned to the user, and the management routines update appropriately all records of used and free blocks in the heap zone. The run-time support routines linked with a user's code include 'new()' and 'free()'. When a new record structure is required a call is made to 'new()' with arguments specifying the size of the record required and referencing a pointer variable (that holds the start address of an area of memory reserved for the record structure).

Thus, as illustrated in Figure 15-9, programs typically have three or four quite distinct parts: code, statics, heap zone, and stack. The code itself may be separable into distinct parts; even ignoring the underlying operating system support routines, there will be at least two distinct parts to the code of a program: the run-time support routines and the user's code. (It is sometimes helpful to envisage a further division of the code into separate parts.)

Figure 15-9.   **Programs in memory are comprised of several different parts: code, statics, heap, and stack**

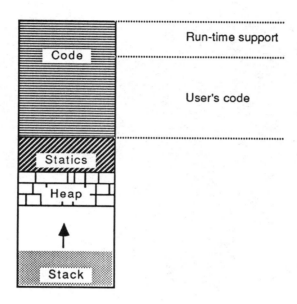

Segmenting a program

The various parts of code and data have quite different patterns of use. Controls on use are appropriate. For example:

1. If subroutine parameters and linkage data are placed onto the stack, then all code can be *read-only*; any attempt to write into the code represents a detectable error.
2. The stack should not grow into the heap zone; any overlap should be a detectable error.

In principle, the compiler could generate distinct addresses for such different objects as labeled instructions, static data elements, and heap pointers. Many machines now have hardware address-decoding circuitry which allows for such *segmentation*. The different component parts of the code and the data areas of a program can be allocated to separate *segments*. The hardware of the address-decoding circuitry maps these segments into different parts of memory and checks that the usage of each segment is appropriate. Segmentation is one of the extensions to a machine architecture that is briefly reviewed in Chapter 21.

Section V

Extending the CPU

16

Extensions to the CPU

The CPU of the simul8 machine is adequate to illustrate the basic principles of how machines work. It is however much simpler and more restricted than the CPUs in current microcomputers. A typical CPU has (1) more instructions, that is more data manipulation and combination circuits, (2) more data registers, (3) more elaborate address-decoding circuitry, (4) a more complex control unit, and (5) more elaborate mechanisms for handling I/O. Together, these extensions allow for the more rapid processing of data.

In this chapter, these additional features are justified, typical instruction repertoires for a microcomputer are briefly reviewed, two examples of different register organizations are noted, and some consideration is accorded to specialized data types such as binary-coded decimal and floating-point numbers. Addressing modes are considered in Chapter 17. Chapter 18 deals with extensions to the I/O handling mechanisms.

Additional features

More instructions

A richer repertoire of instructions allows programs to be more concise. For example, a 'compare' instruction and then a 'conditional branch' instruction can do the work of the 'cla', 'tad ...', 'cia', 'tad ...', 'skip-test', 'jmp' sequence of the simulated machine. The reduction in the number of instructions allows more complex programs to be placed in the same amount of memory; it makes execution faster because fewer instructions need fewer fetch and decode sequences.

If more instruction circuitry can be incorporated into the CPU then it is advantageous to have specialized versions of instructions for handling different size data elements. For example, it is useful if versions of the integer arithmetic instructions exist for both 16-bit and 32-bit integers. Then, one can have both *word* integers and *long-word* integers (terminology varies, sometimes *word* (16 bits) is called *half-word* and *long-word* (32 bits) is called *full-word*). Economies can then be achieved in storage allocation because it is possible to allocate only the space really essential for a variable. Commonly, though not invariably, a CPU that can manipulate different size data elements will have distinct fields in its data manipulation op-codes; one group of bits specifies the data manipulation that is to be performed, another two bits specify the size of the data element(s) that is/are to be manipulated.

As well as specialization of instructions to handle different size data elements, it is useful if additional instructions are provided to perform arithmetic on representations of floating-point numbers or binary-coded decimal numbers as well as binary numbers.

More registers

The presence of more data registers in the CPU reduces the requirements for data to be continually copied between CPU and memory. Most programs incorporate short loops where the same data elements are repeatedly utilized (e.g. a for-loop control variable). It is helpful if registers can be reserved for these variables while the loop is being executed; this minimizes the number of loads and stores performed.

There are two differing approaches to the provision of extra registers. Some machines have (typically 16) general purpose registers whose use is almost entirely at the discretion of the programmer. Most microcomputers have sets of registers whose use is predefined; for example, one for an accumulator when doing arithmetic, one for an index register when accessing arrays, and so forth. A suitable compromise is a set of registers for program data manipulation, and a second group for holding address data.

More addressing modes

Much of the work done by a CPU involves computations on addresses. This feature is largely hidden from the high-level language programmer who works in terms of code describing how program data should be changed; for example, adding the contents of fields from two record structures to yield a result in an array element. At the machine level, the addition step in such code is almost the least of one's concerns; most of the code necessary for such a data manipulation consists of calculations to find the addresses both of the particular record fields and of the array element where the result is to be stored.

Although very frequent, calculations on addresses are generally simple. An array access requires adding an index value to the base address of the array to give the address of the desired element. Access to a record structure requires a field's offset value be added to the address of the first field in the record.

The simplicity and regularity of address-data manipulations makes it possible for these to be hardwired into the address-decoding circuitry of the CPU. Then, provided the instruction can specify the required type of address-data manipulations and the necessary information is available, the address calculations can all be performed as part of a single instruction cycle. Instead of simul8's five instructions to load an array element, a single instruction may suffice.

Based upon analyses of the address-data manipulations of example programs, machine designers have identified the most common ways of accessing program data and provided corresponding *addressing modes* in the address decoding circuitry of the CPUs they designed. On many machines, there are distinct addressing mode fields in the instruction words. The CPU's control circuitry first identifies the op-code, and hence the data manipulation required, and then examines the addressing mode (and other bit fields) to determine how to find the data.

However, some machines do not clearly differentiate between instructions' op-codes and addressing modes. The addressing mode may be subsumed into the instruction. Then, there will be families of related instructions that perform similar data manipulations but explicitly identify different sources (or, maybe, destinations) for the data. Thus, there could be distinct 'add-register' (an addition with data taken from a register), 'add-immediate' (an addition on data included in the last few bits of the instruction word itself), and 'add' (an addition with data read from memory). There is rarely any uniformity; for example, although there could also be 'add-halfword-register' and 'add-halfword' there might not be an 'add-halfword-immediate'.

More elaborate control circuitry

Some elaboration of the timing and control circuitry of the CPU is made necessary by the enlarged instruction repertoire and the varied addressing modes. Inevitably, instructions will be of different sizes. Only a couple of bytes are necessary for an instruction that specifies that the contents of two registers are to be compared, whereas 6-10 bytes might be needed in an instruction requiring the comparison of two data values held in memory locations whose addresses are defined explicitly. The CPU circuitry must be capable of determining the length of an instruction, fetch all the various parts of an instruction, and update the PC appropriately.

Additional problems arise when there are instructions taking relatively long times and many memory cycles to complete. Some machines have instructions that cause thousands of bytes to be copied between different regions in memory, or which search through a sequence of memory bytes to find the first occurrence of a particular character. A fast response to interrupt may necessitate the ability to suspend, and subsequently to resume, execution of these time-consuming instructions.

More sophisticated I/O

The I/O mechanisms of simul8 are slow. Many instructions need to be executed in order to identify an interrupting device. There is no flexibility; the setting of a flag on a critical device won't cause an interrupt to code handling a less critical device such as a terminal.

CPUs that need to serve large numbers of devices, or need to guarantee fast response, require additional hardware to speed their handling of I/O.

Instructions

'Move', 'compare', 'bitset', and 'bittest'

The most commonly used instructions don't combine data elements, nor do they manipulate individual data elements – they just move the data around and test data values.

A machine should have some form of 'move <source>, <destination>' instruction(s). Since one may need to move variously bytes, words, or long-words, this instruction should come in several 'flavors'; these variant instructions are most commonly indicated by a suffix on the op-code; for example, 'move.b' (move a byte), 'move.l' (move a long-word). In the general case, a 'move' instruction specifies two memory addresses, and consequently may occupy quite a number of bytes. Even though the instruction may be long, less space is needed than separate load and store instructions and execution is quicker. Other more specialized instructions, of the form 'movechars #bytes <source>, <destination>', may also be worthwhile; such instructions are even longer, with three operands.

Most machines have a set of *condition-code* flag bits. There will be bits indicating a carry, or overflow on the last arithmetic operation; other bits flag a negative or zero result from the last arithmetic operation or load instruction. These condition bits are set by most data-manipulation and data-combination instructions. Some machines have a 'test <destination>' instruction that sets the condition bits according to the value in '<destination>' (without having to combine that value with anything else, or move it anywhere in particular).

The condition bits are also set by 'compare' instructions: 'compare <source>, <destination>' (note, some machines reverse the order of the arguments). These 'compare' instructions, in effect, subtract the value in '<source>' from the value in '<destination>' and set the condition bits appropriately (the result from the 'subtracter' circuit is thrown away). As with a 'move', a 'compare' instruction comes in several flavors to deal with bytes, words, and long-words.

A sophisticated CPU may incorporate specialized instructions that check, clear, or set the values of particular bits in a chosen memory word. These instructions typically have the form 'bittest (or 'bitset' or 'bitclear') <bit-number>,<destination>' (the bit number might be a constant or specified by the value in a CPU register). The zero (Z) bit of the condition codes will be set to 1 if the tested bit was zero. Frequently, a still more specialized 'test-and-set' instruction exists which sets the Z bit of the condition codes according to the value of the high order bit of a specified destination word, while at the same time guaranteeing that this high order bit is set to 1 (setting it if necessary). A 'test-and-set' instruction is used when coordinating multiple activities. Such an instruction is essential on systems where more than one CPU may be running and trying to access common memory; the instruction is useful even on single CPU systems with asynchronous interrupt-driven I/O devices.

Program control

Data moves and tests typically represent 30-40 percent of the code of the program. The next most frequent class of instructions is the program-control instructions, that is, the jumps, branches, subroutine calls, and so forth.

Apart from 'jump' and 'jump to subroutine' instructions as on simul8, most machines have a large repertoire of 'conditional branch' instructions. Branch instructions use relative addressing; the address part of the instruction defines the byte (or, sometimes, the word) offset of the destination location. These relative addresses are local; most machines use a single byte offset and can jump backward or forward by up to 128 bytes. (Locality is subjective – a 68000 has a more expansive attitude; short relative jumps of from -128 to +127 bytes are allowed, but for a couple of bytes more in the instruction it allows branches in the range -32768 to +32767.)

The conditional branch instructions are usually of the form: 'Bcc <label>'. The 'cc' part of the instruction defines the condition tested, that is, it specifies which bit, or combination of bits, must be set in the condition-code flags to cause a branch to occur. The typical repertoire of branch instructions includes: 'bra' (unconditional branch), 'bcs' (branch if carry bit set to 1), 'bvc' (branch if overflow clear, that is, set to 0), 'beq' (branch if 'equal', that is, Z bit set to 1). (The names vary from machine to machine.)

'DO-loop' instructions are commonly provided. The 68000 variants are the 'DBcc <data register>,<relative branch address>' instructions. These will terminate a loop if (1) the condition specified by 'cc' is satisfied, or (2) after decrementing, the contents of the specified data register equal -1; otherwise, a relative branch back to the start of the loop is made. The Intel 8086 machine has similar loop instructions which decrement a register to zero (allowing the loop to terminate), and which can also test for other conditions flagged in the condition bits.

Most current machines are designed to use a stack for their subroutine linkage.The 'jump to subroutine' instruction references a stack pointer register (either a default stack pointer or a register specified in the instruction), and the return address for the subroutine is pushed onto the stack. There will be a 'return from subroutine' instruction that pops the return address off the stack and into the program counter.

Additional instructions may be provided that help organize the use of a stack for procedure calls. There may be an instruction, for example, 'link' on the 68000, which (1) pushes the contents of the frame pointer (held in some designated CPU register), (2) sets the new value for the frame pointer (from the current stack pointer value), and (3) moves the stack pointer through a specified displacement to leave space for local variables of the current procedure. There will be a complementary instruction for tidying the stack and restoring the old frame pointer on exit from a procedure ('unlink' on the 68000).

Other program control instructions will include 'return from interrupt' (akin to 'return from subroutine' but deals with the re-enabling of interrupts and so forth) and 'wait' (the CPU goes to sleep, leaving the bus completely free for use by DMA-type peripheral devices; the CPU remains asleep until a device causes an interrupt). There will also be 'halt' and the various instructions for enabling and disabling interrupts.

Another important program control instruction is 'svc' (supervisor call) (this may be named 'trap'). This instruction is considered later in Chapter 20 where those extensions of a machine necessary for an operating system are considered.

Data-manipulation and data-combination

Once in a while it is necessary to do some computations with the data that have been shuffled around. The extensions to simul8's instruction repertoire are all obvious.

Data-combination circuits include add, subtract, multiply, divide, inclusive or, and exclusive or.

An integer multiply results in a number that may require twice as many bits to represent than the multiplier and multiplicand; for example, the product of two 16-bit numbers may require 32 bits. This requirement is frequently reflected in the machine architecture; the result of a multiplication may be placed into a pair of CPU data registers. Similarly, the division instruction may expect to work with a 32-bit dividend and a 16-bit divisor. The results of an integer division will give both a quotient and a remainder; normally, both values are saved in a pair of CPU registers.

The data-manipulation instructions include negate, complement (not), rotates, and shifts. The rotates and shifts commonly specify the number of places by which the value is to be rotated. So, on the 68000, one might have 'rol.b #3,d1' (rotate left by three places the byte in the low bits of register d1) or 'asr.l #7,d2' (arithmetic shift right by seven places the contents of register d2).

Exotic instructions versus RISC machines

With usually at least one byte allocated to the op-code, some 256 different op-codes are available. There are 50 to 60 basic instructions one might want. Some of these are required in different 'flavors' (e.g. 'move.b', 'move.w', 'move.l'). But even with these variants, a hundred or more op-code patterns may remain after the basic instruction repertoire has been defined.

There is a tendency for the architects of CPUs to fill out all these op-codes with interesting, imaginative data-processing instructions. One may find an instruction that 'might be useful to someone using circular list or queue structures', or one that 'would be great when evaluating polynomials', or an instruction that will (all on its own!) copy a string from a source to a destination while substituting a translation character for each of the source characters and, if necessary, filling out the destination string with a chosen fill character.

The trouble with such exotic instructions is that they are rarely worthwhile. It is only an exceptional assembly-language programmer who can remember the full repertoire of some 250 instructions and recognize the ideal situation for the 'qawxyz' instruction. If full exploitation of esoteric instructions is difficult for the assembly language programmer, then it is almost impossible for the compiler writer. It would require a quite exceptional optimizing compiler to be able to parse a bit of arbitrary high-level language source code, and then recognize (1) that the hardwired queue instructions were appropriate for handling the weird records just concocted by the programmer, or (2) that provided two or three lines of code were suitably rearranged, one has an expression suited to the polynomial evaluator instruction.

Investment in CPU design and complexity may earn a better return by limiting the instruction repertoire to 40-60 basic (but optimized) instructions. The optimizations can focus on the machine use and the consequent expected pattern of instruction usage. Thus, a machine for processing programs written in an Algol-derived procedural language is likely to deal with very frequent, quite deeply nested procedure calls and with requirements for small amounts of temporary workspace for each procedure. Here, optimizations could focus on the instructions for stack-oriented procedure call sequences and for frequent references to arguments located on a stack. Rather than complex extra circuitry for rarely used instructions, the CPU-chip might contain large amounts of temporary storage space for expression evaluation, for procedures' arguments, and so forth. Machines with these characteristics are known as RISC (Reduced Instruction Set Computers) machines.

Example organizations for CPU registers

These two examples of current CPU architectures are both based on micros made by the Motorola corporation. The machines selected are the 6809 and the 68000.

Motorola 6809

The 6809 is a small microprocessor; it is used in systems such as the Tandy 'Color Computer'™. It has a 16-bit address bus and an 8-bit data bus. Mostly it processes one-byte data elements but there are a few instructions that manipulate 16-bit data elements. Apart from the PC and instruction register, the CPU contains a number of other registers as shown in Figure 16-1.

Figure 16-1. CPU registers in the Motorola 6809

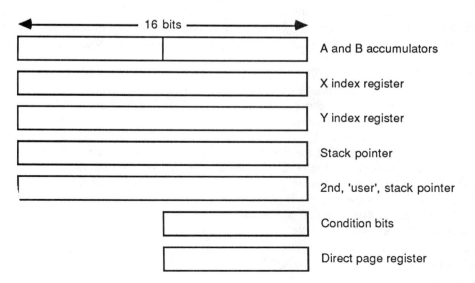

There are two 8-bit accumulators, registers 'A' and 'B', that can be used for arithmetic and logical operations on one-byte data elements. These two registers can also be viewed as a single 16-bit accumulator ('register D') used to manipulate 16-bit data. There are the typical data-combination instructions: 'and', 'or', 'exclusive or', 'add', and 'subtract' (the last two have variants that incorporate any carry digit and thereby simplify manipulations of larger 32-bit numbers). The 8-bit contents of the 'A' and 'B' registers can be multiplied to give a 16-bit result in 'D'. There are limited facilities for manipulating binary-coded decimal data. Data manipulation instructions like 'clear', 'increment', 'decrement', 'rotate', and 'shift' can work either on the contents of one of the 'A', 'B', or 'D' registers, or on data in memory.

There are load and store instructions for data movement. A compare instruction compares byte/two-byte contents of one of the 'A/B/D' registers with memory and sets bits in the condition codes register. The condition bits are also set by all the data manipulation, combination, and load instructions. The usual set of conditional branch instructions tests condition bits and allows for 'local' branches (the 6809 branch instructions can use either 8-bit or 16-bit relative addressing, so a 'local' branch of ±32 kilobytes is possible). There are several additional instructions for setting/clearing chosen bits from the condition codes register.

Although the 6809's data-manipulation/combination instructions extend those of simul8 a little, there aren't any really major differences. However, conditional branches are a significant improvement over simul8's skip tests. The dramatic differences in capabilities relate to the provisions for addressing data. The 6809 has a substantial set of registers for holding and manipulating address data.

There is a stack pointer 'S' which is used in subroutine calls. The subroutine call instruction pushes the return address onto the stack; the return from subroutine instruction pops the address back into the PC. Push and pop instructions allow data to be placed on/retrieved from the stack. The push/pop instructions can use either the 'S' register or the 'U' (user stack) register. Thus, 'U' can be used to maintain a separate stack; it can also be used as an index register or made to serve as a stack-frame pointer.

There are two separate index registers, 'X' and 'Y'. There are instructions to load/store data into/from these registers and it is also possible to add constants to their contents. There are a number of indexed addressing modes that use the contents of these registers.

The direct-page register is described briefly in Chapter 17 on addressing modes. It is really there to allow for shorter forms of instructions by providing a paged-mode addressing scheme analogous to that of simul8. An absolute address on the 6809 requires 2 bytes of address data in an instruction; if a paged-mode address is used, then only one byte of address data is required.

The architecture of the CPU reflects the applications for which the 6809 was designed. It does not have much data processing computing power; that is not needed. The 6809 is for sophisticated terminals, small personal workstations, and hobbyist computers. Rather than raw computing power, these need to be able to shift characters around, to manipulate record structures that represent objects to be displayed, to interpret BASIC and similar languages, and so forth. There is a considerable need for many and varied addressing modes for accessing data structures, and hence the extensive set of registers for address data.

Motorola 68000

The term 'micro' is hardly apposite for the 68000. Current models of this CPU have a 24-bit address space (16 megabytes). The data buses have only 16 bits; but really the 68000 is a 32-bit machine, with all internal data registers having 32 bits and an instruction repertoire including a full complement of instructions for handling 32-bit long-word integer data.

Apart from the PC and instruction register, the CPU contains registers as shown in Figure 16-2.

Figure 16-2. CPU registers in the Motorola 68000

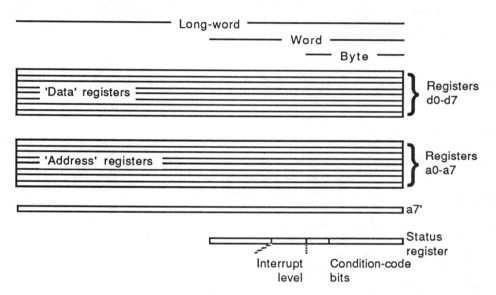

There are 16 (well, really 17) 32-bit registers in two groups. Eight registers, 'd0-d7', are for manipulating and combining program data. Eight more, 'a0-a7', are for address data. Register 'a7' is the stack pointer used in subroutine call instructions and so forth. This 'a7' register is duplicated; one 'a7' register is used for 'user' programs, the other 'a7' is used when the machine is executing (operating system) code in 'supervisor mode'. (The user mode/supervisor mode distinction is discussed in Chapter 20 on machine extensions required for an effective operating system.)

There is a 16-bit status register. In addition to the condition codes this register is used to hold (1) information on the status of interrupts, (2) a flag which indicates whether the machine is running in 'user' or in 'supervisor' mode, and (3) a 'trace' flag that is used in various debugging monitor systems.

The uses of the two groups of registers is obvious. *Address registers* are used to hold base address of arrays, stack-frame pointers, stack pointers, and so forth. *Data registers* are used for the numbers/characters processed by the program. Most two-operand data-combination instructions need to reference a (data) register already holding program data, and also refer to a (address) register that holds some part of the definition of the location of the second operand. If the 16 registers could be completely interchangeable, then each of these references to a register would take up 4 bits in the instruction word. The separation into *data* and *address* register groups makes it possible to identify a register using only 3 bits, and consequently allows for other control information to be packed into each 16-bit instruction word.

There are the usual data-manipulation and combination instructions. All data-processing instructions come in byte/word/long-word variants. Data-combination (two-operand) instructions work on data contained in the CPU registers, or will combine data from memory with data in a CPU register. There is extensive provision for binary-coded decimal data as well as normal binary integers and bit patterns. (The 68000 does not handle floating-point data; such data will be processed by a separate support co-processor. The later versions of the 68000 (e.g. the MC68020) incorporate the interfacing needed for such a co-processor.) Data-manipulation (single-operand) instructions work on the contents of registers or memory locations.

The 'move' instruction is special; both '<source>' and '<destination>' in a 'move' can be memory locations. The great frequency of 'move' instructions inspired the designers of the 68000 to make this the most flexible of the instructions.

The conditional branches, loop-construct, and procedure call instructions of the 68000 have been noted earlier.

The architecture of the 68000 makes possible the compilation of efficient code for a stack-based language such as Pascal or C. There are a reasonable number of registers; it should not be necessary to expend many instructions on the movement of pointers, loop counters, and other data between memory and CPU registers. The large address space simplifies the organization and allocation of memory for data structures. The consistency of the instruction set (with respect to such features as the use of different addressing modes, and the provision for different size data elements) simplifies the code generation sections of the compiler. When supplemented with a floating-point co-processor, a 68000 'micro' will have a computing power comparable with the mainframe machines of the 1960s and early 1970s.

'Advanced data types'

Programming in assembly language is normally appropriate only for applications such as the writing of specialized device handlers and other 'low-level' routines in an operating system. For these applications, characters and binary integer data types suffice.

However, a CPU may also incorporate instructions for handling other data types such as strings, floating-point numbers, and/or binary-coded decimal numbers. Applications written in high-level languages utilize such data types. Compilers must be capable of generating code that correctly represents these data and which uses the appropriate instructions. Although direct use of these data types is rare, it is necessary to be acquainted with their representations.

Strings

Strings of characters may be supported through the provision of a few copying and editing instructions. A commonly available string instruction is one that scans a sequence of bytes, from a given starting address, and stops when it encounters the next instance of a specified character. Such an instruction typically sets one of the CPU registers to the address of that matching byte. These string instructions are chosen to correspond with the primitive string-handling functions defined in certain high-level languages. A compiler can then generate code, for a call to the high-level language's string function, which involves just moving the values for the address of the string argument and the representation of the sought character into registers, and then the string instruction itself.

Binary-coded decimal

Internal to the computer, integer data are best represented and manipulated as numbers in base 2, that is, binary numbers. But, this representation does have a problem: it is costly to convert between the internal binary integer representation and the character strings that represent numbers in decimal notation. The conversion code for input requires a loop with multiplications and additions; output similarly requires divisions. If only a simple addition of a couple of items of numeric data is actually required, then it is an awful lot of trouble (and time) to have to read two character strings representing decimal numbers, convert both to binary, do the one more addition needed, and then do a conversion back from binary.

There are many business applications where large volumes of data must be read, decimal numbers (representing receipts, expenditures etc.) have to be extracted, and simple totals accumulated. Arithmetic processing for such applications should, if possible, use binary-coded decimal rather than binary for the internal representations of numbers.

A major advantage of binary-coded decimal is that it is relatively easy to convert between this representation and character strings. A binary-coded number is represented as a series of bytes in memory. Each byte holds two 4-bit bit patterns, representing individual decimal digits. As illustrated in Figure 16-3, a signed 4-digit decimal number can be represented in 3 successive bytes.

Conversion of the bit pattern 0010100010010111 (interpreted as a binary coded decimal number) to a character sequence is simple. A loop is required that works through the successive bytes; within each byte the two 4-bit bit patterns are extracted in turn and are converted directly to character form by a simple addition. Thus, the bits 0010 are extracted from the first byte (00101000) and the value 00110000 is added to give 00110010 (i.e. the ASCII code for the character '2'); next, the second 4-bit bit pattern (1000) is isolated and converted into the character '8'; the second byte with the next two lower order decimal digits is processed similarly. No divisions are needed; just a simple loop, an 'and', a 'shift', and an 'add'. Input conversions are equally simple. (Many machines provide 'pack' and 'unpack' instructions that can automatically interconvert character string and decimal data.)

Figure 16-3.   Binary-coded decimal data: 3 bytes to represent a 4-digit decimal number

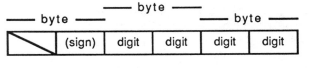

Two binary coded decimal digits can be packed in each byte

e.g.

```
0010 1000        28
1001 0111        97
```

The number of bytes used to represent a binary-coded decimal number can be chosen by the programmer. Consequently, arbitrarily large numbers can be represented if really required (e.g. government budget deficits). Languages like Cobol and PL/1, that were devised for business data processing, allow the applications programmer to declare variables, represented using binary-coded decimal, and specify the number of digits to be accommodated.

Numbers, represented in binary-coded decimal, are combined one byte at a time. Consequently, an addition (or subtraction) of two numbers is coded as a loop. In each cycle through the loop, another pair of bytes is combined to yield one byte's (two decimal digits') worth of the result. There may be 'add binary-coded decimal' and 'subtract binary-coded decimal' instructions that combine two one-byte operands. On simpler machines, only a 'decimal adjust' instruction might be provided. Then, in an addition loop, a byte's worth from each of the two binary coded decimal operands would be added (using a normal binary 'add' instruction) and the one byte result would be 'decimal adjusted' (this adjustment involves checks on 'carry' and 'half carry' bits and then, possibly, changes to the bit pattern in that byte of the result).

The loops for addition and so forth make binary-coded decimal arithmetic slower than binary; but, particularly if there are 'pack' and 'unpack' conversion instructions, the overall processing times are reduced whenever only a few actual computations need to be performed.

Floating-point numbers

Floating-point numbers are used to represent the real numbers of scientific calculations. (Floating-point numbers are not the same as reals; mathematicians can always find a third real number in between any pair of reals; this doesn't always work with floating-point numbers.)

Floating-point numbers are represented as a signed mantissa part and an exponent part. The representation is analogous to conventional 'scientific' notation, as available on pocket calculators, where a number is given in the form $\pm m \times 10^{n}$ (or $\pm m E n$) where m is the mantissa and n the exponent:

Conventional positional number	Scientific notation
+101.5	+1.015E +2
-4095.999	-4.09599E +3
+0.001012	+1.012E -3

There are always *normalization* conventions for such scientific notations. In principle, the number +0.001012 could be represented as +1.012E-3, or +0.1012E-2, or +0.001012E0; there will be a convention that one of these is standard. If a number is given in non-standard form it is converted to comply with the standard.

Floating-point numbers will (at least in these examples) be represented in the form $\pm m \times 2^n$ with m the mantissa (as a binary fractional number) and exponentiation to the base 2 with exponent n. The mantissa will be assumed to be normalized so that (1) the binary point (yes, *binary* point, not decimal point) comes before the bits of the fraction part, and (2) the fraction part represents a number with decimal value v in the range $0.5 \le v < 1.0$.

A typical style for a 32-bit representation for a floating-point number is shown in Figure 16-4. There will be a sign bit, 7 bits for the exponent, and 24 bits for the mantissa. Details of the encoding for the exponent and mantissa differ widely among machines. (Some machines have 8-bit exponents; some do use exponentiation to base 2, others to base 16; some have tricks relating to the representation of normalized numbers that allow them to squeeze 33 bits of data into a 32-bit word.)

Figure 16-4. A possible 32-bit representation for a floating-point number

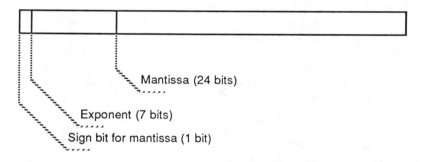

Mantissa (24 bits)

Exponent (7 bits)

Sign bit for mantissa (1 bit)

The exponent value is represented as a signed number in some *excess notation*. A simple case would have the exponent value represented as a binary number in 'excess 64' notation. The binary pattern 0000000 then represents -64, 0111111 represents -1, 1000000 corresponds to zero, and 1111111 is +63.

The mantissa, or fraction part, could be represented as shown in Figure 16-5. The various bit positions correspond to different powers of 2; the left-most bit represents 2^{-1}, the next 2^{-2} etc. (the number is considered normalized if the 2^{-1} bit is 1). A fraction part 1100100... represents the fractional value 0.78125 (0.5+0.25+0.03125).

Figure 16-5. Representation of the mantissa in a floating-point number

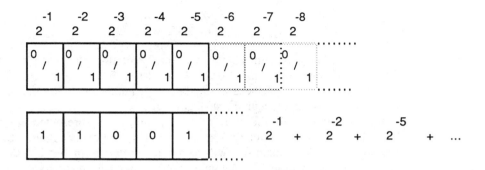

The value of a number with this fractional part depends also on the sign and exponent parts. With positive sign and an (excess-notation) exponent of 1000000, the number is 0.78125; with exponent 1000100 (i.e. +4, after allowing for excess), the value is $2^4 \times 0.78125 = 12.5$; with exponent 0111110 (i.e. -2, after allowing for excess), the value is $2^{-2} \times 0.78125 = 0.1953125$.

Addition and subtraction operations on floating-point numbers require that (1) the smaller number's mantissa is shifted to align their binary points with both having the same exponent, (2) the mantissas are then added (subtracted), and (3) the result is normalized. Multiplication and division require (1) the exponents to be added (subtracted), (2) the mantissas to be multiplied (divided), and (3) the result to be normalized. These operations can all be performed by appropriate hardware circuitry, or simulated through interpretive routines that unpack the various fields of the floating-point numbers and perform the necessary shifts, adds, multiplies, and so forth.

The problems with floating-point numbers almost all relate to the number of bits used to represent them. There are never enough bits in the mantissa. The most common 'single precision' floating-point number representations allow only 24 bits in the mantissa. This is not sufficient for lengthy scientific calculations. When calculations are performed on floating-point numbers, *round-off* errors accumulate.

About the simplest way to envisage problems of round-off in floating-point calculations is to recognize that, really, the floating-point representation allows only certain numeric values to be correctly represented. When calculations are done in floating point, results are changed to the closest representable number.

For example, with a 6-bit mantissa and a 4-bit (excess 8 exponent) one can have the values shown in Table 16-1 (plus the others with the other possible exponents). (Exponent values are across the columns, mantissa values down the rows.) Any calculation using these numbers of bits to represent the parts of the floating-point numbers is forced to yield, as a result, the nearest representable value.

For example, the evaluation of the expression $a.x^2 + b.x + c$ for $x=1.25$, $a=2.8125$, $b=2.3125$, and $c=-6.875$ yields results as shown in Table 16-2. Here, there is about an 8 percent error in the final computed result due to round-off in three multiplications, one addition, and a subtraction. (Probably, the error is larger when one considers the user's actual intention. The values for a, b, and c may have been entered as

Table 16-1. The values that can be represented using a 6-bit mantissa and a 4-bit, excess 8 exponent

Mantissa \ exponents	1000	1001	1010	1011	0111
100000	0.5	1.0	2.0	4.0	0.25
100001	0.515625	1.03125	2.0625	4.125	0.2578125
100010	0.53125	1.0625	2.125	4.25	0.265625
100011	0.546875	1.09375	2.1875	4.375	0.2734375
100100	0.5625	1.125	2.25	4.5	0.28125
100101	0.578125	1.15625	2.3125	4.625	0.2890625
100110	0.59375	1.1875	2.375	4.75	0.296875
100111	0.609375	1.21875	2.4375	4.875	0.3046875
101000	0.625	1.25	2.5	5.0	0.3125
101001	0.640625	1.28125	2.5625	5.125	0.3203124
101010	0.65625	1.3125	2.625	5.25	0.328125
101011	0.671875	1.34375	2.6875	5.375	0.3359575
101100	0.6875	1.375	2.75	5.5	0.34375
101101	0.703125	1.40625	2.8125	5.625	0.3515625
101110	0.71875	1.4375	2.875	5.75	0.359375
101111	0.734375	1.46875	2.9375	5.875	0.3671875
110000	0.75	1.5	3.0	6.0	0.375
110001	0.765625	1.53125	3.0625	6.125	0.3828125
110010	0.78125	1.5625	3.125	6.25	0.390625
110011	0.796875	1.59375	3.1875	6.375	0.3984375
110100	0.8125	1.625	3.25	6.5	0.40625
110101	0.828125	1.65625	3.3125	6.625	0.4140625
110110	0.84375	1.6875	3.375	6.75	0.421875
110111	0.859375	1.71875	3.4375	6.875	0.4296875
111000	0.875	1.75	3.5	7.0	0.4375
111001	0.890625	1.78125	3.5625	7.125	0.4453125
111010	0.90625	1.8125	3.625	7.25	0.453125
111011	0.921875	1.84375	3.6875	7.375	0.4609375
111100	0.9375	1.875	3.75	7.5	0.46875
111101	0.953125	1.90625	3.8125	7.625	0.4765625
111110	0.96875	1.9375	3.875	7.75	0.484375
111111	0.984375	1.96875	3.9375	7.875	0.4921875

data or defined as constants in the source program, for example, 'DATA A,B,C/2.82,2.33,6.85/'. But, these values are themselves rounded to the nearest value that could be represented in the number of bits available; so a=2.82 becomes a=2.8125.)

Of course, with 24 bits to represent the mantissa, errors are not quite so gross. But they are there. Scientific calculations involve thousands of arithmetic operations, not just the half-dozen of the example; although round-off errors are individually much smaller, they still accumulate, so multilength floating-point arithmetic is needed. Floating-point numbers should be represented in 64, or even 128, bits.

Table 16-2.   The effects of round off on a floating-point calculation

	Correct calculation	*Calculations with result at each step rounded-off to representable number*
x^2	1.5625	1.5625
a. x^2	4.39453125	4.375
b.x	2.890625	2.875
a. x^2 +bx	7.28515625	7.25
a. x^2 +b.x+c	0.41015625	0.375

17

Addressing modes and instruction formats

This chapter includes (1) a brief overview, with a few examples, of some of the addressing modes found on current microcomputers, and (2) some examples of the varied op-code formats required when instructions need 0, 1, 2 or more operands, each specified using any one of a number of different addressing modes.

Requirements for addressing schemes

There are a couple of general requirements for addressing schemes. First, it should be possible to access a large amount of memory; consequently, many bits are needed for the address specification. Second, not all instruction words should require large memory-address fields; large address fields make instruction words longer (or require multiple-word instruction formats) with the result that code consumes more of memory and programs run more slowly (because more instruction bytes are read from memory).

 These requirements are conflicting. The conflict can be partly resolved by addressing schemes that allow most instructions to reference address information held in registers (with the instruction word possibly specifying some offset to the value in the register). Then, although such an offset might only require 8 or 16 bits in the instruction word, because this offset is added to a 16-, 24-, or 32-bit value from a register the instruction can still reference any location in an address space of from 64 kilobytes to (in principle) many millions of bytes. In any program, a few instructions may still need to specify a 24- or 32-bit absolute address value as part of the instruction word(s); but most instructions should be capable of being fitted into shorter formats.

 Within these general requirements for large address spaces and short instruction formats, the machine designer can implement addressing modes that accommodate the most frequent types of memory access.

Some of the considerations are as follows:

1. Most programs make very frequent use of small numeric constants, for example, increments for loops, test values, character values. These operands only require a byte of memory, and really could be included in the 'description of operand' part of an instruction word. If such operands are actually located in the instruction word, then there is no need to fetch more data after instruction decoding; the necessary data are immediately available. Such usage both reduces a program's storage requirements and allows for faster execution.

2. On multiple-register machines, both operands for some data-combination instructions could be held in CPU registers. The machine must make provision for such cases even if the majority of data combination steps combine data read from memory with data in CPU registers.

3. Some form of indirect reference is needed. Address values inevitably have to be computed when accessing lists, or other special record structures. Once such an address is computed, it must be stored somewhere and then used in an indirect reference to memory when the required program data are read from that address. It is advantageous if these computed addresses are held in registers; the fetch of program data then uses the address from the register. (It is identical to the use of address pointer variables on simul8, except that generally the pointers are held in CPU registers to avoid the extra memory cycle needed for indirect reference via a pointer in memory.)

4. Programs written in current systems languages, for example, C, and applications programs in Pascal, all use stacks extensively. Push and pop operations are frequent. These operations involve both an indirect memory reference via the stack pointer, and a preceding, or succeeding, updating of the stack pointer. It is worth trying to optimize these operations; possibly by having stack-oriented addressing modes that use registers as address pointers and which appropriately increment and decrement the values held in these address pointers.

5. Another generalization of indirect reference via a register is needed to simplify access to procedural arguments and local variables on a stack, and also to access the fields of record structures. For example, with record structures, the code may need to reference the many different fields within a record (as in Pascal code like 'with p^cell do begin name:=...; val:=...; left:=... end;', where there are fields like 'name' and 'val' in the 'cell' record structure), the address of the start of the record having been previously computed and placed in a register. Rather than changing the value in the address pointer register for each access to a field, since the various fields in the record are all at known offsets from its start, it is more convenient for instructions accessing these fields to refer to the pointer register and specify an appropriate offset. Similarly, when accessing arguments or locals on the stack, it is convenient for instructions to just specify offsets relative to the value in the stack-frame pointer.

6. The need to access data on stacks, or in records, leads to a further yet more elaborate pattern of memory reference. Sometimes, it is necessary to reference a location not at a constant offset from the start of the record or current stack frame, but rather at a dynamically determined offset. Thus, the record or stack frame might include an array

whose various elements must be accessed; depending on an index value, different array elements are, necessarily, located at different offsets from the base address provided by the record pointer. Although it is no longer possible for the instructions to simply specify a fixed offset relative to a pointer, it is still important to try to avoid computing new pointer values at each reference. It is helpful if instructions can specify both a base address in one register and an index value held in another register.

7. If the language supports static arrays, then other simpler forms of indexed addressing are needed. Access to elements of a static array can be made if the instruction word(s) include the base address of the array and also specify a register for the appropriate index value.

8. Most machine designers provide for relative addressing in branch instructions; these allow local jumps to be specified in terms of the number of bytes or words that are to be skipped backwards or forwards. Relative addressing is a special case of an instruction providing an offset to a value in a pointer register; it just happens that the register, used in relative addressing, is the program counter. It may be useful to extend relative addressing so that loads, stores, and compares with constants, or static variables, can be specified using this addressing mode.

The addressing facilities implemented on a machine reflect the designer's perceptions as to which of these and/or other memory access patterns are of sufficient importance to be worth implementing in the logic circuitry.

As noted in Chapter 16, some machines subsume details of the addressing mode into the instruction op-code whereas other machines use separate parts of the instruction words to encode different types of information.

The IBM 360, 370, ... series has distinct instructions for different types of data access. There are, for example, the instructions 'and', 'andregister', and 'andimmediate'. The 'and' instruction combines data from memory with data already in a specified general purpose CPU register. The 'andregister' instruction ands the contents of a second register into the contents of a specified register. The 'andimmediate' instruction ands data included in the instruction with data already in a CPU register. The 'and' instruction has additional information specifying the address of the memory location containing the operand (most memory addresses on the IBM 370 are given in terms of offsets to a value held in an (implicit) base register; additional indexing can be specified).

In contrast, the 68000 uses a 6-bit address specification field in the instruction word. The information in this address specification field determines the appropriate addressing mode for an operand. This 6-bit field consists of two subfields: 'mode' and 'register'. If the mode is 0, then the 3-bit register field specifies a data register that contains the actual operand; thus, one can have the equivalent of an 'andregister'. If the mode and register are 7 and 4 respectively, then immediate addressing is implied. Mode 7, with register 1, allows an absolute address to be specified for the operand. Other modes indicate that the contents of one of the address registers was to be used to compute the effective address of the operand.

Example addressing modes

Absolute addressing mode

The address data provided in the instruction words is the address (defined at linking-loading time) of the required operand. The size of these address data depends on the address space of the computer.

On the 68000, address data require 32 bits (24 bits really, but it is extended to 32). Thus, two extra 16-bit words follow the instruction word. The addressing mode data in the instruction flags the fact that a long absolute address follows in the next two words.

Similarly, on the 6809, with a 64-kilobyte addressing space, an instruction using absolute addressing requires a 1-byte instruction word followed by 2 bytes for the absolute address.

Paged mode

Paged mode allows for shorter addresses in instructions because the instruction word need only provide the *location on page* (7 or 8 bits of data) rather than a full address. This mode (which should be familiar from simul8) is not common; the 6809 is however one current micro which supports a form of paged-mode addressing. The 6809 allows its memory to be viewed as 256 pages of 256 bytes each.

The 6809's 'direct page register' can be loaded with any chosen page number. Subsequently, instructions can specify paged-mode addressing. In these instructions, only one byte is used to specify the location on page of the data. The complete address is generated by the address decoding circuitry (which appends the location on page to the page number from the direct page register).

There are quite a few other machines which make special provision for access to a kind of 'page zero' for globals. Thus, the 68000 has a 'short absolute addressing' mode which specifies 16-bit absolute addresses (interpreted as references to the first 32 kilobytes and the last 32 kilobytes of its 16-megabyte address space).

Register modes

Register modes are available on all machines. Single operand instructions just specify which of any set of data registers is to be operated on (if this is not implicit). Two operand data-combination instructions need to identify a source register and a destination register to contain the result (and which already contains the other operand for the data-combination operation).

Immediate addressing mode

This is the mode where operand data are incorporated in the instruction word or in the immediately following word(s). Typical assembler syntax (for a 68000) is something like 'add.w #100,d3', meaning: add the (decimal) value 100 to the contents of data register 'd3'. The instruction word is encoded with the 'add' opcode, the destination register 'd3', a modifier (saying that this is a word, not a byte or a long word), and the addressing mode ('mode#7,4') that identifies immediate addressing. The value for the constant is held in the following word.

Such encoding is more convenient than something like:

```
add.w kd100,d3
        .
        .
kd100  dc.w 100
```

which represents the generalized way that such combinations with constant data were done on simul8. Apart from simplifying coding, the use of immediate mode does slightly shorten and speed the program: the coding with immediate data requires two words to be read (the 16-bit instruction word and the following word with the immediate data); the alternative coding requires three words (the instruction, one or two following words with the address of 'kd100', and finally the word with the constant data value).

Indirect (register) mode

This is the mode where a register holds a computed address for a list cell, or the address of some Pascal 'var' parameter passed as an argument to a procedure. The required operand is located at the specified address. Its use is equivalent to the use of pointer variables on simul8 but avoids the extra memory fetch that they required. Typical assembler notation is something like 'move.w (a1),d3', meaning: move one word from the location specified by the contents of address register 'a1' into data register 'd3'.

Auto-increment/auto-decrement modes

These addressing modes generalize register indirect to simplify access to variables at the top of the stack (those pushed and popped).

If the stack pointer is to always point to the top of the stack (the lowest location used), then before a datum is stored on a stack the pointer must be pre-decremented. Similarly, when a datum is popped off the stack then, after the fetch, the pointer should be post-incremented.

These facilities are provided by the auto-increment/auto-decrement addressing modes. Typical assembler code for a push is 'move.w d3,-(a7)' (i.e. pre-decrement 'a7', then use it as an address pointer to the location where the contents of 'd3' are to be copied), while the corresponding pop operation is 'move.w (a7)+,d3' (i.e. use 'a7' as a pointer to the address from which data are to be copied into 'd3', then post-increment 'a7').

The updating of the address register takes into account the size of the data element pushed or popped. The movement of a word causes a change of two in the value of the address register used, while a long-word causes a change of four. (Movement of bytes onto, or off, stacks normally causes a change of one in the value of the address register used; but, there are special cases. For example, on the 68000, the address register 'a7', used as the stack pointer in procedure calls, is kept word aligned so that byte movements change its value by two rather than one.)

Based addressing mode

In this mode, the instruction provides a constant offset which is added to the value held in an address register; the result is the address of the required operand. The 68000 provides for a 16-bit, 2-byte, offset to follow the instruction word (the value of the offset is interpreted as a signed number in the range -32768 to +32767). Typical assembler syntax would be 'move.w 16(a4),d3' (move into data register 'd3' the word that starts at the sixteenth byte of the record structure pointed to by address register 'a4'). The 6809 has three minor variants on based addressing; these allow for 5-bit (-16 to +15), 8-bit (-128 to +127), or 16-bit offsets.

Indexed mode

Here, the instruction must provide an absolute address, the base address for the start of the array or whatever, and specify a register whose contents define the index value. The effective address of the operand is given by the sum of the contents of the index register and the base address provided by the instruction.

Based and indexed mode

The effective address of the required operand is given by the sum of the contents of two registers: a base register (whose contents typically define the start of a record structure or array) and an index register (whose contents specify the particular element now required). The assembler code requires a notation like, for example, '(a1,d4)' which identifies the base register ('a1') and the index register ('d4').

Relative mode

The instruction word is followed by an 8-bit or 16-bit quantity that specifies the displacement to be added to the current value in the program counter to determine the effective address of the operand.

Instruction formats

The simple fixed field size 'op-code : operand description' model for an instruction word just does not apply to instructions for sophisticated micros. Their instruction repertoires are too varied.

There are instructions that involve no data, for example, a return from subroutine, or a halt instruction. Other instructions, like shifts and rotates, require several different types of data. Thus, a shift instruction needs maybe 3 bits of information to specify how many places to shift an operand datum; flags, to specify the direction and whether a logical or arithmetic shift operation is to be performed; and a specification of the operand to be shifted. Altogether, a shift may need half-a-dozen bits of data besides the specification of the operand. Quite different data are needed in a relative branch instruction. A relative branch needs, encoded in a set of bits, a specification of the condition to be tested and 8 bits of displacement information. Still another pattern is needed in an instruction that specifies a data-combination operation: a data register must be identified and the effective address of a second operand from memory must be defined.

The instruction repertoire of a machine is divided into groups; each separate group of instructions has a different way of organizing the bits in an instruction word. Instruction decoding becomes more elaborate. Rather than just a simple 'case' statement branching on a fixed size bit pattern, there exists a hierarchy of tests. The first 4 bits classify the instruction into one of 16 instruction groups. Further interpretation of the rest of the word depends upon this initial classification.

The 68000 again serves as an example. As shown in Table 17-1, 16 groups (determined by the first 4 bits of the instruction word) are distinguished in the 68000 instruction repertoire. Note the emphasis accorded to the 'move' instruction; three instruction groups are devoted to them. 'Move' is unique in that the size of the datum moved is considered part of the op-code (in other instructions, there is a special size field). The designers of the 68000 have left two instruction groups, 1010 and 1111, unassigned; these will be utilized in later models to provide for further instructions that might prove desirable (e.g. hardware floating-point instructions).

Table 17-1. The Motorola 68000 instruction groups

0000	bit manipulation etc.	1000	or/div/sbcd
0001	move byte	1001	sub/...
0010	move long	1010	(unassigned)
0011	move word	1011	cmp/eor
0100	miscellaneous	1100	and/mul/...
0101	addq/DBcc/..	1101	add/...
0110	Bcc/...	1110	shift/rotate
0111	moveq	1111	(unassigned)

Some of the 68000's instruction formats are shown in Figures 17-1 and 17-2. The 'move' instructions (Figure 17-1) can move 1, 2, or 4 bytes between any source and destination; both can be memory locations. As noted earlier, specification of the addressing mode in a 68000 instruction consists of a 6-bit 'mode:register' field in the instruction word – the 'effective address'. (The effective address is given as 'mode:register' if it is a source operand, and 'register:mode' if it is a destination.) Some addressing modes require no additional data; for example, no additional address information is required to fetch data from a memory location at an address held in an address register and then push them onto the stack. In other modes, for example, absolute addresses for source or destination, the words following the instruction contain the necessary address data.

The 'add', 'sub', 'or', 'eor', and 'cmp' instructions have similar formats. These instructions all combine data from a data register with a second operand. The op-mode field specifies the size (byte, word, long-word). Furthermore, in instructions like 'add', the mode field also distinguishes whether the data register is to be regarded as a source or destination.

Some of the complexities of instruction coding are illustrated by the instruction pair 'cmp' and 'eor', and the group 'or', 'sbcd', and 'div'. In each of these groups, the instructions share the same 4-bit op-code and the same basic layout of data register, mode, and effective address. The instructions in each group have to be distinguished by special case analyses of op-mode and effective address fields. Thus, 'div' (a 'word sized' operation only) is differentiated from 'or' by the two 'size' bits in op-mode field. The value 11 does not represent a valid operand size (here, 00=>byte, 01 => word, 10 => long-word); if the size bits are 11, then the instruction cannot be an 'or' and must be a 'div' instruction. The 'sbcd' (subtract binary coded decimal) instruction is recognized by an 'address register' being specified as the effective destination address. The 'or' instruction is not allowed to change address registers, so if the effective address and op-mode together identify the destination as an address register then this must be a 'sbcd' instruction rather than an 'or'. Differentiation of 'cmp' and 'eor' is also based upon restrictions on destinations specified in the effective address.

Figure 17-1. Examples of 68000 instruction formats

Move

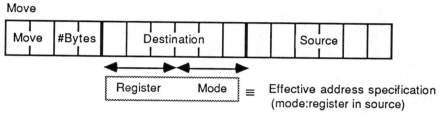

(From zero to four additional words used for address data)

Add, Sub, Or, ...,

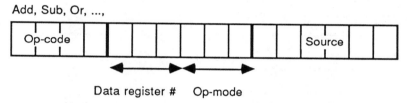

(From zero to two additional words for address data or an immediate operand)

Conditional branch instructions have their own op-code group and format. Apart from the first 4 bits of the op-code, they have a 4-bit bit pattern specifying the condition tested, and have an 8-bit displacement; long branches are encoded by a zero value in the 8-bit displacement field and a 16-bit value in the following word.

The 'not', 'link', 'return from subroutine', and the different 'jump' instructions are all in the 'miscellaneous' group, differentiated by the contents of the next few bits in the instruction word. 'Addq' and so forth are differentiated from the 'DBcc' loop instructions, again, by restrictions on size of operands and prohibitions on the use of address registers as destinations.

The varied pattern of data fields in an instruction word, and the need to fetch from zero to four additional words of immediate data or address specifications, results in a considerably more complex CPU organization. The complexities of the 68000 are by no means atypical. The popular Z80 computer has an even more complex set of instruction formats (partly in consequence of a need to provide for an extended instruction repertoire while still retaining compatibility with the earlier 8080 micro).

Figure 17-2. Additional 68000 instruction formats

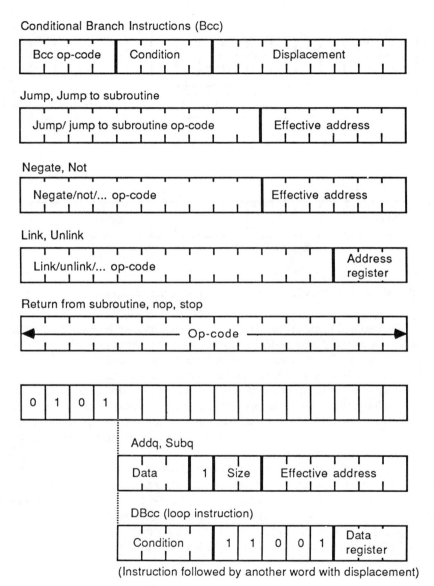

Conditional Branch Instructions (Bcc)

Jump, Jump to subroutine

Negate, Not

Link, Unlink

Return from subroutine, nop, stop

Addq, Subq

DBcc (loop instruction)

(Instruction followed by another word with displacement)

18

Improved input/output handling

This chapter reviews some of the ways in which the I/O handling capacity of a simple CPU can be enhanced, and also introduces methods by which the CPU can delegate responsibility for I/O handling. Changes to and enhancements in the way a CPU handles I/O include:

1. *Memory-mapped I/O.* Memory-mapped I/O represents an alternative design for the CPU's communications with I/O devices. This approach to I/O eliminates the requirement for special I/O instructions. Instead, the move and test instructions, from the CPU's normal instruction repertoire, manipulate data in device registers.The memory-mapped approach provides a cleaner, more consistent instruction set.

2. *Vectored interrupts.* One of the limitations of the interrupt system of the simple computer is the length of time taken to identify the interrupting device. On the simul8 machine, once the CPU state was saved on interrupt, the devices were checked in turn (polled) to find which was responsible for the interrupt. If a system has many active devices, all causing frequent interrupts, then this polling approach can cause intollerable delays.

   A more sophisticated version of polling allows the CPU to ask 'who interrupted?'. The interrupting device replies by placing its device identification number on the bus from where it can be read by the CPU. (If several devices are simultaneously trying to interrupt, then the one 'nearest' to the CPU responds.)

   Vectored interrupts provide an alternative approach in which, instead of using a single interrupt entry-point (location 1 on simul8), there is a unique interrupt entry point for each device. In effect, the devices set the program counter to the start address of their own handler code.

3. *Multiple priority levels for interrupts.* The single-level interrupt scheme of simul8 can be overly restrictive. This single-level scheme is not much of a problem if the handling of an interrupt never requires more than about twenty instructions (because then the CPU's response to interrupt is never delayed too long). But sometimes, as when buffers must be marked as full and new buffers arranged, the response to an interrupt can involve a hundred or more instructions. It is unacceptable for urgent data transfers from a high-speed device to be held up, and data possibly lost, simply because the CPU is performing a mundane housekeeping task on behalf of a

slow-speed terminal. The interrupt mechanism can be extended to allow 'more important' devices to interrupt the handling of 'less important' devices. Instead of having a simple interrupts on/off flag, the CPU has an *interrupt-level* register. If a device is assigned a higher level than the value held in this register, then that device is permitted to cause an interrupt.

4. *Use of a stack for saving CPU state.* As described in Chapter 12, the state of the CPU has to be saved on interrupt and restored before an interrupted task can be resumed. In the simple machine, a fixed set of memory locations sufficed for the register save area. In a more elaborate system, particularly one with multiple levels of interrupts, the use of any fixed set(s) of save locations could be inconvenient. A stack can of course provide a temporary save area, and also any other work space that might be required. Machines that provide instructions for stack-based procedure calls integrate the use of a stack into their hardware interrupt-handling mechanisms.

Memory-mapped input/output

In the simple simul8 machine (and in real machines like the Zilog Z8000 and Intel 8086), I/O is 'isolated'. There are genuine I/O instructions. When these are executed, the control lines of the bus encode information saying 'this is an I/O message'; the address lines contain the 'device identification' (and the data lines carry the data).

As illustrated in Figure 18-1, on the simul8 machine the execution of a 6046 ('tls') instruction sends an 'I/O message to device 4, do a 06 operation' signal on the bus. The teletype (TTY) and other device-controllers must watch for I/O class messages that are placed on the bus, and pick up those that are addressed to them. The data and control registers in the devices are thus accessed in a manner totally distinct from the way in which memory locations are accessed.

Figure 18-1. Isolated I/O as in simul8

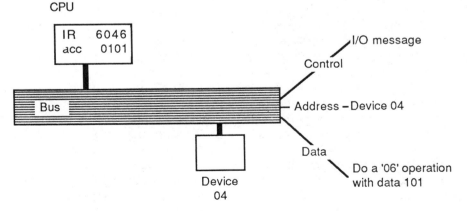

In the alternative memory-mapped I/O methods, device registers are accessed using the same instructions and addressing modes as used for any memory location. The device registers appear as just a special part of the machine's memory. About the first popular machine to use memory-mapped I/O, the PDP-11, with 16-bit addresses (and so a 2^{16}-byte, 64 kilobyte, *address space*), allocated the 8 kilobytes with the highest addresses as device data and control registers. The control and data registers of the PDP-11's teletype output device have (octal) addresses 177564 and 177566. (Such addresses are assigned symbolic names defined by appropriate equates, for example, the assembler directive 'TDATA = 177566' defines a symbolic name TDATA to be the data register for the TTY.) Rather than use a specific I/O instruction, one can access the TTY device's data register using any instruction, for example, 'MOV R0,@#TDATA' copies the contents of register 'R0' to the TTY's data buffer. The scheme is illustrated in Figure 18-2. The memory-mapped approach is now common. Apart from the PDP-11s, this method is used in the Motorola 6809s and 68000s.

Memory-mapped I/O methods are commonly cited as having the advantages of (1) avoiding the need for special purpose I/O instructions, (2) simplifying the bus hardware, and (3) allowing more general data-manipulation of the contents of device's registers.

Figure 18-2. Memory-mapped I/O as in the PDP-11 and the Motorola 68000

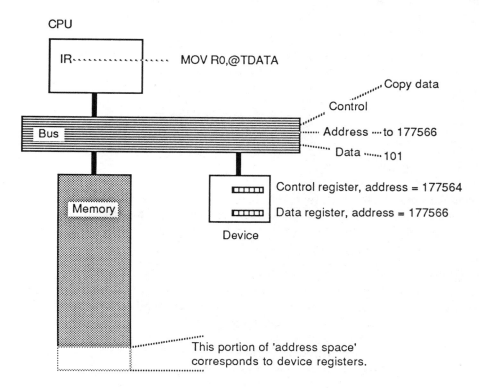

There is a further major benefit in the memory-mapped method. In Chapter 20, requirements for controls on I/O handling and memory access are introduced in relation to operating systems. When 'user' programs are running, the machine should not allow execution of I/O instructions, and only allow access to selected portions of memory. When such constraints are applied, I/O is performed solely by the operating system, and the user cannot overwrite other programs or the operating system. Now, such constraints require two different kinds of check in a system using isolated I/O: check 1; is it an I/O instruction? and check 2; is the address OK? But, with memory-mapped I/O, the same checking mechanism resolves both constraint application problems.

Vectored interrupts

The intent of a vectored interrupt mechanism is to reduce the delay before the CPU starts execution of the handling code appropriate to an interrupting device. The mechanism for implementing vectored interrupts requires minor extensions to the microcode of the hardware response to an interrupt, and more major extensions to the device controllers and their bus interfaces.

The new 'microcode' is:

```
while running do begin
        fetchinstruction();
        decodeintstruction();
        executeinstruction();
        if interrupts_enabled and
                        interrupt_line_set then begin
                                save_cpu_state();
                                periph:=who_interrupted();
                                addr:=entry_size*periph+v_start;
                                pc:=store[addr];
                                interrupt_level:=set_level_for(periph);
                                end
        end;
```

As in the simpler scheme, the program counter must be saved. Further interrupts should be disabled (or, in a multi-level scheme, further interrupts at the same or lower priority levels are disabled). The PC is set to the appropriate value for the next instruction to be the first of the code dealing with the interrupt.

In this example 'microcode', the microprocedure 'save_cpu_ state' is presumed to save at least the PC (and may, on the more sophisticated machines, automatically save several other CPU register values on the stack). The active peripheral is identified, as indicated by the microfunction call 'who_interrupted()'. As in the more sophisticated polling scheme noted earlier, the peripheral controller identifies itself by placing device-identification data on the bus, to be read as part of the hardware interrupt response.

The device identification, 'periph', is converted to an address in memory. A table, or 'vector', stored in some of the first memory locations (those with low addresses) begins at a fixed starting address, 'v_start'. In this table, there will be an entry for each possible device, with length 'entry_size' bytes. The address of a device's entry in this interrupt vector is determined automatically from its identification number, the known start address, and the entry size ('addr:= entry_size * periph+ v_start').

The data in the interrupt vector specifies the address of the appropriate device-handler. Consequently, the next step by the microcode is to fetch this address from the memory location and load it into the PC ('pc:=store[addr]').

The microfunction call 'interrupt_level:=set_level_for(periph)' represents the mechanism for setting the new interrupt level.

The peripheral controllers need the capability of identifying themselves by placing appropriate data on the bus. On some machines, the peripheral controllers also provide data used to establish the new interrupt level.

Although the vectored entry point is fixed once a device identification number has been 'wired into' the circuitry of a device-controller, the programmer is still able to place the actual handler routine almost anywhere in memory. The data in the interrupt vector identify where the handler code is located.

Of course, the interrupt vector must be initialized with the correct addresses for the device handlers that exist in a program. This is usually done in the initiation phase of an interrupt-driven program.

The minimal data in the interrupt vector is the address of the appropriate handler routine. Some machines provide rather more data. Thus, on the PDP-11, the interrupt vector entries are word pairs; one word contains the address of the device handler, the other word contains the new interrupt level/mask. The new interrupt level is then set automatically during the hardware's response to an interrupt.

Sometimes, there may be only a few entries in the interrupt vector, rather than a unique entry point for each device. Devices are grouped and groups share the same interrupt entry point. Thus, one could have a group of keyboards using one entry point, with another interrupt entry point used by printers. The handler routine reached via the interrupt entry point must then poll the various devices, sharing a common entry point, in order to determine exactly which one was responsible for the interrupt.

Multiple priority levels for interrupts

Multiple priority levels for interrupts provide a more certain guarantee of service to important, time-critical devices. The CPU has a register (usually a 3-bit register) whose contents determine the priority level of the code currently being executed. Device controllers have, wired into their circuitry, coded data specifying the level at which they assert an interrupt request.

Typically, ordinary code runs at priority level 0; slow, character-based peripheral devices use level 1; and disks use levels 3-5. As part of the response to an interrupt, the value of the priority level register in the CPU is changed. The following example execution sequence illustrates the various steps that might occur with a CPU working with a keyboard and a terminal (both 'level-1' devices), and a disk (a 'level-3' device):

```
executing main program at priority 0
keyboard-ready flag set, at level 1; interrupt:
                executing keyboard handler;
                teletype-ready flag set, also at level 1; ignored for now;
                continue executing keyboard handler;
                disk-seek flag set, at level 3; interrupt:
                                disk seek handler executed;
                                disk seek handler completed;
                                return from interrupt;
                resume executing keyboard handler;
                keyboard handler completed;
                return from interrupt;
teletype-ready flag, level 1, still set; interrupt:
                executing teletype handler;
                teletype handler completed;
                return from interrupt;
execution of main program resumed.
```

Saving the state of the CPU on the stack

The PDP-11, Intel 8086, Z8000, and the 68000 all utilize a stack in their interrupt handling. Details of how the stack is used, of course, vary slightly. The PDP-11 scheme is typical. Data register 'r6' in the PDP-11's CPU is employed as a stack pointer, and contains the address of the top of the stack (since the PDP-11 stack grows downwards through memory, the top was the lowest address word used by the stack). Data defining a program's procedure call sequence, parameters, and so forth are held on this stack.

On an interrupt, the contents of the PDP-11's processor status word and the PC are pushed onto this stack. (The processor status word contains the condition code bits, the interrupt priority level, and so forth.) The PDP-11 uses vectored interrupts, and consequently the program counter is set to contain the address of the appropriate device handler. The processor status word is loaded with new initial condition code settings and a new interrupt priority level; these data are taken from information in the interrupt vector.

The contents of any of the other CPU registers, 'r0'...'r5', can be explictly pushed onto the stack; the registers whose values were saved are now free to be used in the interrupt handling code. If a higher priority interrupt subsequently occurs, then the stack just grows a little more as a further set of data is saved.

Eventually, when the code of the device handler is complete, instructions are executed to pop the saved register values back into 'r0' etc. Then, a 'return from interrupt' instruction is executed, taking the top elements from the stack and restoring them to the PC and processor status word.

Only a minimal number of registers are saved automatically on the PDP-11. Other CPUs save the contents of all CPU registers on the stack. In yet another scheme, as implemented on the Motorola 6809, different amounts of data are saved automatically for different levels of interrupt request.

More powerful machines tend to have multiple sets of CPU registers so less data have to be saved; instead of saving information, the CPU simply switches to a different set of registers. There may be two stack pointers even on those machines which don't otherwise have multiple register sets. One stack pointer is used for the user program, the second for the operating system, particularly for I/O handling. Memory is then organized as shown in Figure 18-3. Some memory is used for the system's code (all the device handlers and data buffering routines), the I/O data buffers, and the system stack. The rest of memory is used for the code and the data structures of the user's program.

Figure 18-3. **Memory organization for a more sophisticated CPU that has separate user and system stacks**

Memory

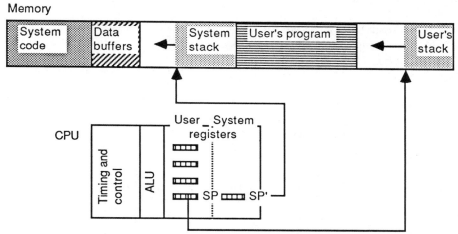

When an interrupt does occur, the program counter and other data are saved on the system stack; and it is this stack that is used for all subsequent device handling code. When interrupt handling is complete, the return from interrupt instruction pops the saved data out of the system stack into the PC etc. and switches the mode back to again employ the user stack.

Delegating responsibility for input and output

If the main CPU is a powerful, costly machine for data processing, then it is not desirable for it to spend any significant amount of time handling peripherals. It is preferable for the CPU to continue with the main data-processing tasks and to delegate some of the responsibility for I/O.

After all, I/O handling can consume a significant number of instructions. For example, a system with 40 terminals and some printers could easily have to deal with a couple of thousand characters each second. (Thirty terminals inputting at 10 characters per second, ten terminals outputting at 100 characters per second, and line printers at 300-

1000 characters per second all add up quickly to a considerable I/O traffic.) If it really took 100 instructions to deal with each interrupt, then some 200,000 instructions, that is, about 20 percent of the CPU's capability, would be expended each second on I/O handling.

All these I/O interrupts could result from 30 'read line' requests, 10 'display line' requests, and a 'print line' request by programs running on the CPU. It can help if the I/O transactions of the CPU are expressed in these conceptual unit operations, with something else attending to all the messy details of single character transfers, updating of buffers, and responses to interrupts.

To achieve this, the overall system is extended so that, as well as the CPU, there is a small *I/O processor / peripheral processor / channel* which has the capability of dealing with the mundane aspects of any data transfer. The basic approach is as suggested in Figure 18-4.

The main CPU connects, via a bus, to memory. Its instructions and data are read in the normal way. The memory is *dual-ported* , that is, there are two entrances (port, from *portal*, a Latin word for a gate or door). The second entrance to memory leads to another bus. The memory has arbitration circuits that only allow one access at any instant.

Figure 18-4. CPU with a separate I/O processor

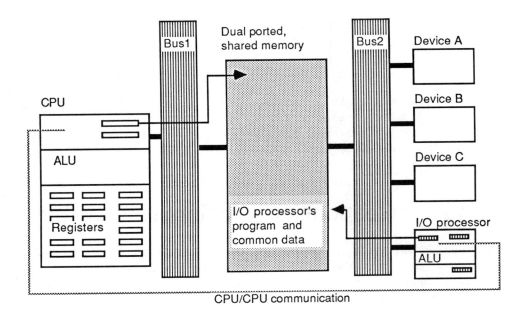

CPU/CPU communication

It is on this second bus that the peripheral controllers and I/O processor are located. The I/O processor shares the main memory. It reads its instructions from there, and arranges for the data transfers between buffers in main memory and devices. Its programs are in a sense composed by the CPU.

When the CPU requires a data transfer, it composes a message describing the transfer. This message is left in memory for the I/O processor. The I/O processor executes code that, eventually, collects the message, interprets the requirements, and determines the actual I/O activities necessary. When the I/O processor has completed the work described in any message, it can interrupt the main CPU and announce the completion of the necessary transfers. For example, the CPU could compose a message requiring that a couple of dozen lines of text be displayed at a terminal. Then, rather than receiving several hundred interrupts (one for each of the individual characters moved), only a single interrupt is received from the I/O processor when all the data have been displayed.

The I/O processor may be just a simple CPU, for example, an 8080 on a machine with a 8086 CPU. Alternatively, as is the case with *channels*, the I/O processor may be specifically designed for I/O handling tasks and have a specialized instruction repertoire. On large IBM computers, there are normally many channels of several different types; there are multiplexor channels designed for handling slow speed character devices, and block channels designed for handling I/O to and from disks and tapes.

19

An example machine

The last three chapters described extensions to the basic architecture of the simul8 machine. Many of these extensions were originally justified in Chapter 15 as needed to make the implementation of compiled languages more practical. This chapter uses a current machine architecture, the Motorola 68000, to illustrate how such an architecture does satisfy the needs of Pascal. In the second part of this chapter, a typical 'educational computer board' is briefly described. Most students will continue from this introductory course onto courses that use such educational computer systems.

Pascal on the 68000

The following examples present Pascal code fragments together with the corresponding Motorola MC68000 assembly language code generated by a compiler. These examples illustrate assembly language code for accessing arrays and records, for preparing arguments and then calling a subroutine, and for various loop constructs and case statements. The examples illustrate based addressing, based and indexed addressing, and relative addressing.

Often the code is not optimal; in some places, careful hand coding, and use of special instructions, might have led to more concise and faster code. Such optimizations, however, require a powerful, multipass compiler to examine the data manipulations in large blocks of code and detect opportunities for optimizations such as the practicality of using a register for a for-loop index in a particular for-loop.

The computational model employed in this Pascal system is illustrated in Figure 19-1. The computer is presumed to have a segmented memory (described briefly in Chapter 15 and in more detail in Chapter 21) with code and data in separate segments. There are two types of data segment: the stack segment and the heap segment(s). The stack segment is the most important in the various data manipulations illustrated in the following examples.

The model presumes three register pointers into the stack segment; in the implementation, three of the 68000's address registers are used. These three register pointers are the stack pointer ('a7'), the current stack-frame pointer ('a6'), and a globals pointer ('a5'). The globals pointer identifies the start of the stack-frame associated with the main program, and hence all the global variables declared in the Pascal program header. Globals can be addressed using based-addressing modes that reference this globals pointer. Variables declared in the current procedure can be accessed using the current frame pointer. The examples do not include any cases where variables in enclosing procedures need to be accessed; such accesses would, as noted in Chapter 15, require chasing through links in the stack-frames.

Figure 19-1. Computational model employed by the Pascal compiler

Memory

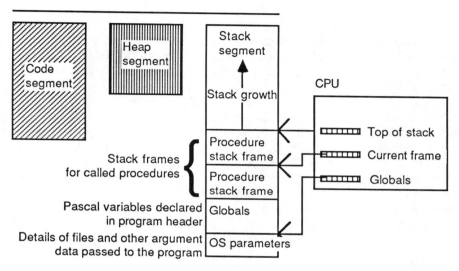

A program using globals and a for-loop

The following Pascal program constitutes a simple first example:

```
program little;
var  j : integer;
  sum : integer;
begin
    sum:=0;
    for j:=1 to 3 do
        sum:=sum+j;
end.
```

There are two global variables on the stack; both are 2-byte integers. The address of variable 'j' is two bytes below where the globals pointer ('a5') points; 'sum' is located four bytes below 'a5'. The assembly language code, for the initialization of the variable sum and the loop, is as follows:

```
*     sum:=0;
            CLR.W           $FFFC(A5)                     1
*     for j:=1 to 3 do
            MOVE.W          #$0001,$FFFE(A5)              2
            BRA.S           L0001                         3
*         sum:=sum+j;
L0002       MOVE.W          $FFFE(A5),D0                  4
```

```
                ADD.W        D0,$FFFC(A5)                  5
                ADDQ.W       #$1,FFFE(A5)                  6
L0001           CMPI.W       #$0003,$FFFE(A5)              7
                BLE.S        L0002                         8
```

Line 1 illustrates based addressing. The address of the (2-byte) word to be cleared is pointed to by 'a5' ('(A5)') as modified by the hexadecimal value '$FFFC'. The hexadecimal constant, '$FFFC', is interpreted as a 2-byte signed integer and, in two's complement notation, represents the decimal value -4. So, this instruction does clear the location reserved for 'sum'. In line 2, the code uses both an immediate operand, the constant '$0001', and based addressing. The use of immediate operand addressing is flagged by the #. The based addressing, '$FFFE(A5)', is interpreted in the same way as in line 1; here the reference is to the variable whose address is given by adding -2 to the value in register 'a5', that is, it is the address of variable 'j'.

Line 3 is an unconditional branch to the statement with the (compiler-generated) label 'L0001'. Pascal requires a for-loop not be traversed if its termination condition is immediately satisfied. Consequently, the compiler always generates a branch to the termination test following the body of the code of the for-loop. The compiler has specified 'short form addressing' in this branch instruction; the number of words to be jumped is small (<128) and, therefore, the branch can be fitted into a one-word instruction. If the destination was more remote, then a long form (two-word) branch instruction is used with 16 bits of offset data.

Lines 4-6 represent the body of the loop. Line 4 moves the contents of variable 'j' into data register 'd0'; again, the variable is referenced using based addressing relative to the globals pointer. Line 5 adds the (one-word, 2-byte) contents of 'd0' to the value in memory at the location for variable 'sum'. The 'ADDQ' instruction in line 6 exploits the 'quick' form of the 'add' instruction; like the short form branch, this is a specialisation that can be used when an immediate constant is sufficiently small (here, <8) to be fitted into the instruction word. This instruction updates the value of the for-loop index, 'j'.

Lines 7 and 8 constitute the termination test at the end of the loop. In line 7, the compare instruction compares an immediate operand, '#$0003', with the contents of memory location '$FFFE(A5)' or 'j'. The results of the comparison are left in the condition bits, and are tested by the 'BLE.S' instruction in line 8. The branch back to 'L0002' is made if either the 'less than' or the 'zero' (or 'equals') bit is set.

There was no need to keep the value of 'j' in the memory location reserved for this variable. Pascal does not require the value of a for-loop index to be defined on exit from the loop. Register 'd0' could be used to hold the index value needed in the loop; this value is discarded once the loop is complete. Such use of a register leads to code that executes slightly faster. One of the other examples illustrates register usage.

Apart from the code illustrated, the compiler also generates a fairly large amount of initialization and termination code. These code sections, which are operating system specific, invoke support routines that (1) arrange for the correct establishment of a stack (setting initial values for 'a7', 'a6', 'a5', and so forth), (2) open default input and output streams, and (3) perform other related housekeeping activities.

A program using a one-dimensional array

This second example illustrates the use of the Motorola 68000's based and indexed addressing mode for array access. Two other points worth noting are the use of 'CHK' check instructions, and differences in the code as compiled for packed and unpacked arrays. The Pascal program is:

```
program help;
var
      thing        : array[1..5] of char;
      i            : integer;
      next         : char;
begin
      thing[1]:='H';
      thing[2]:='e';
      thing[3]:='l';
      thing[4]:='p';
      thing[5]:='!';
      for i:=1 to 5 do begin
            next:=thing[i];
            write(next);
            end;
end.
```

The stack usage for the program is shown in Figure 19-2. On the stack there is an array, an integer, and the variable of type 'char'. All array elements, and the other two variables, are allocated as words, that is, as 2-byte quantities.

Figure 19-2. Arrangement of globals in the stack for program 'help'

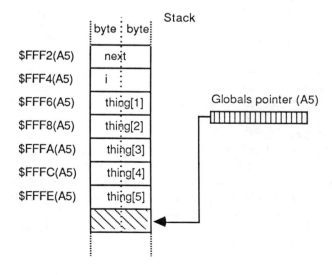

A part of the assembly language code is as follows:

```
*     thing[4]:='p';
              MOVE.W          #$0070,$FFFC(A5)              1
*     thing[5]:='!';
              MOVE.W          #$0021,$FFFE(A5)              2
*     for i:=1 to 5 do begin
              MOVE.W          #$0001,$FFF4(A5)             3
              BRA.S           L0001                          4
*     next:=thing[i];
L0002         MOVE.W          $FFF4(A5),D0                 5
              ASL.W           #$1,D0                        6
              MOVE.W          $F4(A5,D0.W),$FFF2(A5)       7
*     write(next);
              MOVE.L          $000C(A5),-(A7)              8
              MOVE.B          $FFF3(A5),-(A7)             9
              MOVE.W          #$0001,-(A7)                  10
              JSR             %W_C                          11
              ADDQ.W          #$1,$FFF4(A5)                12
L0001         CMPI.W          #$0005,$FFF4(A5)             13
              BLE.S           L0002                          14
*     end;
```

The code in lines 1 and 2 performs initialization of array elements. Although an 'array of char', each element of the array has been allocated one word; so these are word-sized moves. These instructions use immediate mode addressing for the character constants ('$0070' is the hexadecimal code for 'p'), and based addressing for the array elements. The array subscripts are constants in this part of the code, and the compiler has taken advantage of this and generated fixed offsets relative to the globals pointer in these references to array elements.

The code in lines 3 and 4 represents the initialization of the value of the for-loop index and the branch around the body of the loop to the loop-termination test at label 'L0001'.

Lines 5, 6, and 7 represent the code for copying a datum from an appropriate array element into the global variable 'next'. In line 5, the value of the loop index 'i' is moved into register 'd0'. This index is to be used as an offset into the array so that the desired array element will be accessed. These array elements are each 2 bytes in size; consequently, the index value must be doubled before it represents the correct byte offset. The shift instruction in line 6 performs this index-to-offset conversion (an arithmetic shift left by one place doubles a number).

The instruction in line 7 performs a move of a one-word datum. The destination address, '$FFF2(A5)', is just another example of based addressing; it is the address of variable 'next'. The source address, '$F4(A5,D0.W)', is a little more complex. Here, the combined based and indexed addressing mode is used. Register 'a5' is the base; the (word) contents of register 'd0' are the index; a final offset of '$F4' is added. The offset, '$F4', is a signed byte; comparison with the addresses used in other instructions is easier if this is written as a 2-byte offset ('$FFF4').

As shown in Figure 19-2, the array, 'thing', is located on the stack with 'thing[1]' is at '$FFF6(A5)', 'thing[2]' at '$FFF8(A5)', and so on. The address that needs to be generated in the first cycle of the loop is therefore '$FFF6(A5)'. This is the address generated by adding the index value, from 'd0', and the offset '$FFF4' given in the instruction in line 7. On the first iteration, 'i=1', the value in register 'd0' will be 2 (after the shift in line 6). So the address from which data will be moved is '$FFF4' + 2 + (contents of 'a5') or '$FFF6(A5)'.

Here, the compiler has probably done a better coding job than the average assembly language programmer. Most programmers would probably have written code that loads another address register, for example, 'a4', with the address of the first element of 'thing', and then used a based and indexed mode specifying this address register.

Lines 8-10 show data being pushed onto the stack. Each of these instructions uses the pre-decrementing, register indirect mode referencing the stack pointer, '-(A7)'. These are standard push operations; the stack pointer is adjusted and then a datum is copied onto the stack. The first move, a long-word (4-byte) operation, handles information relating to the file used in the 'write' (it is the implicitly declared standard output file that happens to be described by data held just above (A5)). The byte move instruction, in line 9, copies the character from variable 'next' onto the stack. Here, 'next' is identified by '$FFF3(A5)', whereas in the word move operation in instruction, line 7, the address was '$FFF2(A5)'. The difference is that here the code is explicitly referencing the higher address byte of the 2-byte variable. (Although this is a byte-move, register 'a7' is decremented by 2 to keep it word-aligned.) The final move instruction pushes, onto the stack, a constant representing data relating to the print format.

In line 11, there is a call to a subroutine 'W_C' (the '%' sign marks this as a run-time support routine). This is one of the run-time support routines that will eventually be linked with this Pascal-derived code. Lines 12-14 are the instructions that perform the incrementation of the loop index and the loop-termination test.

The compiler used in these examples normally generates slightly more elaborate code for any reference to an array that involves a variable as a subscript. The code reads:

```
*          next:=thing[i];
L0002      MOVE.W      $FFF4(A5),D0                  a
           MOVE.W      D0,D1                         b
           SUBQ.W      #$1,D1                        c
           CHK         #$0004,D1                     d
           ASL.W       #$1,D0                        e
           MOVE.W      $F4(A5,D0.W),$FFF2(A5)        f
```

The extra instructions (b-d) perform *array bound checking*. The objective of the code is to verify that the subscript value used is in the range 1...5 inclusive; if this is not the case, then a run-time error is flagged because the subscript has gone out of range. The test utilises the 'CHK' check instruction; this uses hardware to flag the detection of an error. The setting of this flag causes an interrupt that ultimately is handled by the operating system. The operating system then terminates the erroneous program.

In instruction b, the index value 'i' is copied to 'd1' from register 'd0' (into which it was previously loaded). This is an example of register mode addressing; both source and destination are registers. The subtract instruction (again, a quick mode variant) makes 'd1' hold the value 'i - 1'. Then, the 'CHK' instruction is performed; the value in 'd1 'is checked against an implicit lower bound of 0, and an upper bound, which is specified here as the immediate operand '$0004'. Expressing the range as $0 \le i - 1 \le 4$ rather than $1 \le i \le 5$ simplifies the check due to the implicit test within the 'CHK' instruction.

If the check instruction fails, the program stops. Otherwise, execution continues with the code in lines (e) and (f) that converts the index value still in 'd0' into an offset and moves this data to 'next'. (It is wise to follow the example of this compiler and use 'CHK' at appropriate places in all assembly language programs.)

Allocation of a 2-byte word for each element of an array of characters is a little wasteful, but it is the default action of this compiler. If, however, the array was declared as a 'packed array of char', then the compiler generates code that makes use of more efficient data storage. However, the generated code is a little more involved:

```
*      thing[4]:='p';
              MOVEQ        #$04,D0                      1
              MOVE.B       #$0070,$F9(A5,D0.W)          2
*      thing[5]:='!';
              MOVEQ        #$05,D0                      3
              MOVE.B       #$0021,$F9(A5,D0.W)          4
*      for i:=1 to 5 do begin
              MOVE.W       #$0001,$FFF8(A5)             5
              BRA.S        L0001                        6
*      next:=thing[i];
L0002         MOVE.W       $FFF8(A5),D0                 7
              MOVE.W       D0,D1                        8
              SUBQ.W       #$1,D1                       9
              CHK          #$0004,D1                    10
              MOVE.B       $F9(A5,D0.W),D1              11
              ANDI.W       #$00FF,D1                    12
              MOVE.W       D1,$FFF6(A5)                 13
```

This code has one less conceptual step than that shown earlier; now the index can be used directly as the offset into the byte array and no shift instruction is needed. But, the byte-copying operation becomes more elaborate as the byte is moved into a register, the register is carefully masked, and then a store word operation is performed ('next' is still a one-word, 2-byte variable). Although memory usage might be improved, the code is slower (here, with a very small character array, the extra instructions actually occupy more memory than that saved by packing the character array).

A program with 'while', 'repeat', and 'case' constructs

This example illustrates how some other Pascal programming constructs map into 68000 assembly language. The Pascal program is:

```
program calculator;
var
     entry, result    : longint;
     operator         : char;
begin
     write('>');
     while not eof do begin { main loop }
          result:=0;
          operator:='+';
          repeat { data entry andd combine loop }
               read(entry);
               case operator of
                    '+':        result:=result+entry;
                    '-':        result:=result-entry;
                    '*':        result:=result*entry;
                    '/':        result:=result div entry;
                    end;
               read(operator);
          until (operator='='); { end of data entry  loop }
          write(result);
          readln;
          write('>');
     end { main loop } ;
end.
```

The assembly language code is as follows:

```
*      while not eof do begin
L0008          MOVE.L          $0008(A5),-(A7)              1
               JSR             %_EOF                        2
               MOVE.B          (A7)+,D0                     3
               EORI.B          #$0001,D0                    4
               BEQ             L0001                        5
*      result:=0;
               CLR.L           $FFFC(A5)                    6
*      operator:='+';
               MOVE.W          #$002B,$FFF6(A5)             7
*      repeat
L0007          MOVE.L          $0008(A5),-(A7)              8
               JSR             %R_I                         9
               MOVE.L          (A7)+,$FFF8(A5)             10
*      case operator of
               MOVE.W          $FFF6(A5),D0                11
               SUBI.W          #$002A,D0                   12
               BEQ.S           L0002                       13
               SUBQ.W          #$1,D0                      14
               BEQ.S           L0003                       15
               SUBQ.W          #$2,D0                      16
               BEQ.S           L0004                       17
               SUBQ.W          #$2,D0                      18
```

```
              BEQ.S        L0005                            19
              BRA.S        L0006                            20
*     '+': result:=result+entry;
L0003         MOVE.L       $FFF8(A5),D0                     21
              ADD.L        D0,$FFFC(A5)                     22
              BRA.S        L0006                            23
*     '-': result:=result-entry;
L0004         MOVE.L       $FFF8(A5),D0                     24
              SUB.L        D0,$FFFC(A5)                     25
              BRA.S        L0006                            26
*     '*': result:=result*entry;
L0002         MOVE.L       $FFFC(A5),-(A7)                  27
              MOVE.L       $FFF8(A5),-(A7)                  28
              JSR          %I_MUL4                          29
              MOVE.L       (A7)+,$FFFC(A5)                  30
              BRA.S        L0006                            31
*     '/': result:=result div entry;
L0005         MOVE.L       $FFFC(A5),-(A7)                  32
              MOVE.L       $FFF8(A5),-(A7)                  33
              JSR          %I_DIV4                          34
              MOVE.L       (A7)+,$FFFC(A5)                  35
*     end;
*     read(operator);
L0006         MOVE.L       $0008(A5),-(A7)                  36
              JSR          %R_C                             37
              CLR.W        D0                               38
              MOVE.B       (A7)+,D0 39
              MOVE.W       D0,$FFF6(A5)                     40
              CMPI.W       #$003D,$FFF6(A5)                 41
              BNE.S        L0007                            42
*     until (operator='=');
*     write(result);
              MOVE.L       $000C(A5),-(A7)                  43
              MOVE.L       $FFFC(A5),-(A7)                  44
              MOVE.W       #$0008,-(A7)                     45
              JSR          %W_I                             46
*     readln;
              MOVE.L       $0008(A5),-(A7)                  47
              JSR          %R_LN                            48
*     write('>');
              MOVE.L       $000C(A5),-(A7)                  49
              MOVE.B       #$0003E,-(A7)                    50
              MOVE.W       #$0001,-(A7)                     51
              JSR          %W_C                             52
              BRA          L0008                            53
* end;
L0001
```

The instructions in lines 1-5 constitute the 'while'-loop test. The file identifier for the default input file is pushed onto the stack, and the end-of-file function is called. The result from this function is left on the stack. In line 3, using post-increment register indirect mode, this boolean result value is popped out of the stack into register 'd0'. The 'exclusive or' instruction in line 4 checks the right-most bit. If the right-most bit of the result in 'd0' is 1 (true), then the 'exclusive or' instruction leaves zero in the 'd0' register and sets the 'zero' ('equals') bit in the condition codes. In line 5, the condition codes are tested in a conditional branch to code following the body of the 'while' loop. Here, the normal branch is used because the destination is more than 128 bytes away and the short form of the branch instruction cannot be employed.

Line 6 zeros out 'result'. As this is a 4-byte 'longint' variable, a long-word clear is used. As in the previous example, the variable 'operator' of type 'char' actually occupies a 2-byte word; so, in line 7, it is initialized using a 'move word' instruction.

The instructions in lines 8, 9, and 10 call another of the run-time support routines of this Pascal package. This time the routine is 'R_I', the read-integer routine. Like the end-of-file routine, this 'R_I' is a function that leaves its result on the stack. The instruction in line 10 pops this result off the stack and moves it into variable 'entry'.

The code for the case statement, lines 11-35, consists of a sequence of tests for each possible case value, followed by the appropriate pieces of processing code. If a test is satisfied, a branch is made to the appropriate fragment of processing code. In this dialect of Pascal, an unsatisfied case statement is not an error, execution continues with the statement following the case. This is not standard; usually, the test for the final valid value of the case selector variable is followed by a branch to a run-time error reporting routine.

The compiler has rearranged the sequence in which the tests are performed to achieve a slight local optimization of the code. The value of the case selector, 'operator', is copied into 'd0' by the instruction in line 11. Line 12 subtracts the value for '*'; the conditional branch in line 13 causes a jump to label 'L0002' (i.e. the start of the code for doing the multiplication) if the subtract has set the 'zero' condition bit. The code in lines 14 and 15 tests whether the case selector was '+'. (First, subtract another 1, that is, a total of '$2B' subtracted. In ASCII, '$2B' represents '+'. So, if the result is now zero, a jump is made to the code for addition.) The tests in lines 16-19 are similar. Line 20 is the branch to the end of the case statement that avoids the problems (mentioned previously) of an unsatisfied case selector value.

The code for the addition, lines 21-23, is simple. The value of 'entry', specified using the standard based addressing, is copied into register 'd0'. The value in 'd0' is then added to the value already in 'result' at '$FFFC(A5)'. The code for this particular case is completed, in line 23, with an unconditional branch to the code that follows the body of the case statement. Subtraction, lines 24-26, is similar.

The code for multiplication, lines 27-31, and the code for division, lines 32-35, are a little more complex. The 68000 does have hardware multiply and divide instructions. However, the multiply is limited to obtaining the 32-bit product of two 16-bit values. This instruction cannot be used here, as both 'entry' and 'result' are 32-bit 'longints'. Instead, a multiply subroutine in the Pascal run-time support package must be used. The code in lines 27-30 first pushes the values of 'result' and 'entry' onto the stack, then calls the subroutine 'I_MUL4', and finally pops the product from the stack into 'result'. Similar limitations on the division instruction make it necessary to use the interpretive subroutine, 'I_DIV4'.

The code in lines 36-40 involves another call to a run-time support function, 'R_C' (read character), with the result popped from the stack into 'd0' and thence moved into memory. The comparison and branch instructions, lines 41 and 42, check for termination of the 'repeat' loop; if the termination condition is not satisfied, then the branch back to label 'L0007' is made.

The remainder of the code, lines 43-53, again involves mostly calls to run-time support routines. The unconditional branch, line 53, marks the end of the 'while' loop.

A program that passes the address of a string constant

The Pascal program examples shown so far have called various run-time support I/O functions and procedures. All arguments were passed by value and the calling sequence had only to push values onto the stack. However, frequently, address data must be passed. A rather simple case, illustrated in the following program, is the necessity to pass the address of a string to one of the run-time support routines. The Pascal code is as follows:

```
program greet;
const N=10;
var  j : integer;
begin
     for j:=1 to N do
          writeln('Hello World');
end.
```

This compiler places the constant string, 'Hello World', in the code segment. (The use of a separate statics segment might be preferable.) The assembly language code is as follows:

```
*     for j:=1 to N do
                MOVE.W          #$0001,$FFFE(A5)              1
                BRA.S           L0001                        2
*         writeln('Hello World');
L0002           MOVE.L          $000C(A5),-(A7)              3
                PEA             Cst001                       4
                CLR.W           -(A7)                        5
                JSR             %W_STR                       6
                MOVE.L          $000C(A5),-(A7)              7
                JSR             %W_LN                        8
                ADDQ.W          #$1,FFFE(A5)                 9
L0001           CMPI.W          #$000A,$FFFE(A5)            10
                BLE.S           L0002                       11
                  .
                  .
                  .
Cst001    .BYTE           11                               12
          .ASCII          'Hello '                         13
          .ASCII          'World'                          14
```

The loop construct is the same as that illustrated in previous examples. The new feature here is the need to pass the address of the string to the 'W_STR' (write string) procedure. Of course, the address of the string is not known at assemble time; this address depends on where in memory the code segment that contains the string is finally loaded. The 'PEA' (Push Effective Address) instruction in line 4 provides a way of resolving this problem. The 'PEA' instruction evaluates the address of its source, 'Cst001', and then pushes the result onto the stack. In this case, the address evaluation is based upon the use of PC relative addressing. The compiler and assembler can determine how many bytes, after this 'PEA' instruction, the string 'Cst001' is located. The coding of the source address in the 'PEA' instruction specifies this offset. At run time, the offset is added to the PC to give the effective address of the string. Using this approach, the code is completely position independent; it does not matter where the code segment is placed in memory.

A program with local procedures

When calling a procedure in this implementation of Pascal, the caller's work is limited to pushing a few arguments onto the stack. The rest of the work involved in setting up a new stack-frame must be performed in an initialization phase of the called procedure. Code for building stack-frames is included in the following example:

```
program dosomething;
const N=10;
var   j      : integer;
      t      : array[1..N] of integer;
      procedure sort;
      var i,j,k   : integer;
          temp: integer;
      begin
          for i:=1 to N-1 do begin
                temp;=t[i]; k:=i;
                for j:=i+1 to N do begin
                        if t[j]<temp then begin
                                temp:=t[j];
                                k:-j;
                                end;
                end;
              t[k]:=t[i];
              t[i]:=temp
          end;
      end;

begin
      for j:=1 to N do readln(t[j]);
      sort;
      for j:=1 to N do writeln(t[j]);
end.
```

The assembly language code for some parts of this program follows:

```
*       procedure sort;
*       var i,j,k:integer;
*       temp:integer;
*       begin
SORT            .
                LINK            A6,#$FFF8                       1
                MOVEM.L         D4-D7,-(A7)                     2
*       for i:=1 to N-1 do begin
                MOVEQ           #$01,D7                         3
                BRA.S           L0001                           4
*       temp:=t[i];k:=i;
L0005           MOVE.W          D7,D0                           5
                SUBQ.W          $#1,D0                          6
                CHK             #$0009,D0                       7
                MOVE.L          D7,D0                           8
                ASL.W           #$1,D0                          9
                MOVE.W          $E8(A5,D0.W),D5                 10
                MOVE.W          D7,D4                           11
*       for j:=i+1 to N do begin
                .
                .
                .

*       t[i]:=temp; { at end of i loop }
                MOVE.W          D7,D0                           12
                SUBQ.W          #$1,D0                          13
                CHK             #$0009,D0                       14
                MOVE.L          D7,D0                           15
                ASL.W           #$1,D0                          16
                MOVE.W          D5,$E8(A5,D0.W)                 17
                ADDQ.W          #$1,D7                          18
L0001           CMPI.W          #$0009,D7                       19
                BLE.S           L0005                           20
*       end; { the end statement of i loop }
*       end; { of procedure sort }
                MOVEM.L         (A7)+,D4-D7                     21
                UNLK            A6                              22
                RTS                                             23
*       begin
*       for j:=1 to N do readln(t[j]);
                .
                .
                .

*       sort;
                JSR             SORT                            24
*       for j:= ...
                .
                .
                .
```

The main program consists of a couple of simple loops with calls to run-time support routines. The code for these is similar to that shown in previous examples. The call to the 'SORT' procedure, in line 24, requires only the 'JSR' subroutine call instruction. As 'SORT' works on globals, no arguments need to be pushed onto the stack.

When the code of 'SORT' is entered, the return address is the top element of the stack, previously pushed there by the 'JSR' instruction. If there had been any arguments, these would have been located at higher stack locations.

The code for 'SORT' begins with a 'LINK' instruction. The 'LINK' instruction identifies the stack-frame register, 'a6', and the number of bytes needed for local variables of the procedure. When executed the 'LINK' instruction performs the following operations: (1) the current value of 'a6', that is, the address of the stack-frame of a calling procedure, is pushed onto the stack; and the value indicating the top of stack is then copied into 'a6' from the stack pointer 'a7', and (2) the offset '$FFF8' is added to 'a7' thereby lifting the top of stack to leave space for local variables.

This Pascal implementation treats the first few data registers, 'd0'-'d3', as scratch registers that can be used freely. Other data registers should be preserved across procedure calls. Since the code generated for procedure 'SORT' needs several temporary registers, the next instruction, line 2, saves the current values of 'd4'-'d7'. The 'MOVEM' instruction specifies the source registers and identifies the destination as on the stack (by the 'pre-decrement register indirect' addressing mode on a7). The values in these four data registers are pushed onto the stack when this instruction is executed. The state of the stack is illustrated in Figure 19-3.

Figure 19-3. The top part of the stack after entry to the sort routine

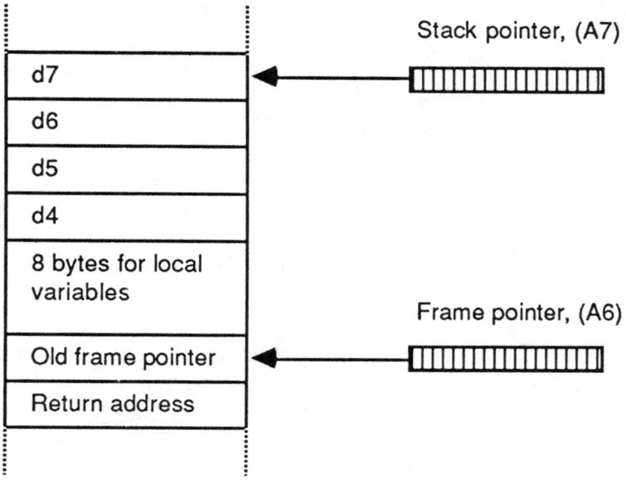

The code for the body of the 'SORT' routine is similar to previous examples using for-loops, except that here the compiler uses data registers for all temporary values. Register 'd7' is used for 'i', 'd6' for 'j', 'd5' for 'temp', and 'd4' for 'k'. Although space for these variables was saved on the stack, that space is never used. Since the code for the sort is sufficiently simple, it is possible to keep active data in registers throughout the body of the loops.

Lines 3 and 4 are the instructions that initialize the 'i-loop' index and jump to the end of the for-loop as in previous examples. Lines 5-10 are the code that first checks if the subscript is out of range, and then loads the value of 't[i]' into 'temp', that is, into 'd5'. Because this code works on the global array 't', the instruction on line 10 uses based and indexed addressing as in previous examples of array access. The 'MOVE', in line 11, uses register mode addressing and copies the value from 'i' ('d7') into 'k' ('d4').

The code in lines 12-17 performs an analogous store back into the array. The code for terminating the 'i' for-loop is shown in lines 18-20. This differs from previous examples only in that the for-loop index is now a register, and consequently register addressing modes are used.

The code in lines 21-23 tidy up and return from the subroutine. First, in line 21, the values for 'd4'-'d7', that were saved on entry, are popped back off the stack and into these data registers. When executed, the 'UNLK' instruction (1) sets 'a7' to the value in 'a6' releasing the space that was saved for locals, and (2) pops data from the stack into 'a6' setting 'a6' back to again point to the stack-frame of the calling procedure. After these operations, register 'a7' points to the stack location holding the return address. Finally, the 'RTS', return from subroutine, instruction pops this return address out of the stack and into the PC.

A program using a record structure

Pascal records may be allocated space on the stack or in the heap. With a declaration like:

```
program xxx;
type account = record
                number : longint;
                value  : integer;
                end;
var  arec = account;
     .
     .
     .
```

the record 'arec' is allocated space in the globals area of the stack. The compiler and assembler derive addresses for the various fields of the record and specify them, using based addressing employing the globals pointer 'a5', in instructions that manipulate data from the record. The code is then fairly similar to that used when accessing a global array as illustrated in previous examples.

Other Pascal records are created dynamically using the Pascal 'new()' procedure. When the operating system starts a program, it allocates a heap segment with a few thousand bytes of memory space reserved for Pascal 'new()' and 'free()' operations. The run-time support routines, linked with Pascal code, incorporate subroutines for managing this heap space. When a new record is required, a call to 'new()' is made; in this call, a

Pascal pointer variable is passed as a 'var' argument. The corresponding run-time support routine (1) finds an unused space in the heap zone, (2) marks this space as allocated, and (3) returns its address in the Pascal pointer variable.

The following example illustrates some aspects of using dynamically allocated Pascal records:

```
program littlerec;
type
     partrecptr = ^partrec;
     partrec = record
          number  : longint;
          cost    : integer;
          sellfor : integer;
          link    : partrecptr;
          end;
var  i,numrecs : integer;
     part,lastpart : partrecptr;
begin
     readln(numrecs);
     lastpart:=NIL;
     for i:=1 to numrecs do begin
          new(part);
          with part^ do
               readln(number,cost,sellfor);
          part^.link:=lastpart;
          lastpart:=part;
          end;
end.
```

The assembly language code illustrating access to the records follows:

```
*       lastpart:=NIL;
                CLR.L           $FFF8(A5)                    1
*       for i:=1 to numrecs do

                .
                .
                BRA.S           L0001                        2
*       new(part);
L0003           PEA             $FFF4(A5)                    3
                MOVE.W          #$000C,-(A7)                 4
                JSR             %_NEW                        5
*       with part^ do readln(number,cost,sellfor);
                MOVE.L          $FFF4(A5),A0                 6
                MOVE.L          $0008(A5),-(A7)              7
                JSR             %R_I                         8
                MOVE.L          (A7)+,(A0)                   9
                MOVE.L          $FFF4(A5),A0                10
                MOVE.L          $0008(A5),-(A7)             11
                JSR             %R_I                        12
                MOVE.L          (A7)+,D0                    13
```

```
        MOVE.W          D0,$0004(A0)                        14
          .
          .
*       part^.link:=lastpart;
        MOVE.L          $FFF4(A5),A0                        15
        MOVE.L          $FFF8(A5),$0008(A0)                 16
*       lastpart:=part;
        MOVE.L          $FFF4(A5),$FFF8(A5)                 17
          .
          .
```

The Pascal pointer variables 'part' (at $FFF4(A5)) and 'lastpart' (at $FFF8(A5)) are both 4-byte variables as they hold addresses. (On the 68000, addresses take 24 bits; 32 bits on the later 68020 model.) Line 1 clears 'lastpart'; the value 0 is used here for the 'NIL' pointer.

The run-time support routine '_NEW' needs the address of a Pascal pointer into which it stores the address of the space allocated for the new record. Once again, it is necessary to calculate the address at run time. The address of 'part' is required, therefore, the 'PEA' instruction, in line 3, evaluates the effective address, working out the actual address from the value in 'a5' at run-time. This address is then pushed onto the stack. The other argument pushed onto the stack, line 4, is the size of record to be created; here it is '$000C' bytes. The '_NEW' routine, called in line 5, sets the address of the new record in 'part'.

Line 6 copies this address into address register 'a0'. Lines 7-8 are the instructions that make the call to the integer reading function in the run-time support. Line 9 pops the result of the read-integer function from the stack, and stores it in the address pointed to by 'a0'. In this instruction, there is a post-increment register indirect on 'a7', and a register indirect via 'a0'. This long-word 'MOVE' copies the 4-byte value into the appropriate number field of the 'part^' record.

Line 10 is a totally redundant instruction; the compiler has not seen that 'a0' already contains the value that this instruction copies into it. Lines 11 and 12 represent the next call to the integer-input function. Processing of the result is slightly more complex this time. The result on the stack is a long-word, 4-byte integer; the value needed in 'part^.cost' is a short 2-byte integer. The long-word result is popped into a data register, line 13; then the word-sized value is stored, line 14. Here, in line 14, based addressing is used with the base being '(A0)' and an offset of '$0004'. This 'MOVE' copies the value into the correct field of the 'part^' record.

Lines 15-17 illustrate further 'MOVE' operations that shift the address pointers around.

Figure 19-4 shows the state of memory at a point part way through the third cycle of the for-loop. Two previously created records already exist on the heap; record 2 has a link back to record 1, while record 1 would have a 0 in its link field. The pointer 'lastpart' holds the address of record 2. A new record has been allocated, and its address is held in 'part'.

Figure 19-4. State of memory during execution of program 'littlerec'

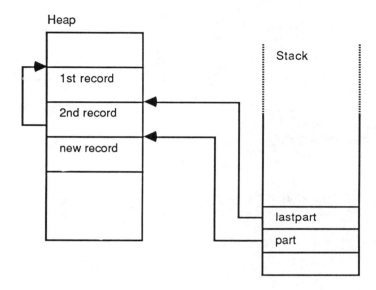

A program that passes arguments to its procedures

The example Pascal program that used a local procedure 'sort' did not need to pass any argument data. Procedure 'sort' worked on a globally defined array. The following example illustrates aspects of the code that handle 'var' and value parameters. The Pascal code is:

```pascal
program histogram;
type
      darray     = array[0..10] of integer;
var
      somnedata : darray;
      procedure initialize(var thing:darray);
      var i : integer;
      begin
            for i:=0 to 10 do thing[i]:=0;
      end;
      procedure readdata(var themarks:darray);
      var mark  : integer;
      begin
            while not eof do begin
                  readln(mark);
                  mark:=mark div 10;
                  themarks[mark]:=themarks[mark]+1;
                  end;
      end;
```

```
        procedure drawone(thedata:darray);
        var i,j     : integer;
        begin
            for i:=0 to 10 do begin
                for j:=1 to thedata[i] do write('*');
                writeln;
                end;
        end;

    begin
        initialize(somedata);
        readdata(somedata);
        drawone(somedata);
    end.
```

In this example, an array is passed to various procedures either by value, or as a 'var' parameter. The assembly language code follows:

```
*       procedure initialize(var thing:darray);
*       var i:integer;
*       begin
INITIALI
                LINK            A6,#$FFFE                       1
                MOVE.L          D7,-(A7)                        2
*       for i:=0 to 10 do thing[i]:=0;
                CLR.W           D7                              3
                BRA.S           L0001                           4
L0002           MOVE.L          $0008(A6),A0                    5
                CHK             #$000A,D7                       6
                MOVE.L          D7,D0                           7
                ASL.W           #$1,D0                          8
                CLR.W           $00(A0,D0.W)                    9
                ADDQ.W          #$1,D7                          10
L0001           CMPI.W          #$000A,D7                       11
                BLE.S           L0002                           12
                MOVE.L          (A7)+,D7                        13
                UNLK            A6                              14
                RTS                                             15
                .
                .

*       procedure drawone(thedata:darray);
*       var i,j: integer;
*       begin
DRAWONE         .
                LINK            A6,#$FFE4                       16
                MOVEM.L         D6/D7,-(A7)                     17
                MOVE.L          $0008(A6),A0                    18
                LEA             $FFEA(A6),A1                    19
                MOVE.Q          #$05,D0                         20
```

```
        MOVE.L      (A0)+,(A1)+                21
        SUBQ.W      #$1,D0                     22
        BGT.S       *-$0004                    23
        MOVE.W      (A0),(A1)                  24
*   for i:= 0 to 10 do begin
            .
            .
* begin { main program }
            .
*   initialize(somedata);
        PEA         $FFEA(A5)                  25
        JSR         INITIALI                   26
            .
            .
```

The code in lines 1 and 2 is standard code for setting up a stack-frame for routine 'initialize'. The 'LINK' instruction updates the stack-frame pointer and claims a couple of bytes of storage for the local variable 'i'; the 'MOVE' saves the value of the one data register needed in this procedure. The state of the stack at this stage is shown in Figure 19-5. The address of the argument array is then on the stack 8 bytes above where the updated stack-frame pointer is pointing.

Figure 19-5. State of the stack after entry to various procedures in program histogram

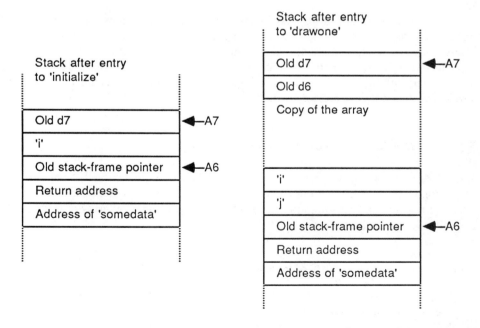

Lines 3 and 4 represent standard code for loop-initialization; once again, the compiler uses a data register 'd7' for the loop index.

The code in lines 5–9 represents the instructions needed to clear a particular array element. The 'MOVE' instruction in line 5 copies the address of the data array into address register 'a0'. Based addressing, relative to the stack-frame pointer, is used in the specification of the source for this 'MOVE' instruction. The next instruction, line 6, performs the array bounds check; then the loop index is converted into an offset address, lines 7 and 8, making allowance for the fact that each array element occupies 2 bytes. The 'CLR' instruction, in line 9, uses based and indexed addressing. The base address is provided by the contents of address register 'a0'; the index is in data register 'd0'. The syntax of the assembler requires specification of an offset with this addressing mode; here, it is zero. The effective address in this 'CLR' instruction represents an element within the (global) array 'somedata'.

The instructions in lines 10-12 complete the for-loop; those in lines 13-15 perform the tidying up and return from subroutine.

The first couple of instructions of procedure 'drawone' are similar to those of 'initialize'. The 'LINK' instruction, though, has to claim much more space on the stack. Here, the array is passed by value; consequently, procedure 'drawone' needs space where it can hold a copy of the array (see Figure 19-5).

In line 18, the address of the argument array 'somedata' is copied into address register 'a0'. Again, the argument is obtained using an addressing mode that employs based addressing relative to the frame pointer. The 'LEA' (Load Effective Address) instruction in line 19 works out the address where 'thedata[0]' is located in the stack, and then loads this address in address register 'a1'. The address for 'thedata[0]' is defined in terms of an offset to the base address for the frame, as defined by the stack-frame pointer 'a6'.

The instructions in lines 20-24 represent a loop that copies the contents of the 'somedata' array into the 'thedata' array. The instruction in line 21 illustrates a slightly different use of an autoincrement register indirect mode from that shown previously. In previous examples the register-indirect and post-increment mode was used only when popping data off the stack. Here, the autoincrementing mode is useful in a loop that works through successive array elements.

A program using a two-dimensional array

In the examples shown so far, the 68000 has consistently demonstrated the appropriate addressing modes and instructions for an effective implementation of the Pascal code. Yet even this machine has its limitations. Access to a two-dimensional array is still painful. The following code illustrates:

```
program mm;
type matrix = array[1..10,1..10] of longint;
var
      d1,d2     : matrix;
      procedure getmatrix(var a:matrix);
      var i,j:integer;
```

```
begin
     for i:=1 to 10 do
          for j:=1 to 10 do read(a[i,j]);
end;
     .
     .
     .
end.
```

The code for the subroutine entry is similar to that previously illustrated. The argument with the address of the array is located 8 bytes above where the stack-frame pointer points. Data registers 'd7' and 'd6' have been reserved for the loop-indices 'i' and 'j' respectively. The code for accessing 'a[i,j]' follows (array bound checking is disabled for simplicity):

```
*     read(a[i,j]);
L0003        MOVE.L        $0008(A6),A0            1
             MOVE.L        D7,D0                   2
             MULS          #$0028,D0               3
             MOVE.L        D6,D1                   4
             ASL.W         #$2,D1                  5
             ADD.W         D1,D0                   6
             MOVE.L        $0008(A5),-(A7)         7
             JSR           %R_I                    8
             MOVE.L        (A7)+,$D4(A0,D0.W)      9
```

In line 1, the base address of the array is collected and saved in address register 'a0'. The value of index 'i' is copied from 'd7' into 'd0' (line 2). This provides the row index and needs to be converted into an appropriate offset that defines where that row starts in the array. Each row has 40 bytes (ten 4-byte elements). Consequently, the value in 'd0' is multiplied by 40 (or, in hexadecimal, $0028) (line 3). Equally, the 'j' index needs to be made into an offset into the row. Each element is 4-bytes, so this time a 2-place left shift is needed (line 5). The two offsets are added to give a total offset relative to the base address of the array (line 6). Lines 7 and 8 represent the instructions needed to call the integer-read function. In line 9, the result is popped from the stack and moved into the array. The destination address specifies based and indexed mode, using register 'a0' with its location for the start of the array, and the index offset value that was computed in 'd0'. The additional offset, '$D4', corrects for the array starting at subscript 1, rather than 0, in both dimensions. The calculations in lines 2-6 locate 'a[1,1]' 44-bytes after the start of the array; however, this is the first element. '$D4' is a signed byte that represents -44, and is used to adjust the computed offset and give the correct address as the final result.

An educational computer board

Students completing this course should go on to obtain practical experience with real microcomputer systems such as those packaged as 'educational computer boards'. Such systems typically contain an MC68000 or comparable CPU, 16 to 32 kilobytes of read-only-memory (ROM), 32 to 64 kilobytes of main memory (RAM), and a few simple memory-mapped I/O devices. These I/O devices certainly include one or more 'Asynchronous Communications Interface Adapters' (ACIAs); these ACIAs represent somewhat elaborate versions of the keyboard and terminal controllers of the simul8 system. A typical configuration for an educational computer board is shown in Figure 19-6. If based on a Motorola 68000 CPU, then the system probably includes Motorola 6850 ACIA interfaces for controlling keyboards and terminals.

The ROM, will contain a line-by-line assembler/disassembler, a debugging monitor for setting breakpoints and examining memory, and a loader that can read object code prepared on another, larger computer system. These object files might be produced on cassettes, or read over a terminal link from a host time-shared computer.

The debugging monitor normally controls the system. It reads commands entered at the keyboard and performs appropriate actions. The command repertoire will include requests for (1) display, and modification, of the contents of registers and memory locations, (2) loading programs (from cassette or remote host), (3) setting breakpoints, and (4) execution of user code. Several different formats will be available for the display of memory including hexadecimal and disassembled instructions (the bit pattern is decoded and the name of any recognised corresponding instruction is printed; unrecognizable bit patterns are shown in hex). The monitor will contain a few utility routines, for example, a read-integer function and a write-integer procedure. Such routines are typically called from the user code by a special trap sequence and the 'TRAP' instruction. Any error interrupts that occur during execution of user code, for example, 'CHK' errors, are trapped and cause the debugging monitor to resume control of the system.

Figure 19-6. An 'educational computer board' system

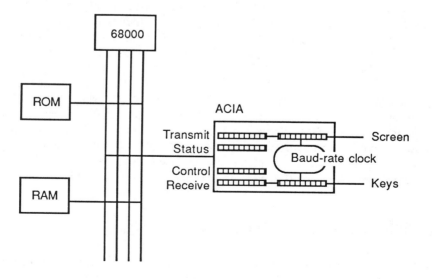

The monitor will set up an initial stack area that can be employed by a user program. The stack is typically used solely for the subroutine call mechanism. Most programs written for such teaching systems use simple static allocation of data space rather than the elaborate stack-based schemes illustrated in the examples of compiled Pascal code. Static allocation of data results in the use of some of the 68000's absolute addressing modes; modes that have not been utilized in the examples of compiled Pascal.

The 'memory modify' commands of the monitor permit programs to be entered directly. However, this is done on a line-by-line basis; there are no labels, and no symbol names except those of the predefined instructions. The user is responsible for working out addresses needed in branch instructions and in references to data elements; these addresses must then be entered in hexadecimal. Thus, the programming environment on the computer board systems is at the level of 'hand assembly' as described in Chapter 13.

Practical exercises require a separate program development system. The most useful exercises are, again, those that focus on I/O handling. There are two major differences from I/O handling on simul8. First, the computer board systems will use memory-mapped I/O devices. Second, the interrupt system will be much more elaborate with both vectored interrupts, and multiple-priority levels for interrupts.

The following example illustrates a simple wait loop approach to the handling of a 6850 ACIA on such a system. The 6850 ACIA combines the keyboard and terminal interfaces of simul8, and includes some additional functionality. Its overall structure is sketched in Figure 19-6. This controller can select the rate and format for serial data transmission. Terminals differ in the number of start and stop bits that they require to frame a character; some require that all characters be transmitted with even parity, others need odd parity. Data-transmission rates range from 110 baud (bits per second) to 19.2 kilobaud. It is inconvenient if changes in such settings require rewiring of the interface. With the 6850 ACIA, changes are made electronically. This interface has an 8-bit control register. Three bits in this register determine the format (number of stop/start bits, parity, and so forth). Another 2 bits select one of the clock rates that the ACIA can use. (There is a baud-rate clock in the interface that will be set to a particular frequency. This is the frequency used to control serial data transmission. Slower rates, +16, +64, can be requested.) When a program starts, it can load the control register of the 6850 ACIA with the bit pattern to define the settings to those needed by the terminal.

The 8-bit status register of the device has 2 bits that correspond to the 'ready' flags of the keyboard and terminal controllers in simul8. The other bits of the status register can flag error conditions, such as the detection of a parity error on an incoming character.

There are two 1-byte data registers: 'receive' for keyboard input and 'transmit' for terminal output. A byte of input data can be read from the 'receive' data register when the receive-bit is set in the status register. As shown in Figure 19-6, these 'receive' and 'transmit' registers are really duplicated. When a byte is written to an initially idle terminal, it goes first into the 'transmit' register from where it is immediately copied into a second register. It is from this second register that the bits are actually transmitted serially to the terminal, at a rate determined by the baud-rate clock.The copying of the byte from the transmit register allows the 6850 ACIA to again set 'receiver ready' in its status flag; and, consequently, allows the CPU to send the next character somewhat sooner. This double buffering feature on both input and ouput goes some way toward making the interface more capable of handling bursty rates of data transfer.

The various control, status, receive, and transmit registers in the ACIA are allocated addresses from the address space of the 68000. A wait loop for the ACIA involves a test instruction that tests a particular bit in the 'memory location' that corresponds to the ACIA's status register. A character is sent by moving it into the 'memory location' corresponding to the ACIA's 'transmit' register. (The 'status' register and the 'control' register share the same address; the 'control' register is used when data are moved to the ACIA, the 'status' register is used when data are moved from the ACIA. Similarly, the receive and transmit buffers also share an address.)

The following code resets the ACIA, defines a transmission rate suitable to a particular terminal, and then sends a null-terminated message:

```
*       The message printing program.
*       First, a few equates:
INIT         =          $15            * the bit pattern that sets terminal
                                       * characteristics as needed
PORTC        =          $10040         * the address of the control
                                       * register on the ACIA
PORTD        =          $10042         * the address of the 'transmit'
                                       * register on the ACIA
READYBIT     =          $1             * the bit in the status register that
                                       * is set when the ACIA can accept
                                       * a character for transmission
RESET        =          $3             * a bit pattern that causes the ACIA
                                       * to initialize itself
TUTOR        =          228            * a magic code, used when returning
                                       * to the on-board monitor when the
                                       * the program has finished
* This ORG directive defines that the code should be located
* at (absolute address) 1000 (hexadecimal). This is in the
* part of memory left to us by the on-board monitor.
* - - - - - - - - - - - - - - - - - - - - - - - -
             ORG        $1000
* - - - - - - - - - - - - - - - - - - - - - - - -
* main program
* - - - - - - - - - - - - - - - - - - - - - - - -
             JSR        INITIAL        * set up ACIA
             MOVE.L     #HELLO,A0      * pick up address of message
             JSR        PRINTIT        * print the message
* all done return to on-board monitor
             MOVE.B     #TUTOR,D7      * magic
             TRAP       #14            * (more precisely, system
                                       * dependent trap definitions)

* - - - - - - - - - - - - - - - - - - - - - - - - -
* routine INITIAL, starts the terminal
* (this not needed if on-board monitor has already initialized
* this particular ACIA port)
* - - - - - - - - - - - - - - - - - - - - - - - - -
```

```
INITIAL       MOVE.B      #RESET,PORTC     * tell the ACIA to reset
              MOVE.B      #INIT,PORTC      * now tell it speed of transfer
              RTS                          * return
* - - - - - - - - - - - - - - - - - - - - - - - - - - -
* routine PRINTIT, print null terminated string,
*         on entry register a0 contains the address of the first
*         character in the string
* - - - - - - - - - - - - - - - - - - - - - - - - - - -
PRINTIT       TST.B       (A0)             * look at next byte
              BEQ.S       PEXIT            * it is the null byte
              MOVE.B      (A0)+,D0
              JSR         PRINCH
PEXIT         RTS                          * return
* - - - - - - - - - - - - - - - - - - - - - - - - - - -
* routine PRINCH, print one character
*         have a wait loop that waits until ACIA is ready to
*         take a character; when it is ready the character is sent
* - - - - - - - - - - - - - - - - - - - - - - - - - - -
PRINCH        BTST        #READYBIT,PORTC  * look at ready bit
              BEQ.S       PRINCH           * it is still zero, not ready
*     when bit is set, can send
              MOVE.B      D0,PORTD
              RTS
* - - - - - - - - - - - - - - - - - - - - - - - - - - -
* Now, the inevitable message
HELLO         DC.B        'Hello World',0
```

The code uses absolute addresses in its references to the registers in the ACIA and also when loading the address of the message into register 'a0'.

20

Requirements of operating systems

The role of an operating system

It is the exception for an applications programmer to have to write new code for low-level I/O handling. Of course, special application-dependent routines are sometimes required. For example, data acquisition code for a laboratory microcomputer might need a new device-handler, or an applications program to control a communications concentrator might consist of an interrupt-handler, the device-handlers, and the data buffering code. But the vast majority of applications programs require only standard device-handling: for example, data input from keyboards, tapes, and disks; and data output to disks, tapes, terminals, and printers.

Given the complexities of code written for I/O handling, particularly code using interrupts and buffering schemes, it is best to relieve the applications programmer from the task of writing low-level I/O. As standard code for device-handling can be written, an interface to this standard code may then be defined in the form of 'readch()' and 'writech()' primitives. Offering a simple synchronous form of I/O, these primitives, if available, allow the applications programmer to no longer be concerned with the details of wait loops and buffering schemes. A program treats the 'readch()' function like a normal function, and can rely on it to return the next input character. Similarly, a return from a 'writech()' procedure call occurs when the character 'was written'. (A programmer working in a compiled or interpreted language uses even higher level routines: 'read(integer, float,string....)' and 'write(integer:format,string,float:format)'. The run-time support functions of the language system translate these calls down to the primitive 'readch()' and 'writech()' calls.)

A user program's calls to 'readch()' and 'writech()' are processed in the interface routines, from where the final calls to low-level I/O handling functions are made. On a very simple operating system, suitable for personal computers, the low-level functions might use synchronous I/O with wait loops. Then 'readch()' really waits for the next input character (and any data entered before the CPU is ready and waiting are likely to be lost), and 'writech()' does not return until the character has actually been sent to the device.

On more sophisticated systems, the low-level routines use interrupts and buffering techniques. A 'writech()' call then appends a character to a queue awaiting output to a terminal or printer; the character is actually transferred at a later time in response to the output device setting its 'ready' flag and causing an interrupt. The 'readch()' function takes the next character from an input buffer and loops until the data arrives if that buffer is empty. The actual input of characters is again handled through an interrupt mechanism, and 'type ahead' is possible.

Such a collection of device-handling code and interface routines constitutes a primitive form of operating system.

An operating system, capable of interpreting high-level I/O requests, redefines the machine programmed. As illustrated in Figure 20-1, instead of a machine with explicit I/O ports and status flags, the applications programmer sees a machine with simple, idealized I/O primitives. The programmer may still have to write different code to handle data read from keyboard from that written to handle data read from disk (as well as 'readch()', there might be a 'readblock()' primitive), and, further, when handling the disk, be aware of its organization into blocks, that is, the need to specify where on disk, the data are located and what data-transfer operations are to be performed.

Figure 20-1. How a simple operating system changes the programmer's view of a machine

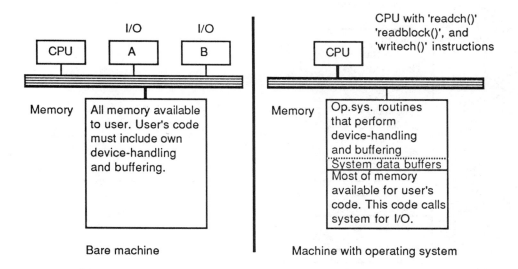

CPU — I/O A — I/O B

Memory | All memory available to user. User's code must include own device-handling and buffering.

Bare machine

CPU with 'readch()' 'readblock()', and 'writech()' instructions

CPU

Memory | Op.sys. routines that perform device-handling and buffering
System data buffers
Most of memory available for user's code. This code calls system for I/O.

Machine with operating system

It is possible for the facilities provided by the operating system to be extended. Additional operating system routines can be included to interpret other high-level user requests and translate them down into the primitive data transfer operations of the machine.

For example, it is possible to define a *file systems* interface. The applications programmer can then work in terms of named files. Interface-routines, such as 'open(filename)', 'create(filename)', and 'close(filename)' could, by looking up filenames in file directories, convert these requests into references to particular block numbers as required for low-level disk 'read's and 'write's.

The applications programmer's view of I/O can also be made device-independent. Single 'read' and 'write' primitives can be provided, with the operating system sorting out the different kinds of operation appropriate for reading from a terminal or for reading characters from a disk file.

An operating system thus adds an interpretive level that comes between the applications programmer and the raw hardware of the underlying machine. This interpretive level defines a new machine, the *virtual machine* , which is closer to the needs of the applications programmer. The virtual machine has a file system instead of a disk with cylinders, tracks, and blocks. The virtual machine has device-independent I/O: all its I/O devices work 'the same way', so the applications programmer need not be concerned with device-specific detail. The virtual machine may appear to have a larger memory than the real machine actually possesses. The operating system may make it appear that there are many CPUs capable of 'simultaneously executing programs' allowing several different applications programs to run concurrently. The effect is illustrated in Figure 20-2.

Figure 20-2. **An elaborate operating system presents the programmer with an idealized virtual machine**

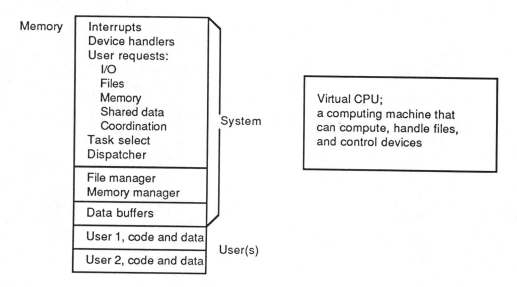

As an operating system is expanded to provide new facilities it acquires numerous managerial tasks. File-systems-manager code must be incorporated. Duties of this file manager include finding space on disk to allocate when a new file is created, and checking that a given user is permitted to open a particular file. If there are many simultaneous users, there has to be a processor manager that controls the allocation of CPU cycles according each user an equitable share. If memory is shared among several simultaneous tasks, then there must be a memory manager that controls the regions of memory allocated to those tasks. An operating system must further include primitives for controlling access to shared data. These managerial aspects are the main topics of introductory texts on operating systems.

The rest of this chapter is devoted to (1) the basic divisions between operating system and user code, (2) how these parts communicate, and (3) the additional hardware required in the CPU to make the implementation of an operating system practical.

The first examples use a single-task, interrupt-driven operating system. This is then elaborated on to allow for multiple tasks.

A single-task, interrupt-driven operating system

For this first example, the operating system is limited to providing the applications level with a simple interface to a set of systems routines for input and output.

The memory of the computer is conceptually divided into two regions. The code (and any data areas) of the operating system are located in low memory.The (single) applications program might be assembled with an origin set at a fixed address beyond the memory areas known to be required by the operating system. Alternatively, this starting address might be provided as a parameter to a linking-loader that prepares each application program for execution. The use of memory, on a machine with such an operating system, is illustrated in Figure 20-3.

The systems code includes a number of user-callable routines: one for reading input data and one for dealing with output data. Other systems functions might include an 'end_of_file' boolean function that indicates when there is no more user data. For now, these routines can be assumed to be called in the normal manner, their addresses predefined and inserted into the user code by the linking-loader.

Such a system might run on a computer with a card reader and a line printer, dealing with applications programs of the form:

```
program XXX(input,output);
var     card : array(1..80) of char;
        line : array(1..132) of char;
        procedure work;
        begin

        end;
begin
        while not eof do begin
                readln(card);
                work;
                writeln(line)
                end;
end.
```

Figure 20-3. Use of memory in a simple operating system that provides I/O handling facilities for a user program

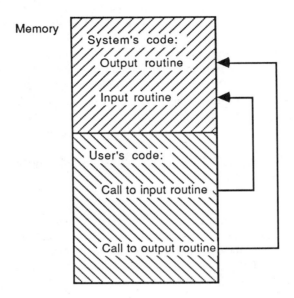

For the applications programmer, this is a typical synchronous program. Only one thing happens at a time: the program is either reading a card, or working on the data, or printing the output.

Now, it is of course possible for the systems I/O routines, called by this application, to perform synchronous I/O. Thus, the 'readln(card)' could be compiled into a call to a systems routine that starts the card reader and then loops, 80 times, calling a wait loop character-input routine with the characters read stored in the 'card' array of the applications program.

But this makes poor use of the machine. A simple card reader can run at 300 cards per minute; a line printer might print 600 lines per minute. Each card read therefore requires $1/5$ second; each line printed takes $1/10$ second.

The work required per card might require only a couple of hundred instructions, for example, for extraction of numeric data and then a little decimal arithmetic. Though some special records might result in additional work, most cards require about $1/1000$ second.

Thus, synchronous I/O makes very poor use of the machine. A typical execution trace for the program is illustrated in Table 20-1. As shown, about 1.2 seconds is used to perform around 0.004 seconds of work (say 0.01 seconds to make generous allowance for the work necessary when reading cards and writing lines). Only about 1 percent of the processing power is effectively utilized.

If the system routines are, however, written to utilize interrupt-driven I/O and to provide buffering, then it is possible to overlap the computations with input and output.

Table 20-1. Trace of activity on a system using synchronous I/O

Time (seconds)			Actions
0			start program and start reading card 1
0	-	0.2	waiting for card 1
0.2	-	0.201	processing card 1,
0.201			start printing line 1
0.201	-	0.301	waiting for line 1
0.301			start card 2
0.301	-	0.501	waiting for card 2
0.501	-	0.502	processing card 2
0.502			start line 2
0.502	-	0.602	waiting for line 2
0.602			start card 3
0.602	-	0.802	waiting for card 3
0.802	-	0.803	processing card 3
0.803			start line 3
0.803	-	0.903	waiting for line 3
0.903			start card 4
0.903	-	1.103	waiting for card 4
1.103	-	1.104	processing card 4
1.104			start line 4
1.104	-	1.204	waiting for line 4
.			.
.			.

The operating system has to be extended by the inclusion of an interrupt-handler, various device-handling routines, data buffering routines, and I/O data buffers. All these components are similar to those introduced in the examples relating to interrupt handling that were discussed in Chapter 12. The systems code and data structures become more complex; memory usage is illustrated in Figure 20-4.

The data flow also becomes more elaborate. As shown in Figure 20-5, the data flow is as follows:

1. Data from the card reader pass via the CPU into input buffers in the systems area of memory.
2. In response to user I/O read requests, data are copied from the system's buffer to the user area.
3. The data are processed with results created in another array in the user area.
4. From there, in response to write calls, data are copied to output buffers.
5. Data pass from the output buffer via the CPU to the printer.

Figure 20-4. Use of memory in a system with a simple operating system that provides for interrupt-driven, buffered I/O handling facilities for a user program

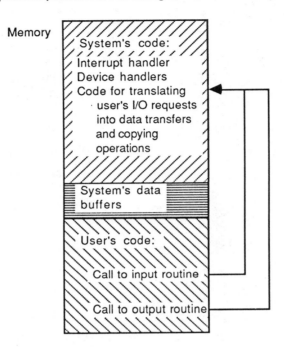

Figure 20-5. Flow of data in a system using interrupt-driven and buffered I/O handling

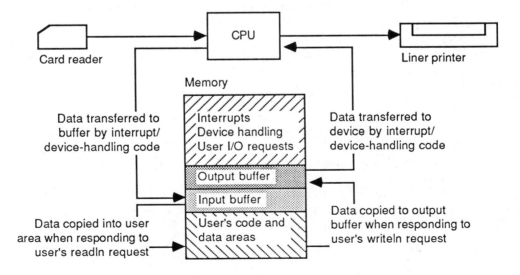

The 'readln(card)' and 'writeln(line)' calls of the applications program compile into calls to systems routines which copy data between data areas in the applications program and I/O data buffers in the system. These systems routines also initiate data transfers and, when necessary, delay the execution of the applications program (e.g. when no input data have arrived or when all output buffers are full).

Since both card reader and line printer are record-oriented devices, double-buffered input and output schemes are appropriate for each. The systems code for the 'write' is something like (this code is incomplete, showing only major steps and omitting some checks):

```
systems_procedure writeln(var line:array[1..132] of char);
var  i : integer;
begin
        { wait until next output buffer is free to be filled }
        while mybuf^.busy do nop;
        { copy data into output buffer }
        for i:=1 to 132 do mybuf^.data[i]:=line[i];
        { mark as in use  and 'queue it for printer', }
        {  if necessary start printer, }
        { − here have variables which will be }
        { shared with interrupt/printer handler code }
        { so must disable interrupts }
        disable_interrupts;
        mybuf^.busy:=true;
        mybuf^.printed:=0;

        { queue(my_buf,printer_queue); }

        if printer_idle then begin
                send_first_character;
                mybuf^.printed:=1;
                printer_idle:=false
                end;

        { claim a new output buffer;  mybuf:=allocate_buffer; }
        { here the code is reduced to a switch between }
        { the pair of buffers }
        tempptr:=mybuf;
        mybuf:=otherbuf;
        otherbuf:=temptptr;
        enable_interrupts
end;
```

The 'write' routine delays the applications program if both output buffers are full. When the next buffer to be used (identified by 'mybuf') is free, it is filled and queued for the printer. The buffers have a data area, for the 132 characters of a line, and various control information. Here it is suggested that control data might include a *busy* flag (indicating if the buffer was full of data, either being printed or waiting to be printed), and a count of characters already taken from the buffer and printed.

In general, some form of queue of buffers has to be maintained for the printer; and, a buffer allocation scheme is needed to select the next buffer to be used by the application. Since only two buffers are used here, simpler *ad hoc* mechanisms suffice.

As in' previous examples, the printer might need to be started by sending it a character. The tests on 'printer_idle' and other common variables need to be done with interrupts disabled (as discussed in earlier examples on interrupts; see Chapter 12).

The handler code is:

```
device_handler printer;
var  i : integer;
begin
        clear_printer_flag;
        i:=printbuf^.printed+1;
        printbuf^.printed:=i;

        if i<=132 then print(printbuf^.data[i])
        else begin

                printbuf^.busy:=false; { free this buffer }
                { switch to other buffer }
                tempptr2:=printbuf;
                printbuf:=otherprintbuf;
                otherprintbuf:=tempptr2;

                if not printbuf^.busy then printer_idle:=true
                else begin
                        printbuf^.printed:=1;
                        print(printbuf^.data[1])
                        end
                end

end;
```

This code is executed (with interrupts disabled) in response to each interrupt from the printer. The printer flag is cleared. If there are more characters in the current buffer then the next character is read from memory and sent. Otherwise, the buffer can be marked as no longer in use (and so refillable). The buffers are switched. If the next buffer is already marked as 'busy', then the first character from its data area is sent. Otherwise the printer can be marked as idle.

The system requires initialization routines that set appropriate values in the various pointers, mark the buffers as not busy, and flag the printer as idle. There would be some form of 'open(input)' and 'open(output)' calls compiled into the applications program which call the intialization routines in the system.

With systems code for handling interrupts and buffering data, the peripheral device operations can proceed *asynchronously* with respect to execution of the application. The code for the application remains unchanged. The applications programmer still perceives a simple synchronous computation and has no concern with details of checks for buffers full or empty, devices running or idle, and so forth.

Such asynchronous I/O handling improves the utilization of the machine. The same job as previously illustrated produces the execution trace shown in Table 20-2. (The processing times have been increased slightly to reflect the fact that some of the CPU cycles are now spent handling interrupts rather than actually working on the data already read.)

As shown by the data in Table 20-2, the overlapping of I/O and processing has allowed the same four cards to be read, analyzed, and results printed in about 0.8 seconds rather than the 1.2 seconds previously. In this example, the improved machine usage is entirely due to the overlapping of the time needed for printing output with the time spent on reading the next card. In a more general case, where a few cards require significant amounts of computation (>0.1 seconds), there are additional time advantages as a second data card is read while the previous one is accorded the lengthy processing.

Table 20-2.   **Trace of activity on a system using asynchronous I/O**

Time (seconds)		Actions
0		start program, init I/O and start reading card 1
0	- 0.2	waiting for card 1
0.2		start reading card 2
0.2	- 0.2015	processing card 1
0.2015		start printing line 1
0.2015 -	0.4	waiting for card 2 (line 1 printed at 0.302)
0.4		start reading card 3
0.4	- 0.4015	processing card 2
0.4015		start line 2
0.4015 -	0.6	waiting for card 3 (line 2 printed at 0.502)
0.6		start reading card 4
0.6	- 0.6015	processing card 3
0.6015		start line 3
0.6015 -	0.8	waiting for card 4 (line 3 printed at 0.702)
0.8		start reading card 5
0.8	- 0.8015	processing card 4
0.8015		start line 4
0.8015 -	1.0	waiting for card 5 (line 4 printed at 0.902)
.		.
.		.

No additional hardware is needed for such an operating system. However, even in this minimal system there are benefits if extra hardware can be provided. The problems with such a system, and their possible hardware-based solutions, include:

1.   Errors in an applications program can result in program data being written over the code or data areas of the operating system (it is not sufficient to put the operating system in read-only-memory; its data must be in read-write memory, and destruction

of control data is as bad as destruction of code). Therefore, it helps if hardware controls can limit memory accesses when the applications code is run, but which still allow unrestricted memory access when running the systems code so that data can be copied between I/O buffers and user data areas.

2. Other errors may result if an applications program (written in assembly language) attempts to execute I/O instructions directly. An application that contains a loop waiting on the setting of a peripheral flag may never terminate (as soon as the peripheral sets its flag, an interrupt occurs, and the systems code takes over and clears the flag). An application that tried to send data to a device would most likely corrupt information already sent by the system. An application that starts a device, for example, a clock in order to time the execution of a part of its code, will probably kill the system (the device causes interrupts for which the system may have no response; for example, there may not be a clock handler).

Ideally, restrictions would be imposed upon both the memory accesses made by the user's application program and its use of instructions. Some areas of memory should be protected from the user's program. Some instructions, for example, I/O instructions, should be prohibited.

Although desirable, the additional hardware is not essential in this situation. Only a single applications task is carried out by the computer; if that application bombs, then no wider damage occurs. The user's application is lost (which happens even if there was error detection), and the system needs reloading.

The operating system developed so far still makes very poor use of the system's resources. This interrupt-driven system is better than one with synchronized I/O but still only a small proportion of the CPU cycles is used. In the example application, although the job can be pushed through the machine significantly faster, still only about 2 percent of the CPU cycles are really exploited. The example application is extreme, but it is the case that the majority of programs spend significant portions of their time waiting for data. In a single-task system, the CPU is idle most of the time.

In the 1960s and 1970s, the CPU was by far the most costly component of a system and it had to be kept usefully employed. The only useful employment for a CPU is running jobs for paying customers. Somehow, CPU cycles left unused by one task had to be used on a second 'simultaneously running' task.

Now, with cheap microprocessors, CPU cycles are less critical. Yet, it is still necessary to allow more than one task to proceed simultaneously. For example, it is undesirable to wait half an hour for a personal computer to print one file before one can start editing another; it is preferable if the personal computer can run a couple of tasks, for example, a listing program and an editing program. If the personal workstation is to be incorporated into a local network, then multiple tasks are essential; one task must listen to the network for incoming electronic mail, another task may maintain a status display on one part of the terminal screen, and a third task may run the editor program for the user.

The implementation of multiple tasks requires a much more elaborate operating system, and some hardware aids are essential.

Multiprogramming

For machine usage to be improved, there must be more than one application in memory ready to be run when the CPU is available. Memory has to be divided into a number of regions: some regions are for the operating system's code and data structures (both for I/O buffers and for other control data), and two (or more) regions are available for different applications programs. For simplicity, one can assume that fixed regions of memory (*partitions*) are allocated for the various user programs. The simplest schemes for memory control are based upon the use of *fixed partitions*; but usually, memory allocation is handled by the operating system. The system must then adjust the size of the partitions according to the needs of the various programs.

The main objective of multiprogramming is to keep the CPU busy: whenever one applications program is idle, waiting for I/O, then attention switches to the running of another program. A typical program might spend 40 percent of its time on I/O wait (i.e. if that program was run alone, then 40 percent of the CPU cycles are spent in idle loops waiting for input or output of data). If two such programs are in memory then, when one is delayed, the other may still be ready to run. Of course, it is possible that both might need input from their own peripherals at any particular moment; so the CPU may still spend time idling. But, instead of wasting 40 percent of the CPU cycles, maybe only 16-20 percent will be spent idling waiting for I/O transfers.

The operating system becomes responsible for selecting the piece of code to execute at any time. A basic selection scheme is:

1. While program 1 is ready to run and program 2 is waiting for I/O, the CPU is devoted to program 1.
2. While program 2 is ready to run and program 1 is waiting for I/O, the CPU is devoted to program 2.
3. While both are ready to run, the CPU is 'time-shared' by alternately allocating about 0.1 second to program 1, then about 0.1 second to program 2.
4. While both are waiting for I/O, the CPU idles, waiting for devices to interrupt with the awaited data.

The switching of CPU attention between users' applications may have to occur after an interrupt from the clock, and will occur any time an application program needs to read from an empty buffer or write to a full buffer. The switching is done by software in the operating system.

Once a system has evolved to this point, it becomes appropriate to start formalizing the differences between the user applications and the systems code. The systems code tries to arrange for the most efficient use of the machine and the equitable and secure sharing of the computer resource.

The objectives of individual users can be in conflict with these overall system's objectives. Some (admittedly contrived) examples of conflicts are:

1. A user wants a compute bound FORTRAN program to run to completion as soon as possible; to avoid the job being stopped after 0.1 seconds, the user disables the clock on entry to the main calculation routines.

2.   A student-user on a time-shared university computer would like a program to read the data areas of another program (that just happens to belong to a professor using a text formatter to prepare an exam paper).

Obviously, user programs have to be restricted, and controlled when run in a shared environment. Users must be fenced in, and not be permitted control of I/O devices; nor should their programs be allowed to execute other sensitive instructions, for example, 'halt'. Users must be limited in their access to memory.

Although users must be so restricted, the systems code has to be able to control devices and copy data between arbitrary regions in memory.

Consequently, there has to be (1) a hardware mechanism for flagging whether systems code or user code is being executed, and (2) other hardware for limiting memory accesses and restricting the instruction repertoire available when running a user program.

Supervisor- and user-modes for program execution

Most computers have, built into their CPU, the concept of *user-mode* and *supervisor-mode*. Supervisor-mode is used for operating system's code (the operating system controls, manages, or supervises the use of the computer by applications programs). User-mode is set when the CPU is executing a user's application program.

Code being executed in supervisor-mode can:

1.   Involve access to peripherals.
2.   Reference any part of memory.
3.   Include privileged instructions that define those regions of memory accessible to the next user program.

Ordinary applications programs, run in user-mode, are limited in the following ways:

1.   Attempts to perform I/O are trapped and reported, as user errors, to the supervising operating system.
2.   Instead of I/O instructions, a mechanism exists that allows a user program to request the supervising operating system to perform I/O on its behalf.
3.   All memory accesses made are checked against the supervisor's specification of accessible memory; accesses outside the specified region are trapped and reported as user errors to the supervising operating system.

The supervisor-mode/user-mode distinction can be achieved with two extra components in the CPU. One is a simple boolean variable or flag (*mode flag*). This mode flag is used to indicate whether the CPU is currently running user code or supervisor code. The second component is a form of *memory-management* hardware. The memory-management hardware is employed when in user-mode; this hardware defines where the user program is located in memory, and what parts of memory it is permitted to access.

The setting of the mode flag can be used to control the use of I/O and other restricted instructions. If this flag is set (indicating that the CPU is currently executing code in user-mode), then any attempt to execute a restricted, or *privileged*, instruction is detected as an error. The CPU will not execute the instruction. Instead, the CPU sets an internal *error* flag (this is just like an external device setting a ready flag), causing an *error interrupt*. The interrupt-handling mechanism is invoked in the normal way: the state of the machine is saved, and code is executed to determine the type of interrupt (the internal error flag can be tested in the same way as any external device's ready flag). The operating system's interrupt-handling code finds out that the interrupt is an *illegal instruction error* interrupt, and handles it by termination of the user's job, and selection of a new job that can now be run for another user.

Memory-management hardware

Memory-management hardware can be implemented in many ways. The simplest scheme requires just two extra registers in the timing and control circuitry of the CPU, and extensions to the microcode of the address decoder. The two registers can be loaded with addresses (but the instruction to load these registers is privileged and therefore only available in supervisor-mode). In user-mode, addresses coming from the main address decoder are compared with the values in these registers. One register (*base register*) defines a lower bound on the area of memory available to the user program; the other register (*limit register*) defines an upper bound.

Code in the operating system sets these registers before selecting the next user program to run. As shown in Figure 20-6, before user 2's program is run, these memory-management registers are set to limit access to the appropriate area of memory.

Figure 20-6. CPU with the mode flag and memory management extensions that permit the implementation of an operating system

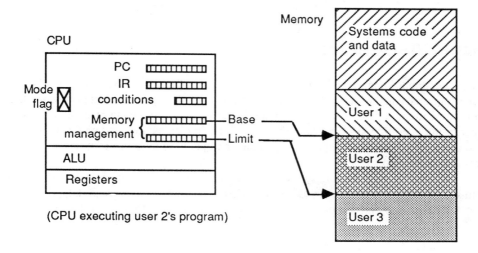

The comparison checks against the base and limit registers are used by the hardware to detect user errors. For example, if user 2 has a program error that resulted in an excessively large positive (negative) subscript for an array, then the address of the array element, as computed by the address decoder, is compared with the limits, and found to lie out of user 2's memory range (positive $\Rightarrow$ address in user 3's space; negative $\Rightarrow$ address in user 1's space). Again, instead of executing the instruction with the illegal address, the CPU simply sets an error flag.

The error flag causes an interrupt; control passes automatically to the supervising operating system's program for interrupt-handling. There the interrupt is identified as an *address error* interrupt. And, again, the appropriate interrupt-handling involves the termination of the user job.

A slight change in the way the base and limit registers are employed allows them to serve a dual purpose. As before, the base register can be set with the address where the user's program starts, but the limit register holds the length of the program. The user's program is assembled to start at address 0 but is loaded into whatever area of memory it is allocated. The linking-loader does not adjust the addresses in the program to reflect the actual starting point in memory. The value of a user's address, coming from the address decoder, is compared against the value 0 and the value in the limit register. If it lies outside this range then an address-error interrupt occurs. If, however, the computed address is within range, it is added to the address in the base register to give the actual address in memory. This scheme allows the user's virtual address to be mapped into the memory of the computer. The scheme simplifies the linking-loading process. More importantly, it makes it possible to move a program in memory. If the operating system is allocating memory space for jobs, rather than using a fixed-partition scheme, then sometimes it will be necessary for existing jobs to be moved. This is simple provided the addresses in the user's code are all implicitly defined relative to the contents of the base register in the memory management part of the CPU. The user's code and data can simply be copied from one area of memory to another and the new value of the starting address placed in the base register for when that user program is next run. As well as defining an allowed window into memory, the base and limit registers can thus be used for the *dynamic relocation* of user's programs.

Supervisor calls

With a user-mode/supervisor-mode flag, and some form of memory managment hardware, user programs can be controlled. They cannot execute instructions that disrupt the working of the machine. They cannot read, let alone overwrite, code or data belonging either to the operating system or to other programs. In fact, as arranged so far, they can't even call subroutines in the operating system (the operating system's routines are not at accessible addresses).

A call to an operating system is inherently a request to change the environment from user-mode to supervisor-mode. When a user program wants to read data, the code executed has to copy information from the system's I/O buffers to the user data areas; the code needs access to arbitrary areas of memory and must therefore be executed in supervisor- mode. Apart from being impractical (because, as noted, the operating system's routines are outside a user's 'address space'), an ordinary subroutine call is inappropriate for a user's request to the system.

Instead, there will be a new instruction, the *supervisor call* instruction ('svc'). When executed, a 'svc' instruction simply sets another internal interrupt flag *user request*. Again, the interrupt mechanism comes into play. The machine state is saved, the machine disables interrupts, supervisor-mode is set (supervisor-mode is set automatically on all interrupts so that the interrupt-handling and device-handling code can control devices), and the interrupt-handler code identifies the type of interrupt as a user request and jumps to the *user handler* or *svc handler*.

The 'svc' handler code must deal with each different kind of user request supported by the system. A user program obviously needs to use the 'svc' mechanism to make calls on the operating system for data to be read or written; it is these calls that are of main interest here. There will be other calls to request that the operating system 'open' and 'close' files, 'create' new files, 'delete' old files, start additional programs (a 'fork' or 'exec' call), read the clock, allocate more memory, and so forth. There has to be an 'exit' request; since a user program cannot execute a 'halt' instruction, it must have another way to terminate.

When an operating system is defined, the various 'svc' requests that it supports are listed and assigned unique integer identifiers or request numbers (e.g. for Unix™, 'exit' = 1, 'read' = 3, 'write' = 4, ...). There is only one 'svc' instruction; the word following the 'svc' instruction in the program code is used to define which particular 'svc' request is made. Typically, other data are encoded in successive words and/or passed in registers; thus, a 'read' call in a user program might be encoded:

```
move.w filenum,d0          register d0 contains file-id#
svc
3                          3=read request
newdata                    address of array where characters are to go
80                         (maximum) number of characters to read
```

Here both registers and memory locations are used to pass arguments to the 'svc' handler. The contents of a register specify which one of a number of input files belonging to this user program is to be read. The other data, in the locations following the 'svc' instruction, specify where in the user program the characters are to be stored and the maximum number of characters to be read.

The operating system's code for a 'svc' handler is going to be based upon a large 'case' statement. The 'svc' handler first reads the request number from the location following the 'svc' instruction (the address of this location is known because it was saved in response to the 'svc' interrupt). Then, based on the request number, the appropriate operating system subroutine is executed:

```
{ handle a svc request }
reqno:=memory[savedpc]; { get request number }
savedpc:=savedpc+1; { update return address!}
```

```
case reqno of
      1: { exit }
                do_exit;
      3: { read }
                do_read;


end;
```

The various system routines fetch any additional arguments from subsequent memory locations, and validate the request. For example, for a 'read' request, validation tests performed by the system routine might include the following: Is it a positive number of characters? Does the file being read really exist? Do addresses, specified for storing the characters, all belong to this user? If the request is validated, the system performs the requested operation.

A simple request in a user program, for example, what time is it? ('time()', 'svc #35'), works as follows:

1. The user program's 'time()' function call will have been compiled to 'svc; 35';' when executed, this 'svc' instruction causes an interrupt.
2. The state of the CPU, with all the registers holding data pertaining to that particular program, is saved. The CPU switches into supervisor-mode (with further interrupts disabled).
3. The interrupt-handler code is executed, the interrupt identified as the execution of an 'svc' instruction, and the 'svc' handler is entered.
4. The 'svc' handler determines (from the request number) that this is a request to find the time, and calls the appropriate system routine.
5. The systems routine determines the time, placing the result at an appropriate location in the user program.
6. Return from interrupt code is executed. This restores the user's data values into the CPU registers and causes the user program to resume execution (in user-mode) at the next executable instruction following the 'svc' instruction and its data.

In these simple cases, the supervisor call works something like an ordinary subroutine call, with just the extra annoyance of switching between supervisor- and user- modes on entry and exit.

Reads, writes, and similar 'svc' requests are, however, more complex. A 'svc' 'read' works just like the previous 'svc' 'time' request provided data are available in the input buffers. But, if there are no data ready, then the supervisor somehow (1) stops execution of the current user program; (2) saves the state of the job; (3) marks the job as waiting for input; (4) finds another job to run instead of the suspended job, and (5) on return from interrupt, loads the CPU registers with data pertaining to the newly selected job so that the CPU resumes the program from the point where it was last suspended.

The operating system's interrupt-handling code, particularly the return from interrupt, requires considerable elaboration.

Processes

By switching the CPU between different user jobs, the operating system of a multiprogrammed computer is really simulating a machine with multiple central processors. Each separate user job is running on its own *virtual processor*. Any analysis of the activities of the machine has to be done in terms of these virtual processors running programs. The term *process* is used to capture this notion of a program running on a virtual processor.

Earlier examples have illustrated how a single applications program can run on a machine using interrupt-driven I/O. When an I/O interrupt occurs, the state of the program is saved, the device-handled, and the computation resumed. All these activities are done in a manner transparent to the application; there is no way to determine when/if the application was interrupted. The interrupt-handling schemes are a way of sharing CPU cycles between the applications program and device-handling code.

Now, these schemes must be extended to share CPU cycles among different processes. A process can be interrupted by an external event like a device setting a ready flag, by a clock tick, or as the result of its making a supervisor call. The state of the process must be saved, the event (device, clock, or 'svc') handled, and the same process resumed (its registers restored and its execution continued from the point where it was interrupted). However, now it is possible for another process to be run instead. Eventually, the original process is given the chance to resume; then, it picks up just as if it was momentarily interrupted, even though it may have been waiting for many seconds.

If the operating system is 'simulating' several CPUs, then it has to maintain several distinct register save areas, one for each virtual CPU or process. When a process is interrupted, the CPU registers are saved in that process's own special save area. If this process is to be resumed on completion of the interrupt-handling, then the CPU registers are restored from this save area. If, however, another process is selected to run, then on return from interrupt the CPU registers are loaded with data taken from the save area of the newly selected process.

As well as memory areas for the applications programs and their data, and areas for input and output buffers, the operating system has to maintain some control data structures. These hold data defining the state of each one of the currently running processes. The organization of the computer's memory is shown in Figure 20-7. The system has code for interrupt-handling, device-handling, dealing with 'svc's, and for managing processes. The system's data areas include I/O buffers and these new control structures or *process control blocks*.

The process control blocks contain data that define the current state of computation for each process. The register-save area for a process is contained in its process control block. The base and limit address values are also saved in the process control block so that the operating system may set them correctly when preparing the CPU to resume execution of the process. Other data include a process-status word which indicates whether the process is ready to run, waiting for I/O or some other event. The general structure of a process control block is illustrated in Figure 20-8; as shown, it contains a register save area, details of a process's allocated areas of memory, status data that define whether a process can be run or is waiting for an I/O transfer, and pointers to the various data buffers associated with the process.

Figure 20-7.   Memory organization for a multiprocess system

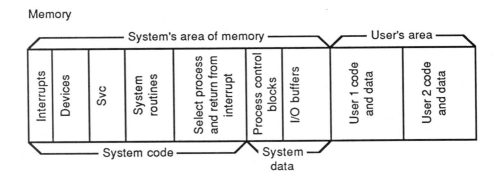

Figure 20-8.   A process control block

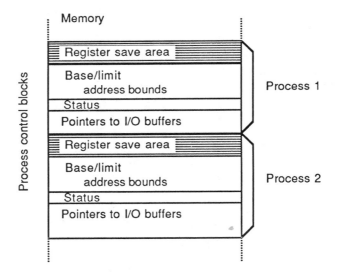

Additional data in the process control block vary from system to system. There might be a count of the amount of CPU time the process has used and details of any CPU time limit; the operating system is then able to detect if a process has used too much time. There might be priority data: if several processes are all ready to run then the operating system may need help in choosing which to run next. There might be pointers to the I/O buffers currently used by the process.

The handling of an interrupt now involves the following steps:

1.   Save the process state in the register save area of its process control block (there will be a system variable set to identify which process is running).

2.   Determine the type of interrupt, and call the device-handler or 'svc' handler as needed.

3. If it is an 'svc' 'read' or 'write' request, attempt to satisfy the user request by copying data between the process's data areas and I/O buffers. If the I/O request cannot be satisfied (because of empty input buffers or full output buffers), mark the process's status as *blocked for I/O on buffer* ..., and set a (boolean) variable to indicate the need for the system to choose another process.

4. If the interrupt is a clock tick, check if the current process has used its share of CPU time. If its turn is ended, then set the variable indicating the need to choose another process.

5. If the interrupt is due to an external device, perform the transfers and buffering of data. Then, check whether the transfer has filled or emptied a buffer; if so, check whether any process is waiting for that buffer and, if one is found, mark it as ready to run and set the variable that indicates the need to choose another process.

6. In the exit from interrupt code, examine the variable that indicates whether selection of a new process is appropriate; if not, continue at step 8 (see below) with the current process.

7. Select a process. Run through the process control blocks and identify all those that are ready to run. Using priorities specified in the process control blocks, rank those that are ready to run. Choose the highest ranked. Change the system's current process pointer to identify the newly chosen process.

8. Resume execution of that process whose process control block is pointed to by the system's current process pointer.

Through mechanisms such as these, it is possible to maintain the appearance of several different user jobs being executed concurrently. The CPU is kept busy, working for the process with the highest priority. A process's stopping to wait for I/O causes an automatic switch to another ready process. If there are no other processes ready, the CPU runs a little wait loop until the next device interrupt.

21

Memory management

A simple 'base and limit' register-pair memory-management scheme does allow for a secure multiprogrammed environment. The processes that run the users' applications programs can be limited to their allocated regions of memory. As described in Chapter 20, base and limit registers may also make possible the relocation of programs in memory.

There are many other more elaborate memory-management schemes. All these schemes define different hardware-assisted ways of mapping a user's address space onto actual memory locations. All allow these mappings to be changed as the program runs, so that the operating system may move programs around in order to make the best possible use of the available memory. All schemes provide some forms of hardware-applied control over a process's use of memory; at the crudest, a process may just be restricted to reading and writing from its own allocated area, but much finer controls are possible. The basic schemes can be extended by a combination of hardware and software, to make the size of the machine's memory appear larger than it really is. Some of the schemes allow different processes to share common code or data.

The schemes differ in their primary objectives. *Segmentation*-based schemes focus first on (1) dividing a program's address space into logically distinct components with distinct memory allocation and usage requirements, and (2) allowing for controlled sharing of common code among processes. *Paging*-based schemes focus first on simplifying the operating system's task of mapping the many, varied sized, address spaces of a set of concurrent processes into the available machine memory. Segmentation and paging schemes can be combined to realize both types of objective.

The hardware and support software of memory-management schemes more properly belong to a course on operating systems. Here, only the simplest versions of segmentation and paged-segmentation schemes are discussed. (The discussion does not extend to consideration of the methods by which an operating system can simulate a *virtual memory* larger than real memory.) Manufacturers of memory-management hardware frequently introduce variations on the standard schemes; consequently, a memory-management chip, available for a particular microprocessor, may not include all suggested features but instead may include some other novelty.

Segmentation

Segmentation is a straightforward generalization of the simple base and limit register-pair, memory-mapping scheme introduced previously. Instead of a single base/limit pair, the CPU's memory-mapping circuits include a small set of *segment registers.*

Each segment register has three fields: 'base', 'limit', and 'use'. The first two correspond to the base and limit registers of the simpler scheme. The third field is a bit pattern that specifies the allowed usage of the segment. Usage bit patterns might distinguish *execute, read-only,* and *read-write* modes.

A user's program is broken up into distinct segments. One division is the separation into code, statics, heap, and stack (see Figure 21-1). Instead of having a single large program comprising all these parts and occupying a single contiguous area of memory, the system using segmentation allows all these parts to be made distinct. The separate segments are individually mapped into the computer's memory; different usage attributes may be associated with the different segments.

Figure 21-1.   Distinct segments of a user's program are separately mapped into the computer's memory

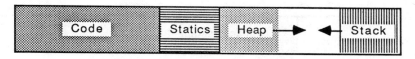

Program occupying a single contiguous area in memory

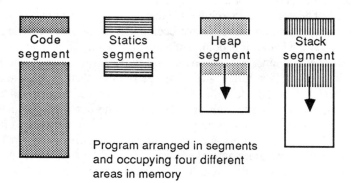

Program arranged in segments
and occupying four different
areas in memory

There are obvious advantages if the parts can be separated. If the program is composed as a single part, then there is no way the code can be protected from being overwritten at run time, for example, by an assignment to an array element with an erroneous subscript, or an assignment via an erroneous pointer. Similarly, apart from costly interpretive checks, there is no way to guarantee that the stack will not overrun into the heap. If, however, these components can be defined as separate segments, each defined by a base/limit/usage value, then one can have hardware checks. The code can be made read-only (provided, of course, that all subroutine arguments, return links, and so forth go on the stack). The limits on addressing data in other segments can be used as a basis for hardware detection of programming errors involving subscripts or pointers.

Finer distinctions may be appropriate. For example, rather than allocate all dynamic data structures from a single heap, it might be preferable to assign different data elements to separate data segments. It might be useful to divide the code into separate segments. For example, a compiler might have separate segments with the code to process variant records, the code for error recovery, and so on. Then, it might be possible to avoid loading all the different segments unless they were needed (so saving on memory usage).

In a segmentation-based system, there are two distinct parts to each user address, as illustrated in Figure 21-2. One part defines the segment, the other part defines the location in segment. The construction of these two part addresses is accomplished at compile time (and/or linking load time). Thus, the compiler could (1) recognize a reference to code (as in a 'jump' instruction) and specify segment 0, (2) recognize a reference to a static array and specify segment 1, and so forth.

Figure 21-2. Segmentation-based system with two-part user addresses

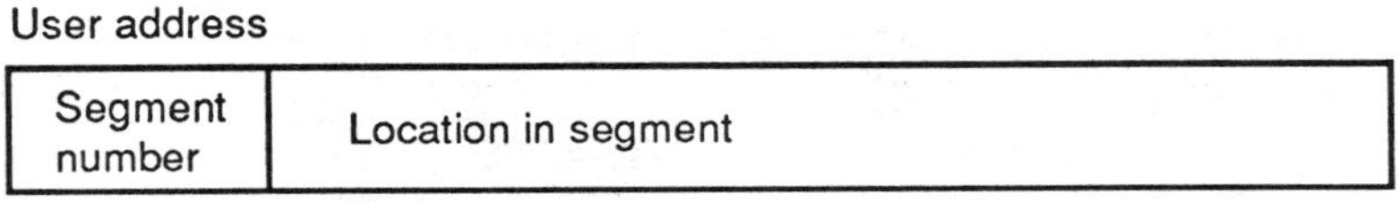

User address

Segment number	Location in segment

At run time, when the addresses come from the main address decoder, the segment number part is split out and used to select the particular segment register that is to be used. The location in segment value is compared with the limit value in that segment register, and an address error occurs if it is out of range. The usage is checked. The CPU knows whether it is doing an instruction fetch, a data fetch, or a data write, and hence can check against execute, read, and write permissions in the usage bits. If the location in segment is in range, and the usage is valid, then the base address given in the segment register can be added in to determine the actual memory address. Usually, the various segments of a program are allocated quite separately and may be scattered throughout memory with intervening areas allocated to other programs or left free.

The CPU's memory-management system is illustrated in Figure 21-3. The memory-management unit contains segment registers, comparator, and addition circuits. When running in user-mode, the address decoders in the main timing and control part of the CPU pass decoded addresses to the memory-management unit, together with information specifying the operation to be performed (read data, write data, or fetch instruction). The segment number is extracted and used to select one of the segment registers. The desired usage is then checked against the use bits in the segment register, while comparator circuits perform the range checks. If all is well, the final address is composed by the adder circuit that combines base and location in segment to derive a location in memory. Finally, the memory read or write is performed.

Figure 21-3. The memory-management system in a system using segmentation

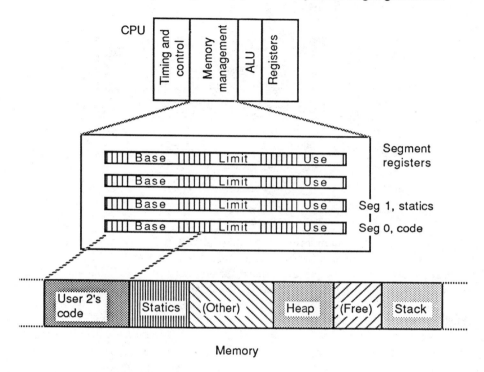

Memory

The areas allocated to the different segments of a program, and their permitted usages, are stored in the process control blocks described in Chapter 20. The operating system loads the segment registers with data from a PCB when starting a process. Different processes can share execute and read-only segments. The operating system must then arrange that the same addresses of the shared segments be entered into the appropriate segment entries in each of the different processes' control blocks.

Paged-segmentation

Segmentation has one real disadvantage. It makes it difficult for the operating system to manage the allocation of memory.

As processes start and terminate, they claim and then eventually release space needed for their different segments. Segments are, of course, totally arbitrary in size. One process may claim a 60-kilobyte segment; when it finishes these 60 kilobytes might be reallocated to other processes requiring 40 kilobytes and 15 kilobytes (and leaving 5 kilobytes unclaimed). After the system has been running for some time, the machine's memory will be occupied by the widely scattered segments of the current processes, interspersed with free areas of memory too small to be of use. The effect is illustrated in Figure 21-4.

Figure 21-4. The fragmentation of free areas of memory into unusably small regions

Memory

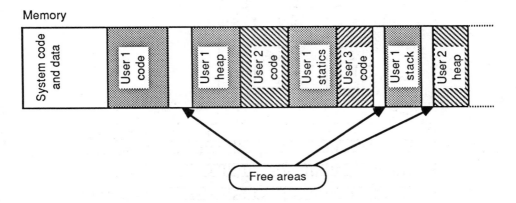

Free areas

The operating system might find that, although it has in total about 200 kilobytes of free space, this is all split up into small 5-kilobyte and 10-kilobyte blocks. Although there could be sufficient total space for another process to start running, the space might be so badly fragmented that none of that process's segments could be loaded into memory. The system then either has to wait for current processes to terminate, or laboriously copy segments belonging to other processes around in memory.

Paging provides a solution to such memory-management problems. With paging, a segment does not have to be allocated a single contiguous area of memory; instead, it can be mapped out over whatever scraps of free memory are available.

Conceptually, a paging system divides memory up into blocks, or *page frames*, each of a fixed size (typically, around 1 kilobyte). The address space of (each segment of) a user program is divided up into 1-kilobyte blocks or *pages*. As shown in Figure 21-5, a mapping scheme is then used to allow individual pages of a user's program to be placed into any page frame.

Details of the mapping are recorded in data structures in memory. For each segment, in a multi-segment program, these data structures record the size of segment, its usage, and provide a *page-map* table, as shown in Figure 21-6. This page-map table is held in memory as a part of one of the data structures associated with a process's process control block. The entries in the page-map table specify the page frame that holds each particular page of the segment. In Figure 21-6, page 3 of segment 0 is in page frame 208 and page 0 of segment 1 is in page frame 500. (Page 3 corresponds to user's byte addresses 3072-4095.) Typical programs in the 200-400 kilobyte range have in total 200-400 different pages.

A user address is regarded as having three parts: segment number, page number, and location on page. The address-decoding process is illustrated in Figure 21-7. The segment number determines the appropriate page-map. The page number provides an index into the map, and the appropriate page-frame number can be retrieved from this map entry. The final address can be composed from the page-frame number, representing the high-order bits, and the location in page identifying the low-order bits.

Figure 21-5. A mapping scheme that describes how pages of a user's program are allocated to particular page frames in the computer's memory

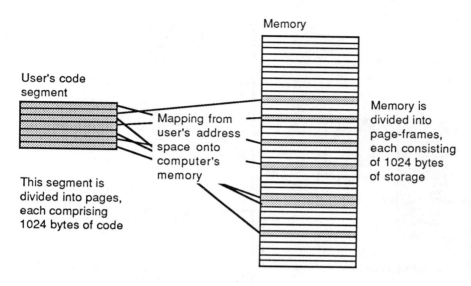

Memory

User's code
segment

Mapping from
user's address
space onto
computer's
memory

This segment is
divided into pages,
each comprising
1024 bytes of code

Memory is
divided into
page-frames,
each consisting
of 1024 bytes
of storage

Figure 21-6. Part of a process's page map

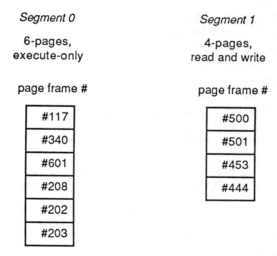

Segment 0

6-pages,
execute-only

page frame #

#117
#340
#601
#208
#202
#203

Segment 1

4-pages,
read and write

page frame #

#500
#501
#453
#444

This paged-segmentation scheme simplifies the allocation of main memory. There is no need for a large contiguous area of free space for a segment. Any sufficient sized collection of free page frames serves to hold the pages of a segment loaded into memory.

Figure 21-7. The address decoding process for paged- segmentation

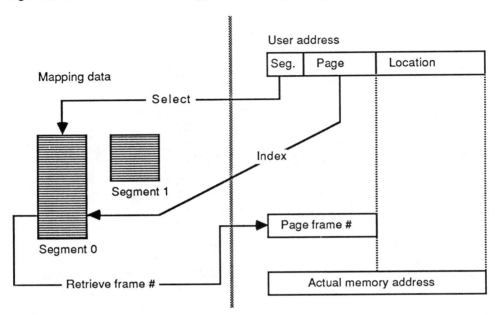

However, there is a major problem with these elaborate mapping schemes. The maps are too large; they have hundreds of entries for reasonably sized programs. It is impractical to arrange for hundreds of mapping registers in the memory-management part of the CPU. Instead, the map that defines the page frames of each page of each segment must be held in memory.

If the map was only held in memory, then every access to the user's virtual memory involves two accesses to real memory. First, it is necessary to retrieve the appropriate page frame by accessing the map. Only then, when the final address is determined, is it possible to fetch the instruction/data for the user program. This represents an intolerable interpretive overhead.

Systems using paged-segmentation require very elaborate *dynamic address translation* circuitry in their CPUs. The dynamic address translator keeps a summary of the main map in a special associative store in the CPU. This summary map contains details of the page-frame numbers for the most frequently referenced segment #/page # combinations. References to addresses in these pages can be mapped immediately onto actual memory locations.

The dynamic address translation unit also has a pointer to the current process's main map in memory. When a user address references a segment #/page # that is not described in the summary map, the dynamic address translator accesses main memory and retrieves the relevant mapping details. These details may be used to update its summary map. The approach is illustrated in Figure 21-8.

Using such mechanisms, it is possible to achieve a paged-segmented system without paying too high an overhead in terms of extra indirect accesses.

Figure 21-8.   A dynamic address translation system for paged- segmentation

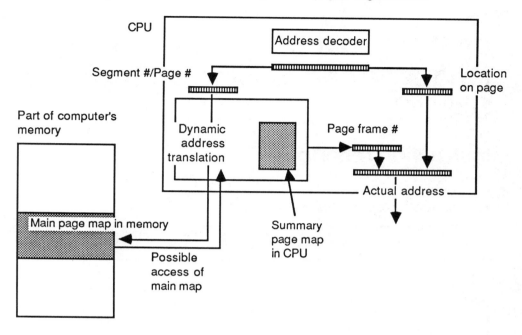

Appendix A

Instruction repertoire, assembly language and coding examples for Simul8

Instruction repertoire

Predefined op-codes for the simulator

Symbol	Class	Value	Symbol	Class	Value
adcrb	iot	6601	adsf	iot	6602
adstrt	iot	6604	and	memref	0000
cia	opr	7041	cla	opr	7200
clkcf	iot	6501	clksf	iot	6502
clkt	iot	6504	cll	opr	7100
cma	opr	7040	cml	opr	7020
dca	memref	3000	dlma	iot	6410
dlsk	iot	6400	drd	iot	6411
dscf	iot	6402	dssf	iot	6401
dtcf	iot	6414	dtsf	iot	6412
dwrt	iot	6415	hlt	opr	7402
i	'indirect'	0400	iac	opr	7001
iof	iot	6002	ion	iot	6001
iot	iot	6000	isz	memref	2000
jmp	memref	5000	jms	memref	4000
krb	iot	6036	ksf	iot	6031
nop	opr	7000	opr	opr	7000
ral	opr	7004	rar	opr	7010
rtl	opr	7006	rtr	opr	7012
skp	opr	7410	sma	opr	7500
sna	opr	7450	snl	opr	7420
spa	opr	7510	sza	opr	7440
szl	opr	7430	tad	memref	1000
tcf	iot	6042	tls	iot	6046
tpc	iot	6044	tsf	iot	6041

The classes are: 'memref' = memory reference instruction, 'iot' = input/output instruction, and 'opr' = operate instruction.

Memory reference instructions

and   'and'

Logical 'and' of the contents of accumulator with contents of the referenced memory location.

>   acc:= acc & memory[effective address];

dca   'deposit and clear acc'

Store the contents of the accumulator in the referenced memory location, then clear (i.e. zero) the accumulator.

>   memory[effective address] := acc;
>   acc:=0;

isz   'increment and skip if zero'

Increment (add 1 to) the contents of the referenced memory location, storing the new value back into the location. If the new value is zero, then increment the program counter skipping the next instruction.

>   memory[effective address] := memory[effective address] +1;
>   if(memory[effective address] = 0) then pc:=pc+1;

(*Note*: this does not involve the accumulator whose contents are not changed by this instruction.)

jmp   'jump'

Change program counter so that next instruction is taken from the referenced memory location.

>   pc:= effective address;

jms   'jump to subroutine'

First, store the current value of the program counter in the referenced memory location (establishing the link needed when returning from the subroutine). Then change the program counter so that the next instruction is taken from the following memory location.

>   memory[effective address] := pc;
>   pc := effective address + 1;

tad   'two's complement add'

Form the sum of the contents of the accumulator and the contents of the referenced memory location. If there is a carry out of the leftmost bit, then the value of the 'link' bit is complemented. There is no hardware detection of arithmetic overflow.

    acc := acc + memory[effective address];
    if(addition gave carry)then link : = not link;

Operate instructions

cia   'complement and increment acc'
           (i.e. change sign of contents of acc as interpreted in twos complement notation)
cla   'clear acc'
cll   'clear link'
cma   'complement acc'
           (i.e. change each 0 bit in acc to a 1, each 1 to a 0)
cml   'complement link'
hlt   'halt' (terminate execution)
iac   'increment acc'
nop   'do nothing'

ral   'rotate acc left'
rar   'rotate acc right'
rtl   'rotate acc twice left'
rtr   'rotate acc twice right'

skp   'skip the next instruction'
sma   'skip if acc holds minus (negative) number'
sna   'skip if contents of acc non zero'
snl   'skip if non-zero link'
spa   'skip if acc holds positive number (including zero)'
sza   'skip if contents of acc is zero'
szl   'skip if zero link'

It is possible to combine 'operate' instructions in various restricted ways. Combining operate instructions shortens programs and makes them faster. The restrictions on combinations are somewhat complex, and not really important. Typical permitted combinations are:

cla cll   'clear both acc and link'
sna cla   'skip if non-zero acc, clear acc'

All the skip instructions can be combined with 'cla'; this allows computations needed for a comparison to be done in the acc, the result tested with skip and the unneeded temporary result removed from the acc.

Input/output instructions

Analog/digital converter

adcrb   ' A/D read data buffer and clear flag'
adsf   'skip if A/D flag set'
adstrt   'start A/D sampling'

The A/D represents a 9-bit accuracy, single line A/D converter that samples the voltage on an input line and returns a numerical representation of the voltage (accurate to one part in five hundred). This is not a simulation of a real A/D device; control of this A/D is greatly simplified.

Example

Store five samples from the A/D in successive memory locations starting at address 'datum'.

```
        *200
        cla cll
        tad    whered      / set up a 'pointer' to where data  are to be
        dca    ptr         / stored
        tad    howmny      / the number of samples to be read
        cia                / make it negative
        dca    countr      / save in a counter variable
main,   adstrt             / start sampling the next value
wait,   adsf               / wait loop, flag will set when voltage reading ready
        jmp    wait
        adcrb              / read data into the acc
        dca  i ptr         / store in memory
        isz    ptr         / update memory ptr (can assume won't cause skip)
        isz    countr      / increment counter, this will cause skip when have
                           / necessary samples
        jmp    main        / (if not complete, go back for next value)
        hlt                / all done
/ here there are a couple of 'assemble time' constants
whered, datum              / the address where the first data will be stored
howmny, 5                  / it is five samples needed
/ here there are the variables used for counters and pointers
ptr,    0
countr, 0
datum,  0                  / first of locations for data
$
```

Clock

clkcf	'clear clock flag'
clksf	'skip if clock flag set'
clkt	'clock toggle'

The clock is a slightly simplified version of a 'fixed-frequency' clock. Once started, it will set its flag every 'x' microseconds. Starting/stopping of the flag is non-standard. These operations are implemented through the single I/O instruction 'clkt'; if the clock is not running, 'clkt' starts it; if it is running, 'clkt' stops it (i.e. it's a toggle switch).

Example

A loop to cause a fixed delay of 100 clock 'ticks'.

```
          tad    limit        / limit on number of clock ticks to wait
          cia
          dca    count1
          clkt                / start clock
loop1,    clksf               / these two instructions cause wait for
          jmp    loop1        / next 'tick'
          clkcf               / clear flag, start clock counting down again
          isz    count1       / increment count of ticks, skip when have sufficient
          jmp    loop1
          clkt                / switch off clock
          .
          .
          .
limit,    0144                / one hundred decimal
count1,   0
```

Disk

The disk is the most complex of the devices on this simulator, and yet is really extremely simplified in comparison to most disk units. There are two sets of instructions for the disk. The first set is used to cause the disk unit to move its read/write heads to the appropriate block.

dlsk	'load disk block register and start seek'
dssf	'skip if disk seek flag set'
dscf	'clear disk seek flag'

The second group sets the start address in memory for the transfer, and initiates the read or write operations.

dlma	'load disk memory address register (from acc)'
drd	'start reading from disk into memory'
dtsf	'skip if disk data-transfer-complete-flag is set'
dtcf	'clear disk data-transfer-complete-flag'
dwrt	'start writing to disk from memory'

Example

A test program for the disk that will read block 1 into memory is as follows:

```
        *200
        cla cll
        tad     sought      / pick up desired block number
        dlsk                / get disk to start seek
dwt,    dssf                / wait for seek flag to set when block found
        jmp     dwt
        dscf                / clear flag
        cla
        tad     adrbuf      / pointer for data
        dlma                / load disk memory address register
        drd                 / start read
/ if anything is to be done, then could do some work while transfer proceeds via dma
/ but as there is nothing to do,  just wait for  completion of the transfer
twt,    dtsf
        jmp     twt
        dtcf
        hlt
sought, 1
adrbuf, buf
        *400
buf,    0
$
```

Interrupts

| iof | 'interrupts off (disabled)' |
| ion | 'interrupts on (enabled)' |

These instructions are used to control the 'interrupt' system. By default, interrupts are disabled; all I/O necessarily involve wait loops. Interrupts must be enabled at the start of a program using interrupt driven I/O. Interrupts are automatically temporarily disabled whenever an interrupt does occur, and must be re-enabled as part of the code that effects the return from interrupt. The interrupts off instruction can be used to temporarily disable interrupts during a 'critical section' of code, such as code testing a shared variable.

Keyboard

krb   'read data from keyboard buffer to acc, clear keyboard flag'
ksf   'skip if keyboard flag set'

These instructions handle input from a keyboard. Note that there is no instruction to start the data transfer (on keyboard input that is done by the user, not the computer). Here, two instructions suffice: a skip that tests if data are ready in the keyboard control unit's buffer and an instruction that reads those data into the acc and clears the keyboard flag.

Example

Read characters from keyboard, echo to 'teletype', stop when the character zero (0) has been echoed. (The ASCII character zero has the octal value 060.)

```
        *200
copy,   cla cll                 / here we wait for a character to be keyed in
        ksf
        jmp     copy
        krb                     / got one, read it in to acc
        tls                     / forward copy to 'tty (teletype)'
wait,   tsf                     / wait for tty to print character
        jmp     wait
        cia                     / negate value
        tad     zero            / add constant
        sza cla                 / if result zero then task complete
        jmp     copy            / else go back for next character
        hlt
zero,   060                     / ascii code for character zero
$
```

'Teletype' (printing terminal)

tcf   'teletype clear flag'
tls   'teletype load and send (clears flag)"
tpc   'teletype print character'
tsf   'skip if teletype flag set'

Example

Print out a standard message. The message is assumed to be held as a sequence of ASCII characters (i.e. octal constants) stored one per word in successive words of memory. The message is terminated by a word containing the value zero. The example is coded as a subroutine; it is assumed that when called the acc will hold the address where the message is stored.

```
msg,    0                  / location where the return address is saved
        dca   mptr         / save start address of message
mloop,  tad i mptr         / get next character of message
        sna
        jmp i msg          / if it was zero, then at end of message
        tls                / if valid character, then send it
mwait,  tsf                / wait for it to be printed
        jmp   mwait
        cla
        isz   mptr         / update address ptr, assume no 'skip'
        jmp   mloop        / go get next character
mptr,   0
```

The assembly language of the simulator

Character set

Letters (lower case)	: abcdefghijklmnopqrstuvwxyz
Digits	: 0123456789
Comma	: ,
Slash (comment symbol)	: /
Star	: *
Dollars	: $
'White space'	: tab, space
Carriage return	: return

These are the characters used by the assembler program. Other characters (e.g. ", +, =, - , !, and &) are permitted in comments. Upper case letters are converted to lower case.

Octal digits and constants

The octal digits are represented by the characters '0'...'7'. An octal constant consists of a sequence of from one to four octal digits. A constant should be followed by a white space character or carriage return.

$$\text{octal digit} \quad = \quad 0 \mid 1 \mid 2 \mid 3 \mid 4 \mid 5 \mid 6 \mid 7$$

$$\text{octal constant} \quad = \quad \{\text{octal digit}\}_1^4$$

The assembler generates an error message 'too large an octal constant' if given an octal constant of more than four octal digits. The error messages 'syntax error' or 'invalid input' result from illegal characters, for example, '8', being found in a supposed 'octal constant'.

Valid octal constants

```
0123
01
1
1777
7776
2345
```

Invalid octal constants

```
5678
5a3
9
17777
```

User's symbol names

The user's symbols correspond to the labeled instructions, the labeled locations for holding program variables, and the labeled locations holding program constants. Users' symbol names must start with a letter, consist only of letters and digits, and should not exceed six characters in length.

$$\text{symbol\_name} = \text{letter } \{ \text{letter} \mid \text{digit} \}_0^5$$

The assembler generates an error message 'name too long' if given a name exceeding six characters. The error messages 'syntax error' or 'invalid input' results from illegal characters found when a symbol name was expected. Users' symbols must be defined by their occurring as labels at some point in the program text.

Valid names

```
ptr
max
addra
buffb
count1
sub2
```

Invalid names

```
1ptr
mainloop
```

Predefined op-code symbols

The op-codes listed in the op-code summary are predefined; these definitions cannot be changed. Any attempt to redefine a standard op-code, for example, by labeling a location with the name of one of the op-codes, results in the assembler reporting a 'doubly defined' symbol.

Comments

A comment is introduced by a slash character, '/', and includes all characters up to the next carriage return.

comment   =   /   { any characters} carriage return

Labels

A label should occur at the start of a line. A label consists of a (unique) users' symbol name with a terminating comma.

label   =   symbol_name ,

The assembler has two error messages concerning labels. 'Doubly defined' label means that the same name has been used when labeling two different memory locations. 'Undefined symbol' errors relate to references to users' symbols for which there are no corresponding label definitions.

Origin directive

An origin directive is used to specify the address of the memory location for the next instruction or program datum assembled. An origin directive should occur on a line by itself. It takes the form of a star and an octal constant specifying the address.

origin directive   =   *octal constant

Valid origin directives

*2
*200
*6000

Invalid origin directives

```
*800
*14000
```

The assembler may report errors 'number too large' or 'invalid input' if given bad data in an origin directive.

End directive

A dollar symbol by itself at the begining of a line marks the end of the program text.

Forms of assembly language statements

The following types of statement are processed by the assembler:

Memory-reference instructions
Input/output instructions
Operate instructions
Specifications of constants (including address constants)
'Declarations' of variables

Any instruction can be labeled. Locations used for specifications of constants and reserved by declarations of variables must be labeled.

There are no strict formatting requirements; it is not necessary to leave a particular number of spaces at the beginning of a line. Usually, a statement should start with a label or a tab character. In memory-reference instructions, the op-code/[indirect symbol]/operand should be separated by one or more spaces.

Memory-reference instructions

[optional label] memref_op-code [indirect symbol] symbol_name

The memory-reference op-codes are 'and', 'tad', 'isz', 'dca', 'jms', and 'jmp'. Indirect addressing, when needed, is indicated by the character 'i' between the op-code and the 'symbol_name'. The 'symbol_name' must correspond to the name used in one of the labels in the program.

Direct memory references

Instruction	Interpretation
and mask	Form the logical 'and' of the data in the acc and the data from the location labeled ' mask'; place the result in the acc.
tad sum	Form the sum of the data in the acc and the data from the location labeled 'sum'; place the result in the acc.
isz lcount	Increment the contents of the location labeled 'lcount'; if the incremented value is equal to zero then increment the PC to skip the next instruction.
dca result	Store the contents of the acc in the location labeled 'result'; then clear the acc.
jms subone	Call the subroutine that starts at the location labeled 'subone'; store current value of PC in the location labeled 'subone'; change the PC so that next instruction is taken from the location following 'subone'.
jmp loop1	Change the PC so that the next instruction is taken from the location labeled 'loop1'.

Indirect memory references

Instruction	Interpretation
and i pmask	Form the logical 'and' of the data in the acc and data from the location whose address can be found in the location labeled 'pmask' (first fetch the address from 'pmask', then fetch the data from that address); place the result in the acc.
tad i pdata	Form the sum of the data in the acc and data fetched from the location whose address can be found in the location labeled 'pdata' (first fetch the address from 'pdata', then fetch the data from that address); place the result in the acc. Usually used when working through the elements of an array.
isz i ptcnt	Increment the contents of the location whose address is held in the location labeled as 'ptcnt' (fetch the address from 'ptcnt', then operate on the contents of the location with that address); if the incremented value is equal to zero then increment the PC to skip the next instruction.

Indirect memory references – continued

Instruction	Interpretation
dca i bufptr	Store the contents of the acc in the location whose address is held in the location labeled 'bufptr' (first fetch the address, then store the contents of the acc in the location with that address); then clear the acc. Mainly used when storing data in arrays.
jms i psub1	Call the subroutine that starts at the location whose address is held in 'psub1' (first, fetch this address from 'psub1', then store the current value of PC in the location having this address; change the PC so that the next instruction is taken from the following location. Mainly used when calling a subroutine located on another page.
jmp i xx	Change the PC so that the next instruction is taken from the location whose address is held in the location labeled 'xx' (first, fetch the address from 'xx'; then use this address in the jump). Most frequent use is in returns from subroutines, for example, 'jmp i subone'.

Valid memory reference instructions

(That is, valid if all the symbols referenced have been defined.)

```
        tad    alpha
ndif,   dca    result
```

Invalid memory reference instructions

```
        tad beta i      Indirect symbol in wrong place.
        dca isz sum     Two op-codes?
lp      tad datum       No comma, label field will be misinterpreted.
```

Input/output instructions

[optional label] io-opcode

An I/O instruction should occur by itself, though of course the instruction can be labeled, and may be followed by a comment.

Valid I/O instructions

twait,	tsf	/ check tty flag
	krb	

Invalid I/O instructions

disc	dscf	No comma after label, label field will be misinterpreted.
	krb datum	I/O instructions don't take operands.

Operate instructions

[optional label] operate_op-code

The majority of operate instructions involve a single instruction op-code, possibly labeled and possibly followed by a comment. There a few permitted combinations of two (or more) operate op-codes. For these the instruction format is of the form '[optional label] operate1 operate2' (the order of the individual operate instructions in such a combined instruction does not matter). Since the restrictions on combining operate instructions are complex, use of combinations should be restricted to those combinations given as examples in the main text.

Valid operate instructions

loop1,	cla cll
	sna cla
	hlt

Invalid operate instructions

	cla count	Operate instructions don't take operands.

Constants

Individual constants (representing limit values, characters, bit masks, and so on) will appear in the assembly-language source code in the form:

label octal-value

The assembler cannot interpret decimal numbers, signed numbers, or text strings for character sequences. If a negative number is required, then the octal pattern corresponding to the two's complement representation of that negative number must be given.

Arrays of constant data (most commonly, these will be required for text strings) will appear in the assembly-language source in the form:

```
label    octal-value
         octal-value
         octal-value
         0
```

A conventional way of terminating a string is to place a zero word at the end.

Valid constants

```
limit,    0012          / limit for loop is ten (decimal)
mask1,    0177          / mask for seven bit character
minus2,   7776          / value -2
msg1,     123           / S
          165           / u
          155           / m
          040           / space
          075           / =
          040           / space
          0
```

Address constants are a special case. They are required in constant pointers, for example, a pointer to a subroutine located on another page, and base address values referencing arrays.

```
label  symbol-name
```

The assembler processes these constant declarations by filling in the values for the addresses of the symbols (once these addresses have been determined).

Examples of address constants

```
psub1,    subone        / pointer to subone
addrb,    buffb         / address of start of 'buffer b'
```

Variables

Variables are defined in the source assembly language program by constructs of the form:

```
label  0
```

This defines the symbol used in the label field and reserves one memory word for the variable with that symbol name. For example:

```
ptr1,    0                    / pointer used when accessing characters in array ...
sum,     0                    / location for sum
```

Such statements, in an assembly-language source program, define the variables 'ptr1' and 'sum'. (When the final object code is loaded, the locations corresponding to the variables 'ptr1' and 'sum' are set to zero. As in a FORTRAN 'DATA' statement, other initial values can be defined for program variables. However, this 'initialization' is a load-time operation; the zeroing-out or value-setting of the variables is not repeated at run time. If the program is restarted, such variables have whatever values they possessed at the end of the previous run of that program. Memory locations for program variables that need to start as 0 should be explicitly cleared in the initialization phase of any program.)

Declarations of arrays are achieved as in the following example:

```
/ save 100 octal words for array buf1 starting at 1000
         *1000
buf1,    0
         *1100
/ now have 40 octal words for array ob1
ob1,     0
         *1140
```

An origin directive is used to define where the array starts. A label is defined at that location. Another origin directive then identifies the first location following the array.

Layout of a program

Simple programs should have the following organization:

```
/ This program ...
```
                                    Each program should start with a few lines of
                                    comments explaining the task it accomplishes.
```
         *20
```
                                    An origin directive should be used to place the first of
                                    any global variables at location 0020. Comments
                                    should identify the use of each variable and constant.
```
buff1,   buffb                 / address of a buffer
kd100,   0144                  / decimal value 100
char,    0                     / last character read
```
                                    It is best to group separately the variables, constants,
                                    and address pointers.

```
        *200
```
The start of the main program should be located at address 0200; so the *200 origin directive is always needed.

```
/ start of main

/ main loop,
/ get next datum & ...
lp,      cla
             jms sub
/ zero values are special
/ so ...
             sna
```

Do not comment every instruction as it only clutters the program listing; instead insert a comment every few lines of code explaining the role of the next few instructions in the overall task being handled by the program.

The code of the main program should be followed by its constants, address pointers, and then local variables.

```
             .
             .

             .
done,    cla
             hlt           / end of program
lim,     0050          / max iterations for ...
psub2,   sub2          / output routine on page 2
asum,    0             / number of ...
```

If several routines are located on the same page, then they should be clearly separated.

```
/ - - - - - -
/ sub, get data from a/d
/ and ...
sub,     0
             .
```

A new origin directive is needed at the begining of each page.

```
/ - - - - - - - - - -
        *400
/ - - - - - - - - - -
/ Here we have the page 2 routines which include ....
```

Code should occupy the first few pages in memory with any data arrays located at higher addresses.

```
/ - - - - - - -
```

```
            *1600
/ - - - - - - -
/ On this page have two 64(dec) word arrays for data being analyzed and ..
arr1,       0
            *1700
arr2,       0
```

The program should terminate with an end directive, that is, the '$' symbol.

```
$
```

Program structures

While loops

The following code typifies the structure of a while loop:

Pascal

while (x <> 0) **do begin**

    .

    .

    .

    end;

Assembly language

```
            .
whl1,       cla cll
            tad     x
            sna     cla     / test if x non zero
            jmp     whe1    / if it is zero, jump to the  instruction following the while loop
            .
            .                / body of while, corresponding to code between
            .                / begin and end
            .
            jmp whl1         / jump back to head of while loop
whe1,       cla
                             / code following while
```

For loops

A for loop can be constructed in a style similar to that used for the while loop; a variable can be allocated for the loop control and the termination test can check whether this variable contains a specified limit value. However, if the value of the loop index is not needed in the loop, then the following assembly language coding is slightly more efficient:

```
/ initialization,
/  set a counter to hold, as a negative number, the
/  number of times the loop is to be cycled
            tad     lim             / pick up required cycle count
            cia                     / negate it
            dca     cntr            / store in counter
/ head of loop
/ return to this point at start of each iteration
loop1,      cla cll
            .
            .                       / body of loop where computation performed
            .
/ termination test and jump back to head of loop if not finished
            isz     cntr
            jmp     loop1
            .
            .
```

If ... then ...;

Simple if tests are coded by having a jump over the body of the if code (the parts 'then begin ... end;').

Pascal

```
  if (z=0) then begin

          .
          .
          .
          end;
```

Assembly language

```
            cla cll
            tad     z
            sza cla
            jmp     ifnd
            .                       / body of if statement
            .
            .
ifnd,       cla                     / code following if
            .
```

If ... then ... else ...;

The code for the simple if ... then ...; construct has to be extended with additional jumps.

Pascal

if (alpha>=3) **then** count1:=count1+1 **else** count2:=count2+1;

Assembly language

```
        cla
        tad     three
        cia
        tad     alpha       / (alpha-3) in acc
        spa cla
        jmp     elsebt      / jump over 'then' clause to get to else
        tad     count1
        iac
        dca     count1
        jmp     endif       / jump over 'else' clause to get to end of if statement
elsebt, tad     count2
        iac
        dca     count2
endif,  .                   / code following if
        .
        .
        .
three,  3
```

Comparisons

The simulated machine lacks a *compare* instruction (and the condition bits that are needed to record the results of a comparison). Consequently, as in the example above where it was necessary to test if alpha>=3, a calculation must be carried out where one value is subtracted from the other, the result left in the acc, and the result tested in a subsequent skip operation.

Procedure's structure and declarations

The arrangement of code for a subroutine differs from the layout of a typical Pascal procedure. Attempts to follow Pascal too closely (by having a procedure entry, declarations of variables and constants, and then code) are likely to result in errors.

The following fragment illustrates the difference in layout. It is a procedure to swap the values of two variables, 'alpha' and 'beta'; in the Pascal version these variables are assumed to be globals; in the assembly code they are page zero variables.

Pascal

```
procedure swap;
var temp:integer;
begin
   temp:=alpha;
   alpha:=beta;
   beta:=temp;
end;
```

Correct assembly language version of swap

```
swap,     0                          / location for return address
          cla
          tad     alpha
          dca     temp
          tad     beta
          dca     alpha
          tad     temp
          dca     beta
          jmp i   swap
temp,     0                          / location for temporary results in subroutine swap
```

Incorrect assembly-language version of swap

```
swap,     0                          / location for return address
temp,     0                          / location for temporary results in subroutine swap
          cla
          tad     alpha
          dca     temp
          tad     beta
          dca     alpha
          tad     temp
          dca     beta
          jmp i   swap
```

If the incorrect code is executed, the first 'instruction' of the subroutine 'swap' is determined by the contents of 'temp'. The first time the routine is called, this would be zero; zero interpreted as an instruction is an 'and' (which would probably not do much harm). Then the current value of 'alpha' (e.g. 5100 octal) is stored in 'temp', from where it is later copied into 'beta'. The next time the 'swap' routine is called, the value 5100 octal left in 'temp' is executed as an instruction (this time it causes a jump to location 100 and wrecks the program).

Don't let variables or constants become mixed into the code of the routines!

Looping and accessing successive elements of an array

A 'pointer', initialized to contain the address of the first element of the array, is used to access array elements. The pointer is incremented on each cycle through the loop. (It is easiest to think in terms of arrays with an index starting at zero, rather than at 1; so an array with 'lim' elements is really **var** datum : array[0..(lim-1)] of integer;).

Example

Sum the values in all elements of array:

Pascal

```
sum:=0;
for i:=0 to (lim-1) do sum:=sum+datum[i];
```

Assembly language

```
            .
            .
            / set up loop
            tad     lim             / number of elements in array
            cia
            dca     cntr
            tad     addtm           / address of element zero of array datum
            dca     ptr1
/ use acc to 'accumulate' the sum
loopz,      tad i   ptr1            / add next element to partial sum
            isz     ptr1            / update ptr1
            nop                     / (Don't want that isz ever to cause a skip)
            isz     cntr            / increment count of elements processed
            jmp     loopz
            dca     sum             / store resulting sum in appropriate variable
            .
            .
            .
```

Access to random elements of an array

Access to random elements of an array requires the complete process of constructing the address of the particular array element required and then accessing the memory location having this computed address. On the simulator, the final access to memory to fetch or store the required datum requires the use of a pointer variable which is also held in memory.

So, to access an arbitrary memory element one needs to fetch the address of the start of the array, and add the index value to get the address of the element required. This address must be stored in a pointer. An indirect access using this pointer is made to access the required data.

Example

Count the number of occurrences of each different ASCII character in a sequence of 512 characters read from the keyboard.

The program consists of two loops. In the first of these, the array of counts must be cleared; here, each array element is accessed in sequence permitting the simple incrementing pointer method to be used for array access. In the second loop, the 512 characters are read and each is used to increment an appropriate count in the array of counts.

Pascal

```
program ascii;
var  chars :array[0..127] of integer;
     cntr,temp:integer;
     ch:char;
begin
        for cntr:=0 to 127 do chars[cntr]:=0;
        for cntr:=1 to 512 do begin
                read(ch);
                temp:=ord(ch);
                chars[temp]:=chars[temp]+1
                end;
end.
```

Assembly language

```
        *200
/ count ascii,
/ - - - - - - - - - - - - - - - - - - - - - - - - - - - - - - -
/ first, must 'zero' out the array which will hold counters
        cla cll
/ set up the loop controls, a -ve counter in cntr, and a pointer
        tad     limit       / number of different ascii characters
        cia                 / negate
        dca     cntr
        tad     addr        / address of where the counts are stored
        dca     ptr
/ start the clearing loop
clear,  dca  i  ptr
        isz     ptr
        nop
        isz     cntr
        jmp     clear
/ - - - - - - - - - - - - - - - - - - - - - - - - - - - - - - -
```

```
/ now initialize count for number of characters to process
        tad     numchr      / number of characters to be read
        cia
        dca     cntr
/ - - - - - - - - - - - - - - - - - - - - - - - - - - - - - - -
/ ok, initialization complete, get characters
loop,   ksf
        jmp     loop
        krb
        and     mask        / mask down to 7 bits (just in case!)
/ - - - - - - - - - - - - - - - - - - - - - - - - - - - - - - -
/ Here is where the random access is made to the array of character counts.
/ now have what is really an index value in acc
/ add in base address of array
        tad     addr
/ and save the resulting final address in a pointer
        dca     dptr
/ ok, dptr holds address of character count value that is to be incremented
        tad i   dptr        / get current value
        iac                 / increment
        dca i   dptr        / store back
/ (that could have been done as isz i dptr)
/
/ ok, processing of current character complete
/ go back for more if necessary
        isz     cntr
        jmp l   oop
        hlt
/ - - - - - - - - - - - - - - - - - - - - - - - - - - - - - - -
/ - - - - - - - - - - - - - - - - - - - - - - - - - - - - - - -
/ variables, pointers etc for character count program
dptr,   0                   / used as pointer holding address of array   element
ptr,    0                   / used as pointer into array when clearing it
cntr,   0                   / used as counter for loops
addr,   chars               / address of array containing character counts
mask,   0177                / make certain only 7-bit ascii codes
numchr, 1000                / 512 decimal
limit,  0200
        *0400
chars,  0       / start of array for character counts
$
```

ASCII character values

|000 nul	|001 soh	|002 stx	|003 etx	|004 eot	|005 enq	|006 ack	|007 bel |
|010 bs	|011 ht	|012 nl	|013 vt	|014 np	|015 cr	|016 so	|017 si |
|020 dle	|021 dc1	|022 dc2	|023 dc3	|024 dc4	|025 nak	|026 syn	|027 etb |
|030 can	|031 em	|032 sub	|033 esc	|034 fs	|035 gs	|036 rs	|037 us |
|040 sp	|041 !	|042 "	|043 #	|044 $	|045 %	|046 &	|047 ' |
|050 (	|051)	|052 *	|053 +	|054 ,	|055 -	|056 .	|057 / |
|060 0	|061 1	|062 2	|063 3	|064 4	|065 5	|066 6	|067 7 |
|070 8	|071 9	|072 :	|073 ;	|074 <	|075 =	|076 >	|077 ? |
|100 @	|101 A	|102 B	|103 C	|104 D	|105 E	|106 F	|107 G |
|110 H	|111 I	|112 J	|113 K	|114 L	|115 M	|116 N	|117 O |
|120 P	|121 Q	|122 R	|123 S	|124 T	|125 U	|126 V	|127 W |
|130 X	|131 Y	|132 Z	|133 [	|134 \	|135]	|136 ^	|137 _ |
|140 `	|141 a	|142 b	|143 c	|144 d	|145 e	|146 f	|147 g |
|150 h	|151 i	|152 j	|153 k	|154 l	|155 m	|156 n	|157 o |
|160 p	|161 q	|162 r	|163 s	|164 t	|165 u	|166 v	|167 w |
|170 x	|171 y	|172 z	|173 {	|174 |	|175 }	|176 ~	|177 del |

Appendix B

A simple assembler

Source of a Pascal version of a simple, two pass assembler program

The following is a listing of the source of a Pascal version of a two pass assembler for the assembly language of the simulator. This version is written for 'Berkeley Pascal' running on a Unix™ system. There are a few incompatibilities with standard Pascal, for example, the 'reset()' and 'rewrite()' functions take optional arguments that define a file name.

The assembler requires a file with a list of the predefined op-code symbols and their values (this file is listed after the text of the program). After reading this file of predefined op-codes and constructing its symbol table, the assembler reads an assembly language source code program and produces both a listing and an ASCII text file which contains an octal representation of the machine code generated. This version of the assembler stops on the first error that it encounters. If an error is encountered in the assembly-language source, then an error message is printed together with details of where the error occurred.

```
program smap(input,output,source,object,symbols);
{    Simple Minded Assembler Program.
    This program is intended as a simple illustration of a two pass
assembler producing code for an absolute loader. The target machine
is a PDP-8.
    SMAP is not sophisticated, and does not include much in the
way of error checking. (In particular, it makes no attempt to validate
microcoded combinations of PDP-8 operate instructions.)
    SMAP only allows for a couple of assembler directives:
    *     origin directive
    $     end directive
}
```

```
const
     dd      =   1;      { error number for doubly defined symbol        }
     ln      =   2;      {          for too long a name                  }
     lo      =   3;      {          for too large an octal constant      }
     sx      =   5;      {          for some obscure syntax error        }
     undef   =   6;      {          for an undefined symbol (pass 2)      }
     xp      =   4;      {          cross page reference (pass 2)         }
     mask177 =      127;
     thispage =     128;
     mask7600 =    3968;
     SYMBOLSFILE = '/CS-3/symbols';  { Name of file containing the predefined symbols }

type
     symbol = packed array[1..6] of char;   { Symbols are up to 6 characters long }
     symtype = (label8,mri,iot,opr,indir);     { Classification of symbol types }

     { Record structure for each entry in  symbol table }
     entry  = record
                   name : symbol;
                   stype : symtype;
                   value : 0..4095;
                   end;

     { Classification of tokens in input stream used in basic lexical analysis }
     token = (labels,comment,octal,origin,ending,identifier,null,errors);

     { More detailed classification of input  tokens used in pass 2 }
     xtoken = (xlab8,xcomment,xoctal,xorigin,xending,xnull,xerrors,
                   xvariable,xmriopcode,xiotopcode,xoropcode,xindirectbit);

var
     error       :    boolean;            { Flag set to true on any fatal error }
     ended       :    boolean;            { Flag set to true when reach end of source
                                           on current pass }
     line        :    array[1..120] of char; { Where we store a line of source program }
     numchars    :    integer;            { Number of characters in this line }
     posn        :    integer;            { Where we are on line }

     symtab      :    array[1..512] of entry; { The symbol table }
     numsym      :    1..512;             { The number of defined symbols }

     where       :    0..4095;            { Location counter }

     source      :    text;               { File with source text of PDP-8 program }
     object      :    text;               { File for object code generated in pass 2 }
     symbols     :    text;               { File with standard symbol definitions }
```

```
newsym        :    symbol;            { Name of most recently read identifier }
newval        :    0..4095;           { Value of most recently read octal # or value
                                        of newsym }
printval      :    0..4095;

passno        :    integer;           { Pass number }
```

```
{ - - - - - - - - - - - - - - - - - - - - - - - - - - - - - - - - - }
{        Utility functions                           }
{ - - - - - - - - - - - - - - - - - - - - - - - - - - - - - - - - - }


    procedure octwrite(x : integer; d : integer;var f : text);
    var temp : 0 .. 7;
       ch : char;
    begin
       if d > 1 then octwrite(x div 8, d - 1,f);
       temp:= x mod 8;
       ch:=chr(ord('0') + temp);
       write(f,ch)
    end;
{ - - - - - - - - - - - - - - - - - - - - - - - - - - - - - - - - }
    function octread(var ff : text) : integer;
    var v: integer;
    begin
             { skip over anything other than valid octal digits }
             while not (ff^ in ['0'..'7']) do get(ff);
             v:=0;
             { consume valid octal digits }
             while (ff^ in ['0'..'7']) do begin
                      v:=8*v + (ord(ff^) - ord('0'));
                      get(ff)
                      end;
             { force into an appropriate range }
             octread:=v mod 4096
    end;
{ - - - - - - - - - - - - - - - - - - - - - - - - - - - - - - - - }
    function orintegers(alpha,beta : integer) : integer;
    var result,bits : integer;
    begin
    { Very frequently we will need to combine specific bits of some integers.
    Of course, this is not allowed in Pascal. Hence, this contrived routine for
    performing the task. It is written to handle just 12 bits, as required for our PDP-8;
    Many dialects of Pascal have an 'OR' function; this should be used if available }

             alpha:=alpha mod 4096; { just in case, make them 12-bit numbers}
             beta:=beta mod 4096;
             bits:=2048;
             result:=0;
             while bits>0 do begin
```

```
                        if ((alpha >= bits) or (beta >= bits)) then
                                result:=result+bits;
                        If (alpha >= bits) then alpha:=alpha-bits;
                        if (beta  >= bits) then beta:=beta-bits;
                        bits:=bits div 2
                        end;
                orintegers:=result
        end;
{ - - - - - - - - - - - - - - - - - - - - - - - - - - - - - - - - - - }
        function andintegers(alpha,beta : integer) : integer;
        var result,bits : integer;
        begin
                alpha:=alpha mod 4096; { just in case, make them 12-bit numbers}
                beta:=beta mod 4096;
                bits:=2048;
                result:=0;
                while bits>0 do begin
                        if ((alpha >= bits) & (beta >= bits)) then
                                result:=result+bits;
                        if (alpha >= bits) then alpha:=alpha-bits;
                        if (beta  >= bits) then beta:=beta-bits;
                        bits:=bits div 2
                        end;
                andintegers:=result
        end;


{-------------------------------------------------------------------}
{ Error reports, and other output routines                          }
{-------------------------------------------------------------------}

  procedure errs(errno,passno : integer);
  var i : integer;
        { Same error can sometimes generate multiple messages; only take the first }
  begin
   if not error then begin
        error:=true;
        writeln; writeln;
        writeln('Assembly error detected in Pass ',passno:3);
        writeln; writeln;
        writeln('Error occurred in or about the line: ');
        writeln;
        for i:=1 to numchars do write(line[i]);
        writeln;
        for i:=1 to (posn-1) do write(' ');
        writeln('^');
        for i:=1 to (posn-1) do write(' ');
        writeln('|');
        writeln;
        writeln;
        write('Error type: ');
```

```
        case errno of
                xp         : writeln('Cross Page Reference.');
                dd         : writeln('doubly defined symbol, ',newsym);
                ln         : writeln('too long a name, ',newsym);
                lo         : writeln('too large an octal constant');
                sx         : writeln('syntax error');
                undef      : writeln('undefined symbol, ',newsym);
                end;
      end
  end;
{----------------------------------------------------------------------}
  procedure andsymtab;
  var i: integer;
     e: entry;
   begin { This procedure appends the symbol table to the object file }
      writeln(object,numsym);
      for i:=1 to numsym do begin
                e:=symtab[i];
                with e do begin
                        write(object,name,' ');
                        case stype of
                                label8    : write(object,' 0 ');
                                mri       : write(object,' 1 ');
                                opr       : write(object,' 2 ');
                                iot       : write(object,' 3 ');
                                indir     : write(object,' 4 ');
                                end;
                        octwrite(value,4,object);
                        writeln(object)
                        end;
                end;
      writeln(object,'$')
  end;
{----------------------------------------------------------------------}
  procedure printsymtab;
  var i: integer; e: entry;
  begin { This procedure prints the symbol table in the assembly listing }
      writeln; writeln('Symbol table: '); writeln;
      writeln('Name  Type     Value      Name   Type     Value'); writeln;
      for i:=1 to numsym do begin
                e:=symtab[i];
                with e do begin
                        write(name,' ');
                        case stype of
                                label8    : write('label    ');
                                mri       : write('mri      ');
                                opr       : write('opr      ');
                                iot       : write('iot      ');
                                indir     : write('indirect  ');
                                end;
```

```
                        octwrite(value,4,output);
                        end;
              if 0 = (i mod 2) then writeln
              else write('        ')
              end;
     end;
{------------------------------------------------------------------------}
{ Output utilities for tabbing (leaving spaces), printing a line etc.  }
{------------------------------------------------------------------------}
  procedure tab(tabpos : integer);
  var i : integer;
  begin
      i:=1;
      while i< tabpos do begin write(' '); i:=i+1 end;
  end;
{----------------------------------------------------------------}
  procedure dumpline;
  var i : integer;
  begin
      i:=1;
      while i< numchars do begin write(line[i]); i:=i+1 end;
      writeln
  end;
{----------------------------------------------------------------}
{Procedures used to read assembly language source }
{----------------------------------------------------------------}
  procedure skipline;
  begin { used when need to skip rest of input line, e.g. have recognized a comment line }
      posn:=numchars+1
  end;
{----------------------------------------------------------------}
  procedure getline;
  var ch: char;
  begin
      numchars:=0;
      while not eoln(source) do begin
                read(source,ch);
                numchars:=numchars+1;
                if ((ch >= 'A') and (ch<='Z')) then
                        ch:=chr(ord(ch)-ord('A')+ord('a'));
                line[numchars]:=ch;
          end;
      readln(source);
      line[numchars+1]:=' ';
      line[numchars+2]:=chr(0); { null character marks end }
      numchars:=numchars+2;
      posn:=1
  end;
```

```
{----------------------------------------------------------------------}
{ token recognition routine – as diagrammed in Ch.13   }
{----------------------------------------------------------------------}
```
function nextsym: token;
> {   Here we have one of those simple transition state type lexical analyzers.
> This function is intended only to classify the type of the next symbol as a comment,
> label, origin directive, end directive, an octal constant, an identifier, null line, or
> obvious syntactic error.
> Nextsym is used directly by PASS1; Nextsym is also used indirectly, via Xnextsym,
> from PASS2.
> During the first pass, when merely building up the symbol table, the symbol
> classifications produced by Nextsym are adequate; a more refined classification is
> needed by Pass2.
> Characters being read by "smap" fall into the following categories:

1) $ special end directive character
2) *   special origin directive character
3) ,   distinctive mark for a label, turns a preceding identifier into a label
4) 0..7   valid characters in an octal constant
5) a..z,0..9 valid characters in an identifier
6) space delimiter (tab is taken as a space)
7) null   (special 0 character inserted into line buffer) end of line marker
8) /   comment marker

We can distinguish the following states:

> start   beginning to process next symbol
> inoct   reading an octal constant
> ident   reading an identifier (or maybe a label)

The transitions can be summarized as follows:

> ! => set readsym to type of symbol specified
> % => set state to state specified
> # => state:=done

symbol state	1	2	3	4	5	6	7	8
start	# !ending	%inoct !origin	# !errors	%inoct !octal	%ident !identi	%start 	# !null	# !comment
inoct	# !errors	# !errors	# !errors	build octal number	# !errors	#	#	# !errors
ident	# !errors	# !errors	# !label8	extend name	extend name	#	#	# !errors

```
}
    type lexstate = (start, ident, inoct, done);
    var
        state       :       lexstate;
        ch          :       char;
        octdigit    :       boolean;
        alphabetic  :       boolean;
        numeric     :       boolean;
        dollars     :       boolean;
        comma       :       boolean;
        star        :       boolean;
        slash       :       boolean;
        space       :       boolean;
        endln       :       boolean;
        readtype    :       token;
        octval      :       0..4095;
        symlength   :       integer;
        symbuf      :       array [1..7] of char;
        errno       :       integer;
        i           :       integer;

    begin
        state:=start;
        octval:=0;
        symlength:=0;
        for i:=1 to 6 do symbuf[i]:=' ';
        while state<>done do begin
                if posn>numchars then getline;
                ch:=line[posn];
                posn:=posn+1;
                alphabetic:=(ch in ['a'..'z']);
                numeric:=(ch in ['0'..'9']);
                octdigit:=(ch in ['0'..'7']);
                dollars:=(ch = '$');
                star:=(ch = '*');
                slash:=(ch = '/');
                space:=((ch = ' ') or (ord(ch)=9)); { 9 should be tab character }
                endln:=(ch = chr(0));
                comma:=(ch = ',');
                case state of
                        start: begin
                                if star then begin
                                        readtype:=origin;
                                        state:=inoct
                                end
                        else
                        if slash then begin
                                state:=done;
                                readtype:=comment
                        end
```

```
                else
                if dollars then begin
                        state:=done;
                        readtype:=ending
                        end
                else
                if alphabetic then begin
                        readtype:=identifier;
                        state:=ident;
                        symlength:=1;
                        symbuf[symlength]:=ch
                        end
                else
                if octdigit then begin
                        readtype:=octal;
                        octval:=ord(ch)-ord('0');
                        state:=inoct
                        end
                else
                if endln then begin
                        readtype:=null;
                        state:=done
                        end
                else
                if not space then begin
                        errno:=sx;
                        readtype:=errors;
                        state:=done
                        end
                end;

inoct:  begin
            if octdigit then begin
                    if octval>= 512 then begin
                            errno:=lo;
                            readtype:=errors;
                            state:=done
                            end
                    else begin
                      octval:=octval*8 + (ord(ch)-ord('0'));
                      end
                    end
            else
            if space or endln then state:=done
            else begin
                    errno:=sx;
                    readtype:=errors
                    end
            end;
```

```
                        ident: begin
                             if alphabetic or numeric then begin
                                    symlength:=symlength+1;
                                    if symlength <= 6 then
                                          symbuf[symlength]:=ch;
                                    if symlength>6 then
                                          begin
                                             state:=done;
                                             pack(symbuf,1,newsym);
                                             errno:=ln;
                                             readtype:=errors
                                          end;
                                 end
                             else
                             if space then state:=done
                             else
                             if comma then begin
                                    state:=done;
                                    readtype:=labels
                                 end
                             end
                        end;
                  end;
        if readtype=errors then errs(errno,passno);
        if readtype in [ labels , identifier ] then pack(symbuf,1,newsym);
        if readtype in [ origin, octal ] then newval:=octval;
        nextsym:=readtype
      end;
{----------------------------------------------------------------------}
  function findposn :integer;
  var top,bottom,sposn: integer;
      found   : boolean;
  { Find the index number in symtab for "newsym" – either the index of where it already
exists or  the place where it should go if things are to be kept ordered. }
  begin
      top:=numsym; bottom:=1;
      found:=false;
      while not found do begin
                sposn:=((top-bottom) div 2) + bottom;
                if newsym=symtab[sposn].name then found:=true
                else
                if newsym>symtab[sposn].name then begin
                       bottom:=sposn+1;
                        sposn:=bottom
                     end
                else top:=sposn-1;
                found:=found or (bottom>top)
                end;
        findposn:=sposn
  end;
```

```
{----------------------------------------------------------------------}
    function xnextsym : xtoken;
    { Need a more detailed classification of tokens in input stream when
    doing Pass2. Nextsym's classes are mostly OK, except its class
    identifier must now be more precisely defined. Identifiers must now
    be catagorized as:

            variables
            mem-ref opcodes
            iot opcodes
            operate opcodes
            (indirection symbol)

    Information needed to do this reclassification is provided by data in symbol table.
    So when read an identifier,
        find it in symbol table and return a categorization based on the data there
        if it is not in the symbol table, then generate an error message for undefined symbol.
    }
    var   temp : token;
          sympos : integer;
          xtemp : xtoken;
    begin
        temp:=nextsym;
        case temp of
                labels: xtemp:=xlab8;
                comment: xtemp:=xcomment;
                octal:  xtemp:=xoctal;
                origin: xtemp:=xorigin;
                ending: xtemp:=xending;
                null:   xtemp:=xnull;
                errors: xtemp:=xerrors;
                identifier: begin
                        sympos:=findposn;  { Find where symbol should be }
                        if symtab[sympos].name <> newsym then begin
                            { Symbol missing, record an error and print }
                            { message for an undefined symbol }
                            xtemp:=xerrors;
                            errs(undef,passno);
                        end
                    else begin
                            { Set xtemp according to type of symbol }
                            case symtab[sympos].stype of
                                label8:  xtemp:=xvariable;
                                mri:     xtemp:=xmriopcode;
                                iot:     xtemp:=xiotopcode;
                                opr:     xtemp:=xopropcode;
                                indir:   xtemp:=xindirectbit;
                            end;
```

```
                                          { Set newval to value from symbol table }
                                          newval:=symtab[sympos].value
                                          end;

                              end;

                    end;
          xnextsym:=xtemp
    end;



{--------------------------------------------------------------------}
  procedure insertsymbol;
  var sposn: integer;   { Position where symbol should go in table }
    n   : integer;
  begin
      sposn:=findposn; { Find where it should go }
      if newsym=symtab[sposn].name then { doubly defined symbol }
              errs(dd,passno)
      else begin      { Insert a new symbol in sequence }
              n:=numsym;
              while n>=sposn do begin
                      symtab[n+1]:=symtab[n];
                      n:=n-1
                      end;
              symtab[sposn].name:=newsym;
              symtab[sposn].stype:=label8;
              symtab[sposn].value:=where;
              numsym:=numsym+1
          end;
  end;
```

```
{------------------------------------------------------------------}
  procedure pass1;
  {
       In pass 1, we need to identify and process origin directives,
     an end directive, and labels. Comments can be ignored. Other input
     lines are accepted unchecked (some more syntax checking done in
     pass 2) and serve only to increment counter "where".
  }
  begin
     reset(source);  { Get ready to read file with source code. }
     where:=0;       { Initialize origin for code/data. }
     ended:=false;   { Mark not yet at end of source text. }
     numchars:=0;
     passno:=1;
     posn:=1;
     while not (ended or error) do begin
             case nextsym of
                     comment:        skipline;
                     origin:         where:=newval;
                     labels:         insertsymbol;
                     ending:         ended:=true;
                     octal,identifier:  begin
                                               where:=where+1;
                                               skipline;
                                        end;
                     null,errors:
                     end;
             end;
     writeln;
     writeln;
     if not error then begin
       writeln('SMAP   Pass 1, Symbol table listing:');
       writeln;
       writeln;
       printsymtab;
       writeln;
       writeln
     end;
  end;
```

```
{-----------------------------------------------------------------------}
  procedure writecode(cval: integer;next : xtoken);
  {
       Write code value, cval, to object file; generate listing.
      Also check that nothing is left on input line, for that would be  a syntax error.
  }
  begin
    write(object,' ');
    octwrite(cval,4,object);
    writeln(object);
    octwrite(where,4,output);
    tab(4);
    octwrite(cval,4,output);
    tab(8);
    dumpline;
    where:=where+1;
    if not (next in [xcomment,xnull]) then errs(sx,passno)
    else skipline
  end;

  procedure iots;
  {    IOT instructions should occur by themselves, but do have the
       possiblity of the following:

       iot 632
       (meaning opcode 6632)

       so allow nextsym to be null or octal, others are errors.
}
  var next: xtoken;
  begin
      printval:=newval;  { will have been set by xnextsym }
      next:=xnextsym;
      while next = xoctal do begin
                printval:=orintegers(printval,newval);
                next:=xnextsym
                end;
      writecode(printval,next)
  end;
```

```
procedure operate;
{ Will allow any sequence of successive operate instructions or operate
  instructions and octal constants }
var next : xtoken;
begin
    printval:=newval;
    next:=xnextsym;
    while next in [xoctal,xopropcode] do begin
            printval:=orintegers(printval,newval);
            next:=xnextsym
            end;
    writecode(printval,next)
  end;


procedure memrefs;
{ Memref <i> variable/octal, or  Memref variable/octal, nothing else allowed }
var next : xtoken;
   temp : 0..4095;
   pcp  : 0..4095;
   dp   : 0..4095;
begin
    printval:=newval;
    next:=xnextsym;
    if next=xindirectbit then begin
                    printval:=orintegers(printval,newval);
                    next:=xnextsym
                    end;
    if not (next in [xoctal,xvariable]) then errs(sx,passno)
    else begin
            { have to check for page 0, this page or erroneous }
            { cross page references  }
            if newval<128 then begin
                    { page 0 }
                    printval:=orintegers(printval,newval);
                    writecode(printval,xnextsym)
                    end
            else begin
                    pcp:=andintegers(where,mask7600);
                    dp:=andintegers(newval,mask7600);
                    if pcp <> dp then errs(xp,passno)
                    else begin
                            temp:=andintegers(newval,mask177);
                            temp:=orintegers(temp,thispage);
                            printval:=orintegers(printval,temp);
                            writecode(printval,xnextsym);
                        end;
                    end;
            end;

end;
```

```
procedure pass2;
begin
    reset(source);  { Get ready to read file with source code. }
    ended:=false;  { Mark not yet at end of source text. }
    numchars:=0;
    posn:=1;
    passno:=2;
    rewrite(object);
    where:=0;

    writeln;
    writeln;
    writeln('SMAP     Pass 2 Assembly listing.');
    writeln;
    writeln;

    while not (ended or error) do begin
            printval:=0;
            case xnextsym of
                    xcomment: begin tab(20);
                                        dumpline;
                                        skipline; { skip over comments }
                                end;
                    xorigin: begin
                                { want to output equivalent of an }
                                { origin directive for the loader }
                                write(object,'*');
                                octwrite(newval,4,object);
                                writeln(object);
                                where:=newval;
                                tab(20);
                                dumpline;
                                if xnextsym <> xnull then errs(sx,passno)
                                end;
                    xoctal,xvariable: begin
                                { just copy octal constants to output }
                                writecode(newval,xnextsym)
                                end;
                    xmriopcode: memrefs;
                    xiotopcode: iots;
                    xopropcode: operate;
                    xending: ended:=true;
                    xnull,xerrors,xlab8: { do nothing }
                    end
            end;
    writeln(object,'$');
    if error then rewrite(object)
    else andsymtab

end;
```

```
procedure initialize;
  var i,j: integer;
begin
    error:=false;

    { Read standard symbols from an ordered file }
    reset(symbols,SYMBOLSFILE);
    readln(symbols,numsym);
    for i:=1 to numsym do begin
            with symtab[i] do begin
                    for j:=1 to 6 do read(symbols,name[j]);
                    read(symbols,j);
                    case j of
                        0:          stype:=label8;
                        1:          stype:=mri;
                        2:          stype:=opr;
                        3:          stype:=iot;
                        4:          stype:=indir;
                        end;
                    value:=octread(symbols);
                    readln(symbols);
                    end;
            end;
  end;



{------------------------------------------------------------------ }
{                                                                   }
{     Main program here,                                            }
{------------------------------------------------------------------ }
begin
    initialize;
    pass1;
    if not error then pass2
end.
```

Symbols

These data represent the predefined op-code symbols with which the assembler's symbol table is initiated. The first datum in the data file is the number of symbols. The symbols themselves follow – mnemonic name, type, octal value. (There should only be one symbol per line of the input file; a multicolumn form is used here for convenience.) The types are 1 = memory reference instruction op-code, 2 = "operate" op-code, 3 = input/output op-code, and 4 = indirect symbol.

50

adcrb	3	6601	adsf	3	6602	adstrt	3	6604
and	1	0000	cia	2	7041	cla	2	7200
clkcf	3	6501	clksf	3	6502	clkt	3	6504
cll	2	7100	cma	2	7040	cml	2	7020
dca	1	3000	dlma	3	6410	dlsk	3	6400
drd	3	6411	dscf	3	6402	dssf	3	6401
dtcf	3	6414	dtsf	3	6412	dwrt	3	6415
hlt	2	7402	i	4	0400	iac	2	7001
iof	3	6002	ion	3	6001	iot	3	6000
isz	1	2000	jmp	1	5000	jms	1	4000
krb	3	6036	ksf	3	6031	nop	2	7000
opr	2	7000	ral	2	7004	rar	2	7010
rtl	2	7006	rtr	2	7012	skp	2	7410
sma	2	7500	sna	2	7450	snl	2	7420
spa	2	7510	sza	2	7440	szl	2	7430
tad	1	1000	tcf	3	6042	tls	3	6046
tpc	3	6044	tsf	3	6041			

Appendix C

Simul8 user manual

Using simul8 on the Macintosh

Starting

1. Insert the simul8 systems disk.
2. Double-click on the disk icon to open it. The screen display then appears as illustrated in Figure C-1.
3. The simul8 system comprises:

simul8

The program that simulates the PDP-8 computer.

SimDisc

A file that serves as the disk in the simulated system.

Demonstrations

A set of demonstration programs.

4. Double-click on the demonstrations folder to open it and gain access to the demonstration programs. While the screen display should be similar to that shown in Figure C-2, there may be a different selection of demonstration programs.

Figure C-1. Screen display for the simul8 system disk

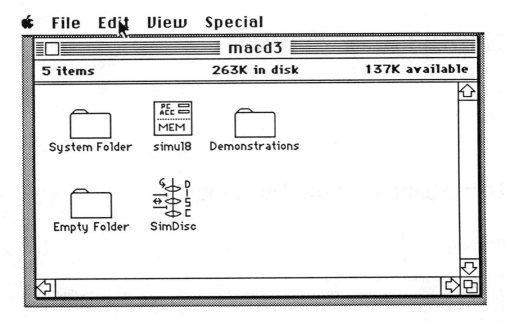

Figure C-2. The demonstrations folder contains a number of example programs (the 'Get Info' command should be used to obtain descriptions of each program)

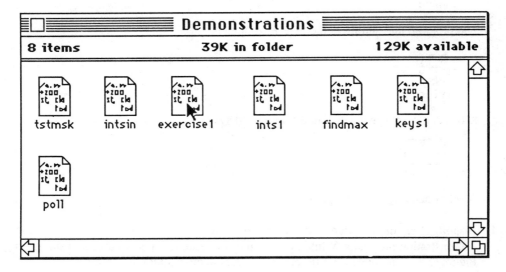

Exercise1

Open the file 'exercise1' (double-click on the excercise1 file icon). When the simul8 program starts, the display appears as illustrated in Figure C-3. The display includes:

1. A menu of commands: 'File', 'Edit', 'Assemble', 'Run', 'Stop'.
2. A window containing a portion of the text of the assembly-language program.
3. A window used to display any text output generated by the assembly-language program, and output from memory dumps.

Figure C-3.   The display created by the simul8 program

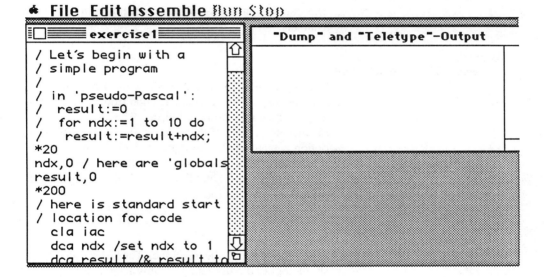

Menus

The menu system follows the conventions for Macintosh programs. Command menus can be 'pulled down' by the mouse. Some of the menu choices are initially disabled – the 'Run' menu is disabled until a program is successfully assembled. Individual menu choices may also be disabled at particular times; for example, the 'File-Save' option is disabled unless a program has been changed since the previous save.

File
New, Open

'New' creates a new document file into which the text of a new assembly language program can be entered. 'Open' allows previously created source files to be read.

Close, Save, Save As..., Revert to Saved

> The 'Close' command closes the window with the current program. 'Save' rewrites the program to file. 'Save As...' creates a copy of the program in a new file. 'Revert to Saved' rereads the original program file.

Page Setup,Print

> The program text can be printed, in a suitable page format, through the use of these commands.

Quit

> Exit from the simulator system.

Edit

Cut, Copy, Paste, Clear

> The conventional cut-and-paste editing commands are available.

Assemble

Assemble, Assemble & List

> The 'Assemble' command invokes the assembler; this attempts to generate executable code from the assembly-language source code program. The assembler will identify any errors. If there are no errors, the Run menu option is enabled. The 'Assemble & List' command will, if assembly is successful, open an additional window that will contain the assembly listing. This listing may be printed, or saved to file.

Run

Reset

> Reset the state of the machine. The 'Reset' command should be used before an assembly language program is to be rerun from its start.

Dump

> Produce an octal dump of the contents of the memory of the simulated machine.

Breakpoints

> Insert or remove breakpoints in the code.

Go, Step, Step-Step

> These commands cause the program to be executed. The 'Go' command is used for fast execution with no displays. 'Step-Step' gives continuous execution with displays of CPU and peripheral device activies. 'Step' is for single-step execution.

Stop
Pause

Pause suspends execution.

Examine

The Examine command permits inspection of the contents of selected memory locations.

Single Step

One instruction is executed each time this menu command is used or the 'command-s' key combination is keyed in.

Do Single Step/Do Step-Step

Switch between single step and step-step mode.

The program window

The program window appears as shown in Figure C-4. The text of the assembly language program is displayed within this window.

Figure C-4.   The program window as displayed by simul8

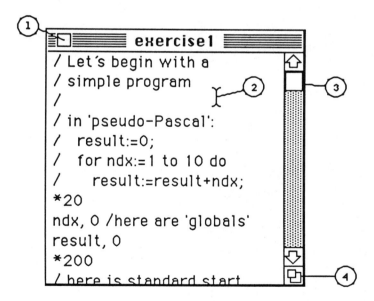

Other features of the program window include:
1.   *The 'Go Away' box.* Clicking in the 'Go Away' box has the same effect as using the 'File-Close' menu command.

2. *The insertion point.* Move the mouse and click the mouse button to set the insertion point. Dragging the mouse, with the mouse button held down, selects text for Edit menu commands. (*Note*: the program window will not scroll if an attempt is made to drag beyond the displayed region. The 'shift-click' control sequence must be used to make selections that extend beyond the window display.)

3. *The vertical scroll bar control.* It is possible to scroll through the program document by moving the 'thumb' with the mouse, or by clicking in the scroll arrows.

4. *The size box.* Drag the box to make the window larger or smaller.

The code of 'exercise1'

```
/ Let's begin with a
/ simple program
/ in 'pseudo-Pascal':
/   result:=0;
/   for ndx:=1 to 10 do
/     result:=result+ndx;
            *20
```

Lines like these, starting, with a '/' are comments.

An asterisk, '*', is used in origin directives. These directives specify the location in memory where the next program datum or instruction is to be located. The '*20' directive causes datum 'ndx' to be located at memory address 0020 octal; the '*200' directive causes the first instruction to be located at 0200.

```
ndx,     0
result,  0
         *200
/ here is standard start
/ location for code
         cla  iac
         dca    ndx
         dca    result
```

/ here are 'globals'

/ set ndx to 1
/ and result to 0

The layout of each line of the program is in the form:

<optional label,> <instruction>.

Thus, the next instruction is associated with the label 'loop'; the instruction specifies that the contents of location 'ndx' be added to the contents of the acc.

```
loop,    tad    ndx
         tad    result
         dca    result
         iac
         tad    ndx
         dca    ndx
         tad    ndx
         cia
```

/ accumulate sum

/ increment count

```
        tad    dec10        / test against limit
        sma cla
        jmp    loop
        hlt
dec10,  0012
$
```

The dollar symbol corresponds to another assembler directive – the end directive. Essentially, it marks the end of the program and is required by the assembler.

Assembling the 'exercise' program

Select either the 'Assemble' or the 'Assemble & List' option from the 'Assemble' menu item. The exercise1 program should assemble without error.

If the 'Assemble & List' option is used, then a new window will appear on the screen once the assembly process has been completed. This window is the active window, displayed in front of all others, and, as illustrated in Figure C-5, contains the assembly listing, a vertical scroll bar, a 'Go Away' box, and size box controls.

Figure C-5. The window used to display an assembly listing

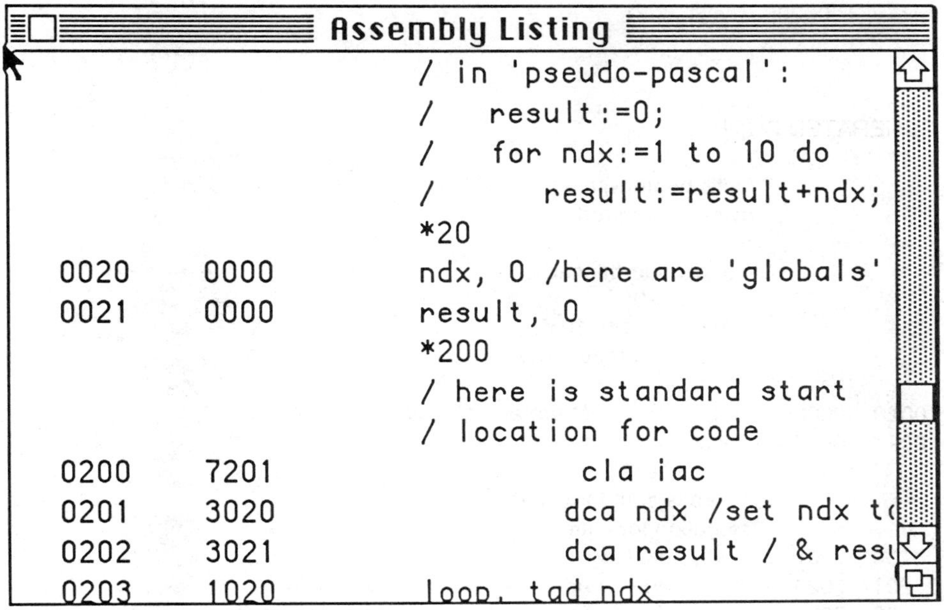

```
═════════════════ Assembly Listing ═══════════

                      / in 'pseudo-pascal':
                      /   result:=0;
                      /   for ndx:=1 to 10 do
                      /        result:=result+ndx;
                      *20
        0020   0000   ndx, 0 /here are 'globals'
        0021   0000   result, 0
                      *200
                      / here is standard start
                      / location for code
        0200   7201        cla iac
        0201   3020        dca ndx /set ndx t
        0202   3021        dca result / & res
        0203   1020   loop, tad ndx
```

The listing is formatted in three columns: address, contents, and assembly-language source statement. The address and contents are shown in octal. Figure C-5 shows that address 0200 contains 7201 (the octal representation of the instruction bit pattern for clearing and incrementing the accumulator).

If the 'Assemble & List' option is used, the listing should be printed using the 'Print' option from the File Menu. A printout, similar to that shown in Table C-1, is obtained. The complete listing comprises a symbol table, giving the correspondence of labels and memory addresses, and the data showing the location and value for each instruction/datum processed by the assembler.

After the assembly listing is printed, close the 'Assembly Listing' window before proceeding to run the program.

Table C-1. Assembly listing of the exercise1 program

```
        Assembled at 14:14 pm.
        Sat. 20 September 1986


SYMBOL TABLE

dec10   0217;  loop   0203
ndx     0020;  result 0021



GENERATED CODE

                / let's begin with a
                / simple program
                /
                / in 'pseudo-pascal':
                /   result:=0;
                /   for ndx:=1 to 10 do
                /     result:=result+ndx;
                        *20
0020   0000     ndx,    0       / here are 'globals'
0021   0000     result, 0
                        *200
                / here is standard start
                / location for code
0200   7201            cla iac
0201   3020            dca     ndx        / set ndx to 1
0202   3021            dca     result     / and result to 0
0203   1020     loop,  tad     ndx
0204   1021            tad     result
0205   3021            dca     result         / accumulate sum
```

```
0206    7001        iac
0207    1020        tad     ndx
0210    3020        dca     ndx             / increment count
0211    1020        tad     ndx
0212    7041        cia
0213    1217        tad     dec10           / test against limit
0214    7700        sma cla
0215    5203        jmp     loop
0216    7402        hlt
0217    0012    dec10, 0012
```

Running 'exercise1'

Reset

Before running the program, the 'Reset' option from the 'Run' menu item should be used to arrange that all peripheral devices are idle, the accumulator is cleared, and the program counter reset to 0200 – the standard starting address for code. The program window is updated by this command; the window scrolls and the instruction at address 0200 appears highlighted.

Step

Start execution of the program in 'Step' mode. The system opens a new window titled 'Simulated CPU'. This window displays the current contents of the accumulator, the value in the program counter, and the disassembled instruction from that location (the next instruction to be executed). Instructions are executed one by one. The 'command-s' key combination must be pressed each time an instruction is to be executed (hold down 'command key', type 's'). When running in 'Step' or 'Step-Step' modes, simul8 maintains a window that displays the contents of CPU registers. In addition, the program source window is scrolled and the next instruction to be executed is highlighted. The form of this display is shown in Figure C-6.

     Try the following:

1. Step through the program and observe the execution of one complete cycle of the loop.
2. Switch to 'Step-Step' mode. The same display is maintained, but instructions are executed continuously. (Execution can be stopped momentarily by pressing the mouse button when the pointer is in the menu bar.)
3. After the loop has cycled through a few times, use the 'Examine' command from the 'Stop' menu item.

Figure C-6.   The appearance of the screen after one instruction has been executed

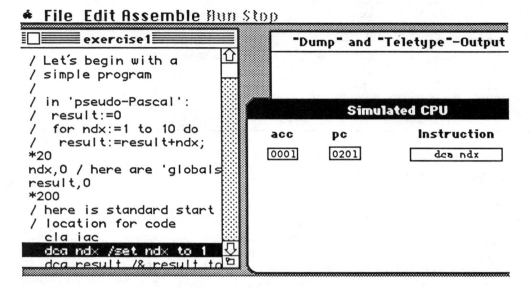

Examining locations in 'exercise1'

The 'Examine' command in the 'Stop' menu item allows for inspection of selected memory locations. When selected, the 'Examine' command opens a dialog box that appears in front of all other windows on the screen. This dialog box has a space where either the octal address of a location, or the label name for a labeled location, can be entered. Once the address is entered, the '=' button should be clicked. The address and contents are then displayed. If the contents of another location are also needed, then the name field should again be selected, the name of the next location entered, and the '=' button clicked. The dialog box has a 'continue' button; clicking 'continue' causes program execution to be resumed.

An example is shown in Figure C-7. Here, the label name 'result' has been entered and display requested. The program's output shows that 'result' is at location 0021 and holds the value 0017.

Use the 'Examine' option to inspect the values of 'ndx' and 'result' at some stage during program execution. Then resume execution and allow the program to run to completion.

Figure C-7. The Examine dialog box

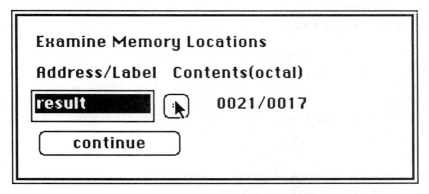

Getting a memory dump for exercise1

When the final halt instruction is executed, the Simulated CPU window is closed and the program window reactivated. Use the 'Dump' option from the 'Run' menu item to produce a dump of the registers and of the contents of memory. The output will appear in the '"Dump" and "Teletype"– Output' window, as shown in Figure C-8.

Figure C-8. Dump output being generated for program exercise1

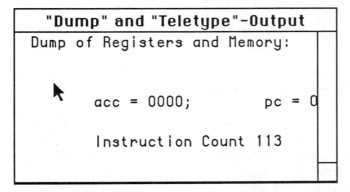

    The '"Dump" and "Teletype"- Output' window should be selected as the current window. A vertical scroll bar and size box will appear and the contents of the window can be scrolled. As illustrated in Figure C-9, the values of chosen memory locations can be seen. The printout displays the contents of eight memory locations on each line. On the left of the line, the octal value given is the address of the first datum printed. The program does not print the contents of memory areas that contain solely zero values. As can be seen from Figure C-9, locations 0020 ('ndx)' and 0021 ('result') can be seen to hold the values 0013 and 0067 respectively. These octal values correspond to 11 decimal and 55 decimal. The program has terminated with the correct sum stored in the location labeled result.

'Dumps' can be requested at any point after execution of a program has been paused. This makes it possible to monitor changes to data structures in memory at various stages of program execution. The complete dump output can be printed by selecting 'File-Print' when the '"Dump" and "Teletype"-Output' window is the current window. When finished inspecting the dump display, reselect the program text window as the active window.

Figure C-9. Scrolling the '"Dump" and "Teletype"-Output' window permits viewing of the values in chosen memory locations

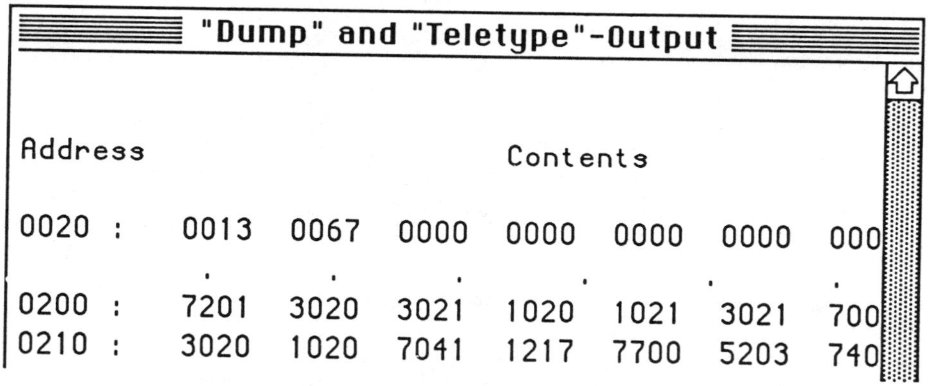

```
 "Dump" and "Teletype"-Output

Address                                   Contents

0020 :    0013   0067   0000   0000   0000   0000   000
           .       .      .      .      .      .      .
0200 :    7201   3020   3021   1020   1021   3021   700
0210 :    3020   1020   7041   1217   7700   5203   740
```

Experiments in editing and assembling

Some experimentation with the use of the cut-and-paste editor and the assembler should be performed after running the 'exercise1' demonstration program.

Most Macintosh applications, for example, MacPascal, incorporate similar editors; consequently, the editing facilities in simul8 should be familiar to students. There are the standard facilities for selecting text: a word can be selected by placing the pointer (insertion cursor) in the word and double-clicking the mouse; a segment of text can be selected by placing the pointer at the beginning of the segment and then dragging with the mouse button held down or moving the pointer to the end of the text segment and 'shift-clicking'. Once a word or text segment has been selected, the options in the 'Edit' menu item are enabled. The selected text can then be cut and copied (and then subsequently pasted). Alternatively, the selected text can be simply overtyped. Figure C-10 illustrates selection of a word and an editing operation.

Figure C-10. The cut-and-paste editor in simul8

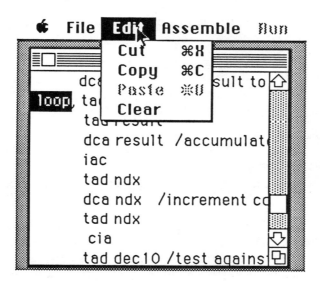

If the assembly-language source is' changed, the 'Run' menu item is disabled. The program has to be reassembled before it can again be executed. This feature guarantees that the code run always corresponds to the source code displayed.

As a first experiment in editing, change the number of times the loop is to be cycled. Select the constant that determines the number of cycles. Overtype with a new octal value. Reassemble. Reset. Run using 'Go' mode. The program then executes quickly without displays. When the program terminates, obtain a memory dump. Check that the values for 'ndx' and 'result' are what you expect.

The next exercise deliberately introduces an error into the program to illustrate the way in which the assembler reports those errors it detects.

Select the word 'loop', where it is used as a label (as illustrated in Figure C-10). Overtype the word with another label name. Then reassemble the program. During reassembly, a 'bug-box' will appear, Figure C-11. This bug-box appears as the top-most window. It contains an error message and an 'OK' button.

The error reported in this example concerns the label 'loop'. Since this label has been replaced in the editing step, it is no longer defined in the program text. However, it is still referenced in the 'jmp loop' instruction. The assembler finds that it cannot assemble this instruction and, therefore, has to generate an error message. As well as displaying the bug-box, the assembler scrolls the program text window so that the position of the error is visible, and highlights the line where the error was detected.

The 'OK' button in the bug-box must be clicked before work can continue. The assembly process is abandoned to permit the error to be corrected immediately.

Figure C-11. A bug-box with an error message from the assembler

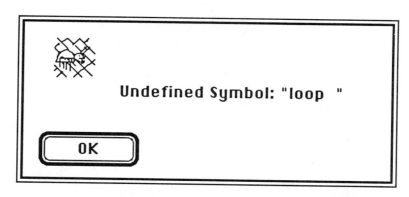

The error messages, generated by the assembler, are summarised in Table C-2. Most errors tend to be mistyped symbol names; these may be corrected by simply changing the erroneous word. Mysterious syntax errors are best dealt with by cutting out, and then retyping, the offending lines.

The execution system may display a similar bug-box. The interpreter that simulates the PDP-8 computer can detect situations where due to program error a jump has been made to a portion of memory that does not contain instructions. (Such errors generally result from an indirect jump using a pointer which has not been set correctly.) The run-time error message specifies 'jump to uninitialized memory'.

Writing and saving new programs

The simul8 program should be opened from the desktop when a new assembly-language program is to be written. Simul8 then starts with an empty document window, named 'Untitled'. The code of the program may then be typed in.

After entry, the new assembly-language program should be saved. Files are created using the 'File-Save' menu option. A standard file dialog box is displayed. As illustrated in Figure C-12, this dialog box contains a field where the file name can be entered, button controls for selecting the disk where the file will be placed, and 'Save' and 'Cancel' buttons for performing or abandoning the filing operation.

After the new program has been saved, the typical development cycle of assemble, edit, assemble, edit, assemble, test run, edit, assemble, etc. should be followed. The source should be saved after each major editing step.

Table C-2.   **Assembly error messages from simul8**

Error message	*Meaning*
Undefined symbol	A reference has been made to a non-existent symbol. Usually, this is the result of mistyping an instruction name or the name of a program label from the code. The error message also results if there is a reference to a variable whose declaration has been omitted.
Doubly defined symbol	This error results when the same name is used to label two different locations.
Syntax error	There is something odd about an instruction specification. Maybe the indirect symbol is in the wrong place; or the comma after a label has been omitted. (It is possible for this error to result from the presence of an illegal (but invisible) character introduced during editing.)
Too long a name	One of the label names used in the program is too long. Label names should be at most six characters in length.
Too large a constant	A constant has been defined having a value greater than 7777 octal.
Invalid input	There is an illegal character in the file; for example, there might be an '8' or a '9' character in an octal constant.
Cross page reference	The code contains a memory-reference instruction using direct addressing that refers to a variable or labeled program location that is neither global nor on the current page. The code is in error. An indirect reference via a pointer is required. (Alternatively, a simple variable might be made global by moving it to page 0.)
Overlayed code?	The organization of code, data, and origin statements is such that two different groups of instructions and/or data values are assigned the same memory locations. This may be due to an error when specifying the value to be used in an origin directive. More typically, it is a result of there being too much code (>128 words) on one memory page. Code from one page has then spilt over onto the next page.

Figure C-12. The standard file dialog box used when saving an assembly-language program to a file on the Macintosh disk

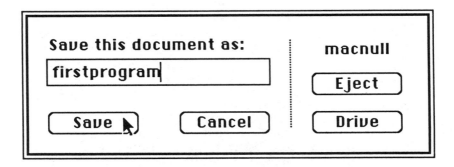

If the current document is closed ('File-Close' on menus or 'Go Away' box clicked), then an alternative program can be opened. The 'File-Open' menu option displays a standard dialog box, as shown in Figure C-13, with a scroll bar for scrolling through files, disk control buttons, and 'Open-Cancel' action buttons. Simul8 will open any file of type 'TEXT'; so, in addition to any files created by simul8 itself, the file list displayed includes 'TEXT' files created from 'MacWrite', 'MacTerminal', 'MacPascal', or other applications. Of course, it is only meaningful to select one of simul8's own files. Simul8 permits previously created assembly listing files to be opened; however, only the 'File-Print' options are then enabled.

Figure C-13. The standard file dialog box used when opening an alternative assembly-language program from a file on the Macintosh disk

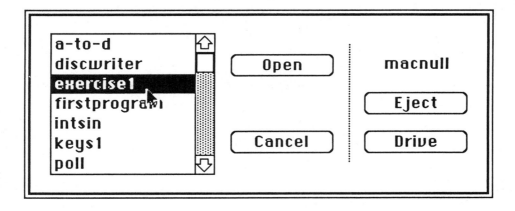

Text can be cut and pasted between different programs. The process involves the following steps:

1. open the document from which the text is to be taken,
2. select the text by positioning the cursor at the start and clicking the mouse button, then moving to the end and 'shift-clicking' the mouse button,
3. copy the text using the Edit-Copy menu command,
4. close the source document,
5. open the destination document,
6. position the cursor to the correct point for text insertion, and click the mouse button, and
7. use the Edit-Paste menu command.

Breakpoints

The simul8 program incorporates a simple breakpoint package. Breakpoints can be set at chosen instructions in the code. Then, when the program is run using 'Go' or 'Step-Step' mode, execution is suspended when the CPU tries to fetch an instruction at which a breakpoint has been set.

The 'tstmsk' program (in the 'simul8' demonstrations folder) can serve as an example of how breakpoints might be used. This program is supposed to read blocks from disk, scanning through the words in each block read, testing for those that when masked with 0077 octal are equal to 0043 octal. A version of 'tstmsk' might be running which, based upon an inspection of a memory dump, seems to read data into memory correctly and find the right number of entries in each block, however, owing to bugs, the program might not print out the block numbers or word values correctly.

It is probable that any error in this version of 'tstmsk' is in the routine that printed octal numbers. One does not want to follow the execution of the entire program in 'Step-Step' mode, for this would take too long. Rather, one wants the program to execute at full speed without display ('Go' mode) for those portions that seem correct, that is the disk-reading routines and the routines that search for words with the desired bit patterns. However, one would want the routine for octal output executed with the display enabled, possibly in single-stepping mode (i.e. 'Step-Step' or 'Step' modes from the 'Run' menu).

Consequently, execution should be suspended when the octal output routine ('octo') is reached so that the execution mode can change from 'Go' to 'Step-Step'. Similarly, execution should also be suspended just before the return from the 'octo' routine allowing the 'Go' mode of execution to be reinstated.

The 'octo' routine is, in part, as follows:

```
        /- - - - - -- - - - - - - -- - - - - - -- -
        /
        / print an octal number passed in acc
        /
0436    0000    octo,   0
```

```
0437    3260          dca    oval
                  / mask out each 3-bit group in turn
                  /
                  / first, pick on bits 0-1-2,
                  / shift these left, via link
0440    1260          tad    oval
0441    7006          rtl
0442    7006          rtl
0443    4261          jms    oput
                  /
                  /

                         .
                         .
                         .

0455    1260          tad    oval
0456    4261          jms    oput
0457    5636          jmp i  octo
0460    0000    oval,   0
                  / - - - - - - - -- - - - - - - - - -- -
```

The first word of a subroutine (the word with the subroutine label) is used to store the return address. The first executable instruction of the subroutine is in the immediately following location. The first point in subroutine 'octo' at which a breakpoint might be set is location 0437 ('3260 dca oval'). When execution reaches this point, the accumulator should hold the value to be printed by the program.

An exit breakpoint for the subroutine could be placed at location 0457 (5636 'jmp i octo').

Breakpoints can be set (and later removed) by using the 'Breakpoints' option from the 'Run' menu. Some initial breakpoints can be inserted prior to program execution; others can be inserted or removed whenever execution is subsequently suspended.

Invoking the 'Breakpoints' option results in the opening of a new window in which are shown the addresses of those locations where the assembler has placed (non-zero) values for instructions (or data elements), together with the contents of these locations and the first few characters of the corresponding assembly-language source statement. The window has a vertical scroll bar; it is possible to scroll down the window to find the point at which a breakpoint is to be inserted (or a previously set breakpoint is now to be removed). This window appears as shown in Figure C-14.

The 'BreakPoints' window appears as the top-most window. Three columns of data are displayed: address, contents, and source statement (which may be truncated). Only those locations filled with non-zero values are shown. The cursor can be used to point to any desired line in this window. Clicking the mouse button then places, or removes, a breakpoint at the corresponding addess. Addresses where breakpoints have been set are tagged by asterisks. When the 'BreakPoints' window is closed (click in 'Go-Away' box), execution can be started or resumed.

Figure C-14. The 'BreakPoints' window

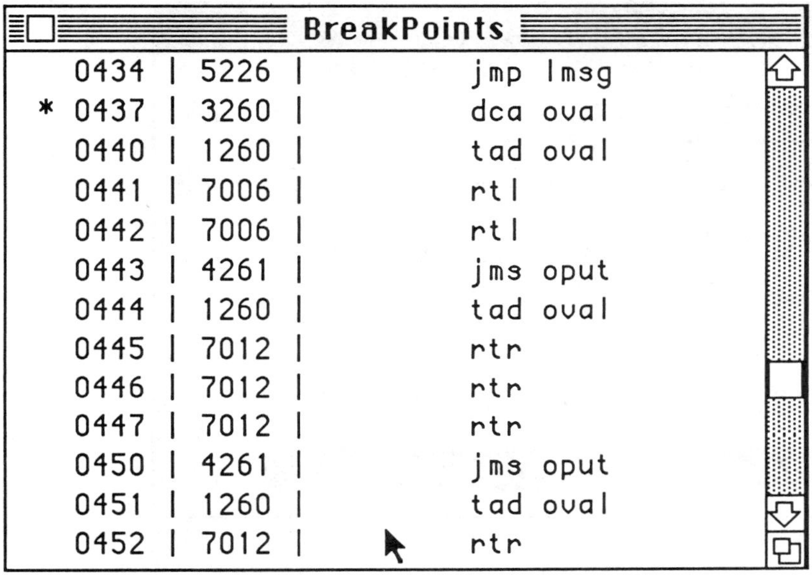

```
╔═╦═════════════════ BreakPoints ═══════════════╗
║ ▤ ║                                           ║
║   0434 | 5226 |         jmp  lmsg         ║ ⬆ ║
║ * 0437 | 3260 |         dca  oval         ║░░░║
║   0440 | 1260 |         tad  oval         ║░░░║
║   0441 | 7006 |         rtl              ║░░░║
║   0442 | 7006 |         rtl              ║░░░║
║   0443 | 4261 |         jms  oput        ║░░░║
║   0444 | 1260 |         tad  oval         ║░░░║
║   0445 | 7012 |         rtr              ║░░░║
║   0446 | 7012 |         rtr              ║░░░║
║   0447 | 7012 |         rtr              ║░░░║
║   0450 | 4261 |         jms  oput        ║   ║
║   0451 | 1260 |         tad  oval         ║ ⬇ ║
║   0452 | 7012 |    ▸    rtr              ║ ⬚ ║
╚═══════════════════════════════════════════════╝
```

Peripherals

The simulated machine has a keyboard, a Teletype™, a fixed-frequency clock, an analog-to-digital converter, and a disk.

The Macintosh's keyboard serves as the keyboard of the simulated machine. When simul8 is executing PDP-8 programs, characters typed in on the keyboard are collected and passed to the simulated machine at a suitably slow rate.

Characters output to the 'Teletype' appear in the '"Dump" and "Teletype"-Output' window.

The clock represents a fixed-frequency clock; it 'ticks' after a fixed number of memory cycles. The A/D reads the x-coordinate of the mouse.

Disk transfers entail transfer of data between the simulated machine and the 'Simdisc' file. The simulated disk can be viewed as having 16 tracks (numbered 0-17 octal); each track holds only one block of 128 words. The disk starts with the heads at track zero. The required track must be sought prior to a data transfer. Seek times are proportional to the distance that the heads must move.

Each peripheral device has a flag that is set when that device is capable of performing an I/O transfer. When set, these flags appear in the 'Simulated CPU' window. The displays are illustrated in Figure C-15, and summarized in Table C-3.

Figure C-15. Display fields for peripheral devices

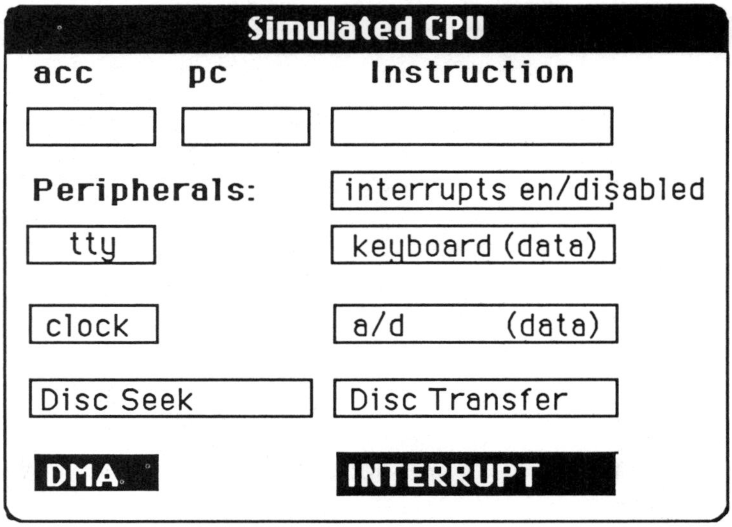

```
┌─────────────────────────────────────────────┐
│              Simulated CPU                    │
│  acc       pc        Instruction              │
│ ┌───────┐ ┌───────┐ ┌──────────────────┐     │
│ └───────┘ └───────┘ └──────────────────┘     │
│                                               │
│  Peripherals:      ┌──────────────────────┐  │
│                    │interrupts en/disabled│  │
│  ┌─────────┐       └──────────────────────┘  │
│  │   tty   │       ┌──────────────────────┐  │
│  └─────────┘       │ keyboard (data)      │  │
│                    └──────────────────────┘  │
│  ┌─────────┐       ┌──────────────────────┐  │
│  │ clock   │       │ a/d       (data)     │  │
│  └─────────┘       └──────────────────────┘  │
│  ┌───────────────┐ ┌──────────────────────┐  │
│  │ Disc Seek     │ │ Disc Transfer        │  │
│  └───────────────┘ └──────────────────────┘  │
│  ████████           ██████████████████        │
│  █ DMA  █           █  INTERRUPT     █        │
│  ████████           ██████████████████        │
└─────────────────────────────────────────────┘
```

The simulated peripheral devices are very fast relative to the speed of the simulated CPU. A real CPU sending data to a real 10 characters per second Teletype terminal might use tens of thousands of instructions in an idle loop while waiting for the terminal to print one character and set its flag indicating readiness to accept another character. Wait loops are still necessary on the simulated machine, but these waits will be in the order of 100-200 instructions rather than many tens of thousands of instructions.

This speeding up of peripherals makes it possible to set simple I/O-handling exercises with wait loops. These exercises do illustrate how I/O may be performed. However, there are two disadvantages associated with the speed up. First, the relative speeds of different types of devices are not accurately modeled. Second, the benefits accrued from using interrupts, to allow overlap of I/O and CPU operations, are less obvious.

Table C-3. The peripheral device displays

Display	Information
interrupts en/disabled	This flag shows whether the CPU has interrupts enabled or disabled. It changes with 'ion' (interrupts on) and 'iof' (interrupts off) instructions, and also when further interrupts are automatically disabled by the hardware response to an interrupt. This disable is only shown for those programs that utilize the interrupt system.
tty	This flag appears when the teletype device has printed a character and can accept further output. The flag is cleared by the next 'tcf' or 'tls' instruction.
clock	This flag appears when the clock ticks. The flag is cleared by the 'clkcf' instruction.
keyboard (data)	This flag appears when keyboard input data are available; the data value is the octal constant representing the character that has been typed. The flag is cleared by the 'krb' instruction.
a/d (data)	This flag appears when the A/D has completed taking a sample; the data value shows in octal the reading that has been taken. This flag is cleared by the 'adcrb' instruction.
Disk Seek	This flag is set when the disk control completes a seek operation and a disk transfer can be started. The flag is cleared by the 'dscf' instruction.
Disk Transfer	This flag is set when a disk transfer is completed. The flag is cleared by the 'dtcf' instruction.
DMA	The DMA field flashes briefly each time a memory cycle is stolen during disk transfers.
INTERRUPT	The INTERRUPT field flashes when, with interrupts enabled, the interrupt line gets set.

Obtaining a printout

Printouts can be obtained of the program source, the assembly listing, and the '"Dump" and "Teletype"-Output'. The document to be printed must correspond to the active window; windows are selected, as is normal on the Macintosh, by clicking the mouse when the pointer is in the window to be activated.

Printouts are obtained through the use of the 'Page Setup' and 'Print' commands in the 'File' menu option. The simul8 system uses the standard dialogs for 'Page Setup' and 'Print'. The wide format output, available with 'Page Setup', is often useful for assembly listings. The 'Print' dialog allows requests for multiple copies and selection of different qualities of printed output.

Once printing has been requested, the simul8 system will display a message stating that output is being 'spooled to disk'. Printing can be cancelled if necessary.

The standard Macintosh commands can be used to obtain prints of the whole screen, or just the active window, and to create 'MacPaint' documents with a screen image. (A 'MacPaint' document is created by 'command-shift/3'. The active window is printed by 'command-shift/4'. A whole screen printout requires 'Caps-Lock', then 'command-shift/4'.)

Printouts are also possible from 'Finder' (the desk-top level of the Macintosh operating system). A document can be selected by clicking it once, and then 'Finder's File-Print' menu option can be used to print it.

Problems with very long programs

Simul8 holds, in the memory of the Macintosh, the text of a program, the text of any listing, and the text of any program dump. On the 128K Mac, space can become short. The system will sometimes not have sufficient memory left to generate a listing for a long assembly-language program containing many comments. If, when memory is short, the 'Assemble & List' option is selected, the system will display a dialog box asking whether the listing should be sent to disk or should be abandoned. This dialog box will have a 'Cancel' button (to abandon the listing) and an 'OK' button (to send the listing to file). If the listing is sent to file, then the file created will be named 'LongListing'; this file can be printed at a later time.

Using simul8 on Unix

A version of the simul8 system is available for use on Unix™. Use on Unix is inevitably more complex than on the Macintosh. Furthermore, the displays produced are generally more limited and less clear than those on the Macintosh.

The simulated system is essentially the same. There is a simple CPU, memory, and the peripheral devices: clock, A/D, disk, keyboard, and printing terminal. The assembly language is identical. The run-time system again has optional displays, and again there is a facility for setting breakpoints and inspecting memory locations. There are, however, some differences, the most important being that the keyboard and terminal devices correspond to files in the working directory (the A/D also differs; on the Unix implementation the A/D is simply a random number generator). Other differences relate to the information shown in displays, and in the methods used to handle breakpoints.

The Unix implementation involves the programs and data files as listed in Table C-4. One of the standard Unix editors must be used to prepare the assembly-language source documents. An assembly-language source file can be assembled using the /CS3/assembler program:

```
$ /CS3/assembler [-l] <filename>
```

The assembler generates a file named 'object' in the current working directory. This file contains the object code printed in octal and a copy of the symbol table. The -l option can be used to request an assembly listing; the listing is produced to standard output and can be redirected to file or to a printer.

Table C-4.   Programs and data files for the Unix implementation of simul8[†]

ed (or other system editor)	An editor is needed to create and modify assembly language programs for simul8.
/CS3/assemble	This is the assembler that processes an assembly-language source program and produces a listing and an object file. The object file can be loaded and run by one of the run-time systems.
/CS3/trace8	A restricted version of the simulator that provides detailed displays of the processes involved in instruction and address decoding.
/CS3/exec8	The full version of the simulator with the comprehensive breakpoint package.
/CS3/assmblgo	This program combines the assembler and the execution system. It permits a somewhat faster development cycle when program listings are not required.
/CS3/disc	This file corresponds to the Simdisc file of the Macintosh version of simul8. A copy of this file should be created in the Unix working directory from which the simul8 system is to be used.
.8.kbd.1	This file in the current working directory, should hold any input character data that are to be read by an assembly-language program run on the exec8 simulator.
.8.tty.1	This file, created in the current working directory, will hold any teletype output from an assembly-language program that has been run on the exec8 simulator.
dumpfile	This file, created in the current working directory, will hold output from any dumps of memory.
/CS3/symbols	A file with the predefined op-code symbols.

[†]The directory that holds the programs is identified here as /CS3; the actual directory name will be determined locally.

There are two run-time systems: '/CS3/trace8' and '/CS3/exec8'. These programs both expect to read the file 'object' from the current directory, and take their control commands from standard input. The programs can be invoked by simply entering their names on the Unix command line:

$ /CS3/exec8

'/CS3/assmblgo' is a variant of exec8. It incorporates the assembler and permits a program to be assembled and then executed in a single step process:

$ /CS3/assmblgo <filename>

Any 'keyboard' input data that are to be read by the simulated PDP-8 program should be in a file in the current directory. This keyboard input file must be named '.8.kbd.1'. Teletype output is generated in a file, named '.8.tty.1', created in the current directory. Any memory dumps are written to a file named 'dumpfile' in the current directory. If a program writes to the simulated disk, then the current directory must contain a copy of the file '/CS3/disc'.

This exec8 version is closest to that implemented on the Macintosh. Exec8 incorporates a conventional assembly-language debugging package and limited displays, whereas the Macintosh implementation focuses on more visual debugging techniques. Trace8 is a limited implementation of the simulator. I/O devices are not implemented in trace8. Instead, this version has the capacity to provide for more detailed explanations of the processes involved in instruction and address decoding. Trace8 can be used for the preliminary exercises involving solely the manipulation of data defined at assembly time. Exec8, or 'assmblgo', should be used for the main series of practical exercises.

Trace8

The '/CS3/trace8' program reads assembled code from the file 'object' in the current directory, requests a few control parameters that must be entered at the keyboard, and then executes the code. It always displays execution. By default, it provides a display of the major steps involved in the execution of each instruction; this can be extended to show even more detailed information concerning the decoding of addresses. Trace8 allows execution to proceed in either single-step or continuous mode. The display produced by trace8 shows the components of the computer: the CPU, the bus, and the memory, as illustrated in Figure C-16. This display is more detailed than the 'Simulated CPU' display on the Macintosh.

The CPU display shows in octal the contents of each of the main CPU registers 'acc', 'link', 'pc', and 'ir'. The contents of the instruction register are printed in octal and as a translated (i.e. disassembled) instruction. Two other text lines in the display give details of the stages of instruction execution. Two additional CPU registers 'mar' (memory address register) and 'mdr' (memory data register) are also displayed.

**Figure C-16. The display produced on a cursor-addressable terminal by the '/CS3/trace8'
Unix implementation of the computer simulator**

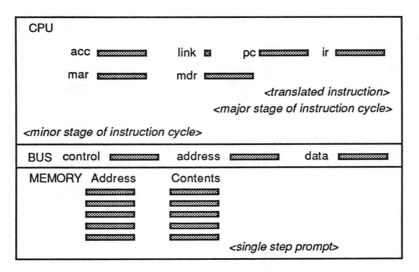

The 'mar' and 'mdr' registers form part of the timing and control circuitry of the CPU. When a memory address is determined (for instruction or data read, or for data store) it is placed in the 'mar' register before the bus read/write operation is initiated. The 'mdr' register is used to hold data temporarily after they have been brought from memory and prior to being sent to 'ir' or 'acc'.

The second part of the display shows the bus. This shows whether a read/write operation is being performed, specifies the memory address where the transfer is taking place, and shows the data value transferred.

The final part of the display shows a 'window' into memory. It shows the location used in the last fetch or store operation together with the two preceding and two subsequent locations. This display changes with every instruction fetch and data fetch/store operation.

The message,'To continue press RETURN', will appear in the bottom right portion of the screen when running in 'single-step' mode.

Trace8's prompts

1. The first request made by trace8 is for a 'delay factor'. Certain display operations are performed rather slowly by the terminals. The Unix time-shared computer must delay before requesting that the terminal proceed with a further display operation. The appropriate delay is rather variable for it depends on the terminal being used, the number of other users on the system, and other extraneous factors. Try a delay factor of 6; smaller values permit the program to run faster but may cause the data on the

screen to be corrupted; larger delays may be useful if you need to slow things down even more in order to follow certain steps.

2. The next prompt from the program will ask 'Do you want the initial contents of memory to be 'dumped' to a file?' A 'Y' response produces a dump of memory prior to program execution.

3. The display shown in Figure C-16 is then presented. The single-step prompt 'To Continue Press RETURN' appears. Run options can be set. The default setting 'single steps' the program; the default is obtained by responding to the prompt with a carriage return.

    The run options are shown in Table C-5. All options act as 'toggle switches', switching displays on or off as appropriate. The displays of activities in bus and memory can be disabled to allow for faster execution. The display of minor cycles of instruction and address decoding shows how op-codes and addressing modes are identified and interpreted.

4. The final prompt from trace8 when the program halts again concerns a dump. A final dump of memory shows changes to memory made by the program.

Table C-5.   Run options for trace8

Option	Effect
b	enable/disable display of bus activity
c	enable/disable display of details of minor cycles of instruction and address decoding
m	enable/disable display of memory
q	quit, exit from trace8
s	switch off single stepping

Exec8

'/CS3/exec8' incorporates a slightly simplified but still fairly typical debugging package. This debugger has facilities for memory inspection and breakpoint controls; however, unlike most debugging packages, it does not permit changes to the code or data. In addition to standard debugging facilities, exec8 also incorporates controls that enable, or disable, the various display windows of the simulator.

When /CS3/exec8 initially starts, or when it subsequently reaches a breakpoint, it (1) clears the screen, (2) prints a message of the form 'Break address : xxxx' (where 'xxxx' is the address of the breakpoint), and (3) prints the prompt 'break>'. At this point, the user is communicating with the built-in debug package and can enter debugging commands. Normally, exec8 runs the program continuously until it reaches the next breakpoint. The Unix 'break' key can be used to force an immediate return to exec8's breakpoint package.

There are three types of commands: (1) those that control the display, (2) those used to place and remove breakpoints, and (3) those used to inspect the contents of memory and registers.

Exec8's display

The form of the display produced by exec8 is shown in Figure C-17. Conceptually, the terminal screen is divided up into a number of windows; displays in these windows are individually enabled or disabled. The CPU window includes the acc, link, and PC registers, and also an approximate time showing how long the program would have taken to execute on a real micro. The 'translated instruction window' shows the disassembled form of the instruction register. There are two windows into memory; one shows where the last instruction fetch was performed, and the other shows where the last data fetch or store operation was performed. The peripherals window shows any peripheral flags that are set, and also provides details of DMA cycles and the status of the interrupt system. If the program runs in single-step mode, then the single-step prompt appears in the bottom right of the screen. Any combination of windows may be displayed.

Figure C-17. The display produced on a cursor-addressable terminal by the /CS3/exec8 Unix implementation of the computer simulator

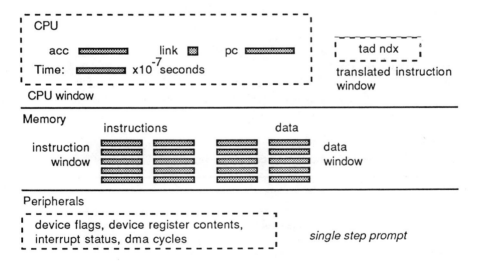

The commands used to enable, or disable, the various display windows are listed in Table C-6. These commands can be entered in response to exec8's 'break' prompt. The commands take the form '+$' and '-$' where '$' may be a character identifying a display window or flagging a special option. A '+' command enables that window or processing option; a '-' disables the window.

Table C-6. The display control commands in exec8

Command	Effect
±c	set/reset CPU display
±d	set/reset memory display for 'data'
±i	set/reset memory display for 'instructions'
±l	set/reset logging of registers on interrupts
±p	set/reset display for status of peripherals
±s	set/reset single step mode
±t	set/reset display of translated instructions

The command '±*' prints a report summarising the status of the various windows. The '±l' command controls the amount of information sent to 'dumpfile'. If this option is enabled, then whenever an interrupt occurs, summary data are printed in the dumpfile.

The '±s' command can be used to set/reset single-step execution. In single-step mode, the exec8 program will display a prompt after each instruction and wait for a carriage return before continuing. (By responding to the single-step prompt with 'q', one can abort execution; 'c' switches back to continuous execution, and 'b' switches control to the breakpoint package.)

Exec8's execution control commands

The second group of commands in exec8 is for setting or removing breakpoints, resuming or abandoning execution of a program, inspecting registers, and other miscellaneous purposes. These commands, listed in Table C-7, can be entered in response to exec8's 'break>' prompt.

Table C-7. The breakpoint and related commands in exec8

Command	Effect
:b	set a breakpoint
:c	continue execution of program
:d	dump registers and memory to terminal screen
:o	show characters sent to 'teletype'
:r	dump registers to terminal screen
:s	list user symbols
:u	remove a breakpoint

The ':b' and ':u' commands respond with the prompt 'Address for breakpoint>'. An address can be specified either as an octal constant or as one of the program labels. Breakpoints can only usefully be set at locations containing instructions that are executed.

The ':c' command terminates interactions with the debugging package and resumes execution of the program being debugged. The ':q' command terminates the entire run. The ':q' command is used when an error in the program has been identified and it is necessary to reedit and reassemble the code.

Exec8 does not have an output window; its output goes to a file. Often it is necessary to know whether characters are being sent correctly (e.g. when it is necessary to check whether a conversion from bit pattern to octal digit character does work). The ':o' command shows the last line of characters sent to the output file.

The ':s' command simply lists the labels from the symbol table. It is useful when working out where to set a breakpoint because it gives the start addresses of subroutines and so forth.

The ':r' and ':d' commands simply dump the values in registers and in memory locations in octal.

Exec8's memory inspection commands

These commands have the following formats:

address/print-style
address,repeat-factor/print-style

The various print-styles are defined by single character identifiers:

:c   print contents of word(s) as an ASCII character
:d   print contents of word(s) as signed decimal numbers
:i   print contents of word(s) as instructions
:o   print contents of word(s) in octal

Some example memory-inspection commands (in italics) and example system responses are:

sum/d	That is, show in decimal the contents of location labeled 'sum'.
sum 0220 / -11	(location 220, labeled 'sum', contains -11 decimal)
loop,4/o	That is, show in octal the contents of 4 locations starting at 'loop'.
loop 0204 / 1022	0205 / 7001
0206 / 3022	0207 / 1022

204,10/o
                      That is, show as instructions the contents of 10 (10 octal, that is, 8) locations starting at 204.

```
loop  0204 / tad ndx        0205 / iac
      0206 / dca ndx        0207 / tad ndx
      0210 / dca i ptr      0211 / isz ptr
      0212 / isz count      0213 / jmp loop
```

Exec8's prompts

1. As with trace8, the first request made by exec8 is for a 'delay factor'.
2. The second prompt asks whether keyboard input is required by the PDP-8 assembly language program that is to be run. If the response is 'Y', then the .8.kbd.1 file is opened and the first character read; this character is passed to the simulated CPU at a later time (causing an interrupt if interrupts are enabled).
3. The third prompt relates to the taking of an initial dump of memory in the dumpfile.
4. The next prompt is from the breakpoint package. The screen is cleared, the start address 0200 printed, and the 'break>' prompt appears.
5. When program execution is complete, there is a final prompt asking whether memory should again be dumped to the dumpfile.

Using simul8 on the IBM PC

The standard Unix version of simul8 can be run using XENIX on the IBM PC-AT; a version that can run on other IBM PCs using DOS has been cross-compiled from the XENIX environment. There are a few minor differences between the Unix and the DOS versions of simul8; most of these differences result from changes in conventions for file-names. The DOS version uses the files listed in Table C-8. The only new file is 'config'; this contains configuration commands that set the monitor in a mode in which it interprets ANSI control characters. The files used to represent the disk, the Teletype output device, and the keyboard input device have been renamed. The IBM DOS disk has the same set of example programs as provided on the Macintosh version; details of these example programs are in Table C-8.

      The trace8 and exec8 systems implemented on Unix and DOS differ only with respect to the prompts: the prompts for a 'delay factor' that are needed in the Unix versions are omitted from the DOS versions of these programs.

Running 'ex1'

The file 'ex1.txt' corresponds to 'exercise1' of the Macintosh version. This file should be assembled:

```
A> assemble -l ex1.txt > prn:
```

Table C-8.   Programs and data files for the IBM PC-DOS implementation of simul8

edlin (or other system editor)	An editor is needed to create and modify assembly language programs for simul8.
config.sys	A file of configuration commands that sets the monitor to a mode in which it interprets ANSI control characters.
assemble.exe	The assembler.
trace8.exe	The restricted version of the simulator.
exec8.exe	The full version of the simulator with the comprehensive breakpoint package and simulated peripheral devices.
assmblgo.exe	The combined assembler and execution system.
disc	This file corresponds to the Simdisc file of the Macintosh version of simul8.
keyboard	This file should hold any input character data that are to be read by an assembly language program run on the exec8 simulator.
teletype	This file will hold any teletype output from an assembly language program run on the exec8 simulator.
dumpfile	This file will hold output from any dumps of memory.
symbols	This file contains the pre-defined op-code symbols.
ex1.txt	The 'exercise1' example program; processing data in an iterative loop.
waitio1.txt	Example program that prints a message using wait loop I/O.
atod.txt	'Reads' data from A/D and stores in memory.
tstmsk.txt	Reads blocks of data from disk and finds words that when masked with 077 are equal to 043; prints summary.
ints1.txt	First example interrupt-driven program. Uses interrupts to monitor clock while performing a computation.
intsin.txt	Read data from keys using interrupts; store in circular buffer; process to find numeric data.
findmax.txt	Reads integers, finds maximum value entered.

This command invokes the assembler, specifying that file 'ex1.txt' be processed, and that the assembly listing be sent to an attached printer. It is usually advisable to redirect output from the assembler to the printer because error messages and listings tend to scroll off the screen rather rapidly. The assembler creates a file, 'object', containing the assembly-language code and a copy of the symbol table.

After successfully assembling the program, run it using the trace8 version of the simulator:

A> trace8

Trace8 asks if the initial contents of memory need to be dumped; reply 'N'. The screen display, shown in Figure C-16, is presented; the 'major cycle' specifies the start of execution at address 0200, the single-step prompt "To continue press RETURN" appears.

Start execution, pressing ENTER for each successive instruction. Figure C-18 shows the display at the stage where the second instruction ('dca ndx') has been read and instruction decoding has commenced. The accumulator contains 1; the link contains 0; the program counter is already updated to the address of the next instruction, 0202; and, the instruction register contains the code 3020. The translated instruction field identifies this as a store, 'dca', instruction; address decoding has not yet started. The data displayed for the bus show that the last data transfer was a read from memory at address 0201; the data transferred were 3020. The memory display shows the region of memory most recently accessed with the entry for address 0201 highlighted.

Figure C-18. The display during execution of 'ex1' on the IBM PC

```
CPU

        acc      1        link   0    pc    0202    ir    3020

        mar               mdr    3020
                                          dca

                                          Decoding instruction


BUS    control   READ       address   0201          data  3020

MEMORY  Address          Contents
        0177             0
        0200             7201
        0201             3020          3020
        0202             3021
        0203             1020
                                  To continue press RETURN
```

Continue execution in single-step mode until the end of the loop is reached at 0215. Switch to continuous execution (type 's', ENTER, in response to the next single-step prompt) and observe the display as the program runs to completion. When the program finishes, at the 'hlt' instruction in location 0216, the trace8 system again asks if a memory dump is required; reply 'Y' to obtain a dump of memory in the output file 'dumpfile'.

Print 'dumpfile'; find the locations in the printout that correspond to 'ndx' and 'result', and verify that these contain appropriate values.

Edit 'ex1.txt' to change the number of times the loop is cycled; rerun the program and produce a new 'dumpfile'; again, check that the final results are appropriate.

After 'addressing modes' have been covered in lectures, this example should be rerun with the more detailed displays illustrating the processes of address decoding. These displays of 'minor cycles of instruction and address decoding' are enabled by responding 'c' ENTER to the first single-step prompt from the trace8 program.

Using exec8

Experiment with the breakpoint package of exec8 using one of the example programs, for example, 'tstmsk.txt'.

The 'tstmsk' program reads blocks of data from disk and searches each block for words that when masked with 0077 octal are equal to 043; it generates a report, identifying for each block, the pairs of <word number>/<word contents> that satisfy this test. The 'disc' file released with the IBM PC-DOS version of simul8 contains several blocks of textual data; in effect, the search is for occurrences of either the '#' character (0043) or the 'c' character (0143) in this text. The 'tstmsk' (test under mask) program has a loop that (1) reads the next block from disk; (2) prints the header 'Disk block : '; (3) uses an octal number output routine ('octo') to print the block number; (4) has an inner loop that checks each of the 128 words of the block; if a word satisfies the test then its index number in the block and its contents are both printed using the 'octo' routine; and (5) prints a terminating carriage return / line feed sequence.

A run of the 'tstmsk' program against the data initially in the 'disc' file involves execution of about 20,000 instructions by the simulated CPU. Visual execution of all these instructions would serve no purpose; however, visual execution of selected program fragments is a very effective approach to debugging during program development. The breakpoint package in exec8 is used to control program execution so that portions of a program can be run, or single-stepped, with detailed displays, while most of the program is executed quickly with minimal displays.

The following exercise introduces some of the control options in exec8:

1. Assemble 'tstmsk.txt' and produce a printed assembly listing. Invoke the exec8 program to process the object file created by the assembler.
2. Reply 'N' to initial prompts from exec8 concerning keyboard input and initial memory dumps.
3. The exec8 system then clears the screen and prints its 'break>' prompt.
4. Inspect the contents of memory near the start of the octal output routine ('octo'):

octo,10/i	Request that 8 (10 octal) words be displayed starting at location labeled 'octo'

436/ and 0	437/ dca oval
440/ tad oval	441/ rtl
442/ rtl	442/ jms oput
444/ tad oval	445/ rtr

5. Request the setting of a breakpoint at the first instruction of the 'octo' subroutine:

.b
Address for breakpoint>*437*

6. Check the default display options:

```
+*
C.P.U.                              TRUE
'Data' Memory Window                FALSE
'Instructions' Memory Window        FALSE
Status of Peripherals shown         TRUE
Single step mode                    FALSE
Translation of instructions         TRUE
```

7. Start the 'tstmsk' program, ':c' command.
8. The 'tstmsk' program reads block 0, the DMA cycles are displayed, and the program can be observed waiting for the disk transfer flag; after the disk transfer is complete, a second loop can be observed in which data are sent to the teletype (this loop prints the header 'Disk block : '). Figure C-19 shows the form of the display during the loop waiting for completion of the disk transfer.

Figure C-19. The display during execution of 'tstmsk' on Unix or the IBM PC

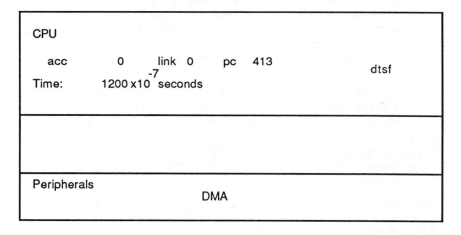

9. The breakpoint at location 437 is reached when the 'tstmsk' program calls the 'octo' routine to print the block number. The screen is cleared and the 'break>' prompt displayed.
10. Obtain a display of the registers (':r'). The display will show that about 930 instructions have been executed; the accumulator contains 0 (the block number), and the program counter is 0437.
12. Check on the most recent output to the teleype (':o'); the text reads 'Disk block :'.
13. Obtain a memory dump (':d'). Data read from disk will have filled the locations from 1200 to 1377. Inspect this data area (the data initially in the 'disc' file on the IBM PC disks do not contain any 0043 or 0143 values in this block).

14. Reduce the detail of display by suppressing the display of CPU registers ('-c').
15. Resume execution (':c'). Execution proceeds with the displays of peripheral status and translated instructions. The display may be too fast to read individual instructions but it will be possible to observe the program executing the loop in which individual words in the first are checked, then the next block of disk is read, and the next header message printed.
16. The breakpoint at 0437 will be encountered for a second time. Again obtain dumps of registers and memory. This second block of data will be seen to contain some words that satisfy the test - the first being the value 0143 held in location 1214.
17. Disable displays of peripherals ('-p') and translated instructions ('-t'), and resume execution (':c').
19. Remove the breakpoint:

    :u
    Address for breakpoint>*0437*

20. Resume execution (':c') and allow the program to run briefly without any displays. Interrupt execution (cntrl-C on IBM PC-DOS; break-key on Unix) forcing entry to the breakpoint package.
21. Inspect memory locations such as 'block' to determine the state of processing at the point where computations were interrupted. Resume execution and allow the program to run to completion.
22. Obtain a final memory dump. Print both the 'dumpfile' and the 'teletype' output files and check these outputs.

Index